AQUAE BRIT

R ediscov~~ering~~

17TH CENTURY SPRINGS & SPAS

IN THE FOOTSTEPS OF
Celia Fiennes

BY
BRUCE OSBORNE ▦ CORA WEAVER

Cora Weaver
Malvern
MCMXCVI

First published in 1996 by Cora Weaver
4 Hall Green, Malvern, Worcs. WR14 3QX

Printed by Aldine Press Limited,
Barnards Green Road, Malvern WR14 3NB

Cover picture: *William Schellinks' view of Epsom Spa in 1662.*

Courtesy of: the Austrian National Library and Picture Archive, Vienna.

Negativ aus dem Bildarchiv der Österreichischen Nationalbibliothek, Wien.

ISBN 1 873809 22 0

CONTENTS

List of illustrations, the authors, acknowledgements, glossary, map showing the spaws of Ceila Fiennes, introduction.

			Page
Chapter	1	Canterbury	1
	2	Tunbridge Wells	11
	3	Epsom	27
	4	London Spas:	65
		Dulwich	
		Shooters Hill	
		Hampstead	
		Hackney	
	5	Barnet	77
	6	Astrop & Great Horwood	89
	7	Buxton	102
	8	Tideswell	120
	9	Scarborough	122
	10	Durham	133
	11	Knaresborough	147
	12	Copgrove	152
	13	Harrogate	160
	14	Wigan	173
	15	Holywell	178
	16	Nantwich and Northwich	189
	17	Droitwich	194
	18	Richards Castle	202
	19	Malvern	204
	20	Bristol	216
	21	Bath	230
	22	Wells	253
	23	Alford	260
		Bibliography	264
		Index	273

i

ILLUSTRATIONS

Introduction   The "Spaws" of Celia Fiennes.

Chapter

1   James Bingley's 1822 map showing Canterbury Wells by the Westgate.

2   An engraving by Jan Kip after a drawing by T. Badslade. Originally published in *The History of Kent* by J. Harris in 1719, this depicts Tunbridge spa as Celia Fiennes would have found it.

Lambert's engraving of Somerhill, 1783, published by J. Sprange.

Lambert's view of Penshurst Place, c.1786, published by J.Sprange.

3   Livingstone's New Wells after Clark (1960).

After an aquatint by Hassell, 1816, showing the clock in Epsom High Street.

Pownall's 1825 picture of Epsom Old Wells.

Simplified Geology of the Epsom District.

5   Author's impression of Barnet Well interior in the late seventeenth century.

Banstead Well, Surrey.

Interior of Barnet Well chamber in 1996.

Barnet Well-house in 1996.

6   Horwood Well, 1996.

St Rumbold's Well, Astrop, erected 1749.

7   The Old Hall, Buxton, from Speed's map of 1610.

The Old Hall and Baths, Buxton, 1996.

8   The Tideswell.

9   Seal on Scarborough mineral water sold by John Fiddes of Covent Garden, 1734.

10   Kepier Hospital, near Durham.

St Cuthbert's Well, Durham.

Bishop Cosin's almshouses, Durham, established 1666.

11   Knaresborough Castle 1836.

      St Robert's cave and grave, Knaresborough, 1996.

12   The lame poor were taken to healing wells in cripple carts
      and hand barrows as illustrated by Cranach (1546).

13   The Tewit Well, the Old Sulphur Well Pump Room and St John's
      Chalybeate Spring, Harrogate, in the twentieth century.

      The Dropping Well, Knaresborough, 1996.

15   St Winefride's Well from R M. Zornlin's *World of Waters*, 1855.

      Crutches left by the healed at the wellside.

      Processional banner of St Winefride.

17   The medieval timbers of St Richard's or the Upwich brine
      pit, Droitwich, revealed during excavations in the 1980s.

19   Malvern Bath c.1750.

20   Part of Jacobus Millerd's plan of Bristol, dated 1673.

      Seal on Bristol mineral water sold by John Fiddes of Covent Garden,
1734.

      Colston's Almshouses, Bristol, built in 1691.

      Ashton Court, Bristol.

21   Bath Abbey or Cathedral as seen today.

      The Kings Bath - a sketch by William Schellinks c.1662.

      The Cross Bath in 1996 showing the spring rising in the centre.

      The Kings Bath today with part of the Victorian floor removed to
show the original spring.

22   The Entrance to Ochie Hole, 1719, after a sketch by Bernard Lens.

23   Alford Well as it may have been at the time of Celia Fiennes' visit.

THE AUTHORS

Dr Bruce Osborne has a long standing interest in springs, spas and holy wells. He has been active in the mineral water and spa industry over many years and was a former chairman of the British Natural Mineral Waters Association. He is based at Sussex University where his interests include research and development related to spa heritage and tourism.

Cora Weaver is a well known author and broadcaster on various aspects of Malvern's history. She has researched the origins of hydrotherapy, both in a local context and on an international scale. Having studied Local History at post graduate level at Oxford University she is currently pursuing research into the origins and evolution of spas.

ACKNOWLEDGEMENTS

This work would not have been possible without the assistance of Dr Peter Ambrose and the resources of the University of Sussex, together with Walter Robinson, Doris & Cyril Prescott, Scarborough; Tristan Gray Hulse, Source Journal; Geoffrey Butler, Roger Farthing, Keith Hetherington, Barry Bassett, John Mitchell, Dr Michael Rowlands, Tunbridge Wells; Jeremy Harte, John Batchelor, Epsom; Dorothy Harding, John Leach, Buxton; Stephen Bird, Bath Museums; Father Bernard Lordan, Holywell; Liz Hogg, Copgrove; Esther Kurland, Bob Penny, Barnet Borough Council; Jennifer Scherr, Bristol University; Katy Jordan, Bath University; Lynn and Martin Emslie, Alford; Peter Ward, Colwall; Linda Cluckie and The British Spas Federation; Ernie Ridgway, Julie Gibbs, Horwood; Amanda Grice; Roland and Chris Bannister; James Rattue; Rev. Dr. Leonard Cowie and many others, including the staff of the various libraries and record offices consulted, whose assistance has been greatly appreciated.

GLOSSARY OF TERMS

Alum -   double sulphate of Aluminium and another element especially
            potassium or iron.

Anhydrite - Calcium Sulphate.

Calcite -   Stalagmites and stalactites - Calcium Carbonate
            resulting from the chemical deposition by
            water, usually underground. **Tufa** is a similar
            deposit above ground. **Lapis calcarius** is where
            the crystals are used as gems. Higher
            temperatures and lower pressures reduce the
            dissolved carbon dioxide giving the following
            reaction:

$$Ca(HCO_3)_2 = CaCO_3 + H_2O + CO_2$$

Calcium Bicarbonate - $Ca(HCO_3)_2$.

Celestine (ite) - Strontium Sulphate, $SrSO_4$.

Epsom salts - Magnesium Sulphate, $MgSO_4.7H_2O$, Epsomite.

Fluorspa - CaF_3, fluorite. Blue John is a purple variety.

Glauber Salts -   Calcium and Sodium Sulphate,
                  $CaSO_4.Na_2SO_4$, Glauberite.

Gypsum - Calcium Sulphate, $CaSO_4.2H_2O$.

Marble - recrystallised limestone resulting from thermal metamorphism.

Silica/quartz - Sulphur Dioxide, SiO_2.

The 'Spaws' of Celia Fiennes

INTRODUCTION

Celia Fiennes was one of a select number of travellers who recorded details of their extensive journeys throughout England during the seventeenth and early eighteenth centuries. Unlike William Camden, John Ogilby, Thomas Fuller and others, Celia's account was a personal diary rather than a reference book for future travellers.

This period was very much one of transition in English history. The unrest of the Interregnum and religious instability of the monarchy was coming to an end. Instead Parliament was becoming the disputed power base and much of what Celia observed was a manifestation of these seventeenth century circumstances. Charles II had ruled from the restoration of the monarchy to 1685 to be followed by James II. James's first daughter and heiress Mary was brought up in the Anglican faith. The birth of a son to his second wife proved unpopular when the boy was brought up as a Catholic. The result was that James II lost the throne to his daughter Mary and William III as joint sovereigns in 1689. Under the Act of Settlement of 1701 Protestant succession was assured. Following the death of Mary in 1694 and then William in 1702, the throne went to Mary's sister Anne, the last of the Stuart dynasty.

As the eighteenth century progressed there was a new impetus for development and commerce. Private capital was playing an important part in pump priming the early industrial revolution. The wealthy industrialist was able to become a person of distinction, if not quality, for the first time. Celia had her own investments, particularly in rock salt, which reflected an interest in new technologies as well as matters underground. The journal of her travels provides an invaluable record of England in transition and this particularly applies to the spaws that captivated her interest.

It is apparent that during this period travel was, for many, an almost everyday occurrence. An infrastructure was well established to service these early tourists. The reasons for travelling were varied; for some it was a quest for health at one of the spas. There was also travel for interest's sake. Tourism was becoming a popular pastime for those who wished to extend their edification through the experience and could afford the costs involved. Travel for pleasure was perhaps the reason for the quantity of travel guides which were being produced in the later seventeenth century. Common phrases in Celia's text and contemporary guide books suggest that Celia Fiennes, or possibly her guides, used these very much as the modern traveller uses a guide book.

Celia's diaries began c.1685, when she was in her early twenties, though she may have travelled extensively prior to this. Being an unmarried lady with financial means she had the time, interest and wherewithal to travel. Since there were no banks, currency was carried on the person and to avoid the risk of robbery people rarely travelled alone. Many would start off as a small party and sooner or later meet with other small groups and continue together for safety's sake. Chaucer's Canterbury pilgrims are a fine example of how individuals congregated and proceeded together.

Cecilia Fiennes (as she was most likely baptised), was born in 1662, the granddaughter of the 1st Viscount Saye and Sele. The family home, which was sold by Celia in 1709, was at Newton Toney, near Salisbury, and it is apparent that this was her destination at the end of some of her travels. Her family background suggested one of Protestant dissent, and Celia herself was a Nonconformist The proceeds of the sale of Newton Toney were invested in commercial funds, only to be lost in the South Sea Bubble of 1720. She visited the rich and prosperous, avoiding anything related to ancient customs and the historic orders within society. She died in 1741 at the age of 78 in Hackney, where her nieces lived.

Although the main body of her work was written in 1702 it is possible to identify with some accuracy the years when she visited specific locations. The contents of the diaries show a repetitive interest in certain aspects of the country. Celia Fiennes was certainly fascinated by natural history, including mineral waters. She liked new and modern things and was inquisitive about the commercial exploitation of nature. She commented at length on the Wonders of the Peak, on various types of mining, on the salt industry, on topographical features such as fen draining, causeways and enclosures, and of the manufacture of items from raw materials. She was intrigued by the Bone Well at Richard's Castle. Apart from topographical features and natural history, she frequently commented upon people's occupations and status, grand houses, cleanliness, social life at the spas and food. She was less interested in animals, clothes or common buildings. She was rarely concerned with ordinary people except in extreme circumstances of unpleasantness. Somerset people were *"a clounish rude people"*; those on the Scottish borders *"seem to be a very poor people which I impute to their sloth"* and at Holywell, where they spoke Welsh, *"the inhabitants go barefoote and bare leg'd a nasty sort of people"*.[1]

The spas in the seventeenth century have not been as well documented by historians and social scientists as the spas in later centuries, and this was one reason why retracing Celia Fiennes' visits appealed so much to the authors. The sixteenth century saw mineral waters as the decayed remnants of the medieval era of holy wells, religious orders and charities. Their healing provision was in disarray. It is possible to put what Celia saw in this historical context.

The seventeenth century was one of gradual change and although many new mineral water sources were discovered, their growth and popularity as then modern healing and leisure centres was slow to materialise. What is apparent is that what Celia observed, in some instances, was the commencement of development and change which was to result in towns and villages later becoming the premier spas of England. Much of what she saw has survived the intervening 300 years and can now be reviewed in a present day context.

During her late seventeenth century tours Celia Fiennes visited 27 active healing mineral waters and springs. A century earlier there had been perhaps only a handful of celebrated healing "spaws", notably the ancient centres of Bath, Holywell and Buxton and the newly-discovered Utkinton in Cheshire. A century later there were over 400 identifiable mineral waters sources dispersed throughout England, Scotland and Wales.[2] John Andrews' 1797 *Map of the Mineral Waters and Bathing Places in England* [3] suggests that the geography of the then active sites had remained unchanged since the 1690s in spite of the vast increase in numbers. The peripheral counties - Devon and Cornwall, Hampshire and Sussex, Norfolk and Suffolk, Hereford and Shropshire - had perhaps two celebrated mineral water wells each, whereas the central counties promoted many more. It is clear that the seventeenth century saw the flourishing of a new national interest in the use of water for healing and that Celia Fiennes was an early pioneer tourist, investigating and recording spa location, development, popularity and curative qualities.

One may ask why Celia was so interested in the spas and mineral content of the waters, since she must have been in remarkably good health to undergo these journeys at all. Her infrequent references to physical ailments support this theory. However, at that time many people sought to avoid illness with prophylactics - by wearing superstitious lucky charms, with regular bleeding by a physician, cold bathing or drinking mineralised water. Mineral waters were an important part of medicine of the day, although the chemistry was little understood. Other cures adopted by the medical profession, which included surgery and the consumption of weird concoctions, were often inclined to do more harm than good. Celia was prepared to undergo considerable inconvenience and hardship to visit the spas and in most cases she was enthusiastic about trying the waters. She visited many more places that were not spas but in this text we have concentrated on the spas where she was without doubt an authority. By the 1680s many of the spa villages, although not well developed, could at least offer food and lodging, and perhaps some entertainment to visitors, so would have been interesting places to stay. However she appears to have avoided the social intrigue which was so often associated with the visits of others. Her concern about propriety in dress at the spas shows that she was not brazen.

It has not been our intention to research a comprehensive history of each of the spas which Celia visited. Instead we have identified and discussed what she saw in both a contemporary and a modern context, thus producing a twentieth century guide to the early history and surviving artifacts. In doing so we have arrived at new interpretations of historical events at many of the locations, particularly as a result of unearthing previously unpublished material. Where this has justified a more comprehensive historical account of a spa, we have broadened our approach by including detail that postdates Celia's visit. As a result the importance and relevance of Celia's journals can be appreciated.

In researching Celia Fiennes' "spaws" we feel we have got to know this indomitable lady very well. This would not have been possible without the work of Christopher Morris who edited the only known surviving manuscripts of her journals. The two manuscripts, which overlapped in time, consisted of an original holographic draft and a version possibly by an amanuensis. Morris's 1947 unabridged text was the first comprehensive published record of the diaries. Prior to this there had been only an imperfectly translated volume of 1888 and a reference in a work of 1812. More recently (1982, 1995) Morris has published illustrated versions of Celia's journals. Although these are abridged they provide invaluable supplementary explanatory text as a result of subsequent research.[4] We have used the 1947, 1982 and 1995 texts in our researches as referenced in the footnotes accompanying each chapter.

In an attempt to reconstruct the sights and atmosphere that Celia experienced we have utilised seventeenth century and early eighteenth century source material, which has included topographical works, diaries, treatises on mineral waters and bathing, maps and illustrations. The text is divided into chapters, one for each locality where Celia explored the waters. These have been ordered as a geographical tour of England, commencing at Canterbury in the east and finishing with Alford in the west. We hope you will enjoy retracing the footsteps of Celia Fiennes as much as we have and, like us, getting to know this adventurous lady who viewed England from a side saddle.

Footnotes:

1   Morris C. (ed.) 1947, *The Journeys of Celia Fiennes*, p.16, 204, 181.
2   Based on a database created by the authors, derived from contemporary publications.
3   Bodleian Library, ref. C 1   6.4 and G.A Fol.B.2.
4   Morris C. (ed.) 1982, *The Illustrated Journeys of Celia Fiennes*, editorial note and introduction.

CANTERBURY

In 1697, possibly in August or early September, Celia Fiennes embarked on a tour of Kent.[1] Her tour began at Amwell in Hertfordshire, about 20 miles north of Hackney which was her usual starting point. Her cousin Susannah had married Thomas Filmer, a successful London lawyer; they were living at Amwell in 1697, so it is possible that Susannah's two daughters accompanied Celia on the tour.

From Tilbury they crossed the Thames to Gravesend, then journeyed via Rochester, Sittingbourne and Faversham, passing extensive hop yards and heavily laden orchards. Six miles outside Canterbury they climbed a hill, and from its summit saw the city away in the distance. Celia's party passed into the city through high narrow gates beyond which were wide, long streets lined with low, well-made brick buildings.[2]

Celia remarked on the city's opulence, created by its great silk weaving production and commensurate trade in the products. In one house alone she saw twenty looms, on which were being worked fine silks showing flowers and figures. Each loom offered employment for a boy whose job was to ensure the unhindered passage of the shuttle. Huge numbers of French were employed in the silk industry, and she encountered them at night in large groups going home after work. She also noted that many of the French were engaged in hop-picking, which suggests her visit was in September, the hop-picking season.

At the spa, the well was surrounded by a wall and rail, and steps led down to a paved area around the well-head, where people could stand to drink. It was very popular - Celia recorded that it was frequented by the same numbers of people that visited Tunbridge. Like Barnet and Epsom wells, Celia disliked Canterbury's well because the water issued so slowly. She preferred prolific springs which bubbled up quickly and were piped away, with fresh water always readily available.

Some people reacted favourably to Canterbury's water, others disliked it intensely. One gentleman, who was staying in the same house as Celia, complained that the water caused him to lose the use of his limbs. Being a chalybeate water like Tunbridge, it should have had the opposite effect - invigorating numbed limbs. It is quite possible that he had taken the water without the advice of a physician; chalybeate waters were known to be unsuitable in some cases. Celia described the water as coming from a mixed soil which affected the taste. She likened it to a mixture of Epsom water and Tunbridge water, though it was a sulphur chalybeate not a saline chalybeate. She tried half a glass but disliked the flavour, so was unable to comment on its effects. Like other spas, Canterbury had its diversions with walks laid out, seats for resting on, and music provided for mental relaxation.

Celia also toured one of the many paper mills. The one she visited was producing brown paper. The multi-functional mill was water powered, and as it pounded the rags in preparation for the paper-making it simultaneously beat hemp and oatmeal, and ground corn for bread. Once the rags and other constituents had been pulped sufficiently, the mixture was tipped into a huge tub. Fine wire meshes framed with wood, the size of the sheets of paper required, were then dipped into the tub and the pulp spread over the mesh. This acted as a seive, so that any pulp which was too liquid ran through and back into the tub. A piece of coarse woollen cloth, the same size as the paper required, was spread on a board and the pulp knocked off the mesh and onto the cloth. Over this layer of pulp was laid another piece of woollen cloth, onto which was tipped another layer of pulp. This process was continued until a large pile had been built up. The pile was carried to a press, a board was placed on the top, and a weight screwed down onto it. This pressed out any lumps in the pulp and squeezed it into the thinness required for paper. The sheets of paper could then be lifted out of the press and laid out to be dried by the wind. Celia discovered that white paper was made in the same way, except that white woollen cloth was used between the layers of pulp.

Of the city's fine buildings she commented on the town hall, which was built above the market, but saved her reveries for the cathedral, *"the finest sight there"*.[3] Finely carved within and without, it was not quite as large as Salisbury cathedral, and had a square tower rather than a spire, but with ornamental spires on the corners of the towers.[4]

Inside the cathedral were two aisles leading to open gates, spiked and made of iron. From the aisles twenty steps, similar to the steps at Winchester, ascended to the choir where the organ was situated.[5] Celia was impressed with the thick, painted glass windows in the choir. Although small, the windows cast wonderful colours into the cathedral. She believed that the art of painting glass had been lost in time. The font was well carved, gilded and painted; the lower part was of grey and white marble with white marble statues carved in relief round the base. The top was carved in a pyramid, and painted. The altar cloth, and the cushions and books on the altar, were all covered in purple velvet with borders of orris work and a knotted fringe of fine gold and purple silk.[6] These all matched the seat and cushion in the Bishop's chair, and all were the gift of Queen Mary during her visit to Canterbury four years earlier, in 1693.

In the cathedral were numerous monuments to monarchs, famous men and ecclesiastics. One of the latter, a bishop, she particularly mentioned as having been inspired to divide up the Bible into manageable chapters. This, she felt, demonstrated the true value of the accumulated learning and wisdom of a man of the church. Another statue of a bishop was of wood, and although it was a hundred years old it was in a sound condition, despite having been defaced by soldiers during the Civil War. There was also one brass statue of a man in armour, though she did not know who it represented.

She saw the chapel known as St Thomas a Becket's Crown, which had acquired its name because the painted roof was carved in the shape of a crown. She also mentioned a pavement, worn into grooves by the knees and feet of scores of pilgrims who had done obeisance at the saint's shrine over the centuries.

In the crypt was a church which had been given over to the use of the many French Protestants who lived in the city. This little underground church was crowded with seats, pushed closely together to accommodate the huge numbers who prayed there. It was quite dark inside, but when the doors were open they allowed in sufficient light. She understood that the accoustics were such that even loud singing below would not disturb the visitors who walked above. The Chapter House she described as lofty, with a ceiling of Irish oak.

COMMENT

Canterbury, in the late seventeenth and early eighteenth centuries, was indeed an affluent city. Celia Fiennes remarked on its opulence during the former period and J. Macky, in the latter period, thought it the metropolis of England.[7] He described the city as being 3 miles in circumference, and the main streets formed an exact cross in the centre, where St Andrew's church stood. There were six wards. The principal street was Westgate Street which housed the Guildhall, where the Court sat every Monday; the gate itself had been a prison since the days of Henry VI. Another street, Newingate, contained a fine conduit which had been erected by Archbisop Abbot for the use of the townsfolk. It was demolished in 1754. In Worthgate were three hospitals, Bridewell Hospital, Maynard's, founded in 1317 and Cotton's, founded in 1580.[8] In Burgate the well-stocked market was held on Wednesdays and Saturdays. Fairs were held on 20 July, 21 September and 29 December, the latter date being the feast day of Thomas a Becket and the anniversary of his death in 1170. Celia Fiennes did not mention any of these town features.

Canterbury's enrichment originated when pilgrims flocked to the cathedral to pay their respects following Thomas a Becket's canonisation by the Pope in 1173. The variety of folk who made the journey - their attitudes to life, love, death, religion and morality, are clearly and rivetingly captured by Geoffrey Chaucer in his late fourteenth-century masterpiece *The Canterbury Tales*. However the religious fervour of pilgrimage to St Thomas's shrine was over before the shrine's destruction at the Reformation in 1539.[9] Celia Fiennes was therefore visiting just another historical monument, admiring the architecture, glass, fabrics and effigies which other people still admire in the twentieth century.

Celia mentioned the twenty steps with the iron gates at the top, which led up to the choir. One can still walk up the steps and through the iron gates. She also mentioned the grooves worn into a pavement by pilgrims. Today it is possible to see a series of grooves in a flight of steps in the south side of the cathedral. These would have led up to St Thomas' shrine, and today are still considered to have been created by the obeisant pilgrims. Celia did not once mention the saint's connection with this feature, treating the cathedral almost as a secular building.

The font, of grey and white marble, was built in 1639 but demolished by Puritans two years later. Fortunately the pieces were secretly saved by William Somner, and reassembled at the Restoration in 1660. The font is now located in the north-west of the cathedral.

The chapel called Becket's Crown is also known as the Corona.[10] It is sited at the east end of the cathedral, access to which was, and still is, through a large arch. It was a circular chapel over the saint's tomb, which was in an undercroft, and was adorned with small compartments of painted glass depicting St Thomas's life. The very top of the crown was not completed until 1748.[11]

The painted glass windows displayed scenes from the Old and New Testament but, once again, Celia avoided any biblical references. Her interest was in the aesthetic value of the colouring and the craftsmanship. The monuments which Celia saw, and which can be identified today, included a *"brass statue in armour"* of Edward the Black Prince (1330-76). His achievements, which are now displayed in a glass case on the south wall, were hanging above his tomb at the time of Celia's visit.[12] She mentioned that one of the clerics, whose monument she saw, had been responsible for dividing the Bible into the chapters in which it is still printed and read. The man responsible was Bishop Stephen Langton (d.1228) who had been consecrated by the Pope in 1207.[13] Langton was buried in the Warriors' Chapel in the south side of the cathedral. The wooden statue of a bishop, which she noted as being one hundred years old, was the wooden effigy of the Franciscan Archbishop of Canterbury John Peckham (1279-1292). His appointment was considered unusual as it was a Benedictine order, not Franciscan, which was attached to the cathedral. The carving, of bog oak, marks the beginning of a decorated style of monument; it was placed in its present position at the end of the fourteenth century, so is indeed much older than Celia Fiennes suggested.

The Chapter House, which she commented on, was built c.1300 and opened off the east side of the cathedral. It measured 92 feet by 37 feet and all round was stone seating backed with arcading and an elaborate barrel-vaulted roof. (Celia described the roof as being made of Irish oak). The Chapter House was originally where the monks had carried out their administration, but was later used for sermons and by 1789 was used for morning prayers.[14] The small, dark Walloon/Huguenot "church" which was sited in the crypt is still used by the French and Walloons for services and prayer.

Following the demise of Canterbury as a prominent place of pilgrimage and the destruction of St Thomas's shrine in the sixteenth century, Canterbury did not slip into decline as one might have anticipated. There were several opportunities for its economic survival. The first came during the reign of Queen Elizabeth I, shortly after the Reformation and the destruction of the shrine. To escape religious persecution, thousands of Walloons fled from the continent to Canterbury where they employed their skills in silk making. Their numbers were swelled when, under the religious tyranny of Louis XIV and the Revocation of the Edict of Nantes in 1685, thousands of French Huguenots similarly fled to Canterbury. They also brought their silk-weaving skills and the city became renowned for its fine silk products which were very highly esteemed in London. The city also prospered on account of the thousands of acres of hopyards which surrounded it, and which Celia Fiennes noted in her journal. Hops were the most time-consuming, unpredictable and expensive of all crops to cultivate, but good harvests could be extremely profitable.[15] Their cultivation was almost totally confined to Kent, Herefordshire and Worcestershire.

CANTERBURY SPA

Canterbury is the Forgotten Spa. Little has been written about it. There is wide acceptance that its apparently short and obscure existence was due to its proximity to its chalybeate rival Tunbridge Wells, which boasted aristocratic and royal connections and an easy travelling distance from London.[16] It is reasonable to imagine Tunbridge Wells being resorted to by those with a view to adventure, amour, excitement and illness. However, Tunbridge is approximately 40 miles from Canterbury, and genuine invalids would not have made the arduous journey to Tunbridge if the same cure could be effected at a more local spa. Far from being overshadowed by Tunbridge, Canterbury springs quickly became popular following their discovery in 1693. By 1700 Dr Scipio des Moulins was treating scores of patients each season, and Celia Fiennes noted that the spring *"is dranck by many persons as Tunbridge and approv'd by them"*.[17] The visitor numbers apparently never became unmanageable. Gosling in his "Walk" noted that the springs had been used to good effect since their discovery *"but never were so much in fashion as to crowd the town with company."*[18]

THE SPRINGS

Canterbury had two medicinal springs, originally situated 7 feet apart - one a purely chalybeate spring, the other sulphur-chalybeate.[19] The springs were discovered accidentally in 1693, when attempts were made to sink a well to find a domestic water supply at a recently acquired house near the Westgate. Several attempts at drilling were thwarted, either by hitting solid rock or by the unsuitability of the water which was found. It tasted unpleasantly of rust. The proprietor soon realised that the water might be mineralised and therefore possess healing qualities, so he carried out various tests. When syrup of violets was added, both waters turned deep green; and when a few drops of spirit of salt were added the green turned a light cherry red.[20] When galls, oak leaves or chips of oak were added, the chalybeate water turned deep blue or purplish black, whilst the sulphur-chalybeate water turned a dark red.[21] An earlier experiment found that a single grain in weight of gall instantly turned $1\frac{1}{2}$ pints a deep red; syrup of violets turned it grass green; an infusion of brasil a deep blue; an infusion of logwood blue-black; flowers of pomegranates a fair violet.[22] The waters discoloured linen which was washed in it, and glasses which were frequently used to hold the water acquired an irremovable yellow staining in the bottom. Both waters were completely limpid when first exposed to the air, but after a quarter of an hour turned whitish, as if milk or lime had been added. This rapid change in composition indicated that the waters should be drunk at source or well-stoppered if bottled.[23] Although usually cold, the water never became frozen in winter. Instead it steamed, and melted any adjacent snow and ice.[24] In calm weather a fatty or oily multi-coloured film developed on the surface. When the water was evaporated the residue felt like butter between the fingers. It was said that a spoonful of the fatty water was as effective as a moderate dose of opium in inducing sleep.[25] The oiliness was most likely due to a certain oily layer of soil containing hydrocarbons which was discovered 3-4 feet down as the well was being dug.

To obtain a suitable public supply, workmen firstly drilled 4 feet through a black earth, rich in decomposed matter; then 2 feet through a sandy soil which was smooth and oily and smelt sulphurous. Next they found $1\frac{1}{2}$ feet of loose, wet sand, and upon digging into this hit the water which gushed 6 feet up into the air. When the jet subsided, the workmen cleared away the loose sand until they reached solid rock, which formed the natural containment of the springs. The well was lined with a 6 foot square of planks. There were two basins; the smaller one, containing the sulphur-chalybeate spring, was originally placed in the south-east corner of the square. Shortly afterwards it was relocated slightly, to within 6 feet of the larger basin, which contained the chalybeate water. There were believed to be 4 feet of water beneath the smaller basin and 6 feet depth of water beneath the larger basin and its surrounding pavement.[26] Celia Fiennes described the wells as being surrounded by a wall and rail. Imbibers descended some steps to the paved area below, where the dipper ladled out the water. This arrangement was similar to that at Barnet and Tunbridge Wells.

Within 3 years of their discovery, the waters were being prescribed for a variety of illnesses by Dr Scipio des Moulins. The Doctor endorsed and promoted its effective properties in a publication of 1700:

"The little well is very useful in diseases of the breast, as in asthmas, coughs, rheums, and catarrhs. It has cured several given over of consumptions of the lungs. Most disorders of the stomach are cured by these waters. It seldom fails in the cure of rheumatic gouty pains of the limbs, or other parts of the body, in the scurvy, and melancholy distempers, jaundice, vapours, all sorts of stoppages, scabs, itch, &c.; but in gravel, cholic, and green sickness, it is a true specific; as also in inward ulcers, if not too far gone."[27]

The little well was beneficial in consumptive cases; the passages became dilated to aid the removal of gravel and stone, and the water was particularly vital in *"The Gout and Rheumatick Pains, for which it is an unparallel'd Remedy"*. It was not recommended in the *"hot, florid, and pletherick Constitutions of some strong young People"*.[28] It was said that the water calmed the stomach (except when it was full) and kept the passages open, although it was not a purger. It stimulated circulation of the blood which made lethargic people feel more lively. Its best use was in infirmities associated with old age.

The water was particularly effective in the relief of agues - a fever characterised by shivering and hot and cold fits and very like influenza. Generally agues were relieved by "the bark", which was the bark of the Cinchona genus of trees from which quinine was made. Canterbury waters were known to have succeeded in curing some cases where the bark had failed.[29]

A contrived "Discourse" between two acquaintances on the merits of the Canterbury waters was published in 1702.[30] One speaker's role was to suggest that Canterbury Spa lacked the qualities of other spas. The other speaker's role was to promote the spa by pointing out the effectiveness of the waters, the various types of entertainment, the presence of many ladies, and the salubrious air of Canterbury itself. A different and sinister "promotional" activity is discussed at great length by the two acquaintances, concerning the effectiveness of the waters in removing stones from the body. It concerned a 12 year old boy who, in immense pain, had voided hundreds of stones after drinking the water. A rumour was circulating that the stones had been forced as far as possible inside the boy's penis so that on occasions curious visitors could watch him passing the stones into a chamber pot, thus witnessing the powerful effects of the water. It was rumoured that the boy's mother was related to the dipper at the spa; that the boy was being used as a tool to promote the waters, attract more invalids and thus more money into the dipper's purse. This story may or may not be true. However it is indicative that specious methods were employed for promoting spa waters.

TAKING THE WATERS

Summer was the season for taking chalybeate waters, and in Canterbury the season lasted from 1 May to 30 September.[31] The dipper served the water every morning, and the recipients walked in the adjacent grounds to promote the effects of their intake. The amount of water taken varied according to sex, age, disability and constitution. As with most chalybeate spas, Canterbury abounded with ladies, as these waters were particularly beneficial in female complaints concerning the blood:

"But this may be observ'd, that after they have drank the Waters a Week or ten days, they look more florid and brisk; and they, whose Countenances at their first coming on, were languid and pale, are in a short time clear'd up, and their Cheeks are ting'd with a pure red."[32]

Celia Fiennes was in good health, and since she disliked the taste of the water only took half a glass. For those with a need to take the waters, three glasses in the first half hour was not unusual.[33] Those seeking a cure would stay for 3 weeks to 3 months, depending on the chronicity of the complaint. Dr des Moulins gave an example of a porter from Bolton who, after consulting many doctors, was finally discharged from St Thomas's Hospital with an incurable bladder ulcer. The condition was cured after 3 months of drinking the Canterbury water.[34]

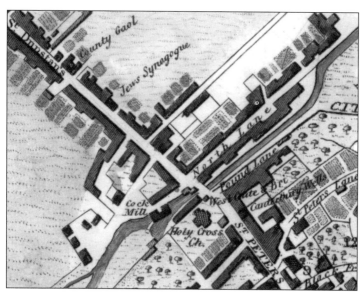

James Bingley's 1822 map showing Canterbury Wells by the Westgate.

SPA FACILITIES

By 1702 there was public music, a coffee house, bowling green, pleasant walks laid out with seats and a dancing room which, although not spacious, was conveniently accessible. Such facilities could be found at almost every spa town and were a necessary adjunct to curing, since both the body and the mind needed relief from stress. The waters relieved the body more quickly following exercise, and the music and dancing created *"Diversions* [which] *relieve the mind from Melancholy thoughts, and overmuch care of Business"*.[35] Canterbury also had its ancient tourist attractions, such as the cathedral and the city walls, though in 1702 there was still no town guide for tourists. Printed guides were unusual in England at that time, though more common on the continent. Three miles east of the city, Barham Downs were ideal for gentlemen to take a canter, and at nearby Bridge Hill was a spacious bowling green and horse racing track. These various types of entertainment attracted Company who might otherwise have travelled elsewhere in pursuit of diversions.

One of the speakers in the "Discourse" on Canterbury Wells suggested that Canterbury had been suffering an economic decline, characterized by the recent demolition of six churches.[36] This innuendo does not comply with Celia Fiennes' remarks on the city's opulence slightly before that time, and J. Macky's complimentary remarks on the wealth of the city shortly afterwards. However, the spa's popularity could beneficially affect the city's future development by stimulating trade and creating employment. It was important for the city to promote its then new-found natural product. The pilgrimage-tourism of former times could be replaced with a new type of tourism. Invalids staying for several weeks or months would create opportunities in the lodging, provision and souvenir industries, and the income used for maintenance of existing buildings and new building projects. The potential for increased wealth was applicable to any township which developed as a spa, so such a status would have been much sought after, particularly by townships with few other means of generating wealth.

The wells were eventually supplemented by a cold bath near the Burgate and a bath called St Rhadgund's Bath outside the North Gate.[37] No pre-1747 documentary evidence of St Rhadgund's Bath has been found. The bath was bought by the city and rebuilt in 1792.

Canterbury does not appear on Joseph Andrews' 1797 *Map of the Mineral Waters and Bathing Places in England*, although over 200 locations, some very minor, are noted.[38] Being mindful that the map may not have been published for some years after it was produced, one may conclude that by the 1790s Canterbury had ceased to be a notable spa. By the early nineteenth century Canterbury's "spa" was situated in a nursery of rare and exotic plants, with well laid out walks. The main entrance was in Pound Lane.[39] The waters had become neglected, but by the 1830s the lessee, Mr William Masters, had rebuilt the wells, provided more modern conveniences and landscaped the walks beautifully. It was unlikely at that date that he was attempting to revive the spa, as in England generally spas had declined in popularity. He had, how-ever, provided a park for the city, a much more modern concept.

TODAY

Much of the old city which Celia saw still exists. There are extensive remnants of the original Roman city wall, and one can get a clear idea of the smallness of the city within these confines. Many of the old buildings still exist, including a pilgrims' inn and a weaver's house. The site of the wells is now lost under a car park. There is still an immense French influence, characterized by day-trippers and parties of French schoolchildren. However, in Celia Fiennes' words, the cathedral is still *"the finest sight there"*.

Footnotes:

1   Morris C. (ed.) 1947, *The Journeys of Celia Fiennes*, p.121-132.
2   This was most likely the Westgate.
3   Morris C. op.cit. p.125.
4   She probably knew Salisbury cathedral well, it being just 8 miles from Newton Toney, her native township.
5   Winchester was approximately 20 miles from Newton Toney.
6   Orris work is a kind of gold and silver lace.
7   Macky J. 1732, *A Journey Through England*, p.100.
8   Camden's *Britannia*, Gough R. (trans.) 1789, p.237, 239.
9   Church R. 1948, *Kent*, p.274.
10   Spence K. 1973, *The Companion Guide to Kent & Sussex*, p.92.
11   Gough R. op.cit. p.238.
12   Morris C. op.cit. p.126.
13   *Dictionary of National Biography*, 1892.
14   Gough R. op.cit. p.238; Spence K. op.cit. p.95.
15   Pitt W. 1813, *General View of the Agriculture of the County of Worcester*, p.117-134.
16   Hembry P. 1990, *The English Spa 1560-1815*, p.73.; Denbigh K. 1981, *A Hundred British Spas*, p.232.
17   Morris C. op.cit. p.125.
18   Gosling W. 1777, 2nd edition, *A Walk in and about the City of Canterbury*, p.54.
19   ibid. p.54.
20   Violets are coloured with a blue pigment which changes to red when acid is applied.
21   Anon. 1702, *Canterbury Wells: or, A discourse upon the mineral waters lately discovered in that city, and the many extraordinary cures which are daily performed by them*, p.23.
22   Anon. 1668, *A Short Account of the Mineral Waters lately found out in the City of Canterbury*, p.4.
23   Gosling W. op.cit. 1825 edition, p.72.
24   Anon. 1668, op.cit. p.3.
25   ibid. p.4.
26   Anon. 1702, op.cit. p.20-21; In Anon. 1668, op.cit. p.2 it was noted that the large well was 8-9 feet deep and the small well 6-7 feet deep
27   *The Canterbury Guide* 1835, 5th edition, p.15.
28   Anon. 1668, op.cit. p.8.
29   *The Canterbury Guide* 1835, p.15.
30   Anon. 1702, op.cit. p.23.
31   *The Canterbury Guide* 1835, p.16.
32   Anon. 1702, op.cit. p.25.
33   ibid. p.2.
34   *The Canterbury Guide* 1835, p.15.
35   Anon. 1702, op.cit. p.11-12.
36   ibid. p.10.
37   Hembry P. op.cit. p.74.
38   Andrews J. 1797, *Map of the Mineral Waters and Bathing Places in England*.
39   Gosling W. op.cit. 1825 edition, p.73.

TUNBRIDGE WELLS

It was in 1697 that Celia made her recorded visit to Tunbridge Wells as part of her tour of Kent.[1] Her acquaintance with the spa is acknowledged in her observation that she had drunk there many years with good effect. She noted several springs emanating from the "*steele*" and iron mines, both in the town and the surrounding countryside. The iron ore gave rise to the Wealden iron works where guns and bells were cast. The waters in the town were "*quick*" in that they flowed from the springs and she cited two springs that had basins set in the ground with holes for the water to bubble up. Being a "*spiriteous*" water it did not travel even short distances. This is a characteristic of chalybeate waters in that oxidisation quickly causes the iron compounds to change in composition.

To Celia Fiennes, Tunbridge was a water against which to judge other mineral waters. It was an "industry standard" and the extensive comparisons that she made with Tunbridge water give us a number of insights into her regard for taking the waters. We may well ask why she was so inquiring about the location and properties of mineral waters. Was she a hypochondriac or did she suffer serious ailments? The importance that she placed on Tunbridge provides a clue as to her quest regarding her perceived physiological needs. It also confirms Tunbridge as one of the premier spas of the time, and one that Celia was exceedingly familiar with.

Comparisons with Tunbridge waters in her journals include Astrop, Horwood, Harrogate, Durham and Canterbury.[2] At the latter she observed that the water was less effective at curing numb limbs than Tunbridge water which was expected to stimulate the blood and aid circulation.

Tunbridge was well developed by the time of Celia's visit and she noted that there was good accommodation. The walk was established in the vicinity of the springs. Provisions could be purchased at the flourishing market by The Wells which sold a variety of produce from throughout the region. The market was located along the walk and here local people sold their produce to visitors, making it inexpensive to stay in Tunbridge. Retailing reflected the general economic prosperity, with a wide range of goods on offer including toys, china, millinery as well as the curious wooden ware for which Tunbridge has subsequently become noted. Coffee houses, lottery and hazard boards occupied the premises adjoining the paved covered walk. This was formed by the upper storeys of the buildings extending over part of the upper promenade, supported by columns.

In dry weather, walking could take place in the open where there was a surface of clay and sand. It was after Celia's 1697 visit that the famous pantiles were laid eventually giving the name The Pantiles to the walking area. In 1697 the young Duke of Gloucester, the sole surviving child of Princess Anne, being top heavy with hydrocephalus, fell over while playing soldiers. Such an accident was of considerable importance as the Duke could have emerged as the sole Stuart heir to the throne. The Princess ordered that proper paving be laid, leaving £100 to defray the costs. Whether through hidden religious agendas or for other reasons the work was not carried out. When the Princess returned, she made suitable revised arrangements to ensure that her wishes were implemented but never returned again, in spite of having previously been a frequent patron.[3] The pantiles were eventually laid in 1700.[4] When Anne came to the throne in 1702 the Queens Grove was planted on the common in recognition of her favours to the town but failed to secure her further patronage.[5]

Celia recorded that at the lower end of the walk, before The Wells proper, there was a broad space with a sun dial giving easy access to the chapel of King Charles the Martyr. As well as a post house for the daily mail there were several apothecaries shops in the vicinity of The Wells. Tunbridge, several miles away was the main post town and there was a penny surcharge for conveyance from there. (Tunbridge town was renamed Tonbridge with the coming of the railway to avoid confusion with the town of Tunbridge Wells around The Pantiles.)

Entertainments at The Wells included numerous bowling greens in the locality and music and dancing either indoors or out depending on the weather. There were also excellent taverns at the walks. Such facilities were available throughout the season. Celia warned of tricksters and rogues who, having gained ones confidence, relieved you of your possessions, often in league with local shopkeepers. Princess Anne, having left money with a local person to pave the walk, was perhaps a victim.

Celia recorded several grand country houses and parks near Tunbridge Wells. Penshurst Place was the seat of the Lords Lester; Eridge was the seat of Lord Abergavenny who had his hunting lodge about three to four miles from The Wells; Ashurst, near Groombridge was the home of the Ashurst family and at Somerhill Celia visited the house of the raffish kin of the last Viscount Purbeck. Travelling, she observed, was pleasant in summer but in winter the roads were impassable, confirming her detailed all year round knowledge of this part of Kent.

COMMENT

When Celia Fiennes recorded Tunbridge in 1697 she found a town already well-established as a social centre and spa. In fact, being so close to London, it rivalled Bath for the premier position. Much of what she saw was the result of recent developments, for example the shops near the spring. She mentioned the bowling greens on Mount Sion and Mount Ephraim, such names bearing witness to the popularity of the locality during the Puritan ascendancy. Her knowledge of the area as a result of many visits is apparent in her descriptions of the localities near Tunbridge Wells. She was in her mid thirties when this part of her journal was written and her description of Tunbridge waters and their expected efficacy, detailed previously when comparing them with Canterbury, gives a possible clue as to why she frequented the spas. Such waters were appropriate for *"poverty of the blood and circulation"*.[6]

Seventeenth century medical theory was partially based on the ancient Greek premise that there were four balanced body fluids, blood, phlegm, choler (yellow bile) and melancholy (black bile). An imbalance brought about disease, and Tunbridge water was particularly effective for curing excess of the black bile. The taking of the waters also precipitated, in many, an excessive display of sexual behaviour. Even during the Queen's presence (Catherine, wife of Charles II) the overt behaviour was viewed with a blind eye, the Queen having decided that court formalities would be dropped during her visits. The sexual excesses were a consequence of the reputation that the water had for enhancing fecundity and resulted in the cure being resorted to particularly by women seeking pregnancy.[7] No doubt the Queen hoped for a future heir to the throne. Often the cure for barrenness was not solely due to the waters, as the following verse, penned just before the time of Celia's visit records.

A Ballad in Tunbridge Wells

You ladies who in loose bodyd Gown
Forsake ye Sneaking City
and in whole shoals come tumbling down
Foul Foolish Fair or Whitty

Some for ye scurvy some ye gout
and some for long disease
Know that those Wells drives it all out
And own what cure you please

They powerfully breake ye stone
and heat consumptive lungs
They'll quicken yr Conception
if you can hold yr tongue

Then you that hither childless Come
Leave yr dull Mary [marriage?] *behind you*
You'll never wish yr selfes at home
Our youth will be so kind to you.

Anon. based on a verse in *Tunbridge Wells, or a Days Courtship*, 1678, Act III, Sc.lll.[8]

13

The waters were also recognised by the medical profession as suitable treatments for anaemia and debility. The ordinary dose was half to three quarters of a tumbler late morning followed by a walk along the Pantiles with a similar dose shortly afterwards. The length of the course was two months.[9] Dr Rowzee noted in the seventeenth century that drinkers would work up to as much as 200 ounces of water in a day, about 10 pints.[10]

Celia Fiennes enjoyed her social interaction with the gentry but appeared to have declined participation in the amusements of Tunbridge. Not for her was the intrigue and scandal of the sexes. Celia Fiennes was an independent woman whose energies were directed at exploration. Her perambulations resemble the famous "progresses" of Elizabeth I and in this respect, and in their apparent celibacy, both women have similarities. In a world dominated by men, independence would have been jeopardised by relationships.

Celia Fiennes was an explorer, pursuing an inquisitiveness of nature and its benefits to humankind. Nature was a storehouse of resources which technology was unlocking. Pestilence, plague and debilitating illness threatened the enjoyment of nature. Her dual aims of enquiry and health came together in her exploration of the natural curing potential of mineral waters, as a preferred alternative to the quackery and incompetence of the medical profession of the time. It was Lord North who observed that there was more danger from the physician than from the disease.[11]

SEVENTEENTH CENTURY TUNBRIDGE WELLS

We owe the account of the discovery of Tunbridge waters to Thomas Benge Burr, the first local historian of Tunbridge in 1766. His *History of Tunbridge Wells* indicates that the chalybeate spring was first noticed in 1606 by Lord Dudley North when riding back to London after a hunting trip at Eridge. Twenty five year old North was recouping from court excesses at the time but the trip did little for his consumptive disorders.[12] Near the perimeter of Lord Bergavenny's (later Abergavenny) estate North noticed a rust coloured pool, beside a stream, in a wooded hollow in Waterdown Forest. Borrowing a wooden bowl to drink the water, he recognised it as similar to water he had drunk at Spa. He returned to London with a sample for evaluation.[13] The physicians declared the water significant and that it had curing abilities. Returning the next year, North took a full treatment to good effect. Lord Bergavenny arranged for the area to be improved, sinking a well and discovering six other springs. By 1608 the source was in a fenced triangular compound with a stone pavement.[14] Dudley, Lord North was also later to "discover" Epsom waters c.1630. In doing so he doubtless scored a political advantage by advocating English spas instead of the town of Spa, then in Germany. To visit the German town produced a balance of trade deficit as well as fuelling religious tensions.[15]

"The use of Tunbridge and Epsom waters for health and cure I first made known to London and the King's people; the Spa is a chargeable and inconvenient journey for sick bodies, besides the money it carries out of the kingdom and the inconvenience to religion."

Quote by Dudley, Lord North.[16]

As the reputation of the Tunbridge waters grew so royalty started to frequent the locality. Charles I's queen, Henrietta Maria, arrived in 1629 and possibly again in 1630 for six weeks after the birth of her son, later to be Charles II.[17] She and the Court camped on nearby Bishop's Down Common. Her fondness for The Wells resulted in the name "Queen Maries Wells" being cited by Dr Rowzee in the first guide to the locality.[18] The name never gained long term usage. Other early names include Frant Wells, a name given in deference to Lord Abergavenny. Eridge is in the parish of Frant.[19]

In 1635 gossip reported that Lord Dunluce had lost nearly £2,000 at ninepins at The Wells. Sir John Suckling, the poet, was the principal beneficiary.[20] In spite of the growing leisure activities of the wealthy it was not until 1636 that necessary facilities were built, one for each sex, no doubt providing needed toilet arrangements as well as a place to relax. Use of the facilities was by subscription.

As the seventeenth century progressed, Tunbridge Wells was not immune to the disturbances of the Civil War. With the outbreak of fighting in 1642 rival troops haunted the Tunbridge area as the local foundries produced the weapons of war. The Royalists formed a base at Southborough between The Wells and Tunbridge town (later Tonbridge), the Roundheads at Rusthall, one mile from The Wells. Both of these hamlets had provided service facilities for The Wells prior to the Civil War.[21] Colonel Brown captured 200 Royalist prisoners at Tunbridge Wells in 1643, releasing parliamentary supporters from custody at the same time.[22] Charles I was executed in 1649 and England became a Commonwealth. Even after the war the spas were viewed as a security risk, harbouring dissidents in the guise of water drinkers. As late as 1659, Colonel Gibbon was ordered to Tunbridge with all the troops that he could muster. Although plots were numerous, for example the capture of Sandwich and Dover Castles were planned at Tunbridge, the spa continued to attract health visitors. John Evelyn, the diarist, arrived with wife and mother in 1652 to escape the smallpox in London.[23]

The Commonwealth period had put a temporary brake on the flourishing spa business, but the town quickly returned to developing further the infrastructure of the spa on the reinstatement of the monarchy in 1660. John Evelyn again visited Tunbridge at this time noting in 1661 the birch trees and the rocks.[24] By now houses, taverns and lodgings were starting to be built near the spring.

At Tunbridge the Bergavennys carried out little other development except around the spring, which lay just inside the Manor of Rusthall, on the perimeter of Bergavenny's estate. This was initially likely due to the early seventeenth century perception of the spring being of medicinal interest rather than a commercial or social resort.[25] It was therefore left to others, particularly the adjacent manor of Rusthall, to exploit the resource once its reputation and potential as a spa had been established. The spring was seen as important for the livelihood of the local populace and to escalate the commerce from cottage industry level would have threatened the welfare of the poor. When John Wybarne, a saddler, attempted to monopolise the source at the Restoration in 1660, this prompted the locals to petition the House of Lords. Wybarne had removed the marble cistern and paving, felled trees in the walk, and generally threatened further destruction unless the spring was solely in his charge. The petition claimed that for upward of 50 years poor women had been permitted to dip and serve the water to the nobility and gentry. This practice was in contrast to Germany where the dippers were organised and dressed as specialist service providers. Referring the case to the Justices, the Lords thereby ordered the restoration of the wells for the public good.[26]

In 1664 the old fencing around the well was replaced by a stone wall, together with a new basin and shelter, all at the expense of Lord Muskerry who lost his life fighting the Dutch the following year. Being the local lord of the manor, his arms were installed on the arch over the gateway to the spring, later to be removed in 1726 during a landlord and tenant manorial dispute.[27] The earlier triangular configuration was retained and the improved facilities would have been what Celia Fiennes saw. Also in 1664 the huge forest of Southfrith was disparked and divided into fifty holdings which included Somerhill estate. The release of land prompted a more commercial approach locally and in turn further development was triggered, attracting venture capital from London.

The London plague of 1665 and the Great Fire of 1666 resulted in the Court arriving in force. Charles II's wife, Catherine of Braganza, had visited in 1663[28] seeking a cure for infertility, according to Denbigh, or an infectious fever according to Sprange.[29] Royal patronage continued and the town developed a reputation for licentiousness ignored by Celia Fiennes. The garden called Fish Ponds was opened for amusement c.1670, low company was admitted and indecencies encouraged. It soon became a place of disrepute, continuing in existence until well into the eighteenth century when Sprange reported it in a ruinous state.[30]

Further deprecation of the character of visitors appeared in the 1678 play *"Tunbridge Wells, or a day's courtship, by a person of quality"*. Performed at the Duke of York's theatre it was considered obscene, lacking in the qualities that determined a good play. It was short lived and was possibly put on at the same theatre as Shadwell's comedy *"Epsom Wells"* following the success of the earlier work.[31]

An engraving by Jan Kip after a drawing by T. Badslade. Originally published in The History of Kent by J. Harris in 1719, this depicts the spa as Celia Fiennes would have found it.

The church of King Charles the Martyr was founded near the spring also in 1678.[32] Its dedication reflected the Stuart patronage of the town. A subscription was opened as early as 1676. This amounted to £1385 by the year the church was established on ground given by Lady Purbeck of Somerhill. Further enlargements took place in 1682 and again later as a result of a second £900 subscription collected between 1688 and 1696. Carey's acidic comment of 1799 noted the close proximity of the springs and church. *"I presume, the chapel was built so near the Well, that, when they had filled their stomachs with the springs from the rock, they might improve it by the spirit of divinity, and, by mixing it, make it into a kind of religious grog."*[33]

The green bank by the well was levelled in 1683 and turned into the promenade that Celia Fiennes described as the peasa (piazza). It was planted with a double row of trees and tradesmen set up stalls and booths. By the time of Celia's account, pillars supported the overhanging upper storeys of permanent shops providing the wet weather walkway that can be seen today. The shops were built after a fire of booths and stalls in 1687, which started in a house at the bottom of the walk. A child died in the fire. Although seen as a disaster at the time it enabled the rebuilding to be carried out on a planned basis with the attractive colonnade. To Celia Fiennes this would have been the equivalent of our modern shopping precinct. Carey in 1799 criticised, in his usual no-nonsense way, the walk which he called the Promenade. It was a bricked pavement over which was thrown a long wooden colonnade or shed, more to keep out the light and fresh air. By 1799 the row of elms that were planted earlier were of considerable size. The result was the imbibing of stagnant air or water with moss adorning the damp brickwork.[34]

Several of the shops on the Pantiles even today have their own springs in the basements, illustrating the profusion of natural water sources in the locality.[35]

The 1680s were a particular boom period and Lord Bergavenny was permitted to change the weekly market to a daily one. The market took place on the Lower Walk and this was supplemented by a weekly cattle market and a fair on St James's Day.[36] Leisure time was excessive for those taking the waters and this led to a flourishing entertainments industry. Shopping, bowling and dancing on the green were regular pastimes.[37]

Scandal mongering continued to be associated with The Wells, particularly involving royalty. The year of 1688 was the date of a possible deception linked with Princess Anne while she was at Tunbridge Wells. The Queen (Anne, wife of James II) had given birth to a son in June witnessed, as was the custom, by 67 persons. The child, who was the male heir to the throne, was unwell. His older half sister, Princess Anne was also pregnant with a possible competing heir to the throne. Princess Anne was at Tunbridge to safeguard her own pregnancy against miscarriage. While there she briefed her equerry, Colonel Sands, to go to Richmond to enquire as to the Queen's child's health. This gave rise to a story that the prince was initially found dead but that later on the same visit he appeared older and in good health. Substitution was suspected. This was used as an argument, amongst many others, to suggest deception in the line of succession. The story lost credibility over time, although such issues continue to vex historians.[38]

Tunbridge Wells still lacked adequate infrastructure in the latter part of the seventeenth century. Building development was underway and as Mount Sion ousted Mount Ephraim as the most fashionable locality to build, building owners mounted their homes and shops on sledges and wheels in order to move with the times. Barton suggests that localised religious prejudice may have motivated such upheaval, coupled with proximity to The Wells.[39] Temporary buildings also attracted less tax.[40]

The season was another limiting factor, being from May to October during the seventeenth century. Tunbridge town, a few miles away, was often relied on for accommodation and frequently overcrowded with visitors.[41] When Robert Harley, who arrived at The Wells on 27 August 1685, was taken ill in October, no physician could be found by then, having departed with the close of the season.[42] This state of affairs lasted from 1660 to 1720 when Tunbridge Wells was seen as the "Courtiers Spa".

Tunbridge Wells quickly developed its own culture and craft heritage. An example is Tunbridge ware. Celia Fiennes noted the curious wooden ware for which the town had become noted. Two families, Wise and Burrows, each claimed to have established their businesses in 1685, twelve years before Celia's visit. The dates of inception lack firm evidence but both businesses continued until Victorian times. Numerous other families manufactured Tunbridge Ware also.[43] Initially the ware comprised undecorated turnery, with painted decoration and marquetry appearing in the mid eighteenth century. Mosaic ware came later c.1830. The origins of the industry certainly predate Celia Fiennes and it is likely that the wooden bowl borrowed by North when he first discovered the spring in 1606 was an early simple example of the craft.[44] The small wooden objects were purchased as souvenirs. Items included snuff boxes, tea chests, punch-ladles and dressing boxes. Sprange gives a clearer idea of this long established industry. Although made elsewhere in England, that of Tunbridge became the finest and many were employed in the production. Made principally from holly which grows in abundance, inlays were added of cherry, plum, yew and sycamore.[45] Often the wood was coloured by soaking in the chalybeate spring water. A principal place of manufacturing this ware was a large house on Bishop's Down Common. Doubt is expressed by Melville as to the extent of the industry due to English goods being less fashionable than those of the continent.[46] Similar craft items had been made at Spa since the early seventeenth century and it is likely that Tunbridge sought to imitate the fashionable continental resort. In due course, the ingenuity and diversity of style of the Tunbridge craftsmen far exceeded that of elsewhere.[47]

THE MINERAL WATERS

The principal spring is situated at the end of the what Celia described as the peasa (piazza) where the company could perambulate. It was after Celia's visit that the area became known as the Pantiles following Princess Anne's instruction to pave it. The spring bubbled up into two basins set below street level and from time to time a dipper dispensed water to passers by, a custom still practised to this day. The Queen's Well was a name applied to one of the springs, that on the left on entering the area.[48] Princess Anne gave a basin for this spring about the time of Celia Fiennes' visit; the lord of the manor gave the other basin.[49]

The water emerges at a uniform temperature of 51° F (10.5° C) indicating that it is not a thermal water. Various analyses have been conducted over the centuries and the following, dated 1892, is consistent with an earlier one by Thompson dated 1857.

Dr Stevenson's analysis of Tunbridge water, 1892.[50]

grains per gallon.

Ammonia (NH_3)	0.006
Potash (K_2O)	0.317
Soda (Na_2O)	1.795
Lime (CaO)	1.749
Magnesia (MgO)	0.448
Ferrous Oxide (FeO)	2.798
Sulphuric Anhydride (SO_3)	3.024
Chlorine (Cl)	2.492
Carbon Dioxide (CO_2) (in combination)	1.792

which may be combined as follows:-

Chloride of Potassium	0.501
Chloride of Sodium	3.379
Chloride of Ammonium	0.019
Chloride of Magnesium	0.264
Sulphate of Magnesium	1.009
Sulphate of Calcium	3.998
Carbonate of Calcium	0.184
Ferrous Carbonate	4.508
Carbonate of Manganese	trace
Silica	0.602
Organic matter	trace

Total   *14.464*

Total solid residue of one gallon experimental - 14.070

Oxygen required to oxidise the organic matter - 0.007
Yield of Albumenoid Ammonia   - 0.006

Specific gravity   - 1.0004

Free Carbon Dioxide - 20.00 cubic inches at 60° F.
Free Nitrogen   - 4.97 cubic inches at 60° F.

The water was found to be clear and not unpleasant to the taste.

There are many other similar springs in the environs of Tunbridge. Described as Britain's only pure "rich chalybeate" spring the water is best suited for drinking. The absence of large amounts of free carbonic acid gas renders the water less suited to bathing than at the continental spas.[51] In spite of this the first cold bath was built shortly after Celia's visit, in 1708 at Rusthall by Mr James Long. A feature of the location was the extensive water works and fountains both inside and outside. Sprange reported that by 1786 it was all lost through decay.[52]

Another celebrated spring in the area is Adams Well. This was noted for curing cutaneous scorbutic disorders. By 1786 it was railed.[53] Burr recorded it as disused in 1766, noting that it was situated a half mile beyond High Rocks and at the time the resort of mangy dogs.[54] Barton in 1937 located the well in a cottage garden a couple of hundred yards north of High Rocks gardens. She considered that its rediscovery in the eighteenth century was faked by a certain Pinchbeck who had aspirations of developing the area as a satellite spa.[55]

The chalybeate waters are a direct result of the geology and physical geography of the area. Situated in the centre of the High Weald anticlinorium, the area is underlain by Hastings Beds, an alternating sequence of sandstones, silts, clays and limestones of the Cretaceous period. Due to the varying nature of the beds, the resulting aquifers are of only local importance. Ironstone occurs in several of the subdivisions of the Hastings Beds, particularly the Weald Clay (lower part), Grinstead Clay and the Wadhurst Clay. This has given rise to the earlier iron industry, of which extensive archaeology survives, and the chalybeate waters. A 1952 analysis indicated that there was 47.9 mg/litre of iron as FeO in the Pantiles Chalybeate spring. The Ardingly Sandstone and Ashdown Beds have produced the notable rock formations which characterise the landscape at such places as Eridge Rocks and Under Rockes Wood near Mayfield.[56]

EFFICACY

In 1769 the Tunbridge waters were described as suited to purging, particularly if a spoonful of common salt were added to the first glass.[57] The efficacy of the mineral water was probably best summed up by the cynical observer George Carey in 1799. *"Of what quality the mineral springs of this place may be is best known to the diplomatist, who, for his own sake, may have analysed them, or the credulous invalid, who may have been complaisant enough to drink them; but we are told, as every quack says of his nostrum, **they are good for all diseases.**"*[58]

LOCATIONS VISITED NEARBY

Somerhill - Celia Fiennes mentioned that she visited Somerhill and it is possible that she stayed there. It served as an aristocratic lodging house during the season.[59] The estate is near Tonbridge, approximately 4 miles from Tunbridge Wells, and is now a school.

The Somerhill estate has had a varied history since being part of the demesnes of Tunbridge Castle. The main part of the house was built in 1614 on land presented by Elizabeth I to Frances, the only child of Sir Francis Walsingham. Evelyn noted that in 1652 the estate had been given to the regicide Bradshaw who had been a participant in the killing of the King. Following a natural death he was later disinterred and hanged before the mob at Tyburn.[60] After the Restoration, Somerhill was returned to Margaret, daughter of Ulick, second Marquis of Clanricarde. She married Charles, Viscount Muskerry, who carried out considerable improvements at The Wells in 1664 as lord of the manor, only to die the following year during the wars with the Dutch.[61]

Lady Muskerry suffered a deformity and was perceived as ugly as a result. She loved dancing and was nicknamed the "Princess of Babylon" following a mischievous prank played on her in 1663 by the Hamiltons. Lady Muskerry responded to a contrived invitation to a Royal Ball, which invited her to dress in Babylonian costume. Her husband eventually persuaded her that she was not invited and that her excessive dress had been in vain.

The estate passed to Lady Muskerry who assumed the title Lady Purbeck when she married Viscount Purbeck, a young rake, half her age and an unscrupulous fortune hunter.[62] She had no right to the title as her later husband had only been the bastard son of the real Lady Purbeck. Later, in 1684, Lord Purbeck, as he described himself, was killed in a duel. Lady Muskerry/Purbeck then married a Jacobite, "Beau" Fielding.

The court visited Tunbridge at least four times during the first decade of the Restoration. This gave rise to another recorded incident of Lady Purbeck's social ineptitude. The unfortunate lady was ridiculed when dancing at Tunbridge whilst pregnant. She unwittingly "gave birth" on the dance floor to a pillow that had been used to adjust her figure to more manageable proportions, an event recorded by Pepys.[63] The unfortunate Lady Purbeck died in 1698, just after Celia Fiennes' visit. Her last husband, Robert Fielding was a character of dubious reputation and gambled extensively at The Wells. In 1705 he sought to make the acquaintance of a wealthy Mrs Deleau but was tricked by servants into wooing and marrying a prostitute. Discovering the ploy too late he then bigamously married a reputed nymphomaniac, the 64 year old Duchess of Cleveland (Barbara Villiers), who had earlier pulled down

Nonsuch Palace, near Epsom, when given it by Charles II. Following ill treatment she complained to the justices and Robert Fielding ended up in the Old Bailey where he was convicted of bigamy.[64]

Lambert's engraving of Somerhill, 1793, published by J. Sprange.

The intrigue and scandal typified spa life. It is difficult to understand why Celia Fiennes chose to be entertained at Somerhill. The family title was dubious and it is surprising that she recognised it.

Penshurst Place - Celia Fiennes mentioned Penshurst Place which has a history dating back to William the Conqueror. The Sidney family have been in possession since 1552 when it was given by Edward VI. Sir Robert Sidney was created Earl of Leicester in 1618. Robert, the second Earl, succeeded to the earldom in 1626. It was to this line that Celia made reference in her journal.

Lambert's view of Penshurst Place c.1786 published by J. Sprange.

The present building features five centuries of architectural styles and the illustration reproduced from Sprange is indicative of how Celia Fiennes would have found it. Penshurst is 5 miles to the north-west of Tunbridge Wells and is open to the public. It is the present day home of Viscount De L'Isle.

Eridge - Located in the parish of Frant, Eridge has two claims to fame relevant to the journeys of Celia Fiennes. She mentioned that it was the seat of Lord Aubergauney (Abergavenny) who was lord of the manor and therefore influential in the manner in which Tunbridge developed. Eridge was used as a hunting lodge. The second claim relates to how it was used by the 25 year old Lord North to recover from 40 days of feasting with King Christian of Denmark. After twelve weeks of simple country life and routine, North decided that an early death from the excesses of court life was preferable and set out to return to the capital on horseback. This journey resulted in him discovering the chalybeate waters which he recognised as similar to those of Spa.[65]

The Eridge that Celia Fiennes and Lord North knew disappeared around 1800 when the second Earl of Abergavenny decided to replace what by then had deteriorated into a ruin. All that remains are the vague references to a substantial lodge, quadrangular in form, surrounded by extensive deer forests.[66] In the outbuildings of the house an ancient drinking basin reputedly survives. A spring supplies water to what was once a cistern, now an ornamental pond, by the stables. One can speculate that North first discovered the chalybeate waters at or near Eridge but that the reluctance of the Bergavennys to accommodate the needs of the common people resulted in alternative springs being exploited at the perimeter of their manorial territory.[67] There is no shortage of chalybeate springs throughout this part of Kent and the selection of one bordering the Manor of Rusthall gives explanation to the skewed early development around the springs.

TUNBRIDGE WELLS TODAY

There are many aspects of the modern town that reflect the era during which Celia Fiennes made her visit. The Pantiles, although modified over the ensuing 300 years, still retain the essential layout with the colonnade that Celia Fiennes would have seen as a modern shopping precinct. The spring at the end of The Pantiles can still be sampled although Muskerry's triangular enclosure has disappeared. The adjoining shop was formerly the Bath House built in 1804. The water is free and there is public access to the second basin. An interesting experiment is to drop a crushed oak gall into a fresh glass of the water. The resulting inky colour replicates the ancient test for chalybeate waters.

The bath is still in situ beneath the chemists shop. Also still to be seen is the church of King Charles the Martyr, the oldest religious building in Tunbridge

Wells. Celia referred to it as the chapel, it being a chapel of ease until its consecration as a church in 1887. Even as a chapel it could seat 800.

The geographical relationship between The Pantiles area and the town centre of Tunbridge Wells can be attributed to Decimus Burton's "new town" plan of the 1820s/30s. Mount Pleasant became the centre of gravity, reinforced by the railway and other nineteenth century developments. It was not until 1909 that the town received its "Royal" prefix. A petition proposing the name "The Royal Kentish Spa" was rejected by the King in favour of "The Royal Tunbridge Wells". The prefix was renewed by Elizabeth II in the 1970s following local government reorganisation.[68]

Accommodation - The Boatwright Calverley Hotel. This hotel is one of the oldest in Tunbridge Wells and its buildings date back to the eighteenth century, when it was often rented for the season to the fourth Duke of Leeds. J. Sprange dedicated his book *The Tunbridge Wells Guide*, published 1786, to the fourth Duke (1713-1789) and the preface includes an ode to this most noble personage.[69] The Princess Victoria and the Duchess of Kent also stayed at the house before it became a hotel in 1840. Today it retains its old style spa semblance but with modern facilities including conference rooms. It is conveniently located in the centre of town adjacent to the Calverley Gardens and within a short walking distance of the Pantiles, museum and other points of interest.

Footnotes:

1   Morris C. (ed.) 1947, *The Journeys of Celia Fiennes*, p.132-137.
2   ibid. p.30, 31, 80, 125, 216.
3   Barton M. 1937, *Tunbridge Wells*, p.168.
4   ibid. p.180.
5   Sprange J. 1786, *The Tunbridge Wells Guide,* p.39-40.
6   Denbigh K. 1981, *A Hundred British Spas*, p.279.
7   Barton M. op.cit. p.70, 139, 150.
8   British Library, ref. Sloane MS 2348, f34, Anon. 17th c. M/S. This transcription varies slightly from the verse in *Tunbridge Wells, or a Days Courtship*.
9   Morris M. Penrose F. 1895, *The Climates and Baths of Great Britain,* a report by a committee of the Royal Medical and Chirurgical Society of London, Vol.l, p.594/5.
10 Melville L. 1912, *Society at Royal Tunbridge Wells*, p.34.
11 Barton M. op.cit. p.47.
12 Savidge A. 1975, *Royal Tunbridge Wells, A History of a Spa Town,* revised edition by Bell C. 1995, p.27-8.
13 Sprange J. op.cit. p.3-10.
14 Denbigh K. op.cit. p.17,18.
15 Melville L. op.cit. p.27.
16 Barton M. op.cit. p.31.
17 There may be some confusion about the second visit which Lennard was unable to authenticate from contempoary sources, see Lennard R. 1931, *Englishmen at Rest and Play*, p.23.
18 Rowzee L. 1632, *The Queenes Wells, that is a Treatise of the Nature and Vertues of Tunbridge Water*, republished in 1658, 1670 and 1671.
19 Sprange J. op.cit. p.18.
20 Calendar of State Papers Domestic, 1635, p.385, see Lennard R. 1931, p.17.
21 Barton M. op.cit. p.75.
22 Hembry P. 1990, *The English Spa 1560-1815*, p.60.

23   ibid. p.61.
24   Melville L. op.cit. p.38.
25   ibid. p.27.
26   Hembry P. op.cit. p.79-81.
27   Sprange J. op.cit. p.27/28.
28   Melville L. op.cit. p.39.
29   Sprange J. op.cit. p.29.
30   ibid. p.32.
31   Barton M. op.cit. p.112.
32   Hembry P. op.cit. p.79.
33   Carey G S. 1799, *The Balnea: or, an impartial description of All the Popular Watering Places*, p.54.
34   ibid. p.51.
35   Elson P. 1995, "Now Tunbridge Feels Distinctly Unwell", *Telegraph*, 14 Oct.
36   Hembry P. op.cit. p.84.
37   Lennard R. op.cit. p.55.
38   Barton M. op.cit. p.155-161.
39   ibid. p.107.
40   Melville L. op.cit. p.49.
41   Sprange J. op.cit. p.15.
42   Hembry P. op.cit. p.85.
43   Gill M A V. 1985, *Tunbridge Ware,* p.27.
44   Sprange J. op.cit. p.9.
45   ibid. p.89.
46   Melville L. op.cit. p.41.
47   Crismer L M. 1983, *The Extraordinary History of the Waters of Spa*, p.60.
48   Sprange J. op.cit. p.39.
49   ibid. p.49.
50   Morris M. Penrose F. op.cit. p.594.
51   ibid. p.594.
52   Sprange J. op.cit. p.41.
53   ibid. p.34.
54   Burr T B. 1766, *The History of Tunbridge Wells*, quoted in Melville L. 1912, p.56.
55   Barton M. op.cit. p.4.
56   Bristow C R. Bazley R A. 1972, *Geology of the Country around Royal Tunbridge Wells*, p.1, 30, 123, plate VII.
57   Russel R. 1769 (5th edition) *Dissertation on the use of Sea Water* with anonymous supplement *A Treatise on the Nature, Properties and Uses of the Mineral Waters*, p.215.
58   Carey G S. op.cit. p.53.
59   Farthing R. 1990, *Royal Tunbridge Wells*, illust 16.
60   Barton M. op.cit. p.127.
61   Melville L. op.cit. p.45.
62   Barton M. op.cit. p.144.
63   ibid. p.143.
64   Barton M. 1937, Chapher 6.; Morris C. 1982, *The Illustrated Journeys of Celia Fiennes*, p.128, footnote 10.
65   Barton M. op.cit. p.41,42.
66   ibid. p.22.
67   Discussion at *Local History Group*, 19 April 1995.
68   Rowlands M. 1996, *personal communication*.
69   Sprange J. op.cit. see preface, armorial and ode dated 1770.

EPSOM

The chronicles of Celia Fiennes' journeys have great significance for Epsom historians. This intrepid lady, who rode side saddle through England at the passage of the seventeenth to the eighteenth century, recorded Epsom in a state of transition. Unlike the other spas that she visited she made two detailed accounts of her visits. The first, sometime in the 1690s, chronicled Epsom as an undeveloped spa with minimal facilities. The second visit, probably about 1712, saw Epsom as a developed spa with new facilities which completely changed the ethos and aura of the town for her.[1]

THE DISCOVERY

Towards the end of the reign of Elizabeth (1558-1603), the pond on Epsom common had become noted for its ability to cure ulcers and other ailments.[2] Physicians who visited the well in 1603 found it to be impregnated with bitter purging salt. This information originated from an editorial in the *Lloyd's Evening Post* of 1769, the significance of which is discussed later.[3]

The presence of surface water on Epsom common was once much more apparent than today. John Speede's map of Surrey engraved by Jodocus Hondius in 1610 shows the substantial Willmore Pond between Epsom and Ashtead in the general area of the common. There is a watercourse draining to the Thames northward. John Seller's 1693 map of Surrey shows the Willmore pond between Epsom and Ashtead to the south of the highway. A watercourse drains the pond to the north, first tracking through Epsom. The pond and watercourse do not appear on John Senex's map of 1729 or thereafter, suggesting that they may have been lost by then.

The traditional explanation for the discovery of Epsom Wells has a typically humble quality. After the Restoration in 1660, but before 1662, Thomas Fuller in *The History of the Worthies of England* outlined the story of Henry Wicker discovering the well at Flowerdale on Epsom Common in 1618. He enlarged a small hole on the common to enable his cows to drink from the water therein, which they declined to do. By experimentation he discovered the efficacy of the waters. Fuller then went on to record that the Aluma based water was initially used as a cleanser and ointment and later taken orally. Exwood points out that this is the earliest and otherwise unauthenticated account of Wicker's discovery. There are several variations to this folklore tale.[4] It may therefore be suspect.[5] Hembry identifies the original well as "Wicker's Well".[6] Certainly by 1618-1620, Epsom waters had been discovered to be medicinal and used by country people for external application to ulcers and internally as a purgative. However it was not until several years later that fame came. In the intervening period, in 1621, a wall was built around the Epsom Well and a shed erected for the benefit of invalids.[7]

By 1629 there were indications of escalating spa activity at Epsom Wells; Abram Booth visited Nonsuch and Epsom Wells and observed that there were always people on the heath who offered visitors the waters in glasses and other vessels. Known as Ipsom-Well it was made accessible by the people of the village of that name nearby. The waters were healthy and promoted effortless purging. After walking up and down the effect became apparent. People came from far away places to drink and collect the waters. The well was supposedly found a few years before Booth's visit. As Clark notes, this is the first authentic account of Epsom Wells.[8]

Dudley North, the third Lord North, was one of the great promoters of both Epsom and Tunbridge mineral waters. It was c.1630 that Lord North first tried the water, soon followed by Maria de Medici (mother-in-law of Charles I), the Earl of Norwich and others. Authority for this stems from Nehemia Grew's writings of the late seventeenth century, of which there is more later.[9] In 1645 Lord North mentioned the wells as being famous and claimed credit for making them so in *Forest of Varieties*.[10] The exit of money from the Kingdom as the wealthy took the inconvenient journey to Spa in the Ardennes, then in Germany, was a sound reason for the establishment and promotion of English spas.[11] Lord North may well have had a hidden agenda therefore in "discovering" new spas, perhaps acting with the support of the treasury. Ironically, although first discovered and used apparently by local peasants, it was the nobility who were able to exploit the Epsom waters to social and commercial advantage.

EARLY YEARS OF POPULARITY (1646-1649)

How did Epsom become one of the most celebrated seventeenth century spas? The fortuitous and legendary cure of a leprous shepherd, an early attribute of the well, was never to be repeated.[12] This can possibly be explained by the fact that leprosy, as known today, died out in England during Tudor times. The term was subsequently used to describe any chronic skin ailment.[13]

After the earlier promotion by Lord North, patronage ensued. In 1648 a London barrister, John Greene, recorded in a manner that suggests it a matter of course, that he visited Epsom for a few days before going on to Tunbridge where he stayed a fortnight. Dr Madden in 1687 was to advocate this procedure of using Epsom waters as a precursor to those at Tunbridge.[14]

Following the wider publicity of Epsom, the declaration of the Commonwealth (1649-1659) threatened any immediate enhancement of the resort facilities. However it did not prevent people from continuing to visit Epsom, as is evidenced by the 1652 letters of Dorothy Osborne who visited the town.[15] Dorothy was the daughter of Sir Peter Osborne. She met Sir

William Temple on the Isle of Wight in 1650. He was born in 1628, the son of Sir John Temple and was eventually to marry Dorothy and pursue a career in public service.[16] Their premarital relationship is recorded in Dorothy's published letters to Sir William.[17]

In January 1653 Dorothy noted that she had needed to drink the waters because of a scurvy spleen. This was a general term used to describe *"a lowness of spirit"*. She had spent the latter part of the summer (of 1652) so doing. Reference to her brother Henry's diary indicates that she had visited Epsom several times in that year.[18] In 1653 Epsom was again mentioned in her letters. June 5th: Dorothy Osborne commented on the proper action of Epsom Waters on the spleen. June 19th: She gave further personal reasons, unconnected with the town, not to visit Epsom. Aug.7th: Dorothy Osborne recorded that Sir William Temple had been to Epsom, drinking the water as she had done previously. Aug.14th: She wrote that Temple had returned presumably from Epsom. Also that when she visited at that time of year the well was low and that she was forbidden to drink the water immediately. When the vessel had stood all night the bottom was covered in an inch thick white clay which had no quality.[19]

"But did you drink them imediatly from the well? I remember I was forbid it, and mee thought with a great deal of reason, for (Especially at this time of yeare) the well is soe low, and there is such a multitude to bee served out on't, that you can hardly gett any but what is thick, and troubled; and I have marked that when it had stood all night (for that was my direction) the bottom of ye Vessell it stood in, would be coverd an inch thick, with a white clay, which sure has noe great virtue int, and is not very pleasant to drink."[20]

It is apparent that The Wells were not of the quality or as prolific as the customers might wish.

Another visitor during the Commonwealth was the great Surrey historian John Aubrey. In 1654/5 he drank the waters and conducted some experiments. Having evaporated the water, it yielded a flakey sediment the colour of Bay-Salt, a similar hue to that of evaporated sea salt.[21] While conducting his trials, Aubrey could well have been rubbing shoulders with prisoners from the Tower. During the 1650s it is recorded that prisoners were released on parole to take a cure at Bath, Tunbridge or Epsom.[22]

With the dissolution of parliament in 1654 England became a dictatorship. Sanctions were taken against Roman Catholics and Royalists who were obliged to meet clandestinely at obscure locations under other guises. Bax identifies the movements of a number of suspect persons removing to and from Epsom in 1656. These included Roger Britterbridge, Baptist Lord Noel Viscount Campden and Richard Lee.[23] Kershaw notes that malcontents held meetings at Epsom during the Commonwealth under the guise of taking the waters.[24]

One of the ancillary attractions to Epsom during its brief period as a fashionable spa was Box Hill, situated between Leatherhead and Dorking and accessible as a place of recreation for visitors. Sometime between 1625-1649, legend suggests that the Earl of Arundel brought box trees from Kent and planted them on White Hill as it was then known. There is also evidence that box existed on the hill in 1602. Normally a shrub, in Surrey and Kent the species grows to a substantial tree.[25] These avenues and glades provided opportunity for early visitors from Epsom Spa to debauch. The involvement of the Earl of Arundel suggests that visitors to Nonsuch may have also taken advantage of the facilities.

During these early years of popularity the manor of Epsom was in the hands of Anne Mynne, the widow of George Mynne of nearby Horton Manor. She was the daughter of Sir Robert Parkhurst and had purchased the manor from Edward Darcy. The manor had therefore come into the Parkhurst family of which more later. Anne Mynne left the manor by will to her daughter Elizabeth, wife of Richard Evelyn, brother of the diarist John.[26] Manorial involvement was to play a crucial role in the future development of Epsom Spa, initially under Richard and then Elizabeth Evelyn and later the Parkhursts.

Although Epsom maintained its role as a spa during the Interregnum, no doubt aided by the intrigues that interrupted everyday life at the time, it was not until after the Commonwealth in 1659 that normality ensued and the spa took on an extended social as well as healing function.

FLOURISHING SPA (1660-1690)

In 1662 we have the earliest known illustration of Epsom Wells. The detail includes a small building located on an otherwise undeveloped common with scrub interspersed by people congregating around the well. In the bushes are those whose imbibing of the waters was giving rise to the renowned purging effect. What is apparent is that the facilities were severely limited. William Schellinks, the artist who drew this early picture of Epsom Well, described the location in his travel journal.[27] Schellinks visited the well on four separate days. He noted that Epsom was by 1662 a pleasant and famous place and that water was sent in stoneware jars throughout the land. There was a spring, with a wall enclosing a raised well and brick paving surround. The well was at the rear of a small house for which was paid a rent of £12 yearly. An old man and woman had it on hire in 1662. Those taking the waters donated what they wished. The practice was to drink the water early on an empty stomach. Some people drank as much as 15-16 pints in one journey, using stoneware mugs. This was followed by a walk with various *"funny"* results, the ladies and gentlemen putting down sentinels in the scrub separately in every direction.

Hot meat broth or ale was often taken after the waters. The water was stronger in summer, being less diluted by rain water, and the well was frequently drunk dry. The 300 beds in the village were inadequate for normal demand. Some visitors stayed several weeks.[28]

Epsom was a town of some prestige by this time.[29] Another visitor in 1662 was George Berkeley, first Earl of Berkeley, who entertained Charles II at Epsom. The King dined at Durdans in 1662 with his brother and Lord Berkeley. This would have been an earlier house than that seen by Celia Fiennes and recorded in her first account of Epsom.[30] The Berkeleys were the keepers of Nonsuch Palace endorsing the constant associations between Epsom and Nonsuch. Other visitors to Epsom included John Evelyn the diarist, who met the King and Queen, the Duke and Duchess of York, Prince Rupert and various noblemen. Charles II came again in 1664.

The arrival of Samuel Pepys on July 25th 1663 was not without problems. Pepys noted that the town was full and had to lodge in Ashtead, an experience which came in for some criticism due to the quality of the accommodation. Visiting Ashtead gave him an opportunity to visit his cousin whose house was not as grand as he recalled as a child. Ashtead was only one mile from the Old Wells, about two from Epsom town. Pepys noted the surprising number of people in Epsom, including some people of quality, with little else to do but drink the water. Epsom town centre facilities, like those at the wells, were clearly limited at this time.[31]

The year 1663 saw the ballad *Merry Newes from Epsom Wells* launched which described life at Epsom.[32] In the same year Richard Evelyn, brother of the diarist, became lord of the manor.[33] Also about this time, according to the Epsom Commons Association, a roughly circular area around the Old Well was cleared and rights of common were curtailed. This encroachment of the manorial commons enabled the crowds to be accommodated. The area was 40 rods in radius, about 450 yards in diameter and can be identified on nineteenth century maps. The earliest map showing this is the 1866 25 inch OS map.[34] It does not appear on the first edition OS map of 1810-17. This enclosure was later to determine the incongruous area of mid-twentieth century housing now surrounding The Wells.

The fact that Epsom provided an easily accessible resort from London is apparent in 1665 when Richard Evelyn, JP. and lord of the manor, was obliged to close the wells due to possible spread of infection from the Great Plague.[35] The instruction, issued by the Surrey Quarter Sessions, directed that the wells be locked and no person permitted to drink the waters. It noted that there had been a substantial influx of visitors to the town from London on the pretext of drinking the waters.[36] By modern day standards Epsom was a small town in spite of its visitor numbers and it is difficult to appreciate the intimacy that must have existed compared with the impersonal indifference that features in modern day urban society. In 1664 Epsom contained only 137 houses liable to the Hearth Tax and yet this made it a notable Surrey town.[37]

By 1667 Samuel Pepys was back in Epsom. He left London at five in the morning to journey to the wells to drink the mineral water at the appropriate time,[38] as well as to fill containers to take home. At the well he learnt from the woman attendant that the well was rented from the lord of the manor for £12 a year, thereby confirming the earlier information recorded by Schellinks.[39] Pepys wrote in his diary in July, *"To Epsum by eight o'clock, to the well; where much company, and I drank the water: they did not, but I did drink four pints. And to the towne to the King's Head; and hear my Lord Buckurst and Nelly (Nell Gwynne) are lodged at the next house, and Sir Charles Sedley with them: and keep a merry house."*[40]

Drinking 4 pints of mineralised water was no doubt a daunting prospect. In the Bohemian spas a custom arose of eating a wafer while taking the waters. This custom remains to this day and the "Kolonada Luxus" continues to be produced locally. Such a practice likely took place in Epsom in order to render the waters more palatable. A wafer iron in the Guildford Museum lends credence to this belief.

In the same year as Pepys' later visit, two convictions for running a disorderly house and another for keeping an unlicensed common tippling house were recorded.[41] Things were without doubt lively in Epsom but it was not only at the spa that one could be relieved of ones money. It was customary for travellers between London and Epsom to be waylaid. The people of Tooting had a reputation for what became almost extortion in an effort to foist their goods and services on the trippers. Such a practice gave rise to the expression "tooting" or "touting".[42]

As the seventeenth century progressed, the year of 1668 saw a number of minor occurrences that give an insight into the activities at the spa. Many doctors advised a visit to Epsom, and the Court of Charles II and other fashionable people visited the town.[43] In Pepys' domestic papers are letters from John Owen requesting 12 days leave to visit the Epsom Wells in June followed by a further request in August.[44] The Court Rolls record that the wall erected by Richard Evelyn around a well near the main Well had been broken down and this was prejudicial to those taking the waters. This suggests more than one well and that the one mentioned was under the control of the manor.[45]

In 1670, Nonsuch Palace was given by Charles II to Barbara Villiers, who rapidly demolished it. The ruins of Nonsuch were subsequently used to beautify the buildings in the town. Thereafter there was no royal palace in the locality of Epsom.[46] Shadwell's comedy, *Epsom Wells*, began a long run at the Duke's Theatre in 1673. Epsom was portrayed as a place of licentious behaviour and scandalous goings on.[47] This suggests that Epsom society had moved "down-market" perhaps following the demise of Nonsuch Palace and abandonment by the aristocracy. Brighton followed a similar sequence in the late eighteenth and nineteenth centuries. Initially it attracted the aristocracy of the Regency period and the Royal Pavilion was built. Later Royalty went elsewhere and the town became a centre for entertainment and pleasure, much of it of a dubious nature.[48]

Another unfortunate event in 1670 was the demise of Richard Evelyn, lord of the manor, who died early in March from calculus, a concretion found in the body. John Evelyn, the diarist, records that his brother's body was opened and a stone not much bigger than a nutmeg was removed from his bladder. In addition his liver and kidneys were faulty, accounting for the intolerable pain that Richard experienced before death. The suggestion is that he died of over consumption of Epsom Waters, having drunk them when in good health, thereby no doubt reducing Lady Elizabeth Evelyn's enthusiasm for the waters.[49] John Evelyn came to Epsom for the funeral.[50] Following her husband's death, Lady Evelyn took over the manorial responsibilities. Elizabeth Evelyn, as lady of the manor, held courts from 1670 to 1691.[51] In the same year, 1670, as a result of a dispute with tenants, she caused the spring to be stopped up, but a new well was discovered at Slyfield, 4 to 5 miles away in Stoke D'Abernon, in 1671. Soon after, the original well at "Ebsham" was reopened with houses to accommodate the reception of strangers.[52] In 1675 the Court Baron recorded that a building solely for the purpose of taking the waters was to be erected on the common annexed to the public wells.[53]

William Head of the Kings Head purchased an acre of land adjacent to the bowling green in 1671. This suggests that the lower bowling green, later noted by Celia Fiennes, was in existence by this date. In 1678, William Glover, the bowling green owner, had died leaving a bowling alley on 2 acres known as Phillips Close. It abutted the Kings Head on the east and the Kings Highway on the north and west. It was therefore on the south side of the present High Street opposite the Clock Tower. The green proved successful and attracted substantial custom from the 1680s as is noted by Clark.[54] A survey of 1688 reveals a further bowling green at Epsom. George Richbell, a yeoman, owned a meadow close to a bowling green. The location was near Summersgate Lane, now Wheeler's Lane, and Clay Hill now West Hill. It was not particularly successful and is not mentioned by contemporary writers. Last record of it was in 1727 when it was described as a former bowling green.[55] The second green was taken over in 1688 by Ashenhurst, who also had an interest in the other. Having secured a monopoly, the second green was closed.[56]

Indications are that, in Epsom, an infrastructure to accommodate and entertain visitors was being developed by the 1670s. The New Inn was mentioned in the Court Baron of 1672. This subsequently became the White Horse in Dorking Road and not to be confused with the later Waterloo House in the High Street.[57] Waterloo House was known as the New Tavern and likely had a long room and bowling green before 1699.[58] Pepys took dinner at the Kings Head in 1667. Other establishments before 1700 included the Golden Ball and the Crown.[59] As communications improved, in 1684 the *London Gazette* announced that the post would go between London and Epsom during the season for drinking the waters.[60] This was the first daily post outside London and could well have resulted in the earlier visits of Celia Fiennes to Epsom.

Also in 1684 a broadsheet was published entitled *An Exclamation from Tunbridge and Epsom against The Newfound Wells at Islington*. This warned readers to beware of interlopers, counterfeit waters and Quack Doctors and was issued to thwart competition from elsewhere.[61] This was a portend of things to come. The same year saw Lady Evelyn securing the right to hold a Friday market and two, three day Fairs yearly. Later Livingstone the apothecary was to lease the concession.[62] Epsom was part of the spa circuit by this time. Sir John Raresby brought his family to Epsom in 1686 and 1688 having in earlier years resorted to Scarborough and Buxton.[63]

In Celia Fiennes' early tours which took place in the 1690s, she compared Epsom with Barnet and complained that the spring was not a *"quick"* spring (i.e. of running water) like Tunbridge and Hampstead Spaw. At Barnet visitors went down to the water which was full of leaves and dirt. She disliked Barnet and, by implication, Epsom. Further comment was made of the *"Sulpher Spaw Epsome"* a little later when she compared it with a spring at Canterbury. She commented on the walled-in well liking *"no spring that rises not quick and runs off apace"*. Further remark comes when she compared Epsom with the springs on Blackheath. Like Epsom, she thought the springs were very quick purgers due to alum.[64]

Later Celia Fiennes expanded her description of Epsom with a narration that also emanated from the 1690s. She described Epsom Well as having waters from alum[65] with no basin or pavement and a dark interior. The spring was often drunk dry and water from elsewhere used to replenish the supply. The efficacy of the water was reduced however unless visitors could consume the waters before they were replenished. There was brick paving around the well to walk in wet weather and where sweetmeats and tea could be consumed. Celia disliked the whole arrangement, likening it to a dungeon, and would not choose to drink there. Near the house which contained the well there was a walk of trees which she considered not particularly pleasant. She noted that most people drank the water at home and that there were lodging and walking facilities in the town.

Accurately dating Celia Fiennes' early comments is difficult. In her account of Barnet and Epsom she referred to the *"Earle of Maulberoug"*. This account is certainly dated before 14 December 1702 when the Dukedom of Marlborough was created.[66]

Further confirmation that these accounts predate 1702 comes from the fact that Lord Berkeley's House, Durdans, is mentioned. It was built with materials from Nonsuch Palace. Berkeley died in 1698 and his son sold the house to Charles Turner in 1702.[67] The narration must predate this, but post date 1684 when Sir Robert Howard built Ashtead House, which she also mentioned.[68] Furthermore, Celia failed to mention the Assembly Rooms which were mortgaged in 1699, suggesting a date prior to this.[69] We are left with a date probably in the early 1690s.

It is apparent that Celia, who had a great interest in mineral springs and wells, disliked Epsom Wells at the time. It was the source that later became known as the Old Wells which she visited. Epsom, like the other spas, was poised to launch into a new era of investment and prosperity. The Wells on the common were still offering only basic facilities and the town remained congested in the season with accommodation stretched. Some amusements were catered for but these remained relatively unsophisticated. The social scene had developed and alongside this the scandals and frolics of the visitors provided ample opportunity for literary amplification. As competition between the spas intensified so did the demand for improved tourist amenities. The proximity to London rendered the town a venue for weekend trips and day excursions. Epsom was ideally positioned for further intensification of commerce to provide an enhanced resort for relaxation, amusement and medicinal healing as the eighteenth century approached. Yet it was already one of the great watering places of the south alongside Bath and Tunbridge when Celia Fiennes recorded her first observations. With the onset of the 1690s much was to quickly change.

SEVENTEENTH CENTURY MINERALISATION OF THE WELLS

Epsom (Old) Wells are situated on the common approximately one mile south west of the town centre, grid ref. TQ 193600. The 6 inch geological map describes it as *"The Old Well, 24ft to Water, Epsom salts"*. The Old Wells were the main focus of spa activity during the seventeenth century and although it will be shown that other wells existed, the Old Wells were where people resorted for "the cure". In spite of the popularity of Epsom Wells however it is apparent that all was not well.

From earlier text it is known that in 1653 Dorothy Osborne recorded that she was forbidden to drink directly from the well and that the waters had to stand overnight to allow the sediment to precipitate. A little later, in 1662, William

Schellinks noted that it was practice to drink the waters early. Probably the reason for this was to avoid the muddied waters after the wells had been dipped. But Schellinks also went on to observe that the wells were frequently drunk dry. This indicates that the demand exceeded the supply with the likely result that more mud than water was dispensed when the waters were low. The further observation made by Schellinks was that rain diluted the mineralised water. This would weaken its efficacy prompting the imbibing of greater quantities.

Another critique of The Wells comes from Celia Fiennes, some years later. In the early 1690s Celia Fiennes described Epsom Well as on clay and gravel with waters from alum. The well was without a basin or pavement and she disliked looking down into the dark interior. The spring was often drunk dry and water was carried from common wells to replenish the supply. The efficacy of the water was reduced however unless visitors could consume the waters before they were replenished. Here Celia Fiennes made an important hydrogeological observation. Not only does this endorse the reason for early morning use, she also records that the well was replenished from elsewhere and that the "natural recovery" of the mineral water level in the well was slow. This in turn indicates slow movement of water through the aquifer strata as well as sources of mineralised and other water nearby for replenishing.

With such problems it is not surprising that other persons sought alternative ways of supplying the demand for Epsom Salts. There was one particular series of events which, although acted out away from the town, was to have a major effect on the future development of Epsom. In the year 1679 Nehemiah Grew, then secretary to the Royal Society, read three papers "*On the Mineral Waters about London*" and the preparation of salts from mineral waters. He referred to Epsom within the papers although he did not make them available for publication.[70]

Nehemiah Grew was born in 1641 in Warwickshire, son of Obadiah, a Nonconformist preacher educated at Balliol College, Oxford. Nehemiah graduated from Pembroke Hall, Cambridge in 1661. In keeping with the prevailing post-Renaissance paradigms, Grew became a naturalist and physician. In 1671 Dr Grew was elected a Fellow of the Royal Society as a result of a paper on the anatomy of vegetables. He then practised medicine in Coventry and continued his botanical studies at the Royal Society. By 1682 he was appointed curator of the Society's museum. This coincided with the publication of his "magnus opus" *The Anatomy of Plants*. On the medical front a purgative was developed containing calomel which became known as Pil.Purg.Grew. At about the same time his interest in Epsom Salts led to the reading of the previously mentioned unpublished papers to the Royal Society in 1679. John Evelyn recorded Dr Grew's discourse in his diary, which he attended after lunch on 19th June.[71]

Turning his attention to sea water, in 1683/4 Grew published observations on making sea water fresh. It is apparent that Grew was continuing his researches into salts, sea water and related matters, no doubt using Boyle's work of 1684 as a primary point of reference. Boyle had sought to analyse and measure the density of Epsom water, together with that of Barnet, Acton etc. in an attempt to identify the salts that gave *"Purgative vertue"*. Chemistry was in its formative years as a scientific discipline and in 1684 Robert Boyle published *Short Memoirs for the Natural Experimentation of Mineral Waters*, in which he made various observations on Epsom Waters.[72]

In 1695 Grew published in Latin *Tractatus de salis Cathartici amari in aquis Ebbeshamensibis* in which the first significant light was shed on the nature of Epsom Salts, especially their artificial preparation. The principal salt was identified as sulphate of magnesia and he clarified its differentiation from sulphate of soda. Grew particularly demonstrated that the salts could be taken without the need to consume considerable quantities of water. In addition he outlined the medical indications.[73] In publishing this paper, Dr Grew was the founding scientist of Epsom Salts.

Although it was not until 1695 that Grew formally went public with his discovery of how to manufacture Epsom Salts artificially, the news of his discovery was to have significant repercussions for a town which relied on the efficacy of its well for its prosperity. Grew, in due course, set up a factory for Epsom Salts at Acton, hoping to make 20,000lbs (9,070 kgs.) per year.[74] The salt was reputedly sold at five shillings an ounce initially.

Realising the implications of Grew's work, others quickly started manufacturing in competition. Francis Moult, a London apothecary (chemist), and his brother George, also a chemist, initially purchased salts from Grew. They investigated other wells near London at Kensington, Dulwich, Lambeth and Richmond. The power of the springs at Shooters Hill was recognised by the Moult brothers and they started using the water for the manufacture of Epsom Salts. They were able to extract greater quantities of salts from Shooters Hill water and undercut Grew's prices. The price fell from sixteen shillings to 3 pence a pound. Dr Hoy shortly afterwards developed a method for extracting the Epsom Salts from the bitterns left after evaporating sea water for common salt.[75] Within a few years salts were being prepared from sea water at Portsmouth, Newcastle and Leamington,[76] and dolomite (magnesium limestone). A similar substance (magnesium sulphate) was later obtained by Hoffman about 1721 from Seidlitz water in Bohemia.[77]

Dr Grew was having difficulty in containing his discoveries, particularly from Francis Moult. An English version of Grew's important paper was published by Grew following a spurious publication in 1697 by Francis Moult using

Grew's name and translated text, but without Grew's authority. In 1697 Grew quickly distributed *A Treatise of the Nature and Use of the Bitter Purging Salt contained in Epsom and other such Waters*. He also secured a patent (No 354) in 1698 for *"making the salt of the purging waters etc..."* This was done by evaporation of Epsom or Ebbisham Waters as was set out in the original Latin publication of 1695. Grew found two drams of magnesium sulphate in a gallon of Epsom Water and for some time this had been the only source of the mineral.

Acrimonious moves and counter moves frustrated Grew's attempts to protect his invention. He was under serious attack by those wishing to challenge his patent on the manufacture of Epsom Salts. He published a defensive document containing testimonials in 1701 and Francis Moult and other infringers were taken to task.[78] Attempts at arriving at a legal arrangement with the Moults were thwarted by claiming that they were now manufacturing on Dr Grew's direction. Eventually the Moults were reprimanded by the Lord Chancellor.

By 1722 the sale of Epsom waters was seen as a cheat. The salts had been expropriated by the Moults and the product on sale was not perceived as the proper salts, as discovered by the worthy physician Dr Grew.

"It is difficult to pass by this article without setting a mark upon that abominable cheat which is now sold by the name of Epsom waters. Dr Grew, who was a most worthy physician and industrious experimenter, made trial how much salt these waters would leave upon evaporation, and found that a gallon left about 2 drams, or near, according to my best remembrance, for I have not his writings with me. He likewise found salt thus procured answered the virtues of the water in its Cathartic qualities. Of this, an account was given before the Royal Society in a Latin dissertation. But by avaricious craft of a certain furnace-philosopher could not let this useful discovery in natural knowledge rest under the improvement and proper use of persons of integrity; but by pretending to make a great quantity for sale; translated the Doctor's lecture into English to give away as a quack-bill."

This testimony was published in *A Compleat English Dispensary* against a background of rivalry between the apothecaries and physicians for the prescription and dispensing of drugs.[79] It clearly identifies the manufactured salts as a cheat and lays blame on the "furnace-philosopher" and translator of Dr Grew's paper. This is without doubt Francis Moult although not named. It is this promulgation that was, arguably, to herald the demise of Epsom's reputation as a legitimate mineralised water and spa.

Dr Grew died in March 1712, aged 71, his patent having been earlier assigned to one Josiah Peter, who defended him during the legal wrangling. Grew was a pioneer in the analytical evaluation of Epsom mineral waters. During the eighteenth century the unravelling of the chemical constituents of mineralised waters was to confuse and baffle those who attempted it. It was not until the early nineteenth century that sufficient knowledge of chemical composition had been secured to give Dr Struve the confidence to manufacture a range of European mineral waters at his German Spa at Brighton.[80] Grew's pioneering approach was no doubt stimulated by the failure to resolve the supply problems at the Epsom Wells and the enormous potential market for the purgative. With the publicity that his efforts received, his findings would have been noted with interest by the medical profession, apothecaries and all interested in the spa industry. One such person was no doubt John Livingstone, more details of whom will be considered in due course.

A NEW ERA (1690-1712)

The evolving commercial infrastructure of Epsom was typical of the principal spas of the time. Tunbridge developed a new shopping mall, now known as The Pantiles in 1687, Bristol benefited from Hotwell House in 1696 and Bath built a new pump room in 1706. Such expansion typified the new commercial approach to spa development which came about following the unsettled times of the Interregnum and subsequent religious instability of the monarchy. A new confidence was apparent and private capital was an essential component in providing facilities that were to attract spa visitors. There is no doubt that Celia Fiennes, who visited Epsom first in about 1690, was attracted to such entrepreneurialism and she in turn invested in a new rock salt mine on the Marbury Estate at Northwich.[81]

In order to understand the evolution of Epsom it is important to appreciate what happened during that vital period between Celia Fiennes' first and second narrations of the town and spa. This period of transition replaced the traditional order with entrepreneurialism although it has been shown that infrastructure investment to accommodate tourists was starting to occur within the town during the second half of the seventeenth century. This earlier investment appears to have been demand led rather that catering for expanded tourism through innovation which typified the transition period. Hampstead underwent a synonymous era of capitalist expansion as entrepreneurs moved in to develop commercial spa enterprises.

For Epsom there were two leading spa entrepreneurs, John Parkhurst developed the wells on the common, to become known as the Old Wells, and one John Livingstone created the New Wells. It was in 1692 that Livingstone, an apothecary, started to make an impact on the local community. Having come to Epsom about 1690, he was appointed by the mayor as Tithingman.[82] In 1695 Livingstone lent £150 secured against a property in Church Street, at the eastern end of the town. Later in 1699, he became the true holder of the property but never developed it.[83]

The increasing importance of the town at this time is apparent in Edmund Gibson's 1695 translation of Camden's *Britannica* which commented on Epsom in an Addendum. It observed that and the medicinal wells, (thereby confirming more than one), were on the common. The water contained *"allom"* and there had recently been considerable development in the parish as a result of the growing reputation of the Spaw.[84] Lady Evelyn held courts until 1691 and died in 1692. The manorial estate was then managed by the Buckles of Banstead as Trustees to Ann, Lady Evelyn's sister. On Ann's death in 1706, John Parkhurst of Northants inherited the manor.[85] This event probably precipitated Parkhurst's serious interest in Epsom, and investment by him followed. As a measure of the town's repute in 1697, 2000 people a day visited Epsom. This comment comes from Grew to illustrate the popularity of Epsom once the salts had been recommended by physicians.[86]

In 1701 there were signs that John Livingstone, the apothecary, was considering developing the western end of the town, while John Parkhurst, lord of the manor from 1707, developed the (Old) Wells shortly after. Livingstone bought a house on a triangular piece of land of about a quarter of an acre in Shoulder of Mutton Close at the end of the High Street. A coachman, one W. Parkhurst had previously erected a house on this site between 1680 and 1686. Livingstone also acquired two small abutting plots. These were all to become "The Grove".[87] Shoulder of Mutton Close had previously been part of Humphrey Beane's estate and it has been erroneously suggested that Livingstone's acquisition included the lease of land with a well from John Symonds.[88] Symonds' property was immediately to the south but the location of any well uncertain.

Shortly afterwards John Parkhurst laid out the town with avenues of trees and built a spa ballroom, 70 feet long at the (Old) Wells. A brick wall with coping surrounded the land.[89] The dating of this as 1690 in the 1769 *Lloyds Evening Post* is suspect. Parkhurst's first court was held in 1707, prior to this the courts were held by the Buckles of Banstead as trustees to Lady Evelyn's will. The date of 1690 raises the question: did Parkhurst lay out the town 17 years before coming lord of the manor? It is unlikely. Furthermore, Celia Fiennes did not comment on the improved facilities until her second narration of 1712; her first narration made no report of Parkhurst's improvements. It is probable therefore that Parkhurst's developments took place about 1707.

Whilst John Parkhurst was developing the town and the (Old) Wells on the common, John Livingstone supposedly sank a new town well and developed a pump room as part of a capital investment programme.[90] The precise location of this pump room and well is uncertain other than it was within the locality of his facilities at the western end of town. When the Manor House, which is in the vicinity, was modernised, beneath the floor of the old kitchen, which was to be converted to the dining room, was a well with pipes. This may have been Livingstone's original well[91] although the Warren's or Symonds Well is a more likely alternative candidate, a point discussed later.

Livingstone's new facility, being far more convenient to the town, was a serious rival to John Parkhurst's Old Wells out on the common. It may have been that the New Wells development prompted Parkhurst to improve the Old Wells. Various authors give testimony to Livingstone's activities at this time. Sunderland records that, c.1706, Livingstone purchased land and erected a ballroom, gambling room, shops and houses as a business speculation.[92] This would have been adjacent to land previously purchased in 1701 and developed as The Grove. Home notes that Livingstone planted a grove and laid out a bowling green at the end of which he sank a well with a pump. By means of pipes the water was conveyed to the assembly room. The development took about two years to complete and was named the "New Wells".[93]

Lehmann gives considerably more detail about the relationship between Livingstone and Parkhurst and it is apparent that in 1707, when John Parkhurst become lord of the manor, inheriting it under the will of Lady Evelyn, he was working closely with Livingstone. Prior to this Parkhurst's history had included some dubious transactions leading to a spell in The Tower. In Parkhurst's first manorial court it is recorded that Livingstone disposed of his Church Street property. In addition the manorial records confirm Livingstone's acquisition, from John Castleton and Sir John Parsons, of a piece of land to the westward of that purchased earlier in 1701. Both acquisitions were once part of Beane estate. The 1701 land was developed by 1707 as The Grove. The further property, purchased in 1707, already contained buildings and a bowling green and was functioning as the New Wells together with Livingstone's adjacent Grove. Livingstone had actually developed the 1707 property before acquisition as a result of an arrangement with Anne Emerson, the tenant. Livingstone's entitlement to be on the land was somewhat dubious and Parkhurst's first manorial courts of 1707/8 enabled Livingstone to secure his position.[94] Often such pre-empting of the final legal agreement came about as a result of the slowness of the legal profession. A similar circumstance is recorded at Hampstead Wells about the same time.[95]

In 1707 the New Wells opened on the 25 April, seven months before Livingstone actually secured his legal title to the land.[96] From Clark's researches it has been possible to piece together a detailed picture of Livingstone's New Wells. The site was a substantial one between the modern West Street and South Street, at the western end of the High Street, east of the railway. The site is mapped by Clark (1960) showing the location of the Upper Green, the Manor House and the Grove. An advertisement for the New Wells appeared in the *Daily Courant* at this time. The waters were free and shops were to let.[9]

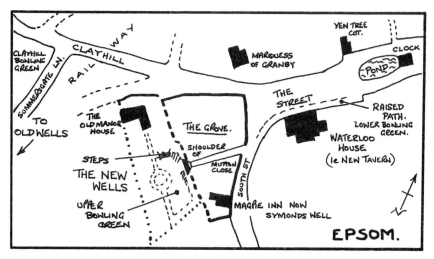

Livingstone's New Wells after Clark (1960).

With two centres for drinking the waters, the Old and New Wells, rivalry was inevitable. In 1710, a German traveller, Von Uffenbach visited Epsom for the horse racing. Visiting the Old Well he drank the water from nasty stoneware jugs, three pints at a time. He also visited the New Wells commenting that the water was very similar.[98] Livingstone appears to have been intent on further securing his position by establishing a monopoly on the mineral waters. In 1711 he supposedly secured the leases on the Old Well, having first engineered a further 21 years extension through the vendors. This done, Livingstone took over the Old Wells which Parkhurst had developed over recent years.[99] The basis for this supposition is the *Lloyds Evening Post* article of 1769.[100] As the article contained inaccuracies it may also be suspect in this respect.[101] Celia Fiennes in 1712 noted that the upper green was kept by the same man as the wells. This tends to confirm the acquisition of the Old Wells lease by Livingstone.

The town was developing fast and it was between 1710-1716 that one Henry North made the Black Spread Eagle a going concern. A valuable general description of Epsom around 1711 comes from John Toland[102]. Living at Woodcote, he wrote that the waters were beneficial in gently cleansing the body, in cooling the head and purifying the blood. Doctors were advocating pleasure as a cure rather than taking the waters. Toland observed above sixty coaches on the ring (racetrack) on the Downs on a Sunday evening. This was on the then new curvilinear course which had replaced the 4 mile straight course down to Banstead Downs.[103] He also commented on the plentiful supply of good food, especially Banstead-down Mutton.[104] Only two to three hours from London meant that commuting was relatively easy. There were topiary porticos and a tiled terrace at Epsom, no doubt similar to the Pantiles at Tunbridge Wells.[105] Two rival bowling greens were mentioned. The Old Wells, a half mile away were not so much in vogue, the waters of the *"village"* being as good. The cold bath, lately erected, was also less popular and he suggested relocating it at Ewell where it could benefit from a more copious supply of water. The Watch House in the High Street was mentioned by Toland and Home confirms that it had a turret with a clock, a fact noted by Celia Fiennes in her second report of Epsom.[106]

We can see therefore that by Celia's second narration of 1712, Epsom was a prospering spa enjoying the benefits of capital investment in infrastructure. Livingstone's New Wells were a success and he secured his position by taking over the Old Wells. The precise whereabouts of Livingstone's new mineral water source remains a mystery. There is little contemporary evidence that it was anything other than a perfectly adequate source of the mineral waters. It was after Celia Fiennes' second visitation that the scene was to change considerably.

CELIA FIENNES SECOND VISIT

How different Epsom was on her later visit, which is dated about 1712, compared with her first. In the second narration of Epsom, Celia Fiennes described the facilities in the town more extensively[107] and noted the curious cut hedges and trees. Durdans was by then *"Lord Guilford's"*. Celia Fiennes observed the rebuilt New Inn on this later visit. Mention of a visit to the Old Wells suggests that at this point in time the Old Wells were still functioning as a spa.[108] The social focus of the time was definitely the town centre and the trip to the Old Wells to take the waters was a less significant part of the proceedings.

Celia observed that the Wells (meaning the Old Wells on the common) were now built about with a large light room to walk in, with a pump put on the well. She does not appear to have taken the waters. A coffee house, gaming rooms and sweetmeats and fruit shops were included in the facilities. There was even organised entertainment with racing of boys, rabbits and pigs. In the town, two greens were used for evening recreation. The Upper Green was kept by the same man as the Wells (Livingstone) and included benches to sit, shops and a gaming or dance room. The Lower Green, in the town centre, was generally warmer, and facilities included a very large room with sash windows with cushions in the windows, two hazard-boards and shops all belonging to the great tavern or eating house. The presence of the large room and a piazza walk with topiary-cut trees suggests that there was a promenade for walking as at Tunbridge Wells. A clock was reported at the *"Crosse in the streete"*.[109]

After an aquatint by Hassell, 1816, showing the clock in the High Street.

COMMENT

Clark, in his 1954 paper, suggested a date for this narration of about 1710 but revised it to later, based on the date of 1716 for the erection of the new New Inn.[110] Clark however was apparently confused on this point, according to Exwood. The then New Inn was the later White Horse public house in Dorking Road and not the building known as Waterloo House in the High Street, erected c.1716.[111] At the time of this second visit Durdans was Lord Guilford's which dates this account after 1708 when John, the Duke of Argyle purchased it. Durdans was then sold by 1712 when Clark, quoting *Victoria County History*, reported that it was in the hands of Lord Guilford.[112] Toland's 1726 description of Epsom further confirmed Durdans was in the hands of Lord Guilford although Toland's original 1711 text did not.[113] A date of 1712 or shortly after is likely realistic for Celia's account.

Morris observed that Celia Fiennes visited the spas more often than she related; she was most familiar with Epsom noting the growth of the weekend habit there.[114] Some aspects of her diary may therefore be difficult to date with precision. Livingstone likely kept the Old Wells open for a while after securing the leases in 1711, certainly they were open when Celia Fiennes made her second visit.[115] Without doubt the improving facilities in the town and the inconvenience of the Old Wells was leading to their reduced popularity. It is known from other documentary sources that the Old Wells had proved unreliable and Epsom Salts were readily available in town either from the apothecaries or the New Wells.

In the full account of her second visit to Epsom, Celia was enthusiastic about the enhanced facilities that she found in the town. The great attraction for Celia in Epsom was the houses of the wealthy by this time. There had been much development that was not present on her earlier visits and this later account was probably an updated replacement for her earlier narration. Fortunately both have survived.

THE ZENITH OF EPSOM SPA (1712-1750)

The period 1712-1750 was the proverbial sunset when prosperity was followed by Epsom's demise as a spa. Livingstone's death in 1727 was a turning point for Epsom and it could be argued that this was partially attributable to the reliance that Epsom by then placed on the New Wells as the principal spa facility.

The town had all the entertainment diversions of a typical spa of the day. John Macky, in 1714, observed that *"Gentlemen and Ladies insensibly to lose their company in the pretty labryinths of Box-wood and divert themselves unperceived....and it may justly be called The Palace of Venus".*[116] Macky also found the Old Wells neglected but still in use.[117] This suggests that the Old Wells were either intermittently closed or just run down and possibly unsupervised. The following year, 1715, John Livingstone having secured the lease on the Old Well eventually locked them, supposedly to avoid undesirable comparisons and competition with his New Wells. As recorded by Exwood, this also coincided with a German visitor being advised that not one dram of salt was produced from Epsom Wells.[118] This suggests that either all the Epsom mineralised water was required for local use and could not be made available for the manufacture of artificial salts or that manufacturing elsewhere had stolen the market. This observation gives a valuable insight as to why manufactured salts were considered a cheat. They did not have a genuine Epsom provenance. Without doubt there was ample supply being made artificially elsewhere by this time, perhaps by Grew at his new factory at Acton or more likely the Moults at Shooters Hill or from sea water.

A good picture of Epsom in 1715 is portrayed by Dudley Ryder, an aspiring practitioner of law, later Attorney-General. In his diary he recorded on June 13 that he had been extremely sick during the night as a result of a meat pie eaten for supper. At 4 am he arose to go to Epsom via his brothers. On arriving, he left the horses at the Inn at Epsom between 9 and 10 am. After breakfast he looked around the town, visiting the bowling green and the long room, observing that some visitors spent all day at the dice tables. They so little valued the heap of guineas that he was tempted to enter the play, feeling confident that their lack of concern over losing would be to his advantage. In the afternoon he saw plays and music at the bowling green. Whilst at Epsom, Dudley Ryder dined with Lady Harrison and her four daughters. The daughter Celia he found particularly agreeable. Lady Harrison was Celia Fiennes' sister Mary. Ryder returned to London later, fearing a possible attempted robbery on the way.[119]

About this time Daniel Defoe published anonymously his account of Epsom but the dating is unreliable. Defoe recorded Epsom in his letter 2, published in 1724. The dating of Defoe's work is the subject of intense speculation, much of his data being an amalgam of personal experience and other authors' work. For example, he or a namesake was a witness to the will of Celia Fiennes and it is not impossible that he was familiar with her journals, although Rogers disputes any connection.[120] The date of 1722 for Defoe's description is taken from Rogers but Clark suggests a date of 1717 or earlier, perhaps coinciding with Celia Fiennes' second visit and Toland's earlier description.[121]

Defoe saw Epsom as a place of pleasure. For a shilling or half a crown one could became a citizen of Epsom for the summer and then drink the waters. Many had the waters brought to their apartments in the morning. Otherwise the day was spent in leisure, available to suit all tastes. The bowling green became the centre of activity in the evening; only one green was mentioned. The character of ladies was often devastated at Epsom, unlike Tunbridge, such havoc being caused through *"tattle and slander"* . For those seeking a country debauch, Box-Hill was a popular excursion venue. Many visitors were business people from London and commuting was a regular practice. The gentry went to Tunbridge, the merchants to Epsom. Defoe saw Epsom as a summer retreat and found it no place for pleasure in the winter.[122] The impression that Defoe's work gives is of a competent updated account of the town as it was in the early eighteenth century. Importantly he made no criticism of the waters. However, Defoe's second edition of 1738 discusses the spa in an historic content rather than current which indicates the demise and its approximate date.[123] Defoe did suggest that Epsom and its environs was the place to debauch, a theme that was to recur continually. It was noted in 1722 that common (loose) women were less likely to be met with at Bath than at Epsom. The suggestion was that this may be attributable to the distance from London.[124]

The people of Epsom had little appreciation of the ramifications of events that were to occur in the year 1727 when Livingstone died, the Old Wells remaining closed until his death. The Old Well was then revived and the rooms improved by Parkhurst the younger, as lord of the manor.[125] Livingstone's estate was left divided between his two daughters.[126] During his lifetime he had given land for almshouses for 12 poor widows in East Street.[127] Livingstone's death appears to have heralded the demise of Epsom as a spa town. The fashionable were no doubt setting their sights elsewhere for whatever reasons. At this point in time there was no substantial allegation that the waters of the New Wells were spurious and it is apparent that visitors continued to come to Epsom.

Evidence indicates that the spa continued for some years after Livingstone's death although Defoe wrote historically about the spa in 1738. The social emphasis appears to change and taking the waters was only one of the attractions. Horse racing and sexual liaisons were overtaking the more traditional appeal. Salmon wrote in 1728 that the mineral waters of Ebesham (Epsom) had resulted in the town being visited by tourists as well as becoming a retirement locality. He noted a new course on the Downs nearer to the wells than the one near Carshalton.[128] This is a reference to the new racing circuit superceding the "straight" to Banstead Downs. The Abbe Prevost, in 1734, recorded that of all the places in the world, those in which pleasures were most lavishly multiplied and continue with least interruption included Epsom. It was also noted that young men visited Epsom to take a course, as it were, in profligacy. Having trained at the regular watering places, Bath became the final stage of the apprenticeship before London.[129]

In 1736, Mrs Mapp the notorious *"female bone setter"* plied her calling at Epsom and gave a fillip to the taking of the waters.[130] In spite of this by 1738 the buildings and facilities at the Old Wells had decayed leaving a single dwelling occupied by a countryman and his wife who carried water around the neighbourhood in bottles.[131]

Pownall's 1825 picture of Epsom Old Wells showing the pump and beyond, to the right, the building containing the long light (Assembly) room that Celia Fiennes observed.

RECRIMINATIONS AND DECLINE (1750-1780)

In spite of its demise there were further efforts to resurrect the spa. In 1754 Epsom Old Well was advertised, by Jane Hawkins, for breakfast, the purging waters being in good order.[132] Epsom Salts were recommended to be taken before breakfast. The one to two hour delay before they took effect suggests that adequate facilities would need to be to hand shortly after breakfast. The advertisement appeared in *Lloyds Evening Post*. In the advertisement the waters were seen to be preparative, prior to taking the waters at one of the major spas, a list being given. The editorial noted that Mr Owen, at his Water Warehouse, sold the waters.[133] The emphasis on the purging waters being in good order echoes the concern about manufactured salts and their provenance that had caused earlier controversy.

Again in 1756 the waters were mentioned. Lucas wrote that the (old) spring had a building and pump set over it but that the quality was superior to those which at present attract attention.[134] About this time Dr Dale Ingram advertised a preparation of magnesia salts obtained from the mineral waters and opened public breakfast rooms at Epsom without success.[135] Dr Dale's magnesia and Epsom Salts were also sold by W. Owen of the Mineral Water Warehouse in London.[136]

By now Epsom Salts were being extensively manufactured artificially for public sale and mineral waters from many locations were widely on sale in prepackaged form from establishments such as W. Owen's. It was a natural progression that artificial mineral water production should start on a large scale. In 1783, Jacob Schweppe commenced commercial production of artificial mineral waters in Geneva thereby, it is argued by some, becoming the founder of the modern soft drinks industry.[137] A more deserving candidate for the title perhaps was W. Owen and his Mineral Water Warehouse. Schweppe was followed in 1825 by Friedrich Struve who founded the German Spa at Brighton based entirely on artificially made mineral waters.[138]

The Mineral Water Warehouse of W. Owen in Temple Bar was initially established by one Henry Eyre, who was the first man to claim to deal solely in mineral waters. By 1727 he is known to have been selling Holt waters and the business was likely founded a few years before this. By 1745 he was selling sea water in London. Eyre died between 1760 and 1762 and William Owen, bookseller and publisher took over the business. Owen ran the business until 1793 when he died.[139]

Owen had a publishing interest which enabled him to promote alternatives to Epsom waters. Both his publishing interest and his mineral water warehouse were to impinge on Epsom. A new author for Owen's business was to appear

48

in the year 1753 who was to have a significant impact on the fortunes of Epsom and the manufactured salts. Richard Russel MD first published, in English, his dissertation of sea water and the virtues of bathing in it. His publication can be seen as a natural extension of the uses of Epsom Salts, an approach similarly pursued by others in the ensuing years. Sunderland suggested that Epsom subsequently fell into disfavour, possibly as a direct result.[140] Pownall also stated that sea bathing precipitated the demise.[141] The reality was somewhat more subtle as is now explored.

W. Owen was the publisher of Dr Russel's dissertation on sea water and the mineral waters of Great Britain. This, linked with the connection between Epsom Waters and sea water, adds credence to the hypothesis that some of Dr Russel's expertise was based on the use of Epsom mineral salts. The 1769 edition of Dr Russel's work carries an advertisement for Owen's wide range of mineral waters which included Jessop's and Stoke waters from near Epsom but did not include Epsom water as such. Neither did the advertisement contain an advertisement for Epsom Salts. It did however carry an advertisement for Acton Salts.[142] This suggests that Acton Salts had been marketed under the name of the spring rather than describing them as Epsom Salts as the Moults and others had done with Shooters Hill salts and those manufactured from sea water.

Dr Russel would have been aware of various developments within the medical fraternity which would have led him to his theories on sea water. He knew that Epsom water was a purgative and that Epsom Salts could be obtained from sea water, which was also a purgative. This information came from *The Domestic Companion* (1730) which he acknowledged reading. Located as he was near Lewes, what would be more natural than to send patients to the nearest coastal town, Brighton, to secure the cure normally afforded by Epsom Salts.[143] The sea, coupled with the availability of manufactured Epsom Salts, would have rendered Epsom Wells largely superfluous as a cure centre. Dr Russel's publication on sea water was to be subsequently republished numerous times and considerably extended and was a significant influence in the extended popularity of sea bathing. By the mid nineteenth century sea bathing was becoming a popular pastime, initially as a curative but later as a low cost recreation.

But Russel merely expanded the application of Epsom Salts in medicine by extending the treatments to include sea water. This was an extension of existing practice rather than an innovative superior alternative and would therefore have unlikely been the main reason for the demise of Epsom as a spa. Substantial written evidence that there was another, more deep rooted, problem comes in 1760, albeit from the same or similar source.

In the year 1760, an anonymous writer, in an extended 4th edition of Russel's *Dissertation on Sea Water*, made various observations about Epsom water culminating in a damning indictment. He stated that many years ago the salt of Epsom water was purported to be counterfeited. When the practice was discovered it was looked upon as a cheat. This however was not so bad, the salt being available through shops.[144] These assertions were repeated in the anonymous supplement to the 1769 edition of Russel's *Dissertation on Sea Water*.[145]

The 1760 author claimed that Epsom Waters were counterfeited and that this point had been long known. A similar theme was also taken up, nine years later, in 1769, by the *Lloyds Evening Post* which indicated that spa related activity persisted at Epsom Well on a minor scale.[146] The anonymous article suggested that the New Wells had not proved as efficacious as the Old Wells and that Livingstone, seeing his custom returning to the common where the Old Wells were located, had closed the Old Wells. It also suggested that substitute Epsom salts were clandestinely brought in and sold as the real thing. The article contains another interesting observation. Experiments indicated that true Epsom Salts contained more calcarious nitre than other waters.[147] This explains why Acton Salts, as originally developed by Dr Grew, were not sold as Epsom Salts by Owen. It also throws light on why manufactured salts from elsewhere were seen as a cheat, because they did not exactly replicate the composition of the true Epsom Salts, in spite of being named Epsom Salts.

This article proved to be a prime source of early detail on Epsom and one that was contributory to establishing a doubtful reputation for Livingstone. This related to the suggestion that the New Wells apparently did not posses the virtue of the Old Wells, to the dismay of visitors, and the suggestion of substitution with manufactured salts. Later criticism of Livingstone was focussed on his closing of the Old Wells thereby denying the visitors access to the true salts.

James Dugdale in 1819, a traveller and chronicler of England said of Epsom, *"...it even rivalled Bath and Tunbridge, till the knavery of one Livingstone, an apothecary, who contrived to get possession of the lease, diminished and finally ruined its reputation."* [148]

This was consolidated into what became an authoritative history by Pownall in 1825.[149]

"The waters... gradually lost their reputation... owing to the knavery of Mr John Livingstone, an apothecary....

From the year 1715, Epsom was gradually deserted, owing to the knavish tricks and frauds of Livingstone the apothecary."

Malden's 1911 *The Victoria History of the Counties of England* pursues a similar vein and this has cemented the derogation of Livingstone's character. Particularly as the juxtapositioning of the text implies incorrectly that the criticism came from Toland in 1711, a "blue chip" source.[150]

"In 1711, Toland, the famous deistical writer, gives a very flowery description of the beauties of Epsom in a letter to "Eudena". But by this date Epsom had come to rely on its general attractions for pleasure seekers, rather than upon its medicinal waters. A quack doctor named Levingstone [sic.] sank a rival well, of no particular quality, near the town in 1706...."[151]

Authors such as Denbigh (1981) have perpetuated this character assassination, following in turn the works of Malden (1911) and Home (1901) who in turn had followed Pownall (1825) and Dugdale (1819). Over two hundred years have elapsed and only now, principally due to the researches of Clark, can Livingstone be viewed in a more accurate light as a major entrepreneur who deployed business acumen and resources into developing Epsom as a major spa. This hypothesis has remained essentially unchallenged since Clark's work in the 1950s and is investigated further in due course.

Summarising, there are two aspects of Epsom's activities that came in for criticism in 1760/9. The anonymous writer in the supplement to Russel and *The Lloyds Evening Post* identified the salts as being counterfeited and The Post article saw the closing of the Old Wells as a means of forcing custom to the New Wells which were less efficacious. The period 1712 - 1780 saw the demise of Epsom as a spa and the blame for this was placed on Livingstone although it was not until some 30 or so years after his death that such opinions were put into print. These issues are discussed further in due course.

Contemporary with the published criticisms of Livingstone was the disposal of the New Wells properties. Plots were sold off for redevelopment. Buildings sold included the New or Upper Long Room, the Old Coffee House, the Booth and the Kings Storehouse together with a Bowling Green and The Grove. No mention was made of a well. This was the end of Livingstone's New Wells.[152]

THE HYDROGEOLOGY AND GEOCHEMISTRY OF EPSOM WELLS

Modern day scientific understanding gives new insights into the problems of the past. Our greater appreciation of the mechanisms which result in Epsom Salts mineralisation enable a greater recognition of Livingstone's problems with his New Wells. Before doing this it is appropriate to consider the state of science in the eighteenth century.

In the 1769 edition of Russel's *Dissertation on Sea Water*, he noted that Epsom water was clear but if left in a vessel for some weeks would stink. A gallon of water would yield between 1 and 1.5 ozs. according to the season. Later he noted that the usual prescribed quantity was two thirds of a pint in summer and half a pint in winter. The salt crystals comprised rectangular prisms with parallelogram planes. Half an ounce of salt was appropriate to induce gentle purging when taken. Some took from an ounce to 10 drams in up to 4 pints of water, with a dram of mace for the same purpose and worked it off with a posset-drink. The writer observed that it could conveniently be added to a chalybeate water like Tunbridge. Poor people once used the water for washing sores to good effect.[153]

The evaporation of ancient salt lakes, usually sea water, when geological strata is being laid down results in saline originated minerals being present in the sedimentary rock. Gypsum is such an evaporite mineral ($CaSO_4.2H_2O$). It is found in clays and limestones, sometimes associated with sulphur. Sodium chloride, ($NaCl$), is widely exploited as a product of marine evaporation, both in geological deposition and by solar evaporation in hot climates. Characteristic geological deposits, which often are changed by the action of ground water, include calcium, magnesium and sulphate ions. The temperature and ion concentration determines the actual substances deposited. Such deposits are usually laid down in reverse order of solubility ie the least soluble first. Epsom Salts ($MgSO_4.7H_2O$), can occur as a secondary product resulting from the transformation of the products of the original evaporite sequence.

Epsom Salt (Magnesium Sulphate), also described as Epsomite, and the sequence of saline deposition in which the salts occur is given by Clarke (1924). It is noted that Epsomite so deposited is commercially valuable.[154] Under natural conditions calcium carbonate is the first solid to separate on evaporation of sea water followed by calcium sulphate. Only when the evaporating body is reduced to 1.54 percent of its original volume do magnesium salts crystalise. The figure may vary according to specific conditions. Natural Epsom Salts are relatively rare because the required conditions are rarely attained.[155]

Epsom lies at the junction of the London Clay to the north-west, hence Clay Hill (the old name for West Hill), and the Chalk to the south-east. At the junction, the Tertiary strata of the Woolwich and Reading Beds and the Thanet Sands surface adjacent to the London Clay and Chalk respectively. This gives a clearly defined NE/SW boundary which extends for many miles. The chalk dips below the Tertiary strata to the north to give an artesian aquifer beneath the London basin.

The Woolwich and Reading Beds and the Thanet Sands contain the sulphates and magnesium necessary for the creation of Epsom Salts together with iron deposits which give a chalybeate water. These Tertiary Beds are therefore the source of ground water containing Epsom Salts. As a result of the artesian pressure of the ground water in the underlying chalk, it seeps to the surface through the Tertiary strata up to one kilometer north of the point where the chalk dips below the Tertiaries. This occurs as a result of discontinuities and fissures in the Tertiary strata and gives rise to ponds and springs.[156] These surface features would likely be charged with Epsom Salts and this explains the original occurrence of the salts in a pond on the common reported by Brayley c.1600.

Any attempt to dig a well in the Tertiary strata would also likely produce water charged with Epsom Salts. This is confirmed by the well digging account of Mr Symonds, reported by Benjamin Allen of 1699, details of which are considered shortly. The selenite bed was seen to overlay a black earth with iron. This is typical of the Tertiary strata. If a well were dug directly in the chalk below however, the water yielded would be charged with calcium carbonate and would not have the characteristics resulting from the higher aquifer in the Woolwich and Reading Beds and the Thanet Sands.

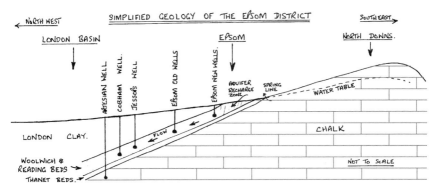

Simplified Geology of the Epsom District.

This sequence and hydrogeological characteristic are confirmed by Stamp who observed the Bullhead bed at the base of the Thanet sands which are water bearing. These in turn overlay the chalk aquifer which is sub-artesian.[157]

The question which now arises is where was Livingstone's well? If it was located in or penetrated directly into the chalk strata, it would not have contained Epsom Salts, in which case he would have had to add the salts by artificial means. If it were dug in the Tertiary sequence he would likely have been more fortunate, although the strength of the well would have been variable according to local geological conditions.

An important geochemical report was fortunately recorded for posterity in 1699. Benjamin Allen in *The Natural History of Chalybeat and Purging Waters of England....* At the newly sunk private well owned by Mr Symonds, he reported selenites (a transparent and beautiful variety of Gypsum) forming columns comprising inequilateral parallelograms. A few feet distant was another well where they were rhomboid as also noted in the public well. Following excavations of the new well, Allen reported a strata of loose rock beneath 7 feet of hard loamy material below the upper earth. In the loose strata, which was 2 feet thick, were small selenites. Below this was a dead, heavy, black earth with iron. The water flowed from the selenite bed. He then described various chemical tests made to determine the nature of the salt, observing that half an ounce purged pleasantly.[158]

The land on which Symonds dug the well can be identified, through the Manorial Survey of 1697, as being that formerly of Humphrey Beane known as "Warrens".[159] This lies at the western end Epsom High Street. The Symonds well is therefore believed to be on the Warrens, near the Magpie Inn. This well should not be confused with the Old Well on the Warren near the racecourse drawing water from the chalk aquifer.

Allen gave more detail of the Symonds well in his 1711 new edition: the well was described as in town and of a depth of about 10 feet. The water oozed in at a rate of a barrel in 24 hours. Lehmann (1973) suggested that Symonds was the well that Livingstone used and this is now discussed.[160]

In 1670, Humphrey Beane bought land in Epsom which included "Warrens" believed to be about 3 acres on the Dorking Road behind the Magpie Inn. In his will, recorded at the Court Barons 1679/80 & 80/81, he left the land to John Parsons, his son-in-law. In 1701 and 1707 Livingstone had acquired land once owned by Humphrey Beane, as mentioned earlier. The latter purchase was from John Parsons. This all became the New Wells and abutted land owned by a John Symonds which was also formerly Beane's land. The Beane will, under which Parsons inherited the estate, recorded a well of water with pipes across the road to his wash house.[161] This is the original Warrens Well. In addition there was the well described as Symonds well, also believed to be on what was formerly Beane's land, which was dug about 1699 and found to contain Epsom Salts.[162]

It can be argued with some confidence that these two sources are the wells that Livingstone relied on for his principal water supply. Livingstone would have been able to transport the water to his New Wells site without traversing a road, possibly by pipeline in the case of the Warrens Well. Unfortunately any mineralisation quality will now be shown to be suspect.

Reference to the 1978 Geological Survey map[163] enables a hypothesis to be constructed. Livingstone's New Wells were situated at the western end of the High Street. This area falls just within the boundary of the London Clay which overlays the Epsomite bearing strata. To the east there is a surface geology anomaly in that the recent Teale Gravels overlay the district. This anomaly is of minor significance in the following argument and is therefore ignored to all intents and purposes. Livingstone's New Wells were therefore sited to be able to secure a well water charged with Epsom Salts, but only just. Inspection of the map indicates that the Old Wells and Jessop's Well, located on the London Clay, are much further from the surface boundary of the Epsomite bearing strata and historically contain more Epsom salts. Can it be argued therefore that there is a relationship between the strength of the well and the distance from the surface boundary of the Epsomite strata?

Exwood recorded a number of historic analyses of Epsom and nearby wells. The analyses have been converted to drachms/gallon, where in other units, for comparison purposes.

date	author	well	contents
1695	Grew	Old Well	6-10 drachms/gallon
1699	Allen	Old Well	7 drachms/gallon
1711	Allen	New Well	0.5 drachms/pint(= 4d/g)
1725	Hoffmann	Epsom	0.5 quentgen/medic.pound
1751	Hales	Epsom	34 grains/pound(avoir)(=4.53d/g)
		Cobham	60-68 grains/pound(=8.53d/g)
		Jessop's	82 grains/pound(=10.93d/g)
1756	Lucas	Old Well	40 grains/pint(=5.33d/g)

Historic analyses of Epsom Salts in various wells.[164]

From the above it can be seen that Cobham and Jessop's were more substantially charged than the Epsom Wells. Also the New Well was less charged than the Old Well. Jessop's Well, which is nearby, would have therefore been a more desirable source for Epsom mineral waters than the Epsom Wells, particularly if the supply were more plentiful and reliable.

The historic analyses are now matched against the distance from the surface boundary of the Upper Chalk and the Thanet Beds.

Old Well (Allan)	- 7 drachms/gallon	- 1.6km
New Well (Allen)	- 4 drachms/gallon	- 0.5km
Epsom (New Well?) (Hales)	- 4.5 drachms/gallon	- 0.5km
Cobham (Hales)	- 8.5 drachms/gallon	- 4.1km
Jessop's (Hales)	- 10.9 drachms/gallon	- 3.9km
Old Well (Lucas)	- 5.3 drachms/gallon	- 1.6km

Epsom salt content of wells and distance from geological surface boundary.

In recent times the artesian mechanism has weakened in effect due to the depletion of the chalk aquifer for public water supplies. As a result any evaluation is dependent on historic analysis. The comparison between distance from the geological boundary and the concentration of Epsom Salts in the water can be graphed out as follows.

The upper line represents the concentration and the lower line the distance. The New and Old Wells analyses are suffixed by a letter identifying the origin of the analysis.

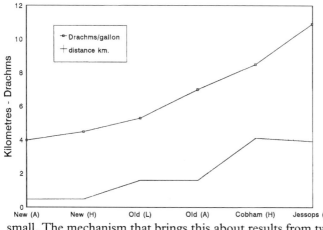

Various Wells

Comparison of Distance and Content

This suggests that there is a correlation between distance and salt concentration although the sample size is small. The mechanism that brings this about results from two considerations. Firstly the recharge zone of the Epsomite bearing strata is where the beds surface, drawing water from the chalk springs along this juncture. Secondly, the further the well is from the juncture, the longer the distance the water travels through the beds and the greater the solution time for the absorption of Epsom Salts. Indications from early literature suggest that the movement of water through the Epsomite aquifer is slow, thereby accounting for the rapid depletion of well contents and the need to replenish the exploited wells, possibly from other mineralised wells nearby.

What is apparent is that Livingstone's New Wells were the weakest of the local celebrated wells and this would be problematical. Firstly he would have been short of the essential mineralised water, if his well flowed at similar rates to that of the Old Well. Every morning the supply of impregnated water, collected overnight, would have been quickly utilised. Secondly, the water that he did secure through natural causes would have been lower in concentration and therefore less effective, requiring larger doses. This would have put further demand on his supply.

The implications of this are considered with hindsight in the ensuing text.

REVIEWING THE DEMISE WITH HINDSIGHT

Innovation was to prove the foundation for the creation of the great English spas of the eighteenth century. For over 100 years Bristol, Tunbridge, Bath and many other spas were to become great social and economic centres of medicine and leisure. It was not until the early nineteenth century that changes in market conditions precipitated a decline in the legendary eighteenth century health resorts. That is with one major exception - Epsom. Epsom suffered a premature demise. By the 1740s Epsom was struggling to survive as a prosperous spa and it is apparent that by the 1770s remedial action was being taken in a forlorn attempt to re-establish any claim that Epsom had of remaining in the spa industry. In attempting to unravel the circumstances which led to this demise it becomes apparent that the period 1690-1730 was critical for the town's development.

Two entrepreneurs were responsible for the development of Epsom Spa at the close of the seventeenth century. Parkhurst, lord of the manor, developed the Old Wells and Livingstone, an apothecary, developed the New Wells. The changes that these two individuals brought about are apparent from the journals of Celia Fiennes which uniquely span this important era. Blame for the demise of Epsom is laid at the feet of Livingstone by many who see him as a knave who had questionable waters at the New Wells and who forced patronage by closing the Old Wells. Others blame a degeneration of moral tone as the reason for the influential choosing to go to other spas. Russel's promotion of sea water is a third alternative. A fourth alternative, which can now be argued, is that Livingstone was an innovative pioneer, ahead of his time in terms of public acceptability. Whilst he was alive, he was able to secure and maintain a market position for his New Wells but his death in 1727, with no comparable successor, also heralded the premature demise of Epsom as a developed eighteenth century spa. This is not the full picture however. Dr Grew's papers on the nature and manufacture of Epsom Salts were also instrumental in changing the public perception of Epsom Salts and Waters.

It has been demonstrated that as a result of the researches of Nehemiah Grew, manufactured Epsom Salts became available at the close of the seventeenth century. The obvious convenience of such a preparation, both in its availability and ease of use, resulted in numerous manufactories being established. By 1711 Toland further observed the fame of *"chymically made"* Epsom Salts throughout Europe.[165]

What was apparent was that Epsom Salts, by the 1720s, were a widely known and sought after medicinal aid. For example, in 1721 when Hoffman identified Seidlitz salts from the Bohemian spring of the same name, now lost due to extensive open cast mining. These bitter aperient salts were similar to those that Grew discovered at the Epsom spring and were unusual for a Continental spring. The salts were present in greater quantities than at Epsom and the evaporated residue became much sought after in England.[166] John Brown, a chemist, stated in 1723, that most Epsom Salt was being manufactured from the *"Bitterns"* left after the crystallisation of common salt from sea water.[167] A substantial industry was emerging producing artificially made Epsom mineral salt.

We also know however from the German visitor cited by Exwood and the *Lloyds Evening Post* (1769) that no Epsom Salts were manufactured from Epsom Wells. The concern expressed underlined an anxiety about the provenance of manufactured Epsom Salts. It has been shown that Grew's patent was under attack by various persons, particularly Francis Moult who contrived to make Epsom Salts at Shooters Hill. It is apparent from the supplement to Dr Russel's work, published in 1760 and 1769, that these manufactured salts were considered counterfeit. The reason for this is given in the *Lloyd's Evening Post* article of 1769. This is that the manufactured salts were a cheat because they did not contain the same amount of calcarious nitre as true Epsom Salts and that they were introduced clandestinely. This explained why Grew's manufactured salts from Acton were sold as Acton Salts rather than Epsom Salts. It also raises the obvious public concern that Moult and others were selling, as Epsom Salts, manufactured salts which were not a true likeness of the genuine article. Hence the accusation of counterfeiting. The statement in the 1754 *Lloyds Evening Post* to the effect that the purging waters at the Wells were in good order was obviously made because of the earlier lack of public confidence in Epsom Waters. The scenario that emerges is one of failing confidence in Epsom Waters because of dissimilar composition salts, but similarly named, being made elsewhere and then being introduced into Epsom. Much of the blame for this lies with Francis Moult and his usurping the patent of Dr Grew. As the *Compleat English Dispensary* has been shown to state in 1722, such a discovery should rest under the proper use of persons of integrity.[168] The resulting conclusion is that Francis Moult was the wicked apothecary. But where does this leave John Livingstone, the traditional villain of the piece?

We know, from the geochemical evidence previously cited, that Livingstone's New Wells source was at best weakly charged with Epsom Salts, if the well existed at all. This is confirmed by the *Lloyds Evening Post* (1769) editorial which suggested fresh water entering the well. Livingstone probably drew water from a well that penetrated the chalk aquifer to supplement any meagre supply of mineralised water, the characteristics of which would have been completely different. It has also been established that the Old Wells on the common were unable to meet demand for salts as early as the mid-seventeenth century. In spite of these limitations, Epsom had responded to capital investment in the early eighteenth century and become one of the premier spas of England.

In order to protect his business investments and the prosperity of the town, Livingstone would therefore have been sorely tempted to resort to artificially made Epsom Salts to fortify the natural supply. This would be a more expedient alternative to topping up the well from elsewhere, as was the practice at the Old Wells. Having closed the Old Wells, Livingstone could later also have used these waters to fortify that of the New Wells, but this is unlikely in view of the negative views on such practices expressed by earlier visitors to the Old Wells. Although the manufactured salts were equally, if not more, effective than the natural product, public attitudes may have continually threatened his enterprise. Information on fortifying the well with manufactured salts would not ideally become common knowledge to serve Livingstone's best interests. Granville later discusses other mineral waters being fortified in this manner. This practice would have been straightforward, especially by an apothecary who would have been well acquainted with the chemistry of the day.

When Livingstone died, his secret had all the signs of dying with him. Others were less able to perpetuate the practice and the reputation of the efficacy of the waters of the New Wells fell into disrepute. This raises the question: was Livingstone a forerunner of the artificial mineral water industry, by using manufactured Epsom Salts to fortify the water from the Warrens Well or the meagre supply of mineralised water from Symonds Well?

The experience of Cheltenham indicates that artificially fortifying the waters was carried out, even if unacceptable to the public, as late as 1809. In that year Henry Thompson settled in Cheltenham and commenced a series of developments which led to the "Great Epsom Salts Swindle". Thompson sank new wells with the intention of finding original sources of mineral water in the town. As a result he was able to offer a range of mineral waters and a new pump room was erected eventually to be replaced by the Rotunda spa building. Doubt was cast on the credibility of Thompson's new sources and it transpired that large quantities of Epsom Salts were thrown into one of the wells daily. A black wagon was noted to travel weekly to Epsom, returning to Thompson's manufactory of Cheltenham Salts. This wagon was believed to be the source of the secret ingredient.[169] An interesting publication appeared in 1820, being a collection of papers presenting arguments for and against the possibility of the Cheltenham Wells being doctored with Glauber and Epsom Salts.[170] The conclusion was that it was better to send patients to take sea water. This reintroduces Dr Russel's theories on sea water expounded during the mid-eighteenth century. Sea water continued to be a rival to the popularity of Epsom Salts.

We can now place the criticism levelled at Livingstone in context. Livingstone's acquisition of the Old Wells was probably purely commercial. It extended his spa interests and when closed focused the spa activity on his New Wells. He is suspected of using his apothecarial skills to ensure that his New Wells contained sufficient mineralisation to satisfy his clientele.

Was the possible doctoring of the New Wells with Epsom Salts, probably manufactured elsewhere, such a trickery that it warranted the character assassination that ensued thirty or so years after his death? We may well argue whether this was a deception or merely good business practice, as later carried on by Struve and Schweppe when they sold artificial mineral salts and waters. Livingstone, in conjunction with Parkhurst, without doubt transformed Epsom, ensuring that it competed in the rapidly developing spa marketplace of the early eighteenth century. Celia Fiennes recorded the transition particularly effectively.

With such proximity to London why then did Epsom fail? Various ideas have already been suggested; however the growing public awareness and unacceptability of artificially fortifying the well would have had a major effect, particularly if Livingstone deliberately deceived his clients. There is no evidence to suggest that this was common knowledge at the New Wells. What became common knowledge was the marketing of counterfeit Epsom Salts from Shooters Hill and elsewhere and then their use to concoct quasi-Epsom Waters. It is probably this point more than any other that led to the breakdown in confidence about Epsom Wells. As a result the crowds departed to spas that could give a quality assurance.

Interestingly, in the anonymous supplement to Dr Russel's work, the point is made that the clandestine use of manufactured salts was not as bad as supposed. Perhaps the visitors found that it was far more convenient and less expensive purchasing salts from the apothecaries than excursioning to Epsom for the purge.

In conclusion, there is no firm evidence to suggest that Livingstone fortified his New Wells. Historians who have viewed him as a knave owe him an apology. That is not to say that there was not a wicked apothecary however. Francis Moult had set about a course of action that undermined public confidence in Epsom Salts and Waters in general. He had deceived the public by naming his manufactured salts as Epsom when they patently came from elsewhere and produced a different mineralisation to the genuine wells. In doing so he had stolen the discoveries of Dr Grew. The mendacity was then extended to other manufacturers and the general use of the salts. This in turn led to a lack of confidence in any mineral source other than the original Epsom Old Wells which Livingstone insensitively closed. Without doubt, following the Lord Chancellor's reprimand, Moult rather than Livingstone justly deserved the title of wicked apothecary. What Epsom doubtless lacked, after Livingstone's death, was a leading entrepreneur who was as enterprising in furthering the spa. But would this have been enough? Perhaps Epsom Wells just lacked an efficacy that could not be bought over the apothecaries counter.

After the demise of Epsom as a spa, evidence that Epsom salts and mineral water was widely recognised as a medicinal treatment was apparent. Dr Monro noted in 1770 that Epsom was a purging water and that a normal dose would be three pints to be taken over 2 - 3 hours or over a day depending on the mildness of the action sought.[171] Although the salts were sought after, Epsom town was not enjoying the benefits of a successful spa.

Footnotes:

1 Morris C. (ed.) 1947, *The Journeys of Celia Fiennes*, p.337-339, 341-353.
2 Home G. 1901, *Epsom, Its History and Its Surroundings*, p.44.
3 Exwood M. 1989, *Epsom Wells*, p.40/1; Lloyds Evening Post, 1769, "British Chronicle" *A concise historical Account of the old Epsom Wells, situated on Epsom Common, in the County of Surrey*, 14-16 August, p.155.
4 Sunderland S. 1915, *Old London's Spas, Baths and Wells*, p.137; Home G. op.cit. Chapter III.
5 Exwood M. op.cit. p8/9.
6 Hembry P. 1990, *The English Spa 1560 - 1815*, p.104.
7 Home G. op.cit. Chapter III.
8 Lehmann H L. 1973, "The History of Epsom Spa", *Surrey Archaeological Collections*, Surrey Archaeological Society, LXIX, p.89; Clark F L. 1960, *The History of Epsom Spa*, p.39; Exwood M. op.cit. p.7.
9 Kirkby W. 1902, *The Evolution of Artificial Mineral Waters*, p.11; Exwood M. op.cit. p.14.
10 Addison W. 1951, *English Spas*, p.15; Sunderland S. op.cit. p.137; Home G. op.cit. Chapter III; Exwood M. op.cit. p.7.
11 Moore-Smith G C. 1928, *The Letters of Dorothy Osborne to Sir William Temple*, Letter 3, p.7, footnote 13 p.211.
12 Toland J. 1711, *The Description of Epsom*, facsimile edition by Silverstone L C. 1978, p.26.
13 Rolls R. 1988, *The Hospital of the Nation*, p.87.
14 "Diary of John Greene" 1929, *English Historical Review*, Vol.XLIV, p.110: Madan P. 1687, *A Philosophical and Medicinal Essay on the Waters of Tunbridge*, reprinted by Harleian Soc. 1808, Vol.I, p.589." See Lennard R. 1931, *Englishmen at Rest and Play*, p.30.
15 Parry E A. (ed.) 1914, *Letters of Dorothy Osborne to Sir William Temple*, p.28.
16 Celia Fiennes' grandmother was Elizabeth Temple of Stowe, which suggests a link with the family of Sir William Temple.
17 Smith G C M. 1930, *Sir William Temple Bt.*, p.5-7.
18 Moore-Smith G C. op.cit. Letter 3, p.7, footnote 13, p.210.
19 Parry E A. op.cit. letters 23, 25, 32, 33, p.95, 103, 127, 130.
20 Moore-Smith G C. op.cit. letter 32, p.70/1.
21 Aubrey J. 1718, *The Natural History and Antiquities of the County of Surrey*, Vol.II, p.191.
22 *Calendar of State Papers Domestic*, 1650, p.259, see Lennard R. 1931, p.31.
23 Bax A R. 1899, "Suspected Persons in Surrey During the Commonwealth", *Surrey Archaeological Collections*, 14, Surrey Archaeological Society, p.164-181.
24 Kershaw S W. 1897, "Surrey During the Commonwealth", *Surrey Archaeological Collections*, 13, Surrey Archaeological Society, p.46.
25 James W. Malcolm J. 1794, "A General View of Agriculture in the County of Surrey", see Marshall W.

26 Malden H E. (ed.) 1911, A History of Surrey, *Victoria History of the Counties of England,* Vol.III, p.272.1817, *County Reports of the Board of Agriculture,* p.380.
27 Schellinks' drawing is now in the National Bibliotek, Vienna.
28 Lehmann H L. 1980, "A Description of Epsom Well, 1662", *Surrey Archaeological Collections,* Surrey Archaeological Society, Vol.76, p.77-79; Exwood M. Lehmann H L. (trans.) 1993, *The Journal of William Schellinks' Travels in England,* 1661-1663, p.87/8; Exwood M. op.cit. p.24/5.
29 Hembry P. op.cit. p.105.
30 Exwood M. op.cit. p.28,37.
31 Smith J. 1924, *Diary of Samuel Pepys,* Vol.I, p.395/6.
32 Sakula A. 1983, "The Waters of Epsom Spa" *Surrey History,* Vol.2, No.5, p.230.
33 Hembry P. op.cit. p.104.
34 Epsom Common Association, 1981, *Epsom Common,* p.16,29.
35 Hembry P. op.cit. p.105.
36 Epsom Common Association, op.cit. p.17.
37 Hembry P. op.cit. p.104.
38 Epsom Salts are a domestic saline purgative which according to the British Pharmaceutical Codex (1954),when taken by mouth decreases the normal absorption of water. This causes bulky fluid contents to distend the bowel, active reflex peristalsis is excited and evacuation of the watery contents of the intestine occurs in one to two hours.
39 Smith J. op.cit. Vol.I, p.290.
40 ibid. p.289.
41 Hembry P. op.cit. p.105.
42 Savidge A. 1975, *Royal Tunbridge Wells, A History of a Spa Town,* reprint by Bell C. 1995, p.94, footnote 3.
43 Sunderland S. op.cit. p.137.
44 Addison W. op.cit. p.15; Home G. op.cit. Chapter III.
45 Clark F L. 1960, op.cit. p.21.
46 Addison W. op.cit. p.16.
47 ibid. p.17.
48 Osborne B E. 1993, *Brighton's Past on Shifting Sands?* unpublished dissertation, University of Birmingham, 2nd edition.
49 De Beer E S. 1955, *Diary of John Evelyn,* Vol.III, p.544; Clark F L. 1960, op.cit. p.22.
50 Sakula A. 1983, op.cit. p.230.
51 Clark F L. 1954, *New Light on Epsom Wells,* p.16.
52 Aubrey J. op.cit. Vol.II, p.191.
53 Clark F L. 1960, op.cit. p.21.
54 ibid. p.23.
55 ibid. p.24.
56 Hembry P. op.cit. p.105.
57 Exwood M. op.cit. p.15.
58 ibid. p.15.
59 Clark F L. 1960, op.cit. p.24.
60 Pownall H. 1825, *History of Epsom,* p.64.
61 Bodleian Library "Ashmole, F5 No. C1XA" reproduced in Lennard R. op.cit. p.36/7.
62 Hembry P. op.cit. p.105.
63 Cartwright J J. (ed.) 1875, *Memoirs of Sir John Raresby,* p.53/4, 187, 363, 399, see Lennard R. op.cit. p.41.
64 Morris C. op.cit. p.121, 125, 132.
65 Alums are a group of sulphate minerals including aluminium.
66 Morris C. op.cit. p.121.
67 Clark F L. 1954, *op.cit.* p.13.
68 Morris C. op.cit. p.339.
69 Exwood M. op.cit. p.15.
70 Lehmann H L. 1973, op.cit. p.90.
71 Sakula A. 1984, "Doctor Nehemiah Grew (1641-1712) and the Epsom Salts", *Acta Academiae Internationalis-Historiae Medicinae,* Radopi, Amsterdam, Vol.19, 1/2, p.1-6,10.
72 Lehmann H L. 1973, op.cit. p.90.
73 Sakula A. 1984, op.cit. p.10/11.
74 Exwood M. op.cit. p.32.
75 Sakula A. op.cit. p.13.

76 The salts in sea water are identified as follows:-

salts	grains/gallon	salts	grains/gallon
Sodium Chloride	1,851.0	Calcium Sulphate	93.0
Magnesium Chloride	221.0	Potassium Chloride	52.0
Magnesium Sulphate	148.0	Calcium Carbonate	3.3

To convert to parts per million divide by 0.07
see Fox C S. 1949, *The Geology of Water Supply*, The Technical Press, London.

77 Kirkby W. op.cit. p.1, 25; Sunderland S. op.cit. p.68/9; Lehmann H L. 1973, op.cit. p.90.

78 Lehmann H L. 1973, op.cit. p.92/3.

79 Sakula A. 1984, op.cit. p.11-13.

80 Coley N G. "Physicians, Chemists and the Analysis of Mineral Waters: the most difficult part of Chemistry", in Porter R. (ed.) *The Medical History of Waters and Spas*, Medical History, Supplement No.10, p.56-66.

81 Morris C. op.cit. p.224, footnote and xxi.

82 Exwood M. op.cit. p.17.

83 Clark F L. 1960, op.cit. p.9.

84 Lehmann H L. 1973, op.cit. p.90.

85 Malden H E. (ed.) op.cit. Vol.III, p.274.

86 Kirkby W. op.cit. p.11; Exwood M. op.cit. p14.

87 Lehmann H L. 1987, *The Residential Copyholds of Epsom*, Epsom and Ewell Borough Council, ref. 1B13; Clark F L. 1960, op.cit. p.13.

88 Anon. 1995, *The Discovery of Symonds Well*, publicity communication, Symonds Well Restaurant, Epsom.

89 Addison W. op.cit. p.16; Home G. op.cit. Chapter III.

90 Addison W. op.cit. p.17.

91 Clark F L. 1960, op.cit. p.15-20.

92 Sunderland S. op.cit. p.140.

93 Home G. op.cit. Chapter III.

94 Lehmann H L. 1987, op.cit. ref.1B7.

95 Potter G W. 1904, *Hampstead Wells*, p.49.

96 Clark F L. 1960, op.cit. p.18.

97 Exwood M. op.cit. p.18; Lennard R. op.cit. p.63.

98 Sakula A. 1983, op.cit. p.234.

99 Clark F L. 1960, op.cit. p.28.

100 a precis is produced by Exwood M. op.cit. p.40-42.

101 ibid. p.26, 40/1.

102 Toland J. 1711, *The Description of Epsom*, facsimile edition by Silverstone L C. 1978, Derek James, Sutton. Also reproduced by Aubrey J. 1718, Vol.II, p.197-213. Home G. 1901, reproduces the 1726 version text, p.51/7.

103 Malden H E. op.cit. Vol.III, p.272.

104 Sunderland S. op.cit. p.140/1.

105 Addison W. op.cit. p.18.

106 Home G. op.cit. Chapter III, p.58; Toland J. op.cit. 1-35.

107 Morris C. op.cit. p.341-351.

108 Clark F L. 1960, op.cit. p.29.

109 Morris C. op.cit. p.349/50; Clark F L. 1954, op.cit. p.12-20.

110 Clark F L. 1960, op.cit. p.29.

111 Exwood M. op.cit. p.15, 19.

112 Morris C. op.cit. p.342; Clark F L. 1954, op.cit. p.13/4.

113 Toland J. op.cit. p.29; Home G. op.cit.1901, *Epsom, Its History and Its Surroundings*, 1971 edition. S R Printers, Yorkshire, see Toland's 1726 text, p.51-57.

114 Morris C. op.cit. p.xxviii.

115 Clark F L. 1960, op.cit. p.29.

116 Macky J. 1714, (5th edition 1732), *A Journey Through England in Familiar Letter from a Gentleman Here to His Friend Abroad*, Vol.I, p.140.

117 Hembry P. op.cit. p.107.

118 Exwood M. op.cit. p.33.

119 Matthews W. 1939, *The Diary of Dudley Ryder 1715-1716*, p.33/4.

120 Rogers P. (ed.) 1992, *Daniel Defoe, A Tour Through the Whole Island of Great Britain*, p.8; Morris C. op.cit. p.362.

121 Clark F L. 1954, op.cit. p.21.

122 Rogers P. op.cit. p.143, 163, 168, 168-71; Cole G D H. 1927, *A Tour of Great Britain by Daniel Defoe*, p.159-163.

123 Clark F L. 1960, op.cit. p.31.
124 Barbeau A. 1904, *Life and Letters at Bath in the 18th Century,* p.106.
125 Sakula A. 1983, op.cit. p.234.
126 Hembry P. op.cit. p.106.
127 Exwood M. op.cit. p.17.
128 Lehmann H L. 1973, op.cit. p.94.
129 Barbeau A. op.cit. p.80, 108.
130 Sunderland S. op.cit. p.140.
131 Hembry P. op.cit. p.241.
132 Home G. op.cit. p.16.
133 Exwood M. op.cit. p.23.
134 Lehmann H L. 1973, op.cit. p.94.
135 Sunderland S. op.cit. p.142.
136 Lehmann H L. 1973, op.cit. p.94.
137 Simmons D A. 1983, *Schweppes, The First 200 Years,* p.12/3.
138 Osborne B. op.cit. p.12/3.
139 McIntyre S. 1973, "The Mineral Water Trade in the Eighteenth Century", *The Journal of Transport History,* Vol.II, No.1, p.3, 6.
140 Sunderland S. op.cit. p.142.
141 Home G. op.cit. p.16; Pownall H. op.cit. p.85.
142 Russel R. 1769.
143 Musgrave C. p.50-3.
144 Russel R. 1760 (4th edition) *Dissertation on the use of Sea Water* with anonymous supplement *A Treatise on the Nature, Properties and Uses of the Mineral Waters.*
145 Russel R. 1769 (5th edition) *Dissertation on the use of Sea Water* with anonymous supplement *A Treatise on the Nature, Properties and Uses of the Mineral Waters,* p.217-221.
146 Lehmann H L. 1973, op.cit. p.94.
147 Exwood M. op.cit. p.40/41.
148 Dugdale J. p.338.
149 Pownall H. op.cit. p.64, 79.
150 Malden H E. p.272.
151 ibid. p.272.
152 Lehmann H L. 1987, op.cit. ref.1C7.
153 Russel R. 1769, op.cit. p.217-221.
154 Clarke F W. 1924, *The Data of Geochemistry,* p.224,243.
155 Mason B. Moore C B. 1982, 4th edition, *Principles of Geochemistry,* p.179.
156 Based on *personal communication* with Vin. Robinson, NRA Reading.
157 Stamp L D. 1946, *Britain's Structure and Scenery,* p.140, 180.Aubrey J. op.cit. Vol.II, p.192-7.
158 Lehmann H L. 1973, op.cit. p.91.
159 ibid. p.93.
160 Clark F L. 1960, op.cit. p.11; Lehmann H L. 1987, 161 op.cit. ref.3A7/3B7.
162 See earlier text: Aubrey J. op.cit. Vol.II, p.192-7.
163 Geological Survey of Great Britain, 1978, *Sheet 286, Reigate,* 1:50,000.
164 Exwood M. op.cit. p.44.
165 Toland J. op.cit. p.26.
166 Kirkby W. op.cit. p.15.
167 Lehmann H L. 1973, op.cit. p.93.
168 As transcribed earlier; Sakula A. 1984, "Doctor Nehemiah Grew (1641-1712) and the Epsom Salts", *Acta Academiae Internationalis-Historiae Medicinae,* Vol. 19, 1/2, p.13.
169 Granville A B. 1841, p.290; Searle M V. 1981, *Spas and Watering Places,* p.122; Hart G. 1981, *A History of Cheltenham,* p.139.
170 Williams G A. 1820, *A Collection of Papers,* held by Cheltenham Public Library, 63G 615.
171 Monro D. 1770, *A Treatise on Mineral Waters,* Vol.1, p.147/8.

London Spas

Dulwich

Celia Fiennes mentioned Dulwich only briefly when discussing Shooters Hill. She described it as a purging spring.[1] It is apparent that Celia was familiar with Dulwich although she did not record precise visits in her published journals.

COMMENT

The wells were located on Westwood Common about 2 miles west of Lewisham parish church. In 1680 it was observed that they were vulgarly called Dulwich Wells and were frequented on Sundays in great profaneness by a rabble of Londoners who drank strong liquors.[2]

It was believed that of the salino-nitrous waters, Epsom's was the first to be discovered c.1618, and Dulwich's the second.[3] The similarity in characteristics suggests that the geochemistry is akin to Epsom. Dulwich waters were first used to treat a local woman who had French Pox in 1648.

The Well's discovery was accidental, according to Dr John Peter who became the principal advocate of its medicinal properties in the seventeenth century. The discovery was due to some venereal ulcers being cured by both drinking the water and washing the afflicted parts in the water. It has been intimated that the spring was originally noticed because it was a congregating point for pigeons, suggesting a saline mineralisation.[4] The location became known as Pigeons Quillet as the birds squabbled for the waters. Pigeons are partial to salt and it was due to them that the saline spring at Alford was discovered.

After its initial discovery the well was apparently dug out and contained with brick and stonework but the water was found to have lost its power. For those who did not have time to visit the well, by 1678 Dulwich water was available in London from a street vendor.[5] By 1680 any moves to enclose the well and charge for its water had been resisted.[6]

In literature there are few references to the Dulwich Well. Of the few, one of the earliest was made in 1653 when Nicholas Culpeper in his *English Physician* of that year, wrote about the juniper bush which *"grows plentifully hard by the New-found Wells at Dulwich"*.[7] Although Dulwich never became a great social centre, the efficacy of its waters attracted the aristocracy, as John Evelyn recalled in his diary of 5 August 1677, when he *"went to visite my Lord Brounker, now taking the waters at Dulwich"*.[8]

THE CURE

Dr Peter in 1680 wrote that the water cured old ulcers either with localised bathing or by applying the curd made from the water mixed with milk. Used externally the water apparently dissolved tumours, cured leprosy, the itch, scabs, pimples and ringworm. It either eradicated or was beneficial in obstructions of the spleen, liver and pancreas; meseraic veins, chlorosis, gravel in the kidneys and bladder, urinary difficulties, haemerroids, black and yellow jaundice, barreness, gonorrhoea and scurvy.

Dulwich water was said to be a quick purger, though slightly rougher than the effect secured with Epsom water. It was best drunk on a clear, dry day during the first hour after sunrise but could be drunk all year. Dr Peter was of the view that although usually drunk cold, it was safest when warm. This avoided it being hurtful to the bones, teeth, sinews, brain and back marrow.[9]

Dr Peter advised a course of the water to last 20 days. Patients should drink 3 pints the first day, increasing the daily intake by half a pint until they were consuming 8-9 pints on the tenth day. Consumption should then be reduced by half a pint daily until the intake was back to 3 pints.[10] The water was clear and had a brackish taste and imparted a bitterness in the throat.[11]

Patients were advised to walk the last mile to The Wells. When there, caraway comfits assisted with the digestion of the waters. The recommended diet gives an interesting insight into the type of foods that Celia Fiennes would have been familiar with in the seventeenth century. Ducks, geese, bacon, tripes, salt fish, eels, old cheese, leeks, onions, cabbage, muskmillions (melons) and cucumbers were to be avoided. By contrast, young, succulent beef, mutton, lamb, veal, chicken, pullet, turkey, partridge, pheasant and young cony (rabbits) were recommended. These were to be eaten with a range of fruits including apples, pears, plums, cherries, ripe gooseberries and raspberries if eaten sparingly. Beer could also be consumed and for those used to them, wines also. Supper would generally be larger than dinner and some 6-7 hours later.[12]

It was little wonder that Dr Peter advised that the services of a skilled physician should be employed to monitor the process of healing by purge. When he was at the Wells he offered his advice without charge.[13]

CONFUSION BETWEEN DULWICH WATER AND SYDENHAM WATER

There has been some confusion between Dulwich Well and Sydenham Wells. The early twentieth century authors Foord and Sunderland suggest that Dulwich Well was not discovered until the mid-eighteenth century (1739/40) and the Dulwich Well referred to above was in fact Sydenham Wells, which had been known since the beginning of the seventeenth century. This hypothesis is doubtful as both Evelyn and Culpeper discuss Sydenham and Dulwich Wells separately. The situation is further complicated by Sunderland who believed that Sydenham Wells were also called Lewisham Wells.[14]

The Sydenham waters were described by Dr Benjamin Allen in *Natural History of the Mineral Waters of Great Britain* (1699), reproduced in Dr Sunderland's book, as *"medicated with salt of the nature of common salt, but with a nitrous quality"* also containing iron pyrites - a compound of sulphur and iron.[15]

Dr Sunderland believed the Dulwich waters had a sulphurous taste and smell, unlike Sydenham[16] and had purging qualities when drunk fresh. The recommended quantity was two and a half pints. Ewart (1895) also described Dulwich waters as sulphuretted and chalybeate (with iron).[17]

Clarification as to which well is which comes from Russel (1769). The water that Celia Fiennes saw was called Dulwich because it rose in the hills surrounding that village. In reality the spring was in the parish of Lewisham, Kent, although Dulwich proper was in Surrey. It was a saline spring with a brackish taste. A second spring was discovered in Dulwich village in 1740, according to Russel. Sydenham Wells were described separately.[18]

Summarising the confusion, a spring near Dulwich, which was technically in Lewisham, was discovered in the seventeenth century. This was supplemented by a spring in Dulwich village in the mid-eighteenth century. Sydenham Wells, although of similar character, were all located in the vicinity of Wells Park Road and St James's Church, Sydenham. It was clearly the spring near Dulwich that Celia Fiennes visited.

Dulwich never became a prosperous social spa of quality. It remained a spa for the common people and joined the plethora of spas that were established around London in the eighteenth century. In due course it was superceded by urbanisation and disappeared.

SHOOTERS HILL

Shooters Hill was a well known haunt of robbers, and travellers were well advised not to cross the hill alone.

Celia Fiennes was up on "Shutershill" when she observed the local springs.[19] It was in 1697 when, having journeyed from Canterbury via Dartford, she surveyed the magnificent prospect from the high ground. This included the numerous villages adjacent to the Thames comprising Greenwich, Erith, Woolwich and Deptford as well as up to one hundred ships sailing by in a single morning. Men o' War were also under sail, it being at the end of the seven year war with France.

The springs were quick purgers containing alum, similar to Barnet, Epsom and Dulwich. She considered these local springs of greater power than those of Epsom and Dulwich.

From Shutershill she went on to Greenwich, about 2 miles away, where she observed a ship which passed her having seen it earlier at Gravesend. She then ferried the Thames and passed through Poplar, Hackney, Tottenham, Enfield and Amwell in Hertfordshire. From Canterbury the journey of 184 miles took 5 days.

COMMENT

Shooters Hill was one of the most prominent features in south-east London being 420 feet above sea level. Shooters Hill Wells lies in Kent, near Greenwich. There were springs at the foot and summit of the hill where ponds existed. The well at the foot, on the north-west side near the Gravesend road, was promoted by one Mr Godbid about 1673 when he published a handbill.[20] This was approximately 25 years before Celia Fiennes recorded the spring. About 1675 the wells acquired the name *"the Purging Wells"* being good for internal and external application with a brisk and bitter taste.[21] John Guy, tenant of the ground on which the wells were located, claimed to have discovered their properties and to have given them the name. The three wells were developed by Guy; two were lined with brick at a cost of 40 shillings in about 1677. One spring or well required a ladder to access, another was at ground level. Guy died in 1699 and was succeeded as tenant by Charles Goodcheap or Goodcheese, yeoman of Plumstead, who erected the well house.[22]

Although the well house was erected over one of the wells no special other diversions were provided. Stabling and accommodation was available however. The spa was essentially rural in nature. John Evelyn, the diarist, drank the waters in August 1699[23] and Queen Anne also imbibed about the same time.

The power of the springs at Shooters Hill was also recognised by the Moult brothers. They were London apothecaries, the sons of a London grocer. When Dr Nehemiah Grew, the discoverer of Epsom Salts, started manufacturing the salts from the Acton spring, the Moults set up a rival manufactory at Shooters Hill. They were able to extract greater quantities from Shooters Hill water and undercut Grew's prices. The price fell from 16 shillings to

3 pence a pound. Not only did the Moults undercut Grew's business, they also plagiarized his treatise *Tractatus de Salis Carartici* (1695) by publishing it in English in 1697.[24]

The waters were still being taken by local invalids as late as 1884.[25] In the nineteenth century the mineral well was recorded as being on the eastern edge of waste ground to the rear of the Royal Military Academy. By 1870 it was said to be under a shed in the garden of a cottage situated at the rear of the Eagle Tavern. A soldier maintained the well and for a small fee dispensed the mineralised waters.[26]

A quart of the water from the mineralised well contained 151 grains of solids of which 58 percent was Epsom Salt. This equates to about 1.5 drams per quart. Epsom Salts were prepared from the water by evaporation about 1700 - for further details of this process see Epsom.[27] The analysis was carried by Mr James Marsh, chemist of the Royal Arsenal.[28]

A further well was reported near the summit of the hill, in the south-east corner of the approach to Severndroog Castle, which was erected in 1784, by Lady James. This well was not considered medicinal, being a dipping well, with one or two steps providing access.[29]

HAMPSTEAD

Celia Fiennes visited Hampstead spa in 1698 with her nephew Fiennes Harrison, her sister's son. She compared the well at Hampstead favourably to that at Barnet. The water at Barnet sat in a hole in the ground, full of leaves and dirt, whereas the spring at Hampstead bubbled up into a fine stone basin before emptying clearly and quickly through a pipe.[30] It is known that when she visited, facilities were rudimentary with only a few modest structures at the well. The Bath Pond was about 100 yards above the well.[31] Like Epsom, which has many similarities, Hampstead was to change dramatically within a short while.

COMMENT

The locality had a reputation for a fresher, healthier climate than London due to its elevation.[32] Most of London is between 20 and 100 feet above sea level whereas Hampstead lies between 180 and 438 feet.[33]

Hampstead is a spa with a mottled history. The carbonated chalybeate spring was described by Ewart in 1902 as having two eras of popularity. The first was during the Heptarchy, the time of the seven Anglo-Saxon Kingdoms following Roman rule. The second era was after the reign of Charles II up to the close of the nineteenth century.[34]

Celia Fiennes found a locality that was already important for its springs of good water and becoming more widely recognised for its chalybeate medicinal well. In fact Hampstead was on the verge of a major era of development as a spa and Celia's account is timely in that it records Hampstead before the imminent changes. Others, such as Daniel Defoe, provide a record of Hampstead during and after the era of development.

THE SPRINGS

It has been suggested that a search for larger and purer supplies of water by the Corporation of London in the reign of Henry VIII led to the discovery of the chalybeate waters at Hampstead. On the eastern side of the hill, because of their unpleasant taste, the chalybeate waters tended to be unsuitable for anything other than medicinal purposes.[35] However the waters on the south and west sides were pure and soft, and prior to the eighteenth century were a source of water for London.

The Hampstead Water Company dates back to 1692 when William Paterson, founder of the Bank of England, with others set out to exploit powers obtained by the City Corporation in 1543 for the utilisation of the Hampstead springs and certain ponds. Although little came of these early efforts further ponds were constructed in the eighteenth century. In 1856 the company was taken over by the New River Company, after which time the pond water was no longer used for domestic purposes. The Metropolitan Water Board eventually disposed of its interest in the properties in the early twentieth century.[36]

Hampstead Heath geologically comprises the Lower Bagshot Sands overlaying the London Clay. A strata of sandy clay and brick earth separates the two. Water in the sands is forced to the surface as it gravitates down through the less permeable sandy clay and meets the impermeable London Clay. The numerous springs give varying chemical content and were once the source of the Fleet River which flowed into London and the Thames.

INITIAL DEVELOPMENT

Shortly after Celia's visit moves were made to protect the medicinal wells and heathland as an amenity which would benefit the community at large, particularly the poor. A special Court Baron was held on 20 December 1698. The Earl of Gainsborough, then an infant, through his mother the Countess, granted 6 acres of land, including the medicinal waters, for the benefit of the poor. Trustees, comprising Sir Thomas Lane and thirteen others, were appointed to manage the charity. A yearly rent was agreed of 5 shillings. This paved the way for the development of spa facilities and the sale of water in containers.

In due course the Trustees appointed concessionaires for the retail trade in the water. By 1700 the Trust was promoting the chalybeate waters of Hampstead, claiming similar nature and virtue to those of Tunbridge Wells.[37] By then the water was available in flasks from Mr Phelps, apothecary of Fleet Street, London. Water was taken from the Bath Pond for this trade rather than the spring in Well Walk. *The Postman* publication carried advertising indicating that the flasks could be purchased for threepence with an additional penny for home delivery.[38]

The Trust granted a building agreement on the 6 acres to one John Duffield in 1701 for the rent of £50 per annum. Duffield committed to spend £300 in the first 3 years improving facilities and if this were effected he could renew his 21 year lease for a further full term after 7 years. The agreement was conditional upon the inhabitants having free access to the waters between 5am and noon. The Trustees also retained the right to retail sales of the waters in containers. As a result of the agreement a pump room, a tavern, assembly rooms and the Sion chapel were built soon afterwards. These buildings were erected in Well Walk. Like Livingstone at Epsom, Duffield built the assembly rooms before the formal lease was granted, a situation attributed to the slowness of the legal profession at the time.[39]

An insight into the development of Hampstead Wells can be gained from Daniel Defoe. He was amazed at the speed with which the tiny village developed into a town, despite the contours of its hilly position being, at first sight, a deterrent to building development. Hampstead's original attraction was its Wells but its appeal soon became its whole aspect - a bracing, pleasant, clean disposition - and other diversions, which attracted visitors. Hampstead Heath, at the summit of the hill, was so high up that the air to Defoe was too rarified for him and he suggested it was best left to a race of mountaineers! The highest part of Hampstead hill is 443 feet above sea level and the view from the hill was spectacular: within sight were Windsor Castle, Banstead Downs near Epsom and Shooters Hill.[40]

The new bowling green, shops and other facilities provided by Duffield brought a great social following to the locality. Dancing, music and gambling became popular pastimes between taking the waters. How different from a few years earlier; when Celia Fiennes went to Hampstead for its mineral waters it was still a village. Its nearness to London, however, meant that it soon became the haunt of loose women and was described as being *"overstock'd with Jews and sharpers"*.[41] By 1709 the locality had acquired a bad reputation and as a result lost its more respectable patronage.[42] By the time Defoe was writing, c.1724, ladies who valued their reputation were steering clear of Hampstead.[43]

In the summer of 1715 Dudley Ryder described his visit to Hampstead with two friends. It was Monday 6th June when he arose between 6 and 7am. He read until breakfast and then mused away the morning playing his violin and contemplating his afternoon trip, especially the dancing. After dinner, at 3pm, he headed for Hampstead with his acquaintances Skinner and Swain. On the journey he was thrown down by a hog but without being hurt, suggesting that travelling by horse was a somewhat precarious pastime or that the incident was in keeping with their high spirits. Arriving at the Wells he drank a pint of wine and went to the dancing. There he found *"tolerable diversion, much company but little genteel"*. The day was a Holy Day, the equivalent of a modern bank holiday, and he thought that this accounted for the dancers being mostly dancing masters and their apprentices. Ryder walked the walks, observed the gamesters and noted how full the place was. He returned home at 10pm.[44] Although at a spa, he makes no mention of taking the waters.

This initial phase of Hampstead's popularity lasted only a short time, largely due to the ineptitude of the Trustees of the land which the Gainsboroughs had given to the poor. By the 1720s the tenant Duffield had paid nothing for some years for the concession of the springs, and the Trustees of the charity had failed to enforce his obligations. By 1726 extended lawsuits were under way which involved sub-leases and re-mortgaged interests by Duffield and it was apparent that the poor of Hampstead had gained little from the bequest of the Gainsborough family 20 or so years previously.[45]

Apart from the Chalybeate Well in Well Walk, there was a separate purging well, which in 1700 the Court Baron ordered should be piped into the town. The ensuing profits were to be used to ease the poor rates, the effect of which would have benefited the rich rather than the poor, by reducing their rates. Eventually one John Vincent, owner of the Hampstead Brewery, laid on a supply including that to his own brewery. Vincent failed to pay the £15 per annum for the lease and it was only after protracted litigation that his son was eventually obliged to honour the arrangement. Up until this ruling the only benefit to the poor had been the privilege of paying to drink beer made with their own water.[46]

The Trustees had failed in their duties during the initial phase of development of Hampstead. By the time that the litigation was in hand in 1726, to bring the situation to order, most of the original Trustees had died. The lawsuits lasted until 1730 and a new Trust and Trustees were then established, thereby bringing to a close this first phase in Hampstead's development as a spa.

Later a new complex of buildings was erected further to the west comprising assembly rooms and other facilities. The Bath Pool was also eventually filled. Sewerage works in Well Walk caused the old spring to fail and a new fountain was erected by the charity Trustees. The fountain lacked a sufficient flow of medicinal water and efforts in 1901/2 to relocate the chalybeate water source were successful, but it proved to be polluted.[47] The old spring is commemorated with an inscription on the stone fountain, erected in 1855, in Well Walk. This is near to the source of the old spring which is situated in the back garden of number 17.[48] The water was bottled and on sale in London up until the end of the nineteenth century.[49]

In spite of Hampstead's era as a flourishing social and medicinal spa, the legend of the waters and their curing abilities lingered on until the 1950s. At that time it was quite common for workmen from Camden and Kentish Town to make a Sunday morning pilgrimage to Hampstead. There they would drink the waters and perhaps take a bottle home, where it could be used for hepatic complaints and as a tonic and eye wash.[50]

ANALYSIS

An analysis of the *Well Walk Spring*, in 1802 by Dr Bliss.

Solid contents in grains per gallon.

Oxyd of iron	1.50
Muriate of magnesia	1.75
Sulphate of lime	2.12
Muriate of soda (nearly)	1.00
Silex (about)	0.38
Total	6.75

Gaseous content in cu. ins.

Carbonic acid gas	10.1
Air, somewhat less than atmospherical	90.9
Total	100.1

Source: Potter, 1904, p.107.

HACKNEY

Although Celia Fiennes was born at Newton Toney in Wiltshire, in later life she preferred to live much nearer the capital. Despite having a house at Barnet,[51] 11 miles north-west of London, she chose to live even closer to the capital, at Hackney, just 2 miles away. She may have been influenced in her choice because two of her nieces lived there.[52] In addition her contemporaries, Ryder and Defoe, also lived there. Celia died in Hackney in 1741.

Hackney began a rise to prosperity soon after the fire of London in 1666. Merchants who prospered after this date began to build modest houses for themselves in a place which was essentially a rural suburb of London, where countryside could still be seen from the windows.[53]

Daniel Defoe in 1724-6, described the town of Hackney as one containing twelve separate hamlets or villages which together formed a substantial parish. Recent years had seen a considerable increase in the number of buildings and, being the retreat of wealthy citizens, it was suggested that there were more coaches than Christians.[54]

Hackney, when Celia Fiennes lived there, was clearly a place where people of consequence had their country seats. Benjamin Capper wrote that Hackney was distinguished by the construction of several fine mansions, including Brooke House. He continued that at one time Hackney was the principal resort of London citizens, suggesting that this was a country retreat, away from the dust and grime of the ever-expanding capital. Indeed, it became so popular with occasional visitors that "Hackney" carriages were introduced for the benefit of the temporary passengers.[55]

In June 1664 Samuel Pepys went to Hackney with his wife. He went first to take the air and then played shuffle-board and ate cherries and cream.[56] On 10 May 1666 he set out once again for Hackney with the intention of taking the air, but on this occasion was thwarted by a silly coachman who took him to Shoreditch, much to the amusement of the party. This suggests that Hackney was indeed resorted to by the London gentry as an antidote to the unrefined atmosphere nearer the centre of London. The salubrious air and the proximity to London are two reasons which almost certainly influenced Celia Fiennes in her choice to live in Hackney.

There were numerous wells at Hackney at this time, including the Pig's Well (or Pyke Well) mentioned by Dr Robinson in his *History of Hackney*, 1842. There was a considerable spring on the Downs which was said never to freeze, and a chalybeate spring, Shacklewell, was recorded as being in Church Street. The Churchfield Well, which gave its name to Well Street, was possibly an ancient mineral spring and its site in Well Street was coeval with the St John's Palace which belonged to the priors of St John of Jerusalem. This monastic association suggests that the well may have had a holy reputation and history. Also that the township was originally established as a result of the social and medical facilities offered by the priory. Another spring was recorded by Dr Robinson at the corner of the old churchyard and Morning Lane. It was a spring of pure water which inhabitants used as a source of domestic water.[57]

The numerous springs at Hackney not only provided pure drinking water, in contrast to the less healthy water supplies in the more densely populated areas, but the mineralisation in some of the springs provided a source of medication for disease. The springs, therefore, are an added reason for Celia Fiennes' choice of residence and may also have triggered her initial interest in medicinal springs.

Footnotes:

1   Morris C. (ed.) 1947, *The Journeys of Celia Fiennes*, p.132.
2   Peter J. 1680, *A Treatise of Lewisham*, see "to the reader".
3   Rutty J. 1757, *A Methodical Synopsis of Mineral Waters*, p.169.
4   Russel R. 1769 (5th edition) *Dissertation on the use of Sea Water* with anonymous supplement *A Treatise on the Nature, Properties and Uses of the Mineral Waters*, p.267-9.
5   McIntyre S. 1973, "The Mineral Water Trade in the Eighteenth Century", *The Journal of Transport History*, New Series, Vol.II, No.1, p.2.
6   Peter J. op.cit. p.76/7.
7   Foord A S. 1910, *Springs, Streams and Spas of London*, p.215.
8   Bray W. (ed.) c.1946, *The Diary of John Evelyn*, p.387,393.
9   Peter J. op.cit. p.81,91.
10 Rutty J. op.cit. p.169-171.
11 Russel R. op.cit. p.267-9.
12 Peter J. op.cit. p.79-82.
13 ibid. p.87.
14 Foord A S. op.cit. p.214; Sunderland S. 1915, *Old London's Spas, Baths, and Wells*, p.120.
15 Sunderland S. op.cit. p.120.
16 ibid. p.118.
17 Ewart W. 1902, "London and Middlesex", in Williams C T. Horton-Smith P., *The Climates and Baths of Great Britain*, a report by a committee of the Royal Medical and Chirurgical Society of London, Vol.II, p.43.
18 Russel R. op.cit. p.267-9.
19 Morris C. op.cit. p.131/2.
20 Foord A S. op.cit. p.203.
21 Sunderland S. op.cit. p.143.
22 Foord A S. op.cit. p.204.
23 Bray W. op.cit. p.574.
24 Sakula A. 1984, "Dr Nehemiah Grew (1641-1712) and the Epsom Salts", *Acta Academiae Internationalis Historiae Medicinae*, Rodopi, Amsterdam, Vol.19, No.1/2, p.12.
25 Sunderland S. op.cit. p.144.
26 Foord A S. op.cit. p.205.
27 Sunderland S. op.cit. p.144.
28 Foord A S. op.cit. p.206.
29 ibid. p.205.
30 Morris C. op.cit. p.121, 141.
31 Potter G W. 1904, reprint 1978, *Hampstead Wells*, Carlisle, p.46.
32 Weber H & F P. 1907, *Climatotherapy and Balneotherapy, the Climates and Mineral Water Health Resorts (Spas) of Europe and North Africa*, p.283.

33   Ewart W. op.cit. p.77.
34   Williams C T. Horton-Smith P. op.cit. p.42.
35   Potter G W. op.cit. p.4-5.
36   Metropolitan Water Board, 1953, *London's Water Supply, 1903-1953*, p.293.
37   Potter G W. op.cit. p.42-44.
38   ibid. p.31-44.
39   ibid. p.40-48.
40   Cole G D H. (ed.), 1927, *A Tour Thro' the Whole Island of Great Britain by Daniel Defoe, 1724-6*, p.384.
41   Morris C. op.cit. footnote p.141.
42   Potter G W. op.cit. p.50-51.
43   Cole G D H. op.cit. p.385.
44   Matthews W. (ed.), 1939, *The Diary of Dudley Ryder*, p29-30.
45   Potter G W. op.cit. p.50-54.
46   ibid. Chapter 6.
47   ibid. p.96-101.
48   Sunderland S. op.cit. p.97.
49   Williams C T. Horton-Smith P. op.cit. p.43.
50   Foord A S. op.cit. p.150/1.
51   Morris C. op.cit. p.362.
52   ibid. p.xix.
53   Hibbert C. 1969, *London, The Biography of a City*, p.92-3.
54   Cole G D H. op.cit. Letter VI, Vol.I, p.381-2.
55   Capper B. 1808, *Topographical Dictionary*.
56   Smith J. (ed.) 1924, *Diary of Samuel Pepys*, Vol.I, p.489.
57   Foord A S. op.cit. p.122-124.

BARNET

Towards the end of her 1697 Northern Journey, having been on the road for seven weeks, Celia and her party reached Barnet, also known as High Barnet, or Chipping Barnet, a large township 10 miles north west of London.[1] The air was "sharp" - excellent for the hordes of valetudinarians who flocked there to take the waters. By this date Barnet had developed its tourist industry sufficiently to cater for the influx, offering large houses for rent where whole families could stay.

Barnet well was situated on the common. The well-house was made partly of brick and a latticework wooden frame ran round the walls like an extended window. Visitors could peer through the latticework and down into the well. The roof was tiled; *"covered like a house"* was Celia's description. Inside, a flight of twelve steps led down to a door which led in to the well, 6 to 9 feet below ground level. Looking through the doorway from the bottom step, Celia, registered her disgust at the sight before her. The well, which was *"walled in 8 square"* was merely a very deep hole in the ground, full of dirt because there was no basin to contain the water.[2] The hole was also full of dead leaves, blown in from outside and never cleared away.

The water issued into two stone-lined sumps set into the floor. Sump 1 is 3 feet 2 inches wide x 2 feet 5 inches long (97 cm x 74 cm) and sump 2 is 3 feet 2 inches wide and 2 feet 7 inches long (97 cm x 79 cm). Both are 1 foot 8 inches (51 cm) deep with water, each being fed by a brick gutter. It was this double rectangle which Celia Fiennes described as *"8 square"* and which can still be seen today (1996).

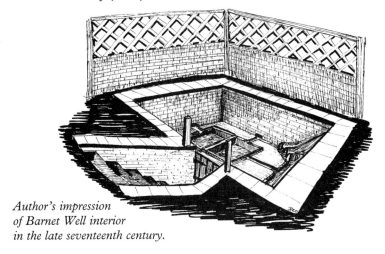

Author's impression of Barnet Well interior in the late seventeenth century.

The spring was not quick-flowing so the well retained its debris, and Celia compared it with Epsom, which she also disliked. Every time water was taken, the remainder became turbid, and had to settle before more could be taken. Despite the well's appearance the water in the glass was clear enough and suitable to drink, although Celia could not be tempted. On this account she was unable to give a first-hand account of its efficacy. She felt sure that no one who saw the state of the well would want to share its contents.

COMMENT

Banstead Well, Surrey. Barnet Well may have resembled this in appearance, except that its walls were brick topped with a wooden latticework "window".

During the seventeenth century High Barnet was a large, dry, pleasant town situated on the main road into London and thus much frequented by travellers. Not only was it notable for the quantity and variety of traffic passing along its dusty road, but also for its swine market, held every Monday. According to Camden, by the end of the sixteenth century the town was already becoming famous for the swine market. Cattle and horse fairs were also held on the eve, day and morrow of St John the Baptist (23-25 June) and St Luke the Evangelist (17-19 October).[3] Richard Blome in 1673 wrote that Barnet was as notable for its medicinal waters as for its Monday swine market, so as a consequence of its flourishing trades the township boasted many good inns by the time of Celia's visit.[4]

THE WELL-HOUSE

The mineral spring, also known as the Physic Well, is situated one mile southwest of Chipping Barnet.[5] The first mention of the spring was in the *Perfect Diurnal* of 5 June 1652, so it was probably discovered at about that time.[6] The well-house was brick, bonded with lime mortar, and tiled according to the churchwardens' accounts for 1656 which record nine shillings and fourpence being expended on *"lyme & bricks & tyles"*.[7]

Interior of the well chamber in 1996.

For over 150 years the well-house remained as Celia had described it. Then in about 1808 a group of local gentlemen raised a subscription to have the well arched over and a pump erected.[8] The "arch" consists of a barrel vaulted brick chamber, 6 feet 8 inches wide, 10 feet 8 inches long and 7 feet 3 inches high (202 cm x 325 cm x 233 cm). The bricks are red: those comprising the wall in English bond, 9 inches x $2\frac{1}{2}$ inches (23 cm x 6 cm). The floor bricks are slightly smaller at 9 inches x 2 inches x $4\frac{1}{2}$ deep (23 cm x 5 cm x 11 cm). The chamber completely encloses the well, and access is through the doorway which Celia Fiennes used. The chamber effectively prevented leaves and other debris from blowing into the water, reducing contamination. The location of the pump is uncertain. It may have been erected on the ground floor, immediately above the chamber, making the water accessible without needing to dip at the source.

In 1812 W M. Trinder described the well as being in a brick building in a little field, near the starting-post of the horse racing track. The well-house was repaired time and again, but was eventually demolished in 1840. The arched brick chamber was covered with soil and an iron pump erected above. This suggests that it replaced the earlier pump, which may have been made of lead.

79

Walter Bell gave a detailed account of how he found the well in the 1920s. In a field next to Well-House Farm he saw an old disused iron pump, and nearby a ladder head was sticking out of the ground. The ladder led into the well to allow maintenance of the pump. Bell descended the ladder through a narrow hole and stood in the well chamber, which had been perfectly preserved by soil. He immediately noticed the small, red, Stuart floor bricks and the two stone-lined sumps set about a foot in the floor. The sumps were fed by the spring which was channelled by gutters and pipes, and Bell noted a continual, though slow, flow. This slow issue accords with Celia Fiennes' suggestion that the water became turbid when dipped because of the shortage of water in the sump. Bell also noted that the chamber had formerly been bricked up and, as a consequence, had filled to the roof with water. The door, which Celia Fiennes mentioned, was no longer there, though the hinges remained.[9] The existence of the sumps, red floor bricks, stairs and doorway makes Barnet very special: it is one of the only spas to have its original well facility, and still in the condition it was built nearly 350 years ago.

MANAGEMENT OF THE WELL

The majority of spas were run by entrepreneurs who leased the wells and the land on which they stood from the local landowners. Barnet well, however, was run and maintained by the parish and the management details were decided at the monthly Vestry meetings. Unfortunately the churchwardens' accounts survive only for the period 1655 - 1691, and those are sparse and intermittant. What we do know is that a man was paid a nominal sum to look after the well: in 1656 "*paid Will Clarke for six nights & days 0-12-0*" (twelve shillings).

At the Vestry meeting on 2 March 1657 it was decided that John Draper should keep the well for which he was paid seven shillings per week. He was obliged to give a weekly account of the money he received in donations and hand it over to the two overseers of the well, Randolph Holmes and Samuel Wilkinson. In the following year it was agreed that Draper should be allowed to sell beer, "*strong water*" and tobacco at the well "*provided hee shuld suffer no disorder*" as a result.[10] This illustrates how Barnet well evolved from being a facility merely for taking the water, to a more refined spa offering extra diversions to visitors, and adding to the well-keeper's income. From May 1659 he was obliged every Saturday to give an account to the overseers of the well of the money he had taken.

INCOME FROM THE WELL

Drinkers were expected to make a donation and the money was handed over to the churchwardens.

Receipts for the years 1658-1658:

1656	8 July - 14 September	£12 11s 10d.
1657	16 May - 15 August	£15 0d 10d
1658	12 June - 21 August	£14 10s 1d

The income was used to pay to the well-house keeper and maintain the building. Any excess was distributed amongst the poor of the parish, particularly to widows. Amounts varied from sixpence to five shillings, though in August 1658 ten shillings was paid to Edward Hughes *"in his extremitie of sicknes"*. In that year eighty poor people benefited from the money taken at the well.

On one occasion the money was used as a short-term loan. In May 1659 it was agreed that Henry Hart and Randolph Holmes, the churchwardens with responsibility for distributing the well income, should lend twenty shillings to Daniel Hart, the money to be repaid by 29 September that year. They lent him a further ten shillings in June. No reasons are given of Daniel Hart's qualifications for the loan and nepotism might be suspected.

REPAIRS TO THE WELL

On 4 April 1655, shortly after the spring's discovery, seven parishioners were elected to oversee the *"worke about the repaire of the Well in the Comon"*.[11] The expenses for repairs suggest deliberate acts of vandalism by people breaking into the well to steal the water. In May 1657 John Draper was paid seven shillings for five locks and three staples, and ten shillings for mending them on several occasions. Three months later ten shillings was paid for a new lock, repairs to the old one, and the carpenter's work. In September 1658 the Vestry agreed to let Draper keep the well through the winter season. In return for giving his bond that he would prevent any damage being done to the well, or that he would repair, at his own expense, any damage which was done, Draper was to be paid either half a chaldron of coal, or fifteen shillings, by the parish officers.[12] This suggests that Draper was keeping the well open during the normal closed season in order to maintain his income, but that he was being held personally responsible for any vandalism.

In April 1676, 25 years after the discovery of the spring, a London alderman, John Owen, gave £270 to the Fishmonger's Company to invest, twenty shillings per annum of which was to be used for the repair of the Physic Well on the common.[13] This was on the understanding that if any obstruction were made to the well's access, or if it should become disused, the twenty shillings should be paid to the schoolmaster of the Queen Elizabeth Boys' School for the teaching of a poor boy, and the remainder to be given to the poor. Owen had already provided money for the education of three poor boys and for the repair of the school.[14] Celia Fiennes would not have concurred that the well was kept in good repair, and one might be a little surprised that she visited at all. Christopher Morris, the editor of Celia Fiennes' diary, believes that she had a house at Barnet which she let out, preferring to live with her married niece at Hackney.[15] Perhaps she inherited or bought the house in later life, for clearly she had not been in the habit of visiting Barnet Well if, by her mid-thirties, she was surprised at the murkiness of the water. It seems incongruous that she was not aware of the state of the place before she visited, since it is not far from Hackney and she was an inveterate traveller. Possibly the well was initially better maintained, since Samuel Pepys quite happily drank there on several occasions in the 1660s, though it is notable that Mrs Pepys appeared not to have taken the water.

The churchwardens' accounts for 1684 show only £4 received in well-money, which was not sufficient to pay the well-keeper. In the 1660s Samuel Pepys mentioned a lady (most likely the well-keeper's wife) who served the water. Celia Fiennes wrote that "*every tyme they dip it troubles the water*" which suggests that by the 1690s there was no longer a dipper and visitors dipped for themselves. It is likely that by that date there was no longer a well-keeper. Fortunately John Owen's endowment covered the costs of maintenance. The lack of income suggests a reduction in the popularity of Barnet Well though a variety of sources, including Celia Fiennes' journal, prove that it was still resorted to for its medicinal water.

It may have been the reduction in income which prompted the churchwardens in 1729 to acquire the Blockhouse at the bottom of Barnet Hill for use as a workhouse for the poor. An Act of 1722 gave parishes the power to hire or buy workhouses where paupers could be sent and put to work. This indoor relief was much cheaper than out-relief because the paupers' work could be sold and the money used to offset the cost of their maintenance.

ENCLOSURE OF BARNET COMMON

In 1716 a clause was inserted in a private Act for enclosing part of the common lying within the manor of Chipping Barnet ensuring that the medicinal well should remain open in perpetuity for the use of the inhabitants.[16] As it was situated on the common, the inhabitants almost certainly exercised their common right to take water from the well.

In a further Act (1728/9) for enclosing more of Barnet common, a right of access at reasonable times of day was allowed to the parishioners of Barnet.[17] This Act provided a potential source of revenue for the poor. It contained a clause stipulating that an annual rent charge should be put into the hands of trustees *"for the benefit of the poor of the parish of Chipping Barnet for ever."*[18] From Lady Day 1731 a rent of £50 was to be paid to the poor in perpetuity, the money to be paid in two instalments - at Lady Day and Michaelmas. One hundred and thirty five acres of common, including the land on which the well stood, was enclosed to form Barnet Common Farm. The farm was owned by James, Duke of Chandos and in 1735 was leased at £30 p.a to James Earle of Welling. The annual rent was paid to the Trustees until 1742, when it fell into arrears. This is reminiscent of Hampstead Well. There, in 1698, the Earl of Gainsborough granted the rent charge to the benefit of the poor. However, for many years the Hampstead tenant paid nothing and the Trustees did nothing to enforce his obligations. At Barnet, £2645 was owing by 1796 and the Trustees took possession of the land until 1833, when the arrears were paid in full. A dispute then arose over the succession to the estate, the Duke of Chandos having died. There was also a problem locating the interest which had accrued on the money handled by the Chandos Charity Commissioners.[19]

THE WATER CURES AT BARNET

Although the Barnet water was first mentioned in 1652, its curative powers were not immediately identified. In a letter of 27 August 1653 to her beau, Sir William Temple, Dorothy Osborne related Lady Diana Holland's trip to Barnet: *"I had a letter the last week from my Lady whoe tell's mee she has bin ill of a Paine at her stomack and that she has bin drinking Barnett waters and has founde her self better since. I thought they had bin soe Lately founde out that nobody had knowne what they had bin good for yett, or had ventur'd to take them; I could wish they were as Proper for the spleen as Epsum, or Tunbridge, they would lye much more conveniently for mee..."*[20]

The rise to fame was speedy. In his 1660 publication promoting Scarborough, Dr Robert Wittie inadvertantly compared Barnet favourably to other major English and German waters.[21] By 1684 there was a *"catalogue of the cures done by this spring"*, an indication that the water's curative properties were well known by the middle of the seventeenth century.[22]

Although the *Perfect Diurnal* (June 1652) described Barnet as a purging water and the strongest of the London springs, it was not as strong as Epsom water. It seems rather odd, therefore, that Samuel Pepys should have found five glasses of Barnet water eminently satisfactory, yet had to consume 4 pints at Epsom. This indicates that by the time he reached Epsom Well, the highly charged water which had collected overnight had already been drunk and the well replenished with water from the ordinary wells nearby.

The presence of allum appears to be a vital ingredient in purging waters. Celia Fiennes wrote that the Epsom waters were from allum.[23] Thomas Fuller also recorded that the medicinal well at Barnet *"springs from Allom-veins"*.[24] Benjamin Allen in 1699 wrote that Barnet's water *"had much the taste of common Pump water, but with the addition of bitterness"* and W M. Trinder described the water, which issued at 55° F, as clear, though somewhat brackish to taste.[25] These descriptions are typical of the variety of adjectives commentators used to describe the same water.

Generally Barnet water was agreeable to the palate but Trinder suggested that if it were not candied caraway seeds should be eaten which would both improve the flavour and prepare the stomach for the water. He weighed a gallon and found that it weighed 7 ounces more than the same quantity of rain water, an indication of the soluble material in the water.[26] Although the water was slightly bitter, with occasionally an unpleasant smell, it did not affect its efficacy. It was clear and sweet when bottled, so could be transported to markets further afield.[27] The water was being transported in competition with other purging waters, such as those of Epsom and Scarborough, though there were problems. At a vestry meeting in June 1659 it was agreed that no well water should be sold or sent away in rundlets or larger vessels until the next monthly meeting.[28] No reason was given for this decision but the most likely explanation is that the water was in shorter supply than usual, possibly due to drought.

Barnet's saline water was generally drunk between May and August, though the season was sometimes extended into September. Two factors may have determined the length of the season. Firstly, as with chalybeate waters, the medicinal effects may have been impaired through dilution by rain; secondly, the route across the common to the well may have been impassable during the colder months. Drinkers could shelter in the well-house during inclement or hot weather, but there is no evidence of there being any of the other facilities commonly found at spas. There was no coffee house, music room, gravel walks, gaming tables or ladies' and gents' rooms. Since the well was on the common, it was no doubt the nearby bushes which offered appropriate conveniences as the water's purgative properties started to work. This lack of refinement may have been a major factor in Barnet's early demise as an elitist venue.

Samuel Pepys, undeterred by the rudimentary facilities, visited on several occasions. He noted in his diary for 11 July 1664 that after having dined with his wife and her friends he and his man, Will, went on horseback: *"to see the Wells, half a mile off; and there I drunk three glasses and went and walked, and came back and drunk two more. The woman would have had me drunk three more; but I could not, my belly being full - but this wrought me very well; and so we rode home, round by Kingsland, Hackney, and Mile End, till we were quite weary - and my water working at least seven or eight times upon the road, which pleased me well."*[29] Many writers attribute Pepys' subsequent sleepless night, and the reason that he *"melted almost to water"* to this imbibing. A closer reading of the diary reveals that his sleepless night was not caused by the potency of the Barnet water, but due to worrying that a burglar was stealing his money![30] The "dipper" who tried to persuade Pepys to drink more water was most likely John Draper's wife.

Pepys visited Barnet again on Sunday 11 August 1667. He was at the well by 7 am and found many others already there. He drank the customary three glasses and afterwards breakfasted on cheese cakes at the Red Lion Inn.[31] This early morning drinking was prescribed by physicians: for maximum purging effect the waters had to be drunk before breakfast. Barnet, like Epsom, was not a quick spring, so those who arrived late would find little water in the well. From Pepys' accounts, however, we know that drinking was carried on throughout the day and that the water was equally effective when taken at a later hour.

According to Trinder in 1812, the water cured a wide variety of complaints. It cleansed the system of viscid, bilious and acrid matter without causing griping pains; it cleared up skin impurities, stimulated both the sex drive and loss of appetite, and the whey was good for cold, fever and rheumatic complaints.[32] Thomas Fuller (1684) had earlier recorded that *"The Water coagulateth Milk, and the Curd thereof, is an excellent Plaister for green Wounds"*, a rare reference to the external application of Barnet's water.[33] Dulwich's saline waters were also curdled with milk and used for curing old ulcers, a remedy recommended by Dr John Peter in 1680.

According to Chauncy, Barnet water was a gentle purgative, of particular benefit to those with a weak constitution or who were hypochondriacal or hysterical. The water was similar to those at nearby Cuffley and Northall, all of which *"dissolve acid tough flegm in the stomach and guts, with sharp choler, much better than other purgers; and are of great efficacy in cholicks, proceeding from both those humours; in short, for most diseases they proceed from sharp and hot humours (if they pass freely) they prove excellent safe purgers."*[34]

The recommended dose was from a pint to a quart taken in two doses, with an hour between. By 1812 the salts could be obtained from Mr Serrell, the local druggist, and if these had been taken to good effect, only half a pint of the water was necessary. It was also recommended that during the summer months a horse ride two or three times round the race track would get the water working. Certain cases benefited from a broth made with the water. Thinly sliced lean beef was added to 3 pints of water and boiled without salt or vegetables but with about a dram weight of isinglass shavings. Half a pint was taken two or three times a day. The water was equally suitable for those who had had a hard night's drinking. Adding a little salt to the broth *"will tend to settle the stomach, and carry off the foul matter of the debauch."*[35]

ANALYSES

Dr Rutty (c.1770) analysed Barnet's mild purging water in Dublin. One gallon yielded 5 drams 28 grains of sediment, of which slightly more than 26 grains were an indifferent calcareous matter, and the other 5 drams 2 grains mostly calcareous Glauber mixed with sea salt.[36] The salt was white, pungent on the tongue and bitter on the throat.[37] The contents are comparable with those of Alford.

An analysis was made by a W M. Trinder in 1812, when he described the water as having been strained through clay. It was the sulphate of magnesia (Epsom salt) and the muriate of magnesia (found in Seidlitz water) which provided the purgative qualities.[38]

Grains per gallon:

Sulphate of magnesia	96
Muriate of magnesia	12
Carbonate of lime	16
Sulphate of lime	24
Extractive matter	7

In 1907 the County Analyst pronounced the water unfit for consumption and as not possessing any medicinal qualities, yet in 1922, according to the Barnet Press, an analysis found that the water still retained its medicinal qualities.[39]

In the 1907 analysis, one gallon was found to contain:

Grains per gallon:

Solids	25.9
Chlorine	0.6
Chloride of sodium	1.0
Free ammonia	0.0157
Aluminoid ammonia	0.049
Nitrogen as nitrates	0.203

These analyses show how the nomenclature of water constituents changed over the centuries.

Barnet's life as a notable spa lasted for approximately half a century. During its heyday 30 coaches stood ready to make repeated trips across Barnet Common, taking visitors out to the well from Chipping Barnet.[40] By 1769 it was said that the spring had formerly been more frequented, and Walter Bell recorded that the well had fallen into disuse by the end of the eighteenth century, although it was repaired with funds from the Boys' School in 1807.[41] In the following year (1808) the barrel vaulted building and pump were provided, suggesting the continued popularity of the well. However these additions were almost certainly for the benefit of the parishioners, who continued to use the water when the gentry went elsewhere; Lysons commented that it was not until the end of the nineteenth century that the well was decayed and little used.[42] W M. Trinder's treatise of 1812 was unlikely to have been an attempt to breathe new life into an ailing spa; it was probably an enthusiastic opportunity to apply the modern advances in chemical analysis and to identify the medicinal virtues of this particular mineral water.

There are various indicators that Barnet's life as a fashionable resort was short-lived. The donations of 1684 were meagre, and following that date the churchwardens' accounts make no mention of an income from the water. This reduced income may have been reflected in the acquisition of the Blockhouse as a pauper institution to reduce poor law expenditure. The rents of Barnet Common Farm which were given to the use of the poor also indicate difficulties in funding their needs. Celia Fiennes' visit of 1697 portrays the well as dirty and unkempt, suggesting that there was no well-keeper. Also, by the end of the seventeenth century the wealthy and educated no longer wrote about Barnet's waters. They wrote of Knaresborough, Epsom, Tunbridge, Islington, Hampstead, Bath and Scarborough; but not Barnet. Daniel Defoe wrote in the 1720s that *"The Mineral Waters, or Barnet Wells, are on the declivity of a hill; they were formerly in great request, being very much approved by physicians; but of late, they began to decline, and are now almost forgotten: other waters at Islington, and at Hampstead having grown popular in their stead."*[43]

Barnet Well-house in 1996.

TODAY

Varying degrees of interest have been shown in the well for almost 300 years, from its discovery until the analyses of 1907 and 1922, though these may have been merely a local authority obligation to ascertain that the water was fit for human consumption. Walter Bell's description of his climb down into the well in the 1920s suggests that an indifferent interest existed at that date. The well was reopened in 1932 as a heritage feature and the present mock Tudor building was erected in 1937. By the 1960s it was under threat of demolition because of vandalism, but it was saved and can still be seen today.[44]

Footnotes:

1   Morris C. (ed.) 1947, *The Journeys of Celia Fiennes*, p.121.
2   ibid. p.121.
3   Camden's *Britannia*, Holland P. (trans.) 1610, p.415. The 1st edition of Camden's *Britannia* was published in 1586 and the 4th edition in 1594. It was probably this later edition which Holland translated; *Victoria County History for the County of Hertfordshire* (1908), Vol.II, p.330.
4   Blome R. 1673, *Britannia*, p.114.
5   Denbigh K. 1981, *A Hundred British Spas*, p.97.
6   Addison W. 1951, *English Spas*, p.44-45.
7   Hertford Record Office, Barnet parish records, ref. D/P15 256 5/2 (microfilm), 2 March 1657.
8   *Barnet Press*, 14 February 1975.
9   Bell W G. 1926, *Where London Sleeps: Historical Journeying into the Suburbs*, p.40-44.
10 Hertford Record Office, Barnet parish records, ref. D/P15 256 5/2 (microfilm).
11 Hertford Record Office, Barnet parish records, ref. D/P15 256 5/2 (microfilm).
12 A chaldron was a measure of coal of 36 bushels or 25.5 cwt. Thus Draper was given 1525 lbs
13 Widdicombe S H. 1912, *A Chat about Barnet and its History*, p.41.   or 692 kg.
14 *V C H for the County of Hertfordshire* (1908), Vol.II, p.79.
15 Morris C. op.cit.p.xix.
16 2 Geo. II cap.19
17 Widdicombe S H. 1912, p.41; Hembry P. 1990, *English Spas 1560-1815*, p.165 notes that this was also the case at other wells situated on common land. At Somersham Spa, in Huntingdonshire, the commoners had rights on Somersham Heath, where the spa was situated, and the poor parishioners were allowed daily access to the water between 5am and 7am.
18 Pickering D. 1765, *Statutes at Large*.
19 Hertford Record Office, ref. 54808 - 54820, Chandos Papers, 1734- 1868.
20 Dorothy Osborne lived at Chicksands in Bedfordshire, about 25 miles north of Barnet and 50
21 The relevant quotation appears in the chapter on Scarborough.   miles north of Epsom.
22 Fuller T. 1684, *Worthies of England*, p.369.
23 Morris C. op.cit. p.337.
24 Fuller T. op.cit. p.369.
25 Allen B. 1699, *The Natural History of the Chalybeate and Purging Waters of England*, p.149.
26 Trinder W M. 1812, *The English Olive Tree; or a treatise on the use of oil and the air bath...3rd edition. To which are subjoined chymical experiments on the Barnet Well Water*, Harts, p.64-65.
27 Russel R. 1769 (5th edition) *Dissertation on the use of Sea Water* with anonymous supplement *A Treatise on the Nature, Properties and Uses of the Mineral Waters*, p.232.
28 A rundlet was a small barrel containing approximately 15 gallons.
29 Latham R C. Matthews W. (eds.) 1971, *The Diary of Samuel Pepys*, Vol.5, p.200-201.
30 According to R C. Latham & W. Matthews this was about £1,000.
31 On the site of 72-76 High Street, High Barnet.
32 Trinder W M. op.cit. p.67.
33 Fuller T. op.cit. p.369.
34 Hertford Record Office, Gerish Collection, Box 13, *General Accounts, Medicinal Waters of*
35 Trinder W M. op.cit. p.68.   *Hertfordshire*, an undated newspaper report.
36 Monro D. 1770, *A Treatise on Mineral Waters*, Vol.I, p.144.
37 Rutty J. 1757, *A Methodical Synopsis of Mineral Waters*, p.95.
38 Trinder W M. op.cit. p.65-66.
39 *Barnet Press*, 14 February 1975.
40 Bell W G. op.cit. p.40.
41 Russel R. op.cit. p.232; Bell W G. op.cit. p.47.
42 Editorial comment in *Letters from Dorothy Osborne to Sir William Temple*.
43 Defoe D. 1724-6, *A Tour through the Whole Island of Great Britain*, Penguin reprint 1978, p.339.
44 *Barnet Press*, 14 February 1975.

ASTROP AND GREAT HORWOOD

It was about the year 1694 that Celia went on a circular tour from London to Sussex. She travelled via Aylesbury, Great Horwood, Hillesden, Buckingham, Banbury, Morton in Marsh, Hailes Abbey, Rowle Stone (Rollright), Broughton and then Astrop. Then via Abingdon, Oxford, Basingstoke and Petersfield, and so into Sussex. The purpose of the journey, which Celia estimated as 220 miles, seems to have been to visit relations and friends. She also visited the two chalybeate springs at Horwood and Astrop, and indulged in the popular pastime of the day, of visiting and criticising country houses.[1]

Celia visited three country houses in Buckinghamshire - the "modern" houses of Hillesden and Stowe, and ancient Thornton. From Aylesbury she went via Great Horwood to visit Mr Denton's estate at Hillesden, which was set on a hill and surrounded by a fine park.[2] Although his house was fairly small, it had an impressive hall and two parlours. Celia particularly admired the garden, with its grass, gravel walks, and excellent fruit and flowering trees. Thomas Denton had acquired the manor of Hillesden in 1547. In 1643 the house was assaulted, pillaged and reduced to ashes by the Parliamentarians. A slightly smaller house, the modern one which Celia saw, was built on the site. It stood at the east end of the magnificent late Perpendicular church but was destroyed in the eighteenth century. Nothing remains of this second house except in the field at the east end of the church, where some depressions near the diapered red brick wall indicate where the cellars lay.

Leaving Hillesden, Celia went to Sir Thomas Tyrrell's large, ancient house at Thornton. The Tyrell family had succeeded to the manor of Thornton in the sixteenth century, though the ancient manor house dated from the thirteenth century. The house was built in the style of other medieval manor houses, and "quadrangled round", Celia noted.[3] She commented on how low it seemed, having few storeys. Despite this, some of the ceilings were very high - presumably extending into the storeys above - and there was a spacious gallery. Once more she was diverted by the gardens, with their gravel walks and arbours, and a river containing fish. In 1850, Thornton was rebuilt in its present Tudor Gothic style, and since 1917 has been a convent school founded by the Sisters of Jesus and Mary.

Celia then made her way to the magnificent country house at Stowe which, she said, Sir Richard Temple had recently acquired. This suggests that the family had not long moved into the area. The Temples in fact had been at Stowe since 1571, and the magnificent pile which Celia saw was built between 1676-83 from designs by William Cleare, Sir Christopher Wren's master joiner.[4]

The house had a lofty, galleried hall, which Celia considered slightly too small for its height. There were many bedrooms and state rooms, an impressive staircase and a gallery which gave access to the "ledds" (roof) through a large "Cupelow" which offered a complete view of the surrounding countryside. What she found on the roof was a flat viewing platform made of lead, and a cupola which was added in December 1688. The cupola was removed about twenty years after Celia's visit, so she captured in writing a rare image of Stowe. The house also had a parlour with a balcony overlooking the gardens, which had been splendidly landscaped by Richard Temple, 1st Lord Cobham.[5] The ornamental gardens were terraced and laid out beautifully, with woods and orchards, and rows of trees stood on the perimeter.

Celia described the garden as surrounding the house in such a way that both the gardens and the landscape could be viewed in all directions from inside the house. In fact the house had been designed like a mini-enfilade, so that from the park one could look straight through the great hall and parlour and out into the gardens on the other side.[6] These original gardens were small, though formal and ornamental. The present vast gardens date from the 1730s and 1740s, and are the work of Nash and "Capability" Brown.[7] The house which Celia saw forms the central part of the present mansion, the whole of which is now the property of Stowe School; the gardens are in the capable hands of the National Trust. From Stowe Celia travelled the six miles to Great Horwood, passing several country houses belonging to Sir Ralph Verney.

At Great Horwood she sampled the waters from a small mineralised well. She "*drank them a fortnight*" and found that they were just like Tunbridge water "*and as good*". She also noted that there were several other chalybeate springs in the area.

The second medicinal water Celia sampled on this journey was the "*Steele water*" at Astrop in Northamptonshire.[8] She described it as being similar to Tunbridge water, though not as strong because of the levels of allum in it. She also compared Astrop water to the chalybeate Sweet Spaw at Harrogate, describing them both as rising "*off Iron and Steele*".

The flow from the spring was meagre, and as there was no basin, it trickled into a dirty well full of moss, which had yellowed by its contact with the water. Despite the meagre supply of water, the spring was much resorted to by the gentry, who stayed either in lodgings adjacent to the well or at nearby Sutton (King's Sutton). The area around the well was a contrast to the well itself, being elegantly landscaped to provide relaxation and diversions for the visitors. A gravel walk had been laid out between very high, smooth-cut, well-tended hedges. Nearby, two rooms were provided, one being "*for the Musick*" which was most likely for the group of string players - a traditional sight at English and continental spas - the other for the visitors to sit and rest.

During this tour of the Midland counties, Celia noted many unusual landscape features, including the Four Shire Stone which stands on the boundaries of Worcestershire, Oxfordshire, Warwickshire and Gloucestershire. She also went to Rowle Stone (Rollright), with its many huge stones similar to those "*at Stonidge*" (Stonehenge). She noted particularly an upright called the King's Stone because it was here that a Saxon King had defended himself against his enemies.

COMMENT

Celia Fiennes did not mention where she stayed during her two weeks in the area, but it was almost certainly at Broughton Castle near Banbury. This was the seat of her grandfather, William the 8th Baron and 1st Viscount Saye and Sele. The Baron's granddaughter described the Castle as "*an old house moted round and a parke and gardens, but are much left to decay and ruin, when my brother came to it...*", a reference to Celia's half brother William, 3rd Viscount.[9] Celia compared the castle with Sir Griffith Boynton's house at Burton Agnes in Yorkshire, of which she said: "*...the front looks very uniform with severall round buildings on each side answerring each other, with Compass windows, and the middle is a round building and the door enters in in the side of that tower which was the old fashion in building, and is like my brother Say's house at Broughton...*"[10]

Using the castle as a base, Celia embarked on several day trips, including one to Oxford. There, relatives showed her round some of the colleges she had not seen before. She also visited New College, which she must have seen on many occasions and where she was entertained by Richard Cross, a fellow of the college and tutor to her nephew Nathaniel Fiennes. New College was founded by William of Wykeham and the Fiennes family, sometimes known as Wykeham-Fiennes, was related to the Wykeham family through William's sister. Broughton Castle, which contains William of Wykeham's chapel, descended to the Fiennes' through Wykeham's sister. This family connection explains Celia's observation that "*...att the Entrance of the Colledge over the gate is the Fiennes's and the Wickhams Arms cutt in stone, sett up there by my Nephew Say when he was at the Colledge before his travels.*"[11] Her nephew, Nathaniel, went on his travels as soon as he succeeded to the title, in 1698. As Celia's sojourn at Broughton was in 1694, this observation about the family arms must have been written retrospectively, four years or more after her visit.

HORWOOD SPA

Great Horwood, situated four miles south-east of Buckingham, is blessed with numerous springs and wells. It is to the south of the village, at Wigwell, that the healing chalybeate spring lies. Evidence of the spring can be seen to the rear of Spring Cottage, Spring Lane.

Almost nothing is known of Horwood Spa. John Harris wrote in 1907 that: *"The mineral springs on the southern slope near Wigwell possessed medicinal quali-ties that were never appreciated"*.[12] The well was certainly appreciated by Celia Fiennes. During her spa tours she sampled many waters out of curiosity, but

 the insignificant Horwood is the only example we have of her taking the waters for a pro-longed period. Unfortunately, she gave no reasons for doing so; perhaps they acted as a gen-eral tonic. The water here would have had the same effects as Tunbridge water, although until recently Horwood spring's reputation was for curing warts.

The chalybeate spring, Great Horwood.

If Great Horwood ever became a spa, i.e a place where people travelled to take the water prescriptively, it had a truncated life, and Celia Fiennes was possibly the only person to record its existence. This may have been as a result of preferential access due to her connections with New College, who were lords of the manor of the land on which the spring is situated. Great Horwood lies only 5 miles from East Claydon, the home of Sir Ralph Verney. Despite this proximity and the water's apparent virtue, Sir Ralph was advised by his doctor in 1686 to take Astrop's chalybeate water.[13] This suggests that Horwood's medicinal spring had not at that time been recognised, sustaining the theory that it was a short-lived spa. Almost certainly it was not endorsed by a physician, neither was an entrepreneur forthcoming to develop it. New College may have been unwilling to allow any great development. The similarly ferruginous waters at Astrop were in easy reach of Buckingham, Bicester and Banbury, all within a 12 mile catchment area. Buckingham was the only major town within a similar radius of Great Horwood. Thus it was probably a combination of factors, i.e its distance from major settlements, competition with similar waters at Astrop, difficulties with site development, and lack of marketing, which caused Horwood's short existence.

TODAY

Behind Spring Cottage three or four steps, now overgrown, lead down to a pool of strong-tasting chalybeate water, the bright orange residue verifying the iron content. The water runs along a ditch and into a rudimentary basin a few yards to the left. The basin is approximately 18 inches (45 cm) square, fashioned out of stones and mortar, and was constructed to enable the cottagers to collect the water. Until recently, various ailments were bathed at the source and water was removed for treating localised complaints, particularly warts. The water today is not used in any way, not even during the severe drought of 1995 when the water continued to flow.

THE ROLLRIGHT STONES

The Rollright circle of stones is thought to have been erected about 3,500 years ago. William Camden described the stones as being an ancient monument standing near the bank of the Isis.[14] He suggested that they were erected by Rollo the Dane, to commemorate a victory fought in this area: possibly the battle between the English and the Danes at Hook Norton, 4 miles north-east of the stones. Known by the local people as the *"Rolle-rich stones"*, each megalith was said to be a man turned to stone.

The tallest was called The King because, before his petrifaction, he was destined to become King of England. To achieve that honour he had only to set eyes on the small nearby town of Long Compton, and he would have succeeded had he taken a few more steps in the right direction. A further five stones standing opposite The King and touching each other, were said to be mounted knights, and the other stones the army. Today the site has mystic associations and is commonly reputed to be the meeting place of witches.

DISCOVERING ASTROP SPRING

Astrop is approximately 3 miles from Banbury, 12 miles from Buckingham and 15 miles from Northampton. The iron-bearing spring was discovered in April 1664 by Dr Richard Lower, a local doctor, at the bottom of a small hill in Sir Simon Stewart's estate. The story goes that as he and his partner, Dr Wills, rode to see a patient, Dr Lower spotted the orange coloured spring water and dismounted to examine it. After several experiments the doctors found the water to be medicinal, and recommended it as a cure.[15]

ST RUMBOLD

The Astrop spring and well were named after the seventh-century baby saint Rumbold (sometimes Rumwold). He was allegedly a grandson of King Penda of Mercia (d. 654), after whom King's Sutton was named. Rumwold was born at Sutton, and an incredible legend is attached to his short life. Apparently he died after three days, but not before repeating several times the phrase *"I am a Christian"*, professing his belief in the Holy Trinity, asking for baptism and communion, preaching a sermon on the Holy Trinity, foretelling his own death, and mentioning where he wanted to be buried. The baby was first buried at King's Sutton, then at Brackley, and finally at Buckingham.[16]

It was unheard of to have a statue of a baby above a well so eventually a statue of St Rumbold dressed as a mature medieval knight was erected in a niche above the spring. People came from far and wide seeking cures, but since this was a Restoration spa it was unlikely to attract the number of Roman Catholics which flocked to the ancient holy wells. The attachment of a saint was probably to add respectability, rather than to suggest divine properties.

VIRTUES OF ASTROP WATER

Astrop's water was described as a brisk, spirituous and clear tasting chalybeate, which at one time was highly recommended by one Dr Moreton. It was effective in curing certain female obstructions, dropsy and jaundice; easing rheumatic pains, freeing gall stones and kidney stones, offering relief in the first and second stages of consumption, and the restoration of the constitution after hard drinking.[17] This suggests it was a cure for a hangover! Some people also asserted that it cured madness and melancholy. One of the earliest accounts of the waters claimed that it was good for stomach, ureter and bladder disorders because *"it penetrates through every occult passage where other Medicines cannot come"*.[18] It cured mesenterie, hypochondria, dried up "Defluxions and Distillations" of the head and chronic headaches, vertigo, palsy and convulsions; trembling and sight disorders and all types of gout. It stopped continuous vomiting, diarrhoea and dysentery and killed and expelled worms. It cured heart palpitations, cured aches and cramp, secured teeth which were about to fall out (a side effect of scurvy) and prevented anal prolapse. It was particularly recommended for women as were, and still are, other chalybeate springs. It suppressed heavy menstruation, prevented miscarriage, and strengthened the womb. At first reading this appears to be an immense list of assorted problems which could be cured, and some modern writers are very cynical about the extremity of this type of claim. However, many diseases manifested several of the symptoms mentioned above. This long list is indicative of the most common types of ailment suffered in the seventeenth and eighteenth centuries. Thus Astrop Wells was noted no less for *"it's* [sic] *noble, volatile, enlivening Chalybeate, than the many truly surprizing cures done, in Comparison of it's Number of Company."*[19]

The waters were taken by drinking, bathing, lotion and injection. The size of the dose which needed to be consumed in order to be effective - between 4 and 10 pints each morning - makes drinking sound an unfavourable option. By about 1680 the prescription for chalybeate waters was that recommended by Fallopius (the Italian anatomist Gabriele Fallopio, 1523-62). Drinkers of these waters began their day with a small quantity, 4 to 5 pints, and increased the dose daily by half a pint every morning for 10 days. For the following 10 days they decreased the amount by half a pint. This was a general outline and varied according to age, gender, strength or debility and type of illness. By 1789 the recommended dose was still high: 3 to 5 quarts in the morning - i.e, 6 to 10 pints.[20]

CURES AT ASTROP

During the eighteenth century, several brief case studies of cures effected at Astrop were recorded.[21] Mr Philip Bird, 25, of Stoney Stratford, had fever, pains in the side, night sweat and trembling. The best physicians in the county could not help him. For 8 weeks he drank 4 quarts daily and went home perfectly cured.

Josiah Diston, aged 66, arrived at Astrop at the beginning of August 1732 suffering from loss of appetite, continual retching and vomiting, jaundice, asthma and dropsy; his legs, stomach and thighs were so swollen that he could not walk. For a fortnight he drank 3 quarts daily, after which he could manage to walk from Sutton to Astrop. Two weeks later he was eating and drinking - perhaps too heartily of the latter - and attending the balls laid on as evening entertainment.

After some years, a slackness in adhering to the dosage crept in. Patients were taking only 3 half pints or a quart in the morning - not sufficient to effect any cures. This caused anxiety amongst those who made money out of the enterprise because if the waters became renowned for being ineffectual the sick would lose faith in them and stop visiting. Dr Short, in 1740, advised that it while was fine to drink so little at spas such as Cheltenham, because the waters were of a much stronger solution and had a quicker effect, the amount was insufficient at Astrop. By 1740 the water had maintained its reputation successfully for 70 years, and there is a hint that it was due to inappropriate consumption that Astrop becoming less frequented.

Bathing at Astrop was used for soothing the nerves, relaxing joints, strengthening broken bones, relieving gout, and preventing miscarriage. By lotion, it helped many eye diseases and asperity of the eye lids, hair loss and running sores of the head. By injection, it was beneficial to diseases of the bladder, fundament and womb.[22] Evidence of bathing survives in sketches of c.1810 by J C. Nattes, which showed a thatched cottage with an adjacent well and the interior of a shed containing a pump, tank and sunken bath.

Despite its popularity, little in the way of analysis of the water survives to suggest what combination of minerals was effecting the said cures. Dr Rutty, publishing in 1757, recorded that when one gallon of the water was evaporated, 17 grains of sediment remained, comprising ochre, a calcareous earth, calcareous Glauber salt and probably some sulphur.[23]

ASTROP AND WELLINGBOROUGH

The new well at Astrop was popular amongst the courtiers, and Dr Peirce of Bath blamed it for eclipsing nearby Wellingborough, the waters of which had been much praised by Richard Banister in his *Breviary of Eyes and Eye Diseases* of 1622.[24] In the early eighteenth century *"a late pevish Humorist of a Physician"* had threatened to put a toad in the Astrop well; he either decided against it, or put the creature in and later removed it, or left the toad in to create one of the most restorative medicines in the country.[25] Perhaps the peeved doctor was from Wellingborough. However, this may have been a specious argument. Hembry noted that the spa declined following Queen Henrietta Maria's visit to Wellingborough in 1628. Since Astrop's medicinal spring was not promoted until 1664, it may only have sealed Wellingborough's fate rather than caused it.[26]

ASTROP WELLS AND KING'S SUTTON

News of the new spring must have travelled rapidly because in 1665, the year after its discovery, Lady Elmes fled to Astrop to escape the plague in London. However the new spa was clearly not ready to receive the Company, as she complained of *"the stink of sour whey and cheese"* in her room and having no coal fire in which to burn perfume to disguise the smell. There was no supper, and she had to borrow a candle because she had not brought her own. Over 20 years later, in 1686, Lady Elmes' ageing brother, Sir Ralph Verney, was encouraged by his doctors to take the waters at Tunbridge, Epsom, Islington and Astrop. Those of Astrop were the most convenient, being as good as the London ones and fairly close to his seats at Middle and East Claydon, near Horwood.[27]

With the well gaining in popularity, facilities were required if the Company were to maintain its interest. Nearby King's Sutton became a fashionable spa township, and at Astrop improvements were made at the well. A strong stone basin was provided for the water, which flowed at about 300-400 gallons per hour. The water flowed through the holes in the bottom of the basin into a freestone gutter which was lined with a pale ochre fur and a coarse variegated scum. The pale ochre was indicative of a mild chalybeate water and accounts for the yellowed moss that Celia saw.

By the 1740s there was a well-house, and from the palisade in front visitors could perambulate under a covered way to a wainscoted room, where they could socialise and take tea and coffee. Behind the well-house was a gravel walk, 140 yards long and 6 yards wide, running between a 12 foot high clipped hedge. The hedge offered shelter from the sun, and benches at each side of the walk provided rest when required. Beyond the walk were some conveniences where the walkers could retire. These may have been rest rooms or lavatories. Beyond the brook which flowed past the well was a tea room, dancing room, shop and kitchen.[28]

LIFE AT THE SPA

Some details of the life at Astrop can be gleaned from the Purfoy letters of 1735-1753.[29] Henry Purfoy (1697-1762) was lord of the manor of Shalstone, situated just one mile from the great house at Stowe which Sir Richard Temple acquired in 1697, and 5 miles north-west of Buckingham. Purfoy was a quiet and reserved country gentleman, rarely straying more than one day's journey from home. He was expected to sit on the Grand Jury at the Quarter Sessions, and as Sheriff of the county he was a regular attender at the Assizes. These duties meant that he was often in the company of the elite members of Buckinghamshire's society. On 8 July 1755 he recorded that at the Buckingham Assizes he had dined, with amongst others, "...*Earl Temple, Earl Verney... Mr Geo Denton...the Viscount Say & Seall.*" These were all familiar names to Celia Fiennes. On her journey to Astrop c.1697, she had visited Sir Richard Temple at Stowe, travelled via Sir Ralph Verney's estates at Middle and East Claydon, called on Mr Denton at Hillesden, and was the granddaughter of William Fiennes, 1st Viscount Saye and Sele. Thus Purfoy and Celia Fiennes mixed in the same company, and would no doubt have engaged in similar pursuits at Astrop.

Purfoy recorded that the gentry from London, Lincoln, Oxford, and as far away as Cornwall, socialised at the little spa. Many went, as Celia did, as part of a wider tour or with friends and relations with whom they were staying. In Purfoy's case it seems that the county gentlemen also made regular visits to relax after the Assizes. His first reference to Astrop was of the season of 1736, which he described as offering "*more diversion than usual*" - suggesting that he was a frequent user - with much dancing and pleasant company amongst the younger folks. Thus Astrop provided food, lodgings, rest facilities and entertainment during the day and evening.

Purfoy's comments also suggest that Astrop was becoming increasingly popular, hence the improvements of 1749 which are described below. In late August of that year, probably at the end of the first season of the modifications, Purfoy met members of the social elite - doctors, counsellors, clerics, and ladies. One or two of them had taken sons and daughters of marriageable age, so perhaps this was also seen as a match-making centre. Again in August, this time in 1750, Purfoy travelled by coach to meet the county families, who at no time seem to have attended for curative purposes.

A New Lease Of Life

In 1749 the water was piped from the well to a new site half a mile away. It was officially opened by Dr Radcliffe of Oxford, suggesting that the proprietors were anxious for Astrop to maintain credibility as a medicinal centre rather than as a place of mere entertainment. The new spring was provided with a stone basin, set at the bottom of a set of steps in a stone-flagged area, with the statue of St Rumbold above. Perhaps it was due to the association with the eminent Dr Radcliffe, or the fact that the location of the spring had been upgraded and made more appetizing, that the gentry soon started to flock here, and King's Sutton expanded in style to accommodate this new influx. Entertainment took on new proportions, with balls being held every Monday and other amusements, notably cards, played at other times.

Thomas Thornton III (1698-1783) of Brockhall visited Astrop almost every year between 1740-82. Some time between 1754 and 1769 he wrote some lengthy doggerel lines which provide a picture of life at Astrop Spa during the eighteenth century.[30]

".... (When you have dress'd you nice & fine)
Go to the Publick room by nine
From that time to the hour of ten
Ent'ring the Beaus & Belles you'l ken;
And if the waters kindly pass
You'l see good Nature in each Face.
When they're assembled you will see
Plenty of butter'd Rolls & Tea,
For which a nine pence you must pay
Because it is a Publick Day.
When ended Breakfast's Noise and Talk
With Friends select you'l take a Walk
Until the Musicks Band is met
And every thing in Order set.
The Ladies all will enter in
And then the Concert will begin....
The Concert ended you may Walk,
On each Performers praises Talk:
Till in due time the Dinners brought,
Such plenty you can want for Nought.
One shilling & a half will pay
For all that you can eat that day,
I mean for all on which you Dine,
And sixpence more will pay for wine..."

From these lines one sees a picture of the Company engaged in traditional spa pursuits. Early in the morning the invalids took the water and promenaded in the walks until the waters had taken effect. At 9 o'clock everyone gathered at the Assembly Room, where for an hour they could meet friends and acquaintances. Or they could watch everyone else walking up and down, noting by the look on their faces how well the waters had worked. A noisy public breakfast of buttered rolls and tea could be had for 9d. Breakfast was often taken publicly at a given time, partly to give the water time to work and partly to promote the social nature of the spa.

For many, water was only taken once a day - before breakfast - so the remainder of the day was taken up with gentle pursuits to prevent boredom. Walks and talks, music, bowling greens, race courses, gambling at cards, visiting local country houses and sights, and clandestine relationships, all provided a sop for boredom. For this reason the healthy also visited spas: visiting friends in an *al fresco* hospital and taking advantage of the multitude of formalised diversions.

After dinner, the visitors either drank wine or tea, or both, gambled or visited the local stately homes, as Celia Fiennes had done. These might be Lord Guildford's gardens at Wroxton near Banbury, or Lord Temple's house and gardens at Stowe. In the evening the Astrop Company might sup wine, talk, or attend a ball, and not get to bed until very late.

Some of Thornton's other lines show that the accommodation was quite suitable for the Company. He noted, for example, that the beds were not damp. Lodgings were of the "ordinary" type: food was 1/6d per day for as much as one could eat, with wine "extraordinary" for an additional 6d.

In August 1783 Thomas Thornton's son, Thomas Lee Thornton, paid a subscription *"to the rooms & wells at Astrop"*.[31] Two years later, in July 1785, a fire destroyed 40 houses. It has been said that the spa seemed unable to recover from this set-back, which effectively ended Astrop's claim to be a society venue. However, Astrop is mentioned on John Andrew's 1797 map of the mineral waters and bathing places of Britain, and Christopher Tongue notes that the Great Room was opened for public entertainment until about 1808. This suggests that the fire did not destroy Astrop's vitality, and that it continued to be popular for a few more years. Many notable English spas changed their character dramatically during the depression caused by the French Wars (1793-1815), and Astrop seems to fit this pattern. By 1914 only the ruins of the Assembly Room and Music Room could be detected.[32]

TODAY

This once lively spa is now forgotten, yet the chalybeate spring continues to flow. One of the early containments lies in a private field: its stone surround is in excellent condition, though the niche is empty of its saintly figure. In front of the stonework lie two conjoined stone sumps, approximately the same size and depth as the two sumps at Barnet Well. This suggests an early date of construction though it was not there when Celia Fiennes visited. The spring rises in the right hand sump, flows through a circular hole into the left hand

sump and from there flows away to the left of the stonework. Three or four steps, now overgrown, lead from the right down to the spring. The water, which tastes very strongly of iron, has left an exceedingly vivid orange deposit between the sumps and the stonework.

St Rumbold's Well, probably the structure which was erected in 1749 and endorsed by Dr Radcliffe: photographed in 1996. This is an excellent and extremely rare example of a containment which was provided during the heyday of an English spa. It lies on private property and is not available to visitors.

In 1857 the owner of Astrop Park Farm closed the path leading to the well, but piped the water to a new site on the King's Sutton to Astrop and Newbottle Road, where he built a replica of St Rumbold's Well.

The stone niche is empty but the spout still dispenses the strong flavoured chalybeate water. It is a County Heritage Site.

Footnotes:

1   Morris C. (ed.) 1947, *The Journeys of Celia Fiennes*, p.31.
2   Probably Mr Justice Denton.
3   Mitton G E. 1901, *Black's Guide to Buckinghamshire*, p.121.
4   Bevington M. 1990, *Stowe, A Guide to the House*, p.64.
5   `Capability' Brown began his career in the kitchen garden at Stowe.
6   Bevington M. c.1990, *Templa Quam Dilecta, Stowe, The South Front*, XI, p.7.
7   Pevsner N. Williamson E. 1994, *The Buildings of England*, p.660.
8   Morris C. op.cit. p.31-2.
9   ibid. p.25.
10 ibid. p.90.
11 ibid. p.38.
12 Harris J. 1907, *Great Horwood, Bucks*, (unpublished), p.7.
13 Hembry P. 1990, *The English Spa 1560 - 1815*, p.70.
14 Camden's *Britannia*, Holland P. (trans.) 1610, p.374.
15 Denbigh K. 1981, *A Hundred British Spas*, p.27-29.
16 Farmer D H. 1978, *The Oxford Dictionary of Saints*, p.377-8.
17 Russel R. 1769 (5th edition), *A Dissertation on the Use of Sea Water* with anonymous supplement *A Treatise on the Nature, Properties and Uses of the Mineral Waters*, p.289.
18 Anon. 1668, *A Brief Account of the Virtues of the Famous Well of Astrop by a learned Physician*, p.2.
19 Short T. 1740, *History of the Principal Mineral Waters*, Preface, p.iii.
20 Elliot J. 1789, *An Account of the Nature and Medicinal Virtues of the Principal Mineral Waters of Great Britain and Ireland*.
21 Short T. op.cit p.47.
22 Anon. 1668, *A Brief Account of the Virtues of the Famous Well of Astrop by a learned Physician*, p.3-4.
23 Monro D. 1770, *A Treatise on Mineral Waters*, p.376.
24 Hembry P. op.cit. p.70.
25 Short T. op.cit. p.45.
26 Hembry P. op.cit. p.46, 70.
27 ibid. p.70.
28 Short T. op.cit. p.46.
29 Mitchell L G. (ed.) 1973, *The Purfoy Letters 1735-1753*.
30 Tongue C. 1970/1, "Thomas Thornton at Astrop Spa", *Northamptonshire Past and Present*, IV, No.5, p.281-285.
31 Tongue C. op.cit. p.284.
32 ibid. p.281-285.

BUXTON

Celia's Northern Journey of 1697 lasted 7 weeks and by her reckoning covered 635 miles. Leaving Yorkshire, the party entered Derbyshire and, ever interested in things underground, she commented extensively on coal mining. At Chesterfield she saw mine entrances which looked like well heads through which the miners were let down and drawn up on a cord. The coal was brought up in the same way, in a basket resembling a hand-barrow.[1] The landscape was riddled with other mines, marble, copper, tin, silver and lead. Celia recorded that, like the coal mines, they were dug like wells, and walled round to stop them caving in. Men were lowered down on a pulley, one at a time, to search for ore. Usually they had to dig some way before striking any, and having found it would excavate horizontally. She saw three or four men at work, all of whom were let down through the well. The work was hazardous and potentially fatal. The men looked pale and yellow - a symptom of lead poisoning - and occasionally workers were killed by unexpected explosions caused by their naked lights and gunpowder. Celia noticed that in digging out the ore they dug out a white crystal-like substance (fluor-spar), which she described as being like *"white Sugar-candy"*, smooth like glass, though cracked, and which was used by doctors for treating colic.

The travellers, ever eager to investigate country houses, spent some time admiring the exquisite beauties of Chatsworth, the Duke of Devonshire's house, before moving on to Haddon Hall near Bakewell. From there they covered the nine miles to Buxton, over craggy hills and roads too narrow for a coach or wagon. There were few hedges, no trees and no fences, and enclosures were made of dry stone walls. All one could see was crest upon crest of steep hills of uneven stone. Travellers in most parts of the county were forced to have a guide to avoid becoming hopelessly lost in the bleak, rocky wilderness. It took 6 hours to cover 9 miles.

At Buxton the most convenient place to stay was in the Duke of Devonshire's house, Buxton Hall (The Old Hall), the largest house in the area. Though *"not very good"*, it was the best place to stay because the bath was in the same building. The disadvantage was the noise of the hordes of other guests, constantly streaming in and out of the bath. All the houses in the town seemed to be lodging houses and run on the same principles i.e they were all "ordinary" - a place where a bed and meal was a fixed price, with a fixed price for servants. At the Old Hall beer was inclusive in the price of the meal, but it was so bad that it was undrinkable; ale and wine were extraordinary. There were two, three or four beds per room so if one party could not fill a room, strangers from another party were put into the same room. Sometimes it was so crowded that three people had to share a bed. Few people stayed more than two or three nights because it was all so inconvenient; to Celia's dismay her party had to stay there for two nights because one of them was ill. Genuinely sick people, however, would have had to tolerate these facilities in their endeavour to find renewed health.

Celia comprehensively described the bath, which was situated in the basement of Buxton Hall. She thought that it was large, and estimated its size as 40 feet x 20 or 30 feet, "*being almost square*". It was paved round the edges and provided with stone benches to sit on. There was a tunnel-like hole in the ceiling, most likely for taking off the rising vapours. Celia complained that it let in the cold, probably as a draught. She would have preferred the bath to be completely open to the sun and air. The bath was fed by eleven or twelve warm springs; they were not as warm as cow's milk but warm enough to open the skin's pores without causing sweating. Despite the water's tepid temperature, Celia complained that it made her shake, suggesting that it was cold. She compared it with Bath waters, which were much warmer.

The water at Buxton bath was deep enough to swim in, and bathers could either stand in the water up to the neck, holding on to a chain fixed to the side, or go in deeper escorted by a guide. The guide was necessary because of the current, which was sufficiently strong to knock people over. Celia did not like bathing here. At Bath, the water was changed every night. At Buxton, the used bath water had only two small overflow pipes to trickle through. She disliked any bath or well where the water did not gush away. Thus she preferred Holywell, Tunbridge and Hampstead to Barnet, Epsom and Buxton.

Buxton water could be drunk at St Anne's Well, which was 10 or 12 yards from the bath. The well was arched over, making it hotter, and it heated the cup which was used to scoop up the water. The water was quite pleasant, about the temperature of milk, and it acted as a diuretic. Celia drank less than a cupful. She drank none at all at Barnet and less than a cupful at Canterbury and Buxton. She preferred the chalybeate waters of Great Horwood and Tunbridge Wells, drinking the former for two weeks and the latter for many years.

As usual, Celia visited the local tourist attractions. At the end of the town was Poole's Hole, a large underground cave. The entrance was so low that visitors had to bend double to get through. Once inside, the cave widened out so that one could stand up and admire the lofty roof and resounding echo. Water dripped from the roof on to the ground and the rocks beneath, creating unusual formations. The local guides interpreted them as a lion wearing a crown, an organ with many keys and pipes, a state chair, and a vast white flitch of bacon. Celia went in as far as the Queen of Scots Pillar, a huge white stone hanging overhead like a canopy, before feeling that she had seen enough. On the way out she had the candle carried to St Anne's Needle, which was white and crystal-like, similar to the other rocks in the cave. The constantly dripping water had caused stalactites and stalagmites to form. Unlike the ecologically minded tourist of today, she had a piece broken off to examine, and described the interior as like mother of pearl.

After Poole's Hole she went on what was clearly a tourist circuit exploring more Wonders. Two miles from Buxton is Elden Hole, an immense cavern running vertically into the ground, which Celia described as the fourth Wonder of the Peak. No one had been able to measure the depth, despite sending down plumb lines. Celia and her companions dropped pebbles into the shaft and listened to them hitting the sides as they bounced down. Putting their ears to the ground approximately 100 yards from the shaft, they could still hear the pebbles striking the stone underground. The fifth Wonder she visited was Mamtour (Mam Tor), "*a high hill*" of stone, one side of which looked perfectly smooth, the other side being completely weather-worn and permanently shedding sand and shale. She noted that no one ever tried to climb the latter side because the loose sand made the surface slippery and dangerous.

The sixth Wonder, at Castleton, 4 miles from Elden Hole, was a hill so steep that no one could climb it. Known as the Devil's Arse, the only way up or down was via a winding road. In the cleft of the hill was a huge cave, and it was probably this cleft and cave formation which earned the hill its title. The cave helped to provide several poor houses, all stone walled and thatched. A Mr Middleton, who was in Celia's party, said that until recently a gentleman and his wife had lived in the cave, despite being fairly wealthy.

COMMENT

THE WONDERS OF THE PEAK

Celia Fiennes was without doubt fascinated by the topography of the Peak District, a landscape determined by the geology of the area. The limestone could not support the traditional English oak tree so birches and limes grew instead.[2] It was also the limestone which provided Derbyshire with its famous natural "Wonders", mentioned by so many early travellers.

POOLE'S HOLE OR CAVERN

Poole's Hole was given the title First Wonder of the Peak by Charles Cotton, a local author, poet and fisherman in 1680, although many people prefer to think of the thermal springs as the First Wonder.[3] It was said that the huge cave was made by a robber named Poole but some said it was caused by mining for marble and crystal. Celia Fiennes preferred the former argument, being unable to reconcile this horizontal "mine" with the deep perpendicular mines she had seen earlier. She was bemused that the roof of the cave could be so high, and not collapse with the weight of earth and stone above it.

One of the clearest pictures of the early entrance was captured by Thomas Short, writing in 1740.[4] He described a rock over the entrance as being 7 yards perpendicular, and the breadth at the outer entry as 9 yards. The doorway itself was two and a half yards wide and 3 to 5 feet high, and he had to stoop quite low for the first 18 yards inside the cave before being able to stand erect. Despite being extremely difficult to negotiate, the mouth of the cave remained very much the same until 1854, when the mass of glacial sediment was removed with dynamite to allow visitors easier access.

Once inside the cave, the temperature was a low 7º C (44º F). Like Ralph Thoresby, who visited Derbyshire in July 1681, Short's attention was drawn by his guides to slightly different aspects of the caves than those to which Celia's attention had been directed. Short's guide concentrated more on the cave as it was used by the robber and outlaw Poole, than on the resemblance of the limestone features to everyday items. Visitors were shown Poole's chamber, which was inside on the right about 5 yards above the level; his parlour and closet, his dining room which extended some way into the rock, and a shelf for his food - a very long and broad flagstone above the entrance. Thoresby was shown the Queen of Scots Pillar and, as Celia Fiennes had done 20 years earlier, broke a piece off. He indicated that many pieces were broken off as souvenirs.[5] Short wrote that the Mary Queen of Scots Pillar was unremarkable, and of the flitch of bacon that *"whoever can see any Resemblance, have a stronger Fancy than I."* He said the whole length of the cave was 230 yards, though a later sightseer described it as twice that length, at about ½ mile long.[6]

Thomas Short noted that 34 yards past the Queen of Scots Pillar was St Andrew's Needle, after which was a very steep and rocky precipice. He advised that visitors wishing to climb should *"be sure your Claws be in good Order, for you must be vastly indebted to them if you return safe, this Ascent being forty Yards above the Level"*.[7] It is possible that St Anne's Needle and St Andrew's Needle were one and the same. It may therefore have been at this juncture that Celia realised that the precipice ahead was not to her liking, and it was this which induced her to curtail her visit.

The cave was dark, and lighting it was the province of the local women, who no doubt received tips from the visitors for their pains. Celia Fiennes did not mention lighting, but as early as the 1670s visitors went in accompanied by guides with lights, and by the early nineteenth century eight women are known to have lighted the way with candles.[8] It was recorded in 1797 that the guides in the cave were local tenants, who fought and jostled each other for the unofficial tours.[9] It was probably just the same in the 1690s when Celia visited. Richard Blome noted another local occupation: on re-emerging from the cave visitors were met by poor women who lived nearby, carrying water and herbs so that the visitors could clean up after having to scramble into and out of the cave.

MAM TOR AND ELDEN HOLE

Mam Tor is about one mile outside Castleton on the right, on the way to Buxton. On his journeysThomas Short estimated the rock as approximately 196 yards high. He also visited Elden Hole *"that terrible perpendicular Gulf or Chasm, Eldine Hole,"* one mile south of Mam Tor and 4 miles east of Buxton. He tried to plumb the depth in seven different places: in six he reached 192 yards and in the seventh 295 yards, of which 40 yards appeared to be in water. He recorded that the best way to check the depth was first to throw a weighty object down it. Then, using Dr Halley's mathematical calculations for the speed of a descending body and ascending sound, calculated it to be 1266 feet or 422 yards deep.[10] William Camden, c.1594, had reckoned Elden hole one of the Wonders of England; he said that the wondrous thing about it was its enormous mouth and exceedingly steep and breathtaking depth. He quotes a verse of unknown date and origin:

"There are in High Peake wonders three,
A deep hole, Cave and Den:
Commodities as many bee,
Led, Grasse and Sheepe in pen.
And Beauties three there are withall
A Castle, Bath, Chatsworth:
With places more yet meet you shall
That are of meaner worth." [11]

These were in contrast to the scathing comments about the "Wonders" made by Defoe, perhaps the only traveller who remained stoutly unimpressed by them. He was not overawed by Buxton's warm springs, having seen plenty at Bath, or by the natural "Wonders" of Poole's Hole and Tideswell. Elden Hole was the only sight which he found impressive.

THE OLD HALL

Buxton's post-Roman history as a spa town starts c.1570, when the landowner, George Talbot, 6th Earl of Shrewsbury, erected a Hall containing lodgings and a bathing house which he improved 1572-3. This "Auld Hall" was first described by Dr John Jones in the early 1570s: *"upon the bathside...Joyning to the cheefe springe, betwene the river, and the Bathe, is a very goodly House, four Square, foure Stories high, so well compact with Houses of Office, beneath and above, and round about, with a great Chambre, and other goodly Lodgings to the Number of 30: that it is and wilbee a bewty to behold: and very notable for the honorable and worshipfull, that shal neede to repaire thither: as also for other".*[12]

The "Houses of Office" would include the kitchen, servants' quarters, still room and store rooms and all the other facilities needed to run a lodging house.

The First Buxton Hall, built c.1560 from Shipton W. 1934, "A History of Buxton"

In 1569, following her defeat and flight to England, Mary Queen of Scots was put under the supervision of the 6th Earl of Shrewsbury. The 1572 improvements to the Old Hall were almost certainly an attempt to convert the building into a sort of garrison for confining the captive Queen during her trips to Buxton for relief of her rheumatism. There is some confusion as to the date that the building work was completed. Dr John Jones's description of the building suggests that it was completed in 1572. However, a letter dated 16 August 1572 from Shrewsbury to Lord Burghley mentioned that Mary Stuart had to postpone her visit to Buxton that year *"as the house is not finished..."*[13] One explanation for this discrepancy is that Jones wrote between 16 August and 24 March following, the last day of the year in the old Julian calendar, and work had been completed during those 7 months. It could also be that some special provision for the Queen was not quite ready by 16 August. The outstanding work must have been completed in 1572, as she definitely visited Buxton in that year. She also visited in 1576, 1580, 1582 and 1584.

The scale of charges at the Old Hall in the mid-sixteenth century had ranged from £5 for a bishop, £3 10s for a duke to 12d for a yeoman.[14] The money provided assistance for the poor, the presence of a physician on their behalf, and possibly some accommodation, according to Dr John Jones: *"Yea, the porest shal have lodgings, & beds hard by, for their uses only."*[15] Such large numbers of poor sick folk visited Buxton and Bath that poor rates in the two townships were very high. As a consequence, a clause appeared in the Poor Law of 1572 stating that poor sick people were not allowed to visit either spa unless their home parish was willing to pay their costs, and a licence obtained from two JPs had to be carried as proof.

In 1610 Speed described the Hall as *"a fair square building of freestone"*, and Jones said of the interior that: *"the ladyes, gentlemen, wyves and maydes, maye in one of the galleries walke"* and he continued: *"Lykewise men feable, the same may also practize in another gallerye of the newe buyldinges"*. This implies that the sexes were segregated and the galleries had been built as places of relaxation and entertainment. After 1610, little more is heard of Buxton until 1665, when Lady Elmes and some friends visited on a tour after escaping from the Great Plague of London. She found Buxton's accommodation "indifferent", yet this was quite a compliment compared to what she had to say about the accommodation at Astrop![16]

In 1990, the Threatened Buildings Section of the Royal Commission on the Historic Monuments of England found substantial remains of the early Hall within the surviving building. A paper was subsequently published detailing the investigations into the parts of the Hall surviving from the times of Celia Fiennes.[17] It was found that the walls of the corridor running the length of the ground floor were as thick as the exterior walls, 0.9m or 3 feet, and each corridor wall contained the flues of approximately six fireplaces. The ground floor was divided into four approximately equal sized rooms, 5m x 5m squares (16½ feet x 16½ feet).

From the front door, a sharp right turn led into a vaulted passage running north, probably into the bath area. The hot spring rises next to the north-east room, and bathers needed access from the Hall to the baths without going outside. This would support Celia Fiennes' theory that people stayed at the Hall because the baths were under the same roof. The first floor was divided into four rooms, though the south-west room, which faced the top of the stairs, was slightly larger than the other three. The second floor had four equal-sized rooms. Between the north-west and south-west rooms is a blocked doorway which formerly opened into a narrow passage beyond. This was most probably the original stairway to the roof: Speed's drawing of 1610 suggests the Hall had a flat roof.

The Old Hall was enlarged c.1670, yet it seems that the accommodation was still insufficient for the number of visitors. Richard Blome wrote in 1673 that despite the waters attracting many people, especially Northern noblemen, the place was backward, with little accommodation and entertainment.[18] By 1686 the inns and ale-houses could still only sleep 39 people and stable 72 horses.[19] The accommodation and facilities at the Old Hall clearly did not meet the expectation of a lady who described herself as a Gentlewoman. Celia Fiennes had complained about there being two, three or even four beds to a room.[20] Her comments reflect Richard Blome's; she thought the facilities were too few and too basic, and it was too crowded and too noisy. This may have been partially due to the change from the original scale of charges operating in the mid-sixteenth century to a fixed price, or "ordinary", which enabled the less wealthy and cultured to stay at the Old Hall.

In 1697 Cornelius White, a barrister at Lincoln's Inn and tenant of the Old Hall, carried out some improvements including new private apartments, but these were most likely for the aristocratic visitors. For the ordinary visitor, the night time arrangements seem to have remained less than satisfactory. Whitaker's *History of Manchester* in 1700 recorded that the sleeping area was one long dormitory, the men sleeping down one end and the ladies down the other, the sexes separated only by a curtain.[21] In its favour, however, J. Verdon writing in 1699 said Buxton was the cheapest place on his travels.

Perhaps, though, it was already showing the signs of mismanagement which caused the following advertisement to appear in the London Gazette in July 1705.

"Whereas the Bath House at Buxton in Derbyshire, so famous in the North for divers cures hath of late years been mis-managed.... this is therefore to give notice to all persons of quality and gentry of both sexes, that care hath now been taken by his Grace the Duke of Devonshire, to remedy the like treatment for the future by sending down from London a fitting and obliging person, sufficiently qualified: So that now all persons resorting to the said bath will meet with civil usage and have the best of everything for man and beast at reasonable rates."[22]

There was other accommodation in Buxton. As early as 1577 it was recorded that there were two inns. The Eagle today stands on the site of the oldest inn, which originally had the Stanley family crest as its sign. Celia may well have seen this as she travelled out and about, and would have been aware how the lodgings on the whole were uphill of the baths, requiring a few minutes walk to the baths for those who could not stay at the Hall. It seems that perhaps, although the Hall was not good, it was better than the alternatives.

SPRINGS

Buxton has Britain's warmest thermal waters, at 28.3° C (82.9° F).[23] The early settlement was known as Aquae Arnemetia, after a minor Celtic deity, which suggests a merging of Roman and Celtic cultures, as happened at Bath. Votive offerings of Roman origin were found in 1975, confirming that the site was a religious shrine as well as a centre for bathing.[24] One Mr Bray in his tour (printed 1783) noted that in 1697, when Cornelius White was driving a level to the bath, 50 yards east of St Anne's Well and 14 yards north of Bingham spring, he found the remains of an ancient bath of lead and timber which had been supplied by Bingham's spring.[25] This was almost certainly the Roman bath.

It was only after the sixteenth century that the amazing healing powers of Buxton waters were extolled by physicians, though the first mention of Buxton as a healing holy well was c.1460. William of Worcester, in his *Itinerarium*, recorded *"that Holywell, the source of the waters of the Wye... makes many miracles, making the infirm healthy, and in winter it is warm, even as honeyed milk."*[26] Buxton's nine springs, eight warm and one very cold, bubbled up out of the rocks within an 8 yard circle and flowed into a nearby running brook.[27] The hot water spring rose on one side of the river and the cold water spring on the other. The effect of this was that a quarter of a mile of the river never froze in winter. There was some debate whether this was the result of the heat or the salt.[28]

Camden wrote that there were nine hot water springs at Buxton well. These legendary springs were confirmed again in 1740 by Short, who indicated that there were four warm springs producing 97,681,800 gallons per annum. The springs comprised a strong spring in the middle, the hot spring, and two small warm springs in the low ground. There was also the prolific cold spring and several very minor ones. Warm springs supplied the natural baths with an estimated 7,770 galls per hour, or $129\frac{1}{2}$ gallons per minute.[29]

There are various unscientific descriptions of the temperature of Buxton water. Celia described it as being the same as milk. It was also likened to a quart of boiling water mixed with a gallon of cold water, in contrast to the water at Bath (40-69° C) which was likened to a gallon of hot mixed with a quart of cold.[30] Floyer (1697) complained that some people, amongst them Dr Jones, erroneously felt that the cold springs were harmful and tried to divert them, but he stressed that cold baths should be used for hot diseases and hot baths for cold diseases; both had a place in curing. One has only to read accounts of the cures effected at the cold waters of Copgrove and Holywell to realise how effective very cold water can be in curing certain ailments.

It was generally agreed that the waters were warm, saline, palatable and not fetid. Although they contained sulphur, it was in significantly smaller quantities than Bath water and did not discolour silver. Drinking the waters enhanced the appetite and removed obstructions;[31] it did not act as a purgative because of the low salt content. Dr Lister took 32lb of water and boiled it to dryness. Just 2oz of salt deposit remained. There were no stone flakes, though the brass vessel he boiled it in was coated with an ash-coloured stone powder. The salt coagulated into common salt crystals, amongst which were some crystals of Lapis Calcarius.[32]

GEOCHEMISTRY

ANALYSES

The following analyses are given in *Wells and Springs of Derbyshire*:[33]

In grains per gallon

	Playfair 1852	Thresh 1880-1882	Hart 1920
Calcium bicarbonate	11.193	14.010	16.596
Magnesium bicarbonate	6.919	6.011	6.426
Ferrous bicarbonate	0.240	0.031	0.054
Manganous bicarbonate	-	0.028	0.029
Potassium sulphate	-	0.621	0.593
Sodium sulphate	-	0.843	-
Magnesium sulphate	-	-	0.784
Barium sulphate	-	0.048	trace
Calcium sulphate	2.323	0.260	-
Potassium chloride	2.500	-	-
Sodium chloride	2.420	3.088	4.061
Ammonium chloride	-	0.002	0.006
Magnesium chloride	0.114	0.953	0.423
Calcium fluoride	trace	0.02	-
Sodium nitrate	-	0.026	-
Magnesium nitrate	-	-	0.087
Silica	0.666	0.949	0.598
Organic matter	-	0.201	trace
Oxygen gas	-	-	0.198
Nitrogen gas	-	0.19	0.331
Carbonic acid gas	-	0.20	0.550
Total dissolved salts	26.375	27.091	29.657

The water has been recorded as flowing at a constant temperature of 81.5° F (31° C) for over 200 years. Variations on this are given from time to time on account of variable cooling as the water nears the surface. For example, in 1929 the temperature of the waters at various points was found to be a constant 82° F (27.7° C).[34] The water rises by hydrostatic pressure via a geological fault from a limestone aquifer at a depth of 5,000 feet. Geothermal heating of the water is thought to be as a result of the depth of the aquifer. The catchment area is generally considered to be to the south and east of the town, over an area of about 20 square miles. If so the water is of meteoric origin and probably about 20 years old. Buxton water is slightly radioactive and has a pale blue hue when seen in large quantities.[35] According to Leach, analysis of the water's tritium content suggests it is geologically ancient and at a great depth, though its exact place of origin is the subject of debate.[36]

THE WELLS

Celia did not mention the warm spring at Bingham's Well, which in the 1730s was gauged at 1758 gallons per hour in drought conditions. The spring rose approximately 63 yards south-east of St Anne's Well and formerly supplied the Roman bath. It was lost when the Crescent was built in the 1780s, but was rediscovered recently. The well was also called Mr Leigh's, because the gentleman in question, who lived 7 miles away, had been frequenting that particular well for many years to good effect. Short found that the temperature remained constant throughout the year despite the temperature of the air outside.[37]

St Anne's Well has been frequented since Roman times. After the Roman occupation the waters were dedicated to St Anne, patron saint of springs and wells, and resorted to by pilgrims and invalids. At the Reformation an attempt was made by Thomas Cromwell to reduce Buxton's image as a holy well and a congregating place for Roman Catholic pilgrims. The mementoes left by the cured - crutches, shirts and shifts - were thrown away and the shrine destroyed. However, the water lost none of its curative properties, so it was seen that the religious attributes were unnecessary.[38] Nevertheless pilgrims still prayed, as Dr Jones recorded in 1572. Prayer is an essential part of the Catholics' healing process, as witnessed at St Winefride's Well at Holywell today.

In 1610 St Anne's Well was described as a hot spring inclosed with four flat stones "*about sixty paces off*", presumably the distance from the Old Hall and baths.[39] The well was enclosed within a Roman brick wall, "*a Yard Square within*" and 3 feet high on the three sides. Dr Leigh visited c.1671 and described the wall as being Roman, cemented together with hard, red plaster as hard as brick. The wall was demolished in 1709 by Thomas Delves, during which process the foundations of a chapel dedicated to St Anne were exposed.

THE CURE

By the 1570s the waters were being used to treat rheums, fevers, headaches, old scabs, weak sinews, ulcers, numbness, cramps, itchings, shrinkings, ring-worms, aposthems, *"Sterility from overmuch Moisture"*, much watery fluor albumen with priapismus, and *"that be parboyled in Venus Gulf"*, tuberculosis, liver inflammations, burning urine; asthma, fluxes, overflowing of the menses, hiccups, vomiting, premature ejaculation, obstructions of the liver and spleen, green sickness, morphew and the stone.[40] Camden wrote that the waters were good for the stomach and sinews - in fact for the whole body.[41] By the mid seventeenth century St Anne's Well had retained notoriety for its ability to cure lameness and infertility, as captured in these doggerel lines:

Old men's numb'd joints new vigour here acquire,
In frozen nerves this water kindleth fire.
Hither the cripples halt, some help to find,
Run hence, their crutches unthanked left behind.
The barren wife here meets her husband's love,
With such success she straight doth mother prove.

From Dr Richard Russel's long list of cures (1769) one can assume that visitors to Buxton were suffering from a wide variety of ailments. He wrote that the waters were effective when used both internally and externally - for gout, vomiting blood, fluxes of the piles, consumption, ring worms, St Anthony's fire, scabs, the itch, hard callous tumours and barreness.[42] It also cured rickets, inflammations, fevers, rheums, headaches, old scabs, weak sinews, ulcers, numbness, impostumes, impotence, priapism and tuberculosis.[43] No wonder the Hall was so full.

The waters could be effectively used internally and externally, as recorded by the Earl of Sussex in August 1582. Despite it being summer, the bath was too cold to use, so he drank the water instead. Starting at 3 pints per day he increased the quantity by one pint per day until he reached 8 pints, then reduced the quantity by one pint daily until he was back to three.[44] This was a similar procedure to that used at Astrop Wells in the late seventeenth century, which was based on the recommendations of Gabriele Fallopio (1523-62), the Italian anatomist. Drinking the waters cooled the body, and Monro in 1770 pronounced them good for rheumatisms, arthritic pains, diabetes, urinary obstructions, colics, dysentery, disorders of the lungs, and cutaneous diseases.

In 1697 Floyer compared the taste of the bath water with that of St Anne's Well. He found no difference in temperature or mineral content, and therefore in taste. Their *"Milky Tepor"* was salt, rank and aluminous. Some people drank up to 4 pints, but this quantity occasionally caused vomiting when drunk quickly. Others were nauseated by its stypticity, saltness and tepor.[45]

Daniel Defoe quoted Dr Leigh's *Natural History of Lancashire*, which detailed the well's remedial effects on scorbitic rheumatics. Many who had previously not been able to move, except with crutches, walked unaided the 16 miles back to Manchester. Leigh also believed that the chalybeate waters at Buxton had the same curative properties as Bath and Bristol, where blood in the urine and diabetes were cured.[46] Defoe was very impressed by the curative properties of the waters, and could not deny the miraculous cures *"especially in rheumatick, scorbutick and scrofulous distempers, aches of the joint, nervous pains, and also in scurvy and leprous maladies"*.[47]

THE BATHS

Celia Fiennes' visit to Buxton in 1697 coincided with major improvements at the Old Hall and baths carried out by the tenant, Cornelius White. He added private apartments, as mentioned above, extra stabling, and a new bath was made for the poor. He repaired and paved the ancient bath and added a new roof. Celia Fiennes mentioned that the roof was partially ceiled, causing a draught. Thus we know that changes were made to the baths immediately after her visit. A pump was installed at the south-east corner of the bath, but it is not known whether this was a pump to help with the emptying of the bath or one for pumping bath water over affected limbs.[48] In his itinerary of 1700, the Reverend James Brome commented that the restored bath was enclosed in a fair stone building (The Old Hall) erected by George, Earl of Shrewsbury, and to which many people resorted in the summer. The water was similar to the Cross Bath at Bath and he described the hot well at Buxton as the sixth Wonder of the Peak.[49]

When Celia stayed at the Old Hall the kitchen was on the north side, next to the bath. White demolished the kitchen and built a new bath on the site. Named White's Bath, it was enclosed by a wall but had no roof. It was 17 feet long, 10 feet 2 inches wide and 4 feet 16" [sic] deep, its water coming from the inner bath. The inner bath had an enclosed roof, was 20 feet 6 inches long, 12 feet 8 inches wide; the lower end was 4 feet 9 inches deep with water and 4 feet 3 inches deep at the head or south end. The water level could be raised a further foot if necessary.[50]

Thomas Short in 1740 described the inner bath as 26 ft 6 inches x 12 feet 8 inches and 4 feet 6 inches deep; the outer, new bath, was 17 feet x 10 feet 2 inches and 5 feet 6 inches deep. Neither of these match the size of the bath that Celia saw, suggesting some reduction in the size of the old bath by White. The bottom of the bath was smooth flagstones; the two chief springs rose up through the rock, but several smaller springs bubbled up through other chinks in the rock and between these flagstones at the bottom. The water was warm, and a sulphurous steam covered the surface of the water. The back of the bath was solid black limestone and the sides were polished freestone. Celia would have recognised the stone benches along the side used by the bathers for dressing and undressing, the smooth flagstones between the benches and the bath, and the stone steps at the corners of the bath leading down into the water.

Short recorded that there was a strong spring in the middle of the bath level, and two large iron chains hung down for the bathers to hold on to.[51] This replicates what Celia Fiennes experienced: *"...you may stand in some place and hold by a chaine..."*[52] At Bath there were also rings for bathers to hold on to. At the north, or lower end, was a large square hole *"in the Foundation of the House Wall"*, which allowed the water to escape into the outer bath. Above this hole, level with the surface of the water, were two small holes in the wall, which is where the dirty or excess water escaped at the time of Celia's 1697 visit. Of the bath water she had complained that: *"...its not capable of being cleansed after every body has been in..."*[53] These overflows were not removed by Cornelius White, and Short noticed them in 1740.[54] After 1697, Mr White's improvements included the addition of a 200 yard long gutter running from the baths to the brook. This enabled the baths to be emptied, washed out, and filled with fresh water daily.[55]

Publishing in the same year that Celia visited and White carried out his improvements, Floyer observed that the spring ran plentifully, and the bath could be emptied in a quarter of of an hour and refilled in just under an hour.[56] Three years later, in 1700, James Brome noticed that *"The Fountain daily purging itself, runs away in a continual Current into the adjacent Meadows, and adds a reeking colour to the other Waters with which it unites its Tepid Streams."*[57] Most likely this was the route that the used bath water took as it was flushed from the bath down Cornelius White's new stone gutter.

This contradiction in the cleansing process underpins the hypothesis that Celia's visit was immediately before Cornelius White's 1697 improvements, and Floyer's visit was just after. Celia most likely visited Buxton at the beginning of the season, perhaps in May, and the alterations were carried out shortly after she left. This was at the height of summer or early autumn, when the water table was at its lowest and the spring flow reduced. Celia's text therefore provides an invaluable description of the baths immediately prior to White's modifications. Used comparatively, the texts of other authors can be dated pre- or post-1697.

Only Dr Granville seems to have shared Celia's dislike of Buxton's baths. On a visit in the 1830s to the bath in the vault under the Old Hall, he noticed a scum on the water at its source, which made him not at all anxious to get in. The bath was free, and attracted *"the pot-bellied farmer of sixty, half palsied, and the lame artisan with his black and callous hands, and the many who suffered from cutaneous disorders - all plunging together, or one after the other in quick succession"* and all using the communal scrubbing brush to scrub off years of dirt.[58] The overflow pipe was not large enough to remove the scum as fast as it was forming, despite the added efforts of a woman who came occasionally with a broom to sweep it out.

BATHING

According to Floyer in the 1690s the bath was contained within a room with very warm air, and a fume rising like boiling water. It fumed most in the winter, probably because the water temperature remained the same but the air temperature was cooler.[59] Some visitors, like Celia Fiennes, used the baths for pleasure and cleansing. Others were suffering from various maladies and bathed for a cure. The recommended time for bathing was in the morning and evening between the beginning of May and the end of September. Dr Robertson suggested the optimum time to spend in the bath was 4-12 minutes. The bath water was 82-86° F and being slightly cooler than body temperature would, in the first instance, make even a healthy bather feel momentarily chilled.[60] Celia complained of this very chilliness in 1697. Defoe also mentioned that the water was barely warm and one felt slightly chilly upon dipping or plunging in. He found that this soon dissipated and that the body quickly became accustomed to the coolness of the water;[61] the feet in particular felt warm. The bath water was so clear that, despite being immersed up to the neck, it was possible to see the bottom of the bath. At many spas, shirts and shifts were provided for visitors but John Floyer, writing in 1697, noted that through custom the sexes bathed at different times, and naked. He voiced his disapproval of the naked bathing, suggesting that the men should wear drawers and the women linen or flannel.[62]

Some sufferers stayed in for almost an hour, keeping constantly on the move to avoid cold setting in. Floyer recommended dipping the head in the water or covering it with a wet cloth, because this both cooled the head and checked the rising fumes. Jones, in his *Auncient Baths of Buckstones* noted that some people said prayers whilst bathing, possibly invoking the name of a saint connected with healing. On leaving the water, bathers dried themselves and went to bed for half an hour. This was the chief benefit of staying at the Old Hall: the fact that patients did not have to go outside to get from the bath to the bedroom. Jones likened the effects of this bath to those at St Winefride's and St Mungo's *"for they strengthen, and cool, and constringe the solid Parts, and cure the hot Cacochymia's of our Blood; ..."*

ENTERTAINMENT

During the day, when the visitors were not bathing, there was entertainment for them to enjoy, apart from going out on the tours of the Wonders. Dr Jones noted that in bad weather the ladies played troll-madam (also troule in madame, troll-my-dame, trou-madame or Lady in the Hole). In Shakespeare's day, troll-my-dame was a game like bagatelle, in which bullets, or balls, were trolled (rolled) into a little arcade. *"The Ladyes, Gentle Women, Wyves and Maydes maye...have in the ende of a Benche eleven holes made, intoo the which to trowle pummetes or Bowles of Leade...or also of Copper, Tynne, Woode..."*[63] The *London Gazette* of 1689 advertised that *"If any Persons have occasion to for Tables, and Table-men... and Troll-Madames, they may be furnished."*[64] The game was still played at the beginning of the nineteenth century. It is highly likely that Celia either played this or watched others playing during her idle moments. The more lively of the Company entertained themselves by playing bowls, shooting at garden butts, bowling, and playing windball and yarn ball.[65] Walks and bowling greens were regular features of seventeenth century spas, and at Buxton these were provided by Cornelius White in 1697.

Despite various seventeenth century attempts to make Buxton more desirable and competitive with other flourishing spas, Celia Fiennes would doubtless have agreed with Defoe, writing in the 1720s. He predicted that unless more facilities were provided in the way of lodgings, bath houses and entertainment, Buxton would never attract as many people as Bath.[66]

TODAY

Buxton developed considerably after Celia Fiennes' visit, and little remains of what she saw. However the Old Hall is still a functioning hotel of considerable character, and a few of its sixteenth-century features can be detected. The only other houses remaining from this period are Yheldt Cottage (1600), Old Hall Cottages (1687) and Golf Cottage.

The Old Hall and Baths, 1996.

The baths in particular have undergone a series of reconstructions, and the late eighteenth century St Anne's Crescent, now undergoing renovation, is the focal point of the spa. The Dukes of Devonshire have been responsible for the considerable development of much of the old spa infrastructure. Near the Crescent are the Dukes' circular stables, which once formed part of the octagonal complex of 1798 providing equestrian facilities for visitors. The stables have been converted into a handsome sanatorium with various bathing facilities. The magnificent domed roof was the largest in the world when erected in 1881.

Buxton's role as a spa continues with the prescriptive use of water at the sanatorium. The town also retains much of its spa heritage: the waters are still consumed at St Anne's Well, often collected in containers to be taken away, and the St Anne's Pump Room is to be opened again as a drinking facility. The baths buildings which flank St Anne's Crescent are at one end converted to a shopping precinct. Inside, some interesting artifacts have been preserved testifying to the building's former function as the Hot Baths. At the other end, the Natural and Thermal Baths, partially situated in the basement of the Old Hall Hotel, are used for the Tourist Information Office. In this building it is possible to see Buxton's premier spring which now supplies the Buxton mineral water bottling works. The museum at Buxton is well worth a visit, as is the swimming pool in St Johns Road, which is filled with 636,440 litres of spa water.

Chatsworth House, mentioned by Celia Fiennes, is a stately home open to the public. The present building dates from 1707 with parts dating from the earlier building that Celia Fiennes would have seen. The house still belongs to the Cavendish family, whose lineage as Dukes of Devonshire dates from the first Duke, a contemporary of Celia Fiennes. Haddon Hall, one and a half miles west of Rowsley, is a beautifully restored English medieval manor.

Poole's Hole is still a popular tourist venue, and can be visited just outside Buxton. A petrifying well is reputed to be nearby. Mam Tor is a well know topographical feature. Elden Hole lies at an altitude of 1,383 feet on the southern slope of Elden Hill. The cave is 245 feet deep and is the largest open pot hole in Derbyshire.[67] It is now a favourite spot for caving enthusiasts (rated grade III).

Footnotes:

1   Morris C. (ed.) 1947, *The Journeys of Celia Fiennes*, p.96.
2   Robertson W H. 1838, *Buxton and its Waters*.
3   Allsop D G. 1992, *Visitor's Guide to Poole's Cavern*.
4   Short T. 1740, *History of the Principal Mineral Waters of Buxton*, footnote p.29.
5   Hunter J. (ed.) 1830, *The Diary of Ralph Thoresby 1677-1724*, p.86.
6   Capper B. 1808, *Topographical Dictionary*, p.128-147.
7   Short T. 1740, op.cit. footnote p.29.
8   Blome R. 1673, *Britannia*, p75; Capper B. op.cit. p.128-147.
9   Allsop D G. op.cit. 1992.
10 Short T. 1740, op.cit. footnote p.33.
11 Camden's *Britannia*, Holland P. (trans.) 1610, p.557.
12 Leach J. 1987, *The Book of Buxton*, p.46; Lennard R. 1931, "The Watering Places", *Englishmen at Rest and Play*, p.5.

13 Thornes R. Leach J. 1994, "Buxton Hall", *Derbyshire Archaeological Journal.*
14 Jones J. 1572, *The benefit of the Auncient Baths at Buckstones.*
15 Quoted from Dr John Jones 1572 in Lennard R. op.cit. p.5.
16 Hembry P. 1990, *The English Spa 1560-1815*, p.94.
17 Thornes R. and Leach J. op.cit.
18 Blome R. op.cit. p.75.
19 Hembry P. 1990, p.94.
20 Morris C. op.cit. p.95.
21 Langham M. Wells C. 1986, *Buxton Waters, A History of Buxton the Spa*, p.49.
22 ibid. p.49-50.
23 At 40-69o C, Bath's waters are considered hot. Buxton's cooler waters are thermal. See
   Luke T D. 1919, *Spas and Health Resorts of the British Isles*, p.19.
24 Langham M. Wells C. op.cit. p.26.
25 Noted by Jewitt A. 1811, *History of Buxton*, p.28.
26 Langham M. Wells C. op.cit. p.21; Leach J. op.cit. p.45.
27 Blome R. op.cit. p.75; Jewitt A. op.cit. p.xv-xvi. quoting from "A Prospect of the most
   famous parts of the World" (1646).
28 Floyer J. 1697, *Hot, Cold and Temperate Baths in England*, p.122.
29 Camden, op.cit. p.557; Stevens J V. 1929, *Wells and Springs of Derbyshire*, p.68.
30 Floyer J. op.cit. p.122.
31 Capper B. op.cit. p.128-147.
32 Floyer J. op.cit. p.122.
33 Stevens J V. op.cit. p.70.
34 ibid. p.68.
35 Langham M. Wells C. op.cit. p.12-19.
36 Leach J. op.cit. p.75.
37 Short T. 1734, 2nd edition, *The Natural, Experimental, and Medicinal History of the Mineral
   Waters of Buxton, and other warm waters in the Peak in Derbyshire*, p.23.
38 Jewitt A. op.cit. p.21.
39 Leach J. op.cit. p.47.
40 Short T. 1740, op.cit. p.39.
41 Camden, op.cit. p.557.
42 Russel R. 1769 (5th edition) *Dissertation on the use of Sea Water* with anonymous supplement
   A Treatise on the Nature, Properties and Uses of the Mineral Waters, p.206.
43 Floyer J. op.cit. p.129.
44 Langham M. Wells C. op.cit. p.43.
45 Floyer J. op.cit. p.122/129.
46 Defoe D. 1927, *A Tour Through England and Wales*, Vol.II, p.166-7.
47 ibid. p.166.
48 Short T. 1740, op.cit. p.43.
49 Brome J. 1700, *Travels over England, Scotland and Wales*, p.93.
50 Short T. 1740, op.cit. p.43.
51 ibid. p.23.
52 Morris C. op.cit. p.104.
53 ibid. p.103.
54 Short T. 1740, op.cit. p.43.
55 ibid. p.43.
56 Floyer J. op.cit. p.122.
57 Brome J. op.cit. p.93.
58 Granville A B. 1841, *The Spas of England, The Midland and South*, p.34-35.
59 Floyer J. op.cit. p.122.
60 Robertson W H. op.cit.
61 Defoe D. op.cit. p.167.
62 Floyer J. op.cit. p.122.
63 Jones J. op.cit. p.12.
64 *The London Gazette*, 1689, No.2503/4.
65 A windball was an inflated sphere, possibly a pig's stomach.
66 Defoe D. op.cit. p.168.
67 Ford T D. Gill D W. 1979, *Caves of Derbyshire*, p.51/2.

TIDESWELL

During her short stay in Buxton, Celia visited some of the local "Wonders", many of which were limestone features. Along with Poole's Hole, Elden Hole and Mam Tor she also visited the seventh Wonder of the Peak, the "Flowing and Ebbing Well", situated between Castleton and Buxton.[1] She recounted how the well was normally calm, except following heavy rainfall when the waters ebbed and flowed like the sea. For the second time during her "Wonders" tour she spoke of Mr Middleton *the man who was with us*, who had witnessed this ebb and flow several times in the space of an hour. Celia found this hard to believe, and thought that the sea must come through the earth to cause the phenomenon, though she added that it was many miles from both the sea and ebb and flow rivers.

COMMENT

Celia rarely mentions untitled people in her journals. When she does, they are people of some status. Mr Armstrong of Beccles in Suffolk was a highly regarded church minister; Mr Darcy at Richmond was Earl Holderness' brother; Mr William Allen was the mayor of Chester; Mr Thomas and Mr Showers of London were probably related to Celia; Mr Wessells alias Mr Scawens was a businessman and Director of the East India Company.[2] It is safe to assume, therefore, that Mr Middleton was a man of status who enjoyed travelling. From Celia's comments one can believe that he had been to this area on previous occasions; he had seen the well ebb and flow, and had also had a meal with some troglodytes at the Devil's Arse near Castleton.

The Ebbing and Flowing Well, Tideswell

Tideswell was situated in the "Peake Forest", near the market town of Tideswell, which took its name from its famous natural feature. By the time of Celia's visit, Tideswell was a low lying, indifferent town with a church, a free school and a market on Wednesdays.[3] By the late sixteenth century, the well was already known as one of the Wonders of the Peak. In the 1730s "Tides-Well" was also known as the Weeding-Well, though there is no explanation for this title. The diameter of the well was about a yard and the depth about the same. The spring ebbed and flowed like the tide, the flux and reflux being about the same.[4] Various travellers saw the well in action, and recorded what they saw. Camden, in the late sixteenth century, recorded that the well ebbed and usually flowed four times an hour.[5] Thomas Short noted that it ebbed and flowed dramatically up to three times an hour after heavy rains, but in dry weather not at all. He was positive that it was not influenced by the sea. He commented that there was nothing remarkable about this ebbing and flowing well *"besides its secret Supply with great Quantities of Water which it throws out in sudden Gluts at uncertain Times in an Hour after great Rains, and not once a Week in dry Weather."*[6]

Mr Grant, in Mavor's *British Tourist* observed that the well was in a little pool beside the road. Within the space of 3 minutes it rose 4 inches and sank again.[7] In wet weather these occurrences were frequent, perhaps every 20 minutes. In dry weather the returns were every 2 to 3 hours; in very dry weather the flow was approximately once a week.

TODAY

The Tideswell is situated in the garden of Craven House, along the Manchester Road. Although the water still ebbs and flows, it is not with the same vehemence as of some years ago. It is possible that local building has disrupted and reduced the flow. The well is no longer mentioned in guide books and brochures on Tideswell and the surrounding area, probably because it is on private property. There is a public well along the Manchester Road, approximately 100 metres north of Craven Cottage.

There are other ebbing and flowing wells in England. Richard Gough recorded Laywell, near Brixham in Devon, which ebbed and flowed about 5 to 6 inches every few minutes, and sometimes bubbled up as if boiling.[8] The water was crystal clear, cold in summer but never freezing in winter, not brackish, and was effective in abating fevers. It appeared to have nothing to do with the sea. He also noted that at Shap, Westmoreland, near the river Loder, was another well which ebbed and flowed several times a day.[9] The Reverend James Brome recorded an ebbing and flowing well at Settle, near Giggleswick, Yorks, which ebbed and flowed several times an hour, flowing to a height of half a yard and ebbing to a low of one inch.[10] These wells work on the syphon principle, which accounts for the intermittant ebbing and flowing. As the chamber fills, it sets off the syphon action which then drains the chamber. When the water has gone, the syphon is broken.

Footnotes

1 Morris C. (ed.) 1947, *The Journeys of Celia Fiennes*, p.109.
2 ibid. p.141, 146, 179, 218, 219, 341.
3 Blome R. 1673, *Britannia*, p.78; Camden's *Britannia*, Holland P. (trans.) 1610, p.558.
4 Macky J. 1732, *A Journey Through England*, Vol.2, p.213.
5 Camden's *Britannia* 1610, p.558.
6 Short T. 1734, *The Natural experiments, and medicinal history of the mineral waters of Derbyshire, Lincolnshire and Yorkshire*, p.34.
7 Quoted in *A Guide to the Watering and Sea-Bathing Places 1813*, p.153.
8 Camden's *Britannia*, Gough R. (trans.) 1789, Vol.1, p.34.
9 ibid. p.148.
10 Brome J. 1700, *Travels over England*, p.217.

SCARBOROUGH

In May 1697 Celia embarked on her Northern Tour. May to October was the best time for travelling; the roads were even less passable in the other months. During the tour she visited Scarborough, which she described as a pretty seaport town built on the side of a steep hill. The hill was fortified on the shore side by a series of tiered ditches and a castle. Of the castle only the ruins remained, and the local inhabitants grazed their cattle on the several acres inside its walls. The church was built on the highest point of the hill, overlooking the rest of the town, and the churchyard was situated at the top of a flight of twenty or so steps.

The harbour consisted of two semi-circular breakwaters, *"resembling the Cobb at Lime in Sommersetshire"* (Lyme Regis in Dorset).[1] At high tide, the sea reached the foot of the 5 - 6 mile ridge of hills which surrounded the town. When the tide was out, it exposed 400 yards of flat, firm, sandy beach, which Celia found was excellent for walking on because her feet did not sink. At low tide it was possible to walk the whole of the length of the hills at their base, and watch the ships sailing up to Newcastle and back down again, with coal bound for London. From this point she spotted about 70 ships, travelling in protective convoys because of the war with France.

When Celia visited the "Spaw Well" it was merely a spring bubbling up in the sand. Despite its rudimentary containment, visitors still drank the *"Iron or Steele minerall"*, which was an excellent purgative. The high tides covered the source, making it brackish, but it was generally believed that the force of the spring soon cleared the saltiness. Despite her reference to the springs being ferruginous, Celia, believed that because of their proximity to the sea, the water of this spring, and all the others bubbling up on the beach, were affected by the sea water. A closer inspection of her phrase *"and there they drank"*, referring to the visitors at the spring, suggests that she did not taste the water, so could not comment empirically on the taste.

Scarborough had no spa facilities, apart from its natural spring, until about 1700, so entertainment was limited. Twice a day, between ebb tide and high tide, visitors could walk across the sands to visit the spring, or could take a boat ride. Celia went out in a small boat but found the sea rather rough, even in the harbour. Sea trips were probably one of the first diversions provided for tourists at Scarborough.

Celia was surprised to find that Scarborough appeared to be a Quaker stronghold, and that the majority of lodgings were in their hands. The lodgings were in private houses and ordinary, i.e a set price for board and bed, with ale extraordinary.[2] She was happy with her own accommodation, which was comfortable and reasonably priced. She mentioned that there were a few inns for horses only, which is indicative of three things. Firstly, that private lodgings did not always have their own stabling; secondly, that there were many day trippers who required temporary stabling and thirdly, that she travelled on horseback rather than in a carriage or coach.

In Scarborough, Celia attended a Quaker meeting, where four men and two women spoke, one after the other.[3] She remarked that the performance seemed incoherent and confused, and felt sorry for their deluded ignorance in spiritual matters, thanking God that others i.e herself, were not so misguided. She wrote that *"their prayers were all made on the first person and single, tho before the body of people, it seems they allow not of ones being the mouth of the rest in prayer to God tho' it be in the publick meetings..."* The interpretation is that their prayers were led by one person who consistently referred to "I" rather than "we", because one person could not be endowed with the responsibility of speaking on behalf of the whole congregation. The participation of women in spiritual matters was welcomed by Nonconformists, a completely opposite approach to that taken by the Anglican church.

Celia provided an unusual and fascinating picture of a regional dish. Large, cod-like fish which had been salted and dried, were soaked and dressed before being strung onto wires and roasted in front of the fire. They were eaten with a sauce, and tasted as tender and sweet as fresh cod. It was advisable to cure the fish well and as soon as possible after they were caught, otherwise they tended to have too strong a flavour.

COMMENT

It was believed that the name "Scaer burg" was of Saxon origin, derived from scar, meaning a steep rock, and burgh meaning a town.[4] The "scar" could refer to the natural cleft running north-east/south-west through the town, or to the inaccessible 330 foot high rock stretching out into the sea to the north-east.[5] The rock was reached by crossing a narrow neck of land on which was a drawbridge over a very deep trench. On top of the rock were approximately 60 acres of ground, including 18-20 acres of meadow. There was also a very deep well hewn through the stone, which appeared to be dry at the bottom.[6] The castle on the rock was originally built by William le Grosse, Earl of Albermarle and Holderness. It had fallen into disrepair and been rebuilt by Henry II.[7] By the time Celia Fiennes visited it was disused, owing to the battering it had received during the Civil War.

The town was quite modest in size, but well built and well inhabited.[8] Government was in the hands of two bailiffs, two coroners, four chamberlains and 36 burgesses, who were elected annually. There was also a commodious quay which protected the shores from the battering of the sea, and numerous trades were carried on round the quay area.[9]

Celia Fiennes mentioned a constant movement of ships trading between Newcastle and London. Other travellers also noted this busy shipping line, which resulted from the development of Newcastle as a coal trading port. The building and maintenance of the quay at Scarborough was vital for the protection of this and other trade, because it was the only harbour for ships between the Humber and the Tyne. To ensure its survival, the town was granted the right to levy tolls on all ships carrying coal from Newcastle to Sunderland. The normal rate was 4d, and 8d was charged for ships over 100 chaldrons.[10]

The town's survival relied on sea trades. The sea, then as now, claimed lives and as a result a hospital was built for poor seamen's widows. It was paid for with £100 contributed by sailors, and the community then supported the poor widows with alms. Every vessel master and every vessel contributed 4d, and everyone in the town earning more than 15s per week contributed 2d; this collection was distributed amongst the widows at Christmas.[11] Celia did not mention the hospital, but it was certainly there when she visited.

The town's main trade was fishing. Herring fishing in particular had been carried on in these waters for generations. At the end of the fifteenth century herrings were only found around Norway, but by the 1590s were migrating as far south as Scarborough. About midsummer, when they were at their fattest, they swam south from Norway to Scotland. Moving further south, they could be caught in shoals between Scarborough and the mouth of the Thames between August and November. In November they moved into the English Channel before moving further round to the west coast of England. On the whole, the English were too lazy to take advantage of this natural gift, but others saw their fortune in it and the *"Holanders and Zelanders use to take mervelous plentie of herrings"* after having first obtained a licence from Scarborough Castle.[12]

Trade around the quay was very brisk during the herring fishing season. Markets were held on Thursday and Saturday, so these would have been particularly busy days.[13] Defoe, often unimpressed by the sights at which others wondered, marvelled at the variety of fish he saw here, which included cod, whiting, herring and mackerel. In particular, he was impressed by the size of the turbots, some weighing as much as three quarters of a hundredweight, and which were very tender when eaten fresh.[14]

DISCOVERY OF THE CHALYBEATE SPRING

The first of Scarborough's two springs to be discovered was the north or chalybeate spring, found c.1626 by Mrs Farrow (or Farrer), who lived in the town.[15] A steep descent led from the town to the spring, which was located a quarter to half a mile south of the town on the sands at the foot of the high cliff. The water emerged vertically from the ground, close to the spring tide level, so consequently it was often inundated by the tide, as Celia Fiennes noted. She also noted that it soon cleared the saltiness from the inundation, which corresponds with Dr Wittie's description of it being a quick spring.[16] Mrs Farrow tasted the water and found that it differed from common water because of its acid (salt) taste. She also noticed that the stones along its water course were russet-coloured, and that galls turned the water purple.[17] She and a neighbour drank the water and found that it *"opened the Belly"* - presumably causing them to evacuate their bowels. Constipation was a perennial problem in this period, proved by the many people who visited springs to cure that complaint and the stress laid on its cure in medical publications. Constipation, or costiveness, could either be the result of diet or it could be a symptom of a greater problem, such as gout.

News of the water's curative property soon reached Dr Robert Wittie in Hull, and he became the first physician to promote the use of Scarborough water.[18] He visited the town from the 1640s and, with his colleague Dr James Primrose, sent patients there to take the water. In 1660 Dr Wittie wrote and published *Scarbrough Spaw*, a treatise on Scarborough water, in which he noted the contents as vitriol, iron, allome, nitre and salt.[19] With such a variety of minerals the water was bound to be effective, and Wittie compared them favourably with other famous waters of the day:

"... moreover let them inform themselves well, concernig [sic] the cures that have been done by the waters at Epsom, Tunbridge, Barnet, Bristol, Knaresborough, etc. This is ours coming not short of (if not exceeding) the best of them all either Germane or English."[20]

In order to justify and support his belief in the nature and quality of the water, Wittie quoted from the Classical writers, such as Seneca, Pliny and Hippocrates.[21] His references to the ancients was accepted in his 1660 work. However by his second version, published in 1667, the knowledge surrounding the chemistry, properties and effectiveness of the waters had noticeably advanced, and the new version seemed very dated. Wittie's work also extolled the temperance cause, promoting the use of water instead of ale and wine. It seems ironical, therefore, that towards the end of his life he was stricken with *"gout in my hands and feet"* - gout being an affliction associated with heavy drinking - also an ailment which he claimed could be cured with Scarborough water.

Wittie found his work opposed by other doctors. They were perhaps jealous that he was not native to Scarborough but had cornered a market there and prospered at their expense. In his *Hydrologia Chymica* of 1669, William Simpson challenged Wittie on the use of his term "vitriol" as an ingredient of Scarborough water. To what sort of vitriol was he referring - iron or copper? Simpson also pronounced that certain sicknesses which Wittie had said were curable with the water - "*Plurisies, Prunella's, Poysons taken in or inbred, Leprosie, French Disease, Morphew, Cancer...*" - were not. Wittie had stressed the importance of drinking Scarborough water for curing ailments, but Simpson and later writers promoted diet, fresh air and exercise as being equally important in treatment.

Wittie counter-attacked, partly to protect his good name and also to denigrate this young upstart who was 30 years his junior. This was a typical battle of ideals between the Classical and the modernist scientific approach. The row gathered momentum via the *Philosophical Transactions* of the Royal Society for Improving Natural Knowledge, and Drs Daniel Foot, Highmore of Sherborne, J. Beale of Yeovil and George Tonstall of Newcastle upon Tyne became autographically involved. Tonstall was greatly disenchanted with Scarborough water. He had taken it in 1669, and within a fortnight was seized with a "*Fit of the Stone*". Upon recovery, he got gout in the big toe which caused him to limp for a fortnight. As the result of his first experience, he promoted the idea that Scarborough was a petrifying water which caused kidney stones.

Tonstall eventually moved to Harrogate. Dr Wittie died in October 1684, by which time a *modus vivendi* existed. Thomas Short, commenting in the eighteenth century, believed that Tonstall was merely furious that Wittie had monopolised Scarborough and that the former's move to Harrogate was enforced. Simpson continued to write, and his *History of Scarborough Spaw* of 1679 lists approximately seventy case histories concerning cures effected with Scarborough water. These included cures for female infertility, gonorrhoea, worms, and mental illness. Simpson later moved to Wakefield and eventually to Leeds.

BOTTLING THE WATER

Chalybeate waters are renowned for changing their properties when exposed to oxygen. When the water reaches the surface, the ferric carbonates, sulphides and silicates dissolved in the water form other compounds. Perhaps the most noticeable change is the production of ferrous oxide, which is insoluble in water and forms a reddish-brown or orange deposit. Because of their changing nature, it was advocated that these waters should be drunk at source. Such an arrangement attracted patients and therefore income to local doctors. In taking up residence in the town during a course of treatment, patients would also provide an income for the corporation and the residents.

126

Despite the recommendations, the water was bottled and transported into the town and further afield. By the 1730s, 70,000 - 80,000 bottles per annum were being sold, if the corporation accounts are a true reflection of the trade. The bitter, ferruginous taste became fetid in bottles that had not been thoroughly cleansed of fermented liquors, although after a while it did become a little more palatable.[22] As owners of the seashore, the spring was the property of the corporation, and in 1684 they imposed a tariff of 6d an anker on water removed in bulk.[23] Quantities of under half an anker were free, as was water for the poor. In 1691 the imposition was doubled to 6d per half anker, but was free if the collector brought a note from the vicar or church-warden stating that *"the saide water is not to be sold but for some sicke p'sone or p'sones that is not able to come and drinke it heare"*.[24] In order to evade the tariff, collectors visited the spring at night. This was the state of affairs at the time of Celia Fiennes' visit. The corporation's response to the nocturnal visiting was to construct a huge cistern, in readiness for the 1699 season, which was kept locked and guarded.[25]

Seal on Mineral Water sold by John Fiddes of Covent Garden, 1734.[26]

THE WATERS

WE whose Names are here subscribed do certify, That the Scarborough Spa Water, filled for Mr. John Fiddes, and sealed with the Corporation-Seal, is constantly taken up from the WELL at the most proper Seasons, and cemented down in the Bottles with a well-adapted Cement, according to our Directions:

CULMER COCKERILL.
PETER SHAW.

The Scarborough Water is delivered at that Town to the Land-Carriers at 4 s. per Doz. and put on Board a Ship at 5 s. per Doz. All the other Waters may be had there at 2 s. per Doz. Advance for Carriage.

In 1699 Benjamin Allen noted only one purging chalybeate spring on the sea shore.[27] By the 1730s the spa consisted of two mineral springs, both saline chalybeate. The first mention of two springs, within a few yards of each other, was made in 1731, when both flowed into stone basins.[28] The waters were clear and crystal-like; they had the same constituents but in different proportions, hence their different effects on the constitution. The south spring, which was furthest from the town, was more purgative. The north spring, which according to Dr Monro was the first to be discovered and therefore the one which Celia Fiennes visited, was the more strongly chalybeate.[29] It produced 24 gallons per hour and never ran dry.[30] Both waters lost their chalybeate properties when exposed to air, though the chalybeate spring retained them longer. Both turned green when syrup of violets were added, indicating an acid (salt) presence. Both waters turned purple with powdered galls, showing the presence of iron. When evaporated, the water left a brown, sandy deposit which was not earth so was indicative of the iron content. Hoffman also noted an ochry scurf when the water was bottled in glass. The specific gravities of the waters were almost identical, though they were slightly heavier than common water. Both specific gravity and medicinal efficacy varied, with rainy seasons diluting the waters more than dry seasons.[31] The temperature of the springs, at 45-46° F (7.5° C), was similar to that of common water. The salts, which acted as a mild aperient, were manufactured from the purgative south well and sold round the country.[32] By 1769 they were being sold for 2/6d per ounce at Owen's Mineral Water warehouse in London.[33]

The *Journal of Excursions* c.1820 discussed the properties of the waters following some basic experiments.[34] When they were poured from one glass to another they threw up air bubbles, and if shaken in a closely-stopped phial, and the phial was opened before the movement had subsided, *"they displode an elastic vapour, with an audible noise, which shows that they abound in fixed air."*

ANALYSES

An analysis of c.1819 found that in one gallon the wells contained the following, in grains.[35]

	Chalybeate Well (north)	Purgative Well (south)
Vitriolated Magnesia	98	128
Vitriolated Lime	54	58
Carbonate of Lime	61	28
Muriated Magnesia	14	16
Carbonate of Iron	trace	trace
Muriated Nitron	trace	trace
Total Content	227	230

An analysis is provided by Richard Phillips Esq.[36] grains per gallon:

	North Spring		South Spring
Azotic gas	6.30	cu.in	7.50
Chloride of Sodium (common salt)	26.64	grains	29.63
Crystallized Sulphate of Magnesia	142.68	"	225.33
Crystallized Sulphate of of Lime	104.00	"	110.78
Bicarbonate of Lime	48.26	"	47.80
Bicarbonate of Protoxide of Iron	1.84	"	1.81
Total Content	323.42		415.35
Specific Gravity	1.0035		1.0045
Temperature	49° F		

Taking The Water

The season was from May to September. This was partly due to the poor state of the roads during the other months; partly because the mineralised water was noticeably diluted by the winter rains, and partly because chalybeate waters were best drunk during warm weather. Upon arrival in the town, patients were recommended to rest for 2 or 3 days, then start their treatment with a course of laxative medicines.[37] Relaxation after a tiring journey, and an aperient prior to taking the waters, was a recognised physical and mental preparation recommended at many spas. Patients rose early to take the waters, 2 or 3 half-pints daily, gradually increasing the quantity to 4 or 5 pints per day. Thus between one and a half and 5 pints were usually drunk.[38] Four to 5 pints of the purging water drunk within the space of an hour would *"give two or three easy motions and raise the spirits."*[39] The chalybeate had a less purgative effect, and then it was mostly through urine, but it apparently raised the spirits more. The appetite was improved if the waters were taken before 10am, which accounts for the early start to the day. Patients were encouraged to measure both the input and output of fluids. In the case of chalybeate waters, it was vital that the body should purge the whole of the morning's intake before food was taken. Measuring also enabled patients to compare their former habits with their improved healthy approach.[40] From as early as 1684 the water was dispensed by local women. Their income ensured that they did not need parish relief, at least during the spa season.

William Simpson in 1679 listed the many complaints alleviated by the waters. They eradicated chronic diseases of the kidneys and skin, and cured in cases where other medicines had failed, though these cases are not mentioned specifically. The waters were beneficial in hectic fevers, weaknesses of the stomach, indigestion, scurvy, hypochondriasis, green-sickness, hysteric disorders, asthma, rheumatism, habitual costiveness, fluor albus, gleets and preternatural evacuations.[41] Digestion was also aided, as was scrofula and other skin diseases.

According to Dr Kelk in 1841 the waters had a *"brisk, pungent, chalybeate taste"*, though the purgative also tasted bitter. Shortly after drinking half a pint from the south spring, an agreeable sensation was felt in the stomach followed by a general warmth: *"...the spirits became exhilarated and he feels himself more inclined to enter into any scheme of amusement or pleasure, which forms the great business of watering places."*[42] This suggests a slight inebriation. Kelk advocated the waters in the treatment of chronic ailments, i.e those of more than 40 days duration, in particular stomach disorders. These included heartburn, indigestion, acidity, loss of appetite, and atonic gout, when almost the whole body is debilitated.[43] Sometimes, when an aperient effect was wanted, it could be taken last thing at night as well as two or three glasses early in the morning. Taking less still acted as a mild diuretic, particularly if it were accompanied by exercise such as walking or riding.

By the 1670s Scarborough spaw was resorted to by foreigners, and some English people travelled over 100 miles to take the waters.[44] A bracing sea air also contributed to Scarborough being a popular spa. Defoe in the 1720s noted that there were many people at the spa, mostly from the north of England but also from Scotland.[45] By the 1770s Dr Monro claimed that the chalybeate waters here were the most frequented waters of their kind in England. He added that despite being the second spring to be discovered, the purging well was the more famous, and was the one generally referred to as the Scarborough water.[46] Scarborough's mineral wells were compared favourably with the continental waters of Pyrmont in Germany and the famous Sprudel of Carlsbad.[47] Many people preferred the Scarborough spa because the waters had a more rapid effect on the system. It was said that Scarborough's waters gave an easier passage to urine and stools than some of the continental waters.[48]

FACILITIES

The first spa buildings were erected in 1700, after Celia Fiennes' visit, and for many decades remained rudimentary. As late as 1732 Sarah Duchess of Marlborough fled for home as fast as she could because of the lack of privacy in the sanitary arrangements. Letters to her grand-daughter, the Duchess of Bedford, give an insight into the type of spa arrangements of which we usually remain peculiarly ignorant. The following extract illuminates the facilities for those taking the purging waters, when the men and the ladies were necessarily segregated.

"There is a room for the ladies assembly, which you go up a steep pair of stairs into, on the outside of the house, like a ladder. In that room there is nothing but hard narrow benches, which is a punishment to sit upon. When the waters begin to operate, there is a room within it, where there is above twenty holes with drawers under them to take out, and the ladies go in together and see one another round the room, when they are in that agreeable posture, and at the door, there is a great heap of leaves which the ladies take in with them... I came home as fast as I could for fear of being forced into that assembly."[49]

The lavatories were clearly communal and the drawers were most likely earth trays to collect the debris which at some time had to be cleaned out. Most towns dictated that such offensive waste should only be removed during the hours of darkness. The leaves were probably the precursor of leaves of toilet paper. Similar arrangements must have been provided at all spa towns, particularly those with purging waters.

In the same year, 1732, it was said that lodgings were always plentiful. However, apart from the occasional private ball there was still no organised entertainment, such as the walks to be found at Bath and Tunbridge.[50] Pastimes at Scarborough included eating, drinking and riding, or playing games on the sand.[51] Years later, by 1819, there were still no amusements - no public walks, no theatre or well-stocked shops and no assembly room. People still came to Scarborough though, because of the fame of its waters - which by that time were used more for sea bathing than drinking.[52]

An early reference to sea bathing for health in England appears in Nicholas Blundell's diary. On 3rd, 4th and 5th of August 1709 his two children *"were put in ye Sea for some outbreaks"* (of spots).[53] By the early 1730s sea bathing was becoming acceptable at Scarborough, where: *"It is the Custom, for not only the Gentlemen, but the Ladies also, to bath in the Sea: The Gentlemen go out a little way to Sea in Boats and jump in naked directly.... The Ladies have the conveniency of Gowns and Guides. There are two little Houses on the Shore, to retire for Dressing in."*[54]

A print showing the South Bay by John Setterington in 1735 depicts the first recorded bathing machine. Also shown are rowing boats with a tent built at the stern to offer a mobile dressing room. This is a clear transitional era in Scarborough's evolution from medicinal spa to thalassic spa.

TODAY

Scarborough is still a very popular town, partly because of its beach, its bracing, healthy air, and the entertainment provided. In 1995 a new spout was installed in a recess in the sea wall a few metres to the north of the original saline and chalybeate springs. A brass spout dispensed its chalybeate water into a brass basin and could be freely drunk - if the public health warning were ignored! The following year, 1996, the spout was vandalised and lost.

Footnotes:

1 Morris C. (ed.) 1947, *The Journeys of Celia Fiennes*, p.91.
2 She also found ordinaries at Buxton.
3 M. Whittaker (1984, *Book of Scarborough Spaw*, p.21) believes that the Quakers' Meeting House was situated in Cook Row; *The Scarborough Heritage Trail* (1984, Scarborough Borough Council Part I, p.13) suggests that the Meeting House was the one which was built in 1676 in Low Conduit Sreet, now Princess Square.
4 Dugdale J. 1819, *The British Traveller*, Vol.IV, p.570; Camden's *Britannia*, Holland P. (trans.) 1610, p.717.
5 This interpretation was promoted by Dr Robert Wittie in his *Scarbrough Spa* of 1660, p.1/2.
6 According to the Rev. James Brome in his *Travels over England* of 1700, p.159-60, it was a small town built of stone and slate and well inhabited.
7 Camden's *Britannia* 1610, p.717.
8 Blome R. 1673, *Britannia*, p.251.
9 Hunter J. (ed.) 1830, *Diary of Ralph Thoresby, 1677-1724*. Brome J. 1700, *Travels over England*, p.159-60.

10 A chaldron was a coal measure of 36 heaped bushels or 25.5 cwt. There were 20 cwt to a ton so these vessels carried over 100 tons.
11 Hunter J. op.cit.
12 Camden's *Britannia* 1610, p.717.
13 Blome R. op.cit. p.251.
14 Three quarters of a hundredweight was 84lbs.
15 Short T. 1734, *Natural Mineral Waters*, p.114.
16 Wittie R. 1660, *Scarbrough Spa*, p.6.
17 Gall nuts (galls) are produced on oak trees by the gall-wasp and the gallic acid obtained from the galls was formerly used for making ink. The efficacy of chalybeate waters was determined by their ability to change colour with galls.
18 Short T. op.cit. p.114.
19 A second edition followed in 1667.
20 Wittie R. op.cit. p.253-4.
21 See Wittie R. op.cit. p.139, 160, 167 and passim.
22 Russel R. 1769 (5th edition) *Dissertation on the use of Sea Water* with anonymous supplement *A Treatise on the Nature, Properties and Uses of the Mineral Waters*, p.211.
23 An anker was 81/3 inperial gallons.
24 Whittaker M. 1984, *The Book of Scarbrough Spaw*, p.48.
25 ibid. p.42.
26 Taken from Shaw P. 1734, *An Enquiry into Scarborough Spaw Waters*, endpiece.
27 Allen B. 1699, *The Natural History of the Chalybeate and Purging Waters of England*, p.151.
28 See Hoffman F. 1731, *New Experiments & Observations upon Mineral Waters*.
29 Kelk J. op.cit. p.viii.
30 Russel R. op.cit. p.211.
31 Hoffman F. op.cit. p.87-94.
32 *A Guide to All the Watering and Sea-Bathing Places for 1813*, by the Editor of the Picture of London, p.358.
   As early as the 1660s Dr William Simpson had been boiling off the water to make salts which he called *"the Essence of Scarbrough-Spaw"* (see Whittaker M. op.cit. p.31).
33 In 1769, 2/6d was one third of an agricultural labourer's weekly wage. (For agricultural wages see Lord Ernle 1919, *Farming Past and Present*, p.468.) Medicinal salts were only for the rich.
34 *Journal of Excursions* 1819-23, p.105.
35 Dugdale J. op.cit. p.570.
36 Kelk J. op.cit. p.10.
37 Whittaker M. op.cit. p.29.
38 1 pint = 0.55 litre
39 Monro D. 1770, *A Treatise on Mineral Waters*, Vol.I, p.389-395.
40 Whittaker M. op.cit. p.30.
41 William Simpson in *The History of Scarbrough-Spaw* (1679) wrote that during the Civil War the majority of the garrison at Scarborough fell sick with scurvy but were cured when Dr Wittie directed them to take the spa water. See Whittaker M. op.cit. p.24.
   Green sickness, or chlorosis, was usually suffered by pubescent girls and was noticeable by a greenish-yellow pallor.
42 Kelk J. op.cit. p.10.
43 ibid. p.3.
44 Blome R. op.cit. p.251; Wittie R. op.cit. p.8.
45 Defoe D. 1927, *A Tour Through England and Wales*, Vol.II, p.247.
46 Monro D. op.cit. p.389-395.
47 Macky J. 1732, *A Journey Through England*, Vol.2, p.239; Kelk J. op.cit. p.3.
48 Short T. op.cit. p.114.
49 Scott Thomson G. (ed.) 1943, *Letters of a Grandmother, 1732-1735*, p.46.
50 Macky J. op.cit. p.239.
51 Whittaker M. op.cit. p.73-79.
52 Dugdale J. op.cit. p.570.
53 Blundell M. 1952, *Blundell's Diary and Letter Book*, p.66.
54 Quoted in Whittaker M. op.cit. p.77, from Ward C. Chandler R. 1734, *A Journey from London to Scarborough in Several Letters from a Gentleman there*, 1st edition 1734, 2nd edition 1736.

DURHAM

In 1698 Celia undertook her Great Journey of 1551 miles which led her from London to Southwold in the east, Newcastle in the north, Flint and Shrewsbury in the west and Penzance in the south-west, returning to London via Dorchester and Windsor. This was a mammoth undertaking considering the state of the roads. It was the poor condition of the roads which was the cause of an accident just outside Arlesford, when Celia's horse slipped and she was sent flying over its head, though she was none the worse for the experience.[1] Fortunately, except for the occasional shower, she only had three wet days throughout the whole tour.

Travelling south from Chester-le-Street, Celia saw Durham up on its hilltop from 4 miles away. On her approach she observed how the course of the River Wear caused the city to be triangular in shape,[2] and almost as a consequence, there were three bridges over the river, each of stone with several arches. She crossed the river, probably via the old, narrow Framwellgate Bridge to the north-west of the city. The bridge dated from 1401 when it was built to replace its earlier counterpart which had been damaged by floods. She entered Durham via Silver Street Gate and would have seen the towers and gates at each end of the bridge. The Silver Street Gate and the battlements were later removed and the bridge widened.

Celia mentioned two bridges into Durham apart from Framwellgate Bridge. Elvet Bridge, to the north-east, was built in the late twelfth century and extensively restored in the late fifteenth century; three of the arches were destroyed by floods in 1771. Prebends Bridge leads into the south-west of the city and was originally a wooden footbridge built in 1574. This was replaced by a stone bridge in 1696, so was new when Celia visited. It was almost totally swept away in the 1771 flood.

The castle and cathedral were, and still are, an impressive sight both from a distance and close up. Celia described the castle and all the cathedral buildings as built of stone and enclosed within a battlemented wall. The whole complex is situated in the middle of the town, on the highest point of the hill. Celia was not sure if this were a cathedral or an abbey, or both, but described it as large, with a respectable organ and a "good" though not extraordinary choir. Her attention was drawn to the elegantly carved chiming clock which showed the seven stars, the changing phases of the moon and the signs of the Zodiac.

She was most impressed with the stained glass windows and variety of carvings, specifically mentioning the carved top to the marble font, which was situated within a high arch of unpainted wood, finely carved, and terminating in a point. The whole resembled pictures she had seen of the building of the Tower of Babel.

Over the altar, taking up the whole window space, was a huge painting depicting a Catherine wheel.[3] The Bishop's throne was approached along a gold carpet and mounted via several steps, and had a seat of crimson damask made during the reign of Charles I. She saw the cloisters remaining from the monastic days, and St Mary's Chapel which was used for the Spiritual Courts.

In the vestry she admired three or four embroidered copes, one far more elaborate than the others, which was used by the dean to celebrate the Eucharist. Its elegant embroidery depicted the nativity, life, death and ascension of Christ. Celia believed Durham's rites and ceremonies made it the highest Anglican church in the country. This very high churchmanship attracted many Roman Catholics whose numbers increased daily according to Celia, a staunch Nonconformist.

The castle, which was also the Bishop's Palace, was surmounted by towers and gave the appearance of being fortified. The hill on which it stood had tiers of grassy-banked walks, rows of trees, and a wall at the bottom. From one of the grassy walks one could enter the palace dining room which gave access to the rest of the building. She described the rooms as stately, with parlours, drawing rooms and an impressive hall, though the best furniture had been removed during the absence of Lord Crew, Bishop of Durham, who was living then at another well-furnished Castle, twelve miles away. This refers to the castle at Bishop Auckland, ten miles away, which was the chief residence of the Bishop of Durham and where at that time Lord Crew was staying.

Near the Castle, on Palace Green, was the *"place for the assizes"*.[4] These courts had been rebuilt by Bishop Cosin in 1664.[5] At the time of Celia's visit Durham had a dean, two archdeacons and twelve prebendaries (canons), who lived in the houses round the Green[6]. She noted that it was possible to see the College and Doctors' houses through two gates which opened on to the Green, though it seems that the area was only open to visitors by appointment, not to wandering tourists like Celia. The houses were supplied with water from a large, elegant conduit in the centre of the Green. The conduit had stone pillars culminating in a high carved stone arch terminating in a stone ball, almost certainly of late Gothic design and Celia described the delightful sound of the water falling into the cistern from four pipes. Unfortunately the conduit no longer exists.

From the castle Celia took a steep, winding descent into the town. There, in the spacious market place, she saw the town hall built on stone pillars. What she saw was a small part of the original town hall of 1555 which had been largely replaced by Bishop Cosin in 1665, and thus was quite a new building at the time of her visit. She also remarked on the large conduit in the market place. In 1450 Thomas Billingham had granted a public water supply to the city, in perpetuity, for 13d rent per annum. It was piped from his manor at Sidgate to a reservoir, or conduit, in the market place.[7] Part of the conduit can still be seen at Sidgate. Near the river she found a Nonconformist meeting house which had attracted a congregation of approximately 300. She thought this a marvellous achievement, given that it was so close to the High Anglican cathedral. Celia Fiennes did not describe the city itself in great detail but John Ogilby in 1698 mentioned that it was well compacted, suggesting that the buildings were fairly densely grouped without being overcrowded.

In the evening Celia crossed from the east to west of the city, north of where the river meandered south. She walked along the river bank and passed Sir Charles Musgrave's house. It had originally been very grand, but she only saw its ruins.[8] The gardens still flourished, as did the fruit trees in them, and the area had become a popular spot for the town gentry to walk in the evenings. There were plenty fish in the river, and even more rocks, and the water cascading over them made a soothing and pleasing sound. There was talk of making the river navigable, but with so many rocks Celia doubted if this were possible.

She walked a mile out of the city to see the spa waters, including a salt spring in a rock in the middle of the river. After half a mile she came across the first well which had a stone basin and a stone arch over it. It was a chalybeate spring which she likened to the Sweet Spaw at Harrogate and the water at Tunbridge. Half a mile further on she encountered a well which tasted like Harrogate's Sulphur Spaw. They were both from brimstone, though Durham's water was not so strong *"for it was a longer tyme before the silver was changed in it"*.[9] From the sulphur well she took a stony and hazardous route down through the bushes to the river bank to see the third spring. She would have liked to turn back but could not and had to make a precipitous descent to the river's edge. She records that the spring emerged upwards from a cleft in the rocks in the river and that during heavy rains the extra water diluted the spring, thus weakening it.

Whilst in Durham Celia found very comfortable lodgings at the Nag's Head, an inn run by two spinster sisters and their brother. She was very taken with the city which, she said, had *"the noblest, cleane and pleasant buildings, streets large well pitch'd...its a noble place and the aire so cleer and healthy that persons enjoy much health and pleasure"*.[10]

COMMENT

THE CATHEDRAL

The present cathedral, which dates from 1093, was built to house the remains of St Cuthbert. It is significant that here at Durham, as at Canterbury cathedral, although describing a multitude of internal and external features, Celia Fiennes did not once mention the saint to whom the cathedral was originally dedicated. John Ogilby, writing in the same year as Celia Fiennes, noted not only that the cathedral was dedicated to St Cuthbert but that there were six other churches in Durham apart from the cathedral.[11] It was possibly that Celia paid less attention to religious establishments because of her Nonconformist beliefs, and here only mentioned the cathedral and the Quaker meeting house.

Celia wrote in some detail about the interior features of the cathedral, many of which can still be seen. She wrote of embroidery, stained glass, wood carving, the Bishop's throne, the clock and the font, but generally without a mention of religion or their religious significance. Only the vestments elicited a mention of Christianity, when she noted that their embroidery depicted scenes from the life of Christ, and that they were used at the Eucharist. At the time she visited, these particular vestments were housed in the vestry. Visitors had to pay a charge to see them, which put them beyond the gaze of poorer people and so made them rather exclusive and special.

There are two copes on display amongst the cathedral's treasures and today, as before, visitors still pay to see them. One of them is the cope to which Celia Fiennes paid particular attention and which depicts scenes from Christ's life. It is medieval, thought to have been made in Italy between 1440-1470, and is now very fragile. It is of blue velvet brocade with silver-gilt thread. Its orphreys are embroidered with silver-gilt and silver thread, with coloured silks, mainly in split stitch and couched work on linen. As one looks at the cope, the orphrey to the left shows, from bottom to top, the Betrayal, the Flagellation, Christ bearing the cross and Christ crucified. The right hand orphrey shows, from bottom to top, the Resurrection, the Incredulity of St Thomas, the Ascension and Pentecost. The hood was extensively altered during the 1630s and 1640s and depicts Christ in Judgement. The threads of red, blue, green, purple, yellow and gold would have been much more vivid when Celia Fiennes saw them.

The other cope is maroon, dates from the 1630s and is associated with Charles I's visit to the cathedral in 1633. It was most likely during this visit that he provided the crimson damask seat for the Bishop's throne. This second cope is extremely unusual; between the Reformation and the nineteenth century elaborate vestments of this nature were rarely made.

The present choir stalls, with their finely carved misericords, were provided by Bishop John Cosin in 1665. They replaced the original choir stalls which were destroyed during the Civil War. The Bishop also provided "*a great carved oak screen carrying an organ*".[12] This was the choir or chancel screen, which separated the choir from the nave, and upon which stood the organ built in 1683 by "Father Smith" and which Celia saw. In 1846, under the direction of Gilbert Scott, the organ screen was removed and part of it resited in the south-west aisle.[13] The front of the organ case was re-erected against the south wall of the south aisle where it can be seen today. Part of the organ was incorporated into the gallery of Bishop Tunstal's Chapel in the Castle when the chapel was restored in 1921.[14] The present choir screen was designed in the 1870s by Gilbert Scott.

The marble font and its canopy, which survive today, were provided by Bishop Cosin in 1663. The font is dwarfed by the extravagance of the carved cover which, as Celia Fiennes noted, resembles the immense Tower of Babel. To the east of the font is a band of black Frosterley marble set into the floor, which marks the boundary over which, during monastic times, women were not allowed to pass. This was to prevent them going too close to St Cuthbert's shrine, giving rise to the common belief that the saint was a misogynist.

The elegant painted and gilded bishop's throne, reputed to be the highest in the Christian world, was erected above the tomb of Bishop Hugh Hatfield (1345-81) as a memorial to himself. It is not known what happened to Charles I's crimson damask seat which caught Celia Fiennes' eye. She was most likely talking about a cushion which had surprisingly survived the Civil War and the Interregnum when other parts of the cathedral were badly damaged. The throne is still in its original position.

In the 1620s and 1630s John Cosin was a canon at the cathedral, becoming Bishop at the Restoration. During his time as canon he spent approximately £3,000 restoring parts of the interior, including repairing, painting and regilding the great clock.[15] This finely carved Gothic masterpiece was installed in the south transept at some point during Prior Castell's time (1494-1519). The clock stands on wooden columns painted to resemble marble, and the richly painted and gilded dial is supported on carved pinnacles and crowned by a dome with a tall finial. As Celia Fiennes described, it shows the seven stars and the changing phases of the moon. Following the battle of Dunbar in September 1650, Cromwell sent 4,000 Scottish prisoners to Durham and incarcerated them in the cathedral with little food and no heating. The prisoners destroyed almost all the wooden fixtures which they used as fuel. The clock survived, perhaps because it had a Scottish thistle carved on it, or perhaps the prisoners felt that the Zodiacal signs boded well for them. Originally the clock only had one hand; a minute hand was added at the end of the nineteenth century. At the same time the chimes were removed because they interrupted the services. Possibly the only record of the clock ever having chimed is in Celia Fiennes' journal. Despite the nineteenth century rearrangement, the original mechanism still exists and is wound up once a week.

THE CASTLE

Begun in 1071, this Norman fortification has been modernised many times during its history. The current exterior is eighteenth century and masks the earlier stone features which Celia Fiennes saw. However she did see the huge solid oak and iron doors which are still closed every night, leaving access only through a wicket gate. The dining room into which she entered, and several of the other rooms, were fashioned out of the lower hall by Bishop Tunstal from 1530-59.[16] During his term of office, Bishop Crewe (1674-1721) extended the sixteenth century chapel eastwards, though he retained the original east window, which can still be seen. In 1832 the Castle became part of the University and Bishop Auckland became the sole See of the bishops, though they retain the right to use the state apartments at Durham.[17]

KEPIER HOSPITAL

On her walk out one evening, Celia passed the old Kepier Hospital which, at the time she visited, was a ruined mansion, the property of Sir Charles Musgrave. Its foundations were twelfth century though most of the stonework was fourteenth century. At the Reformation the Kepier Hospital property was confiscated and was acquired in 1569 by a wealthy Protestant merchant, John Heath.[18] A mansion adjoining the southern medieval buildings was built by his son, also named John Heath, sometime between 1591 and 1618. It remained in the Heath family until 1630 when the house, gardens and orchards were sold to Sir Ralph and Sir Nicholas Cole, who kept it until 1674, when it was taken over by Lord Musgrave of Carlisle. He never lived there

and appears to have bought it as an investment. Today, in an isolated spot beside the river, one can still see the the gatehouse and the extensive orchards. Visitors can see the remains of two stone arches and a square window.

Kepier Hospital, near Durham.

138

THE SPRINGS

St Cuthbert's Well, Durham.

When Celia visited the springs she walked south, though there is confusion about her starting point and her estimation of distances between identifiable places. After half a mile she recalled passing a well with a stone basin and an arch over it. This strongly suggests St Cuthbert's Well (Grid ref NZ 272422), now situated near the Galilee Well on the banks of the river and accessible by a narrow path. The well still has a stone basin and a substantial stone surround with an inscription *"Fons Cuthbert"* and the date 1690 engraved in the stonework.[19]

She described the water at the well as being like Harrogate's Sweet Spaw, or Tunbridge water, i.e chalybeate. From a variety of texts it is widely known that the prominent chalybeate spring in the area was at Butterby, one and a half miles south of the cathedral. It is doubtful whether Celia would have remarked on an isolated fountain such as St Cuthbert's rather than a thriving curative spring. It may have been that the Sweet Spaw water was known as St Cuthbert's spring and was dispensed through the fountain we now see. Also, that when Butterby's chalybeate spring was destroyed by mining activity the fountain was perhaps removed from the Sweet Spaw and resited in its present location.

Celia's details of distances is further evidence to suggest that she did not see a fountain on the present site of St Cuthbert's fountain. She walked half a mile before arriving at the Sweet Spaw, though she does not indicate where she started her journey. It was a further half mile before she reached the Sulphur Spaw. If it had been the present St Cuthbert's fountain she saw, on the present site, then she had a further mile and a half to the Sulphur Spaw, not just half a mile. Although her judgement of distances is sometimes inaccurate, it is not so askew as to confuse half a mile and one and a half miles.

In the late sixteenth century William Camden described Butterby as a little village lying just over a mile south of Durham city, and it was here that Celia Fiennes saw the mineral springs. The first documentary evidence of springs located here was in 1675, when only the chalybeate spring was mentioned.[20]

By 1684, according to Mr Hugh Todd in *Philosophical Transactions*, the "springs" were much frequented.[21] This might account for the provision of the "Fons Cuthbert" in 1690.

THE SWEET SPAW (Grid ref. NZ 268394)

This spring was "*a short but delightful walk*" from the city, and set in a deep, romantic dell overshadowed by woods.[22] Dr Clanny in 1807 found the water issuing at 50° F and containing lime suspended in carbonic acid gas. He commented on its purity and that it cured the same types of ailments that Matlock's waters cured: internally, problems with kidneys, bladder, urinary calculi, hectic fever and fistulas, and externally, cutaneous eruptions.[23] Dr Granville described the spring as being a pure water with a small amount of carbonate of lime, and having almost no taste, an indication that it had curative properties but was not unpleasant to taste or smell.[24]

The water contained spirit of sulphur and a vaporous spirit associated with coal, and 20 years before Celia's visit, it was known to be used for curative purposes.[25] The most explicit details on the medicinal use of these waters come from Dr Edward Wilson in 1675. His recommended dosage was three half pints per visit and was most beneficial in chronic (long-term) diseases.[26] It is believed to have cured dropsy, black and yellow jaundice, diarrhoea, gonorrhoea, disentery, scurvy, fluxes of the abdomen, rickets, green sickness (chlorosis) and King's Evil.[27] It was a powerful diuretic; prevented and cured epilepsy, carus, apoplexy, cephalaea, vertigo and cephalagia; it helped in nervous diseases, cramps, and barrenness in women, though pregnant women were not advised to be take it. It eased itchy and prickly skin and eye problems such as inflammation; eased wounds, sores, scabs and ulcers, "*being both drank and outwardly applied*".[28] By 1807 Dr Clanny was recommending only half a pint, although a quart could be taken with safety, and that it was beneficial as a laxative and for scrofula and cutaneous eruptions.

Effecting a complete cure could take two to four weeks, depending on the nature of the disease and the age and constitution of the invalid. One must assume that since Butterby is so isolated, visitors stayed in Durham and made a daily journey out to the spring. The best months to take the waters were June to August, when the weather was hot and dry, so the walk would have been pleasant and relaxing. Relaxation and gentle exercise were important constituents of spa healing. Before drinking, Dr Wilson advised that certain precautions should be observed, including preparation of the body. This meant purging, or excreting, either naturally or artificially. Then, three half-pint glasses of water should be consumed, unless the stomach could not take quite that amount. The patient then exercised for a quarter of an hour, either riding or walking, but not sufficiently briskly to generate sweating. Orange chips, lemon or lime pills, candied elecampane roots or caraway confits were also recommended to settle the stomach.[29] This was followed by three or four more glasses and a further fifteen minutes exercise. This formula was repeated until the stomach could not hold any more without vomiting. Those with a strong digestion were allowed to drink a further half the quantity in the afternoon, about four or five hours after dinner, but should then eat little or nothing at supper time. The following day saw the same regimen with the exception that the dose was three glasses more than the previous day. The daily consumption continued until three quarts (12 glasses) to a pottle was being taken in a day.[30] Then the intake was reduced by three glasses each day.[31] It was strongly advised that if the body found the water disagreeable drinking should be terminated immediately.

Dr Wilson stressed that the water should be consumed at the fountain head, as soon as possible after it emerged; therefore, like most chalybeate waters, it was unlikely to have been bottled and transported to the home or lodgings except in the case of the bedridden. Food was not to be consumed until the water had been flushed out of the body and this could be detected by the urine turning a darker colour. There is no information on toilet facilities; it may be that the bushes were used, or rudimentary toilets provided. The regimen included diet. Salt meat, goose, eels, salmon and all fatty foods were not recommended. "Cold" stomachs could manage strong ale or sack whereas hotter, stronger stomachs should stick to weaker drinks.

It is difficult to imagine this now defunct spa ever having the capacity to cure invalids. All that remains today are some stone ruins in a cattle yard, a ditch and what appears to be a spring, though as late as 1841, when Dr Granville was writing, Butterby was still considered a spa. Dugdale talks of a narrow road being made for the use of a local quarry so it could well have been late nineteenth century mining or quarrying activities which disrupted the spring's flow. Today there is evidence of a roadway running parallel to the river, near the site of the sulphur spring.[32] It is quite overgrown with grass and bushes, but the disturbance in the landscape is indicative of a track.

THE SULPHUR SPAW (Grid ref. NZ 271396)

About 200-300 yards further along the river bank from the Sweet Spaw was the sulphur spring which, according to Dr Elliot in the 1790s, was similar to the Harrogate sulphur spring in its effectiveness.[33] Thomas Short confirmed that the spring rose out of a bore in the rock on the north bank of the river Wear and lay at the side of a brook at the foot of a steep bank.[34] Dr Clanny believed the spring was discovered by workmen digging for coal in 1684. The medicinal water was reached at twelve and a half fathoms.[35] At the beginning of the nineteenth century it was recorded as issuing at 30 gallons per hour and at 50° F, several degrees less than the normal air temperature of 63° F.[36]

141

ANALYSES OF THE SULPHUR SPRING

An analysis of the Butterby sulphur spring was carried out by Dr Clanny in 1807.[37] It was said that following this analysis the sulphur spring was much resorted to by invalids, though there is now no visible evidence to show any such popularity.[38]

Amount in grains and thousandth parts of a grain of the mineralizing ingredients held in solution in the eighth part of an imperial gallon.

M = muriatic acid   S = sulphuric acid   C = carbonic acid

Soda	with M	7.06
	with S	-
	with C	-
Lime	with M	0.62
	with S	0.44
	with C	1.62
Magnesia	with M	0.56
	with S	-
	with C	-
Alumine		-
Silica		-
Oxide of Iron	pure	-
	with C	-
Iodine		-
Bromine		-

Sulph.hydr.gas in cub. inches	1.44
Carb.hydr.in cub. inches	-
Azote in cub. inches	0.37
Free carb.gas in cub. inches	1.00

Dr Clanny analysed the water on a second occasion, with the following results.[39]

Amounts in grains per wine gallon:

Muriate of soda	56.6
" lime	5.0
" magnesia	4.5
Carbonate of lime	8.5
Sulphate of lime	3.5
	78.0

Gas in cu ins.

Carbonic acid	8.0
Azotic	3.0
Sulphurated hydrogen	11.5
	22.5

142

Dr Short in 1734 evaporated one gallon of water from the sulphur spring. The sediment contained 56 grains, 18 of which were earth and 38 sea salt.[40] Dr Granville noted that despite being sulphurated the water was not unpleasant to taste. It was clear and colourless, with no sediment and few bubbles. After standing for a few hours the bubbles disappeared and the sulphurous taste and smell were reduced.

Celia Fiennes, having encountered other sulphur springs on her travels, carried out her own experiment to determine how concentrated the sulphur was, by noting how long it took to discolour silver. It took some time for the discolouration to be visible, hence she knew the sulphur content to be weak. Experiments by others resulted in a residual rust-like powder after the water was boiled, and a fine brown scurf encrustation on polished silver which had been immersed.[41]

Dugdale's comment on the road being made for quarry access sustains Fordyce's observation that the sulphur spring was lost through mining.[42] There are still indications of open quarrying in the same field, possibly the result of small-scale coal extraction, and these almost certainly resulted in the spring's failure. In 1995 when the authors visited, the sulphur spring was dry, though there was evidence that it had flowed into a steep gully down to the river.

THE SALT SPRING

The River Wear below the sulphur spring is rocky with white water. The third spring which Celia noted sprang from a fissure in one of the rocks in the river bed, about 40 feet from the shore and 20 yards south-west of the Sulphur Spaw.[43] It was a considerable spring which, according to Granville, was a mixture of some iron and plenty of common salt. Because the river inundated the spring it was difficult to ascertain how much salt it contained, but a series of experiments found that it was twice the amount found in sea salt. In the summer, when the river was low, a reddish salt water could be seen springing out from between the stones in the river. When the water had dried on the stones it left a red tinge caused by oxides of iron and the thick incrustation remaining was gathered and used as salt by the local inhabitants.[44] Some local people boiled the water to produce baysalt which was just as useful as ordinary salt though not quite so palatable.[45] William Marshall in 1818 identified the spring, which issued into an ancient excavated basin. It was still only accessible at low water, and since the output was so trifling the proprietors were never likely to consider exploiting it.[46]

The water contained sulphate of magnesia or Epsom salt and was drunk as a purgative.[47] It was also reputedly good for the diseases caused by the fumes associated with the smelting and refining houses of the lead industry, and half a pint was deemed sufficient for the strongest constitution.[48] Dr Clanny believed that if the sulphur spring and the salt spring waters were mixed together, when drunk they would cure tape worms, apoplexy, herpes, piles, elephantiasis and leprosy.[49] Dr Granville thought that the salt spring water on its own was so diluted by the river water that its medicinal qualities were severely impaired. But, like Dr Clanny, he thought a combination of the saline and sulphur waters would be immensely beneficial and mused that Nature must have deliberately placed the two springs near each other.

THE FRESH WATER SPRING

Two authors mention a fourth spring in the vicinity. Dugdale, publishing in 1819, records that the sulphur spring and a fresh water spring were discovered accidentally by workmen digging for coal. At 80 feet they found the sulphur spring, and 300 feet away at about the same depth they discovered a fresh water spring. Both springs then emerged from their man made holes.[50] Thomas Short, writing nearly 80 years earlier, noted that about 200 yards from the salt spring, and nearly opposite, was a sulphurous spring, a chalybeate spring and a spring of fresh water, all springing up through the rocks.[51]

OTHER SPRINGS IN THE AREA

In addition there were a number of springs in the immediate environs of the city of Durham.[52]

The Banks Mill spring is recorded by Allen (1824). This was located a few yards past Banks Mill, on the west side of the Wear. It was a powerful chalybeate spring issuing from a fissure in the rock. The water was considered a healing water and much visited. The well is now lost. (Grid ref NZ 272422)

The Galilee Well is located beneath the west wall of the cathedral. To reach it, take the path from Windy Gap to Watergate. A metal grille gives access to the well which is now dry. (Grid ref NZ 272422)

St Mary's Well was highly praised during the nineteenth century. It was located on the south bank below South Street. There is a well in the locality which comprises an arch of stone walling with a small hollow where water collects. It is a short distance from Prebends Bridge. Today it is known as South Street Well. (Grid ref NZ 271419)

St Oswald's Well is in a large cavern in the rock outcrop overlooking the cathedral. Located on the bank of the Wear below the church tower, it is approached via a footpath from St Oswald's churchyard to Prebends Bridge. The well head was destroyed by nineteenth century vandals. (grid ref NZ 275419)

There was also a Flass Well, the location of which is lost.

On the pathway beside the river just below St Cuthbert's Well is a fountain which is most likely an overflow from the larger structure above. A group of small holes in the stonework suggests that it formerly sported an ornamental animal's head, perhaps a lion or a dolphin.

TODAY

It is possible to drive out to Butterby and park fairly close to the springs. A walk by the river is recommended. It is still romantic and one can appreciate the steep slope that Celia clambered down to the river's edge. Major disruptions in the landscape caused by quarrying and mining can also be seen quite clearly. The area has been subjected to extensive coal mining operations during the nineteenth century and this has certainly disturbed the hydrogeology of the locality. The presence of coal also explains some of the more exotic characteristics of the water mineralisation.

Celia's journals mention very little about the city centre, but one feature survives. The town hall, which was altered in the eighteenth century, was demolished and rebuilt in 1851. However, the old rectangular market underneath it was retained and can now be seen incorporated amongst the stalls of the new market.

In Castle Green are two buildings which Celia would have seen - the old Grammar School of 1661 and Bishop Cosin's almshouses. The latter was established in 1666 for four poor men and four poor women, but is now part of the University.

Bishop Cosin's almshouses, established 1666.

Although the castle is now closed to visitors, much of what Celia Fiennes saw remains, especially in the cathedral, to be rediscovered by today's traveller.

Footnotes:

1   Morris C. (ed.) 1947, *The Journeys of Celia Fiennes*, p.273-4.
2   ibid. p.213.
3   The Catherine Wheel window has been replaced with a Rose window.
4   Morris C. op.cit. p.215.
5   They were replaced by the Diocesan Registry in 1820.
6   Brome J. 1700, *Travels Over England*, p.169.
7   Proud K. 1992, *Durham City*, p.67.
8   Kepier Hospital
9   Morris C. op.cit. p.216.
10 ibid. p.215.
11 Ogilby J. 1698, *Britannia*, p.5.
12 Pitkin Pictorials, *Durham Cathedral*, p.18.
13 ibid. p.21; Johnson M. 1992, 6th edition, *Durham, Historic and University City*, p.6.
14 Johnson M. op.cit. p.2.
15 *Pitkin Pictorials, Durham Cathedral* 1988, p.17.
16 Johnson M. op.cit. p.1-2.
17 Thorold H. 1980, *County Durham*, p.88.
18 Johnson M. op.cit. p.27.
19 The flow has been intermittant since the University Library was built.
20 Wilson E. 1675, *Spadacrene Dunelmensis, treatise on the vitrioline spaw near Durham.*
21 Clanny W R. 1807, *History and analysis of the Mineral Waters at Butterby*, p.24; Lowthorp's Abridgement of Philos. Trans. Vol.II, p.333.
22 Granville A B. 1841, *The Spas of England: The North*, reprinted 1971, p.243.
23 Clanny W R. op.cit. p.28-31.
24 Granville A B. op.cit. p.243.
25 Wilson E. op.cit. p.50/51.
26 Chronic diseases were those of more than 40 days duration.
27 Wilson E. op.cit. p.74/77.
28 ibid. p.70-77.
29 Elecampane was widely grown for its medicinal root which was converted to a sweetmeat.
30 A pottle was half a gallon, or 4 pints.
31 Wilson E. op.cit. p.78-81. At Astrop's chalybeate well the dose was increased or decreased by half a pint daily; the dose at Durham was likely to have been the same, not the three glasses suggested by Dr Wilson.
32 Dugdale J. 1819, *The British Traveller*, Vol.II, p.272.
33 Elliot J. 1789, *An account of the nature and medicinal virtues of the principal mineral waters of*
34 Short T. 1734, *History of Mineral Waters*, p.61.   *England and Ireland*, p.175.
35 80 feet, or 24 metres.
36 Clanny W R. op.cit. p.31.
37 Dr Clanny of Sunderland was physician to the Durham Infirmary. His analysis of the Butterby springs is published in Dr Granvilles's *Spas of England, The North*, 1841.
38 Fordyce W. 1857, *History of Durham*, Vol.1, p.391-2.
39 Clanny W R. op.cit. p.40/41.
40 Monro D. 1770, *A treatise on mineral waters*, Vol.I, p.202.
41 Wilson E. op.cit., p.51; Clanny W R. op.cit. p.51.
42 Fordyce W. op.cit. p.391-2.
43 Short T. op.cit. p.61.
44 Clanny W R. op.cit. p.51-60; Camden's *Britannia*, Holland P. (trans.) 1610, p.739.
45 Surtees R. 1816-40, *The history and antiquities of the County Palatine of Durham*, reprinted 1971, Vol.4, p.110, footnote k.
46 Marshall W. 1818, *Review and abstracts of the County Reports to the Board of Agriculture*, p.140.
47 Dugdale J. 1819, *The British traveller*, Vol.II, p.272; Monro D. op.cit. Vol.I, p.202.
48 Dugdale J. op.cit. Vol.II, p.272.
49 Clanny W R. op.cit. p.51-60.
50 Dugdale J. op.cit. p.272.
51 Short T. op.cit. p.61.
52 Hunt L. 1987, "Ancient, healing and holy wells of Durham", *Source, The Holy Well Journal*, No.7, p.10/11.

KNARESBOROUGH

Celia Fiennes visited Knaresborough during her Northern Tour of 1697.[1] From York, she travelled the 4 to 5 miles to Bishopsthorpe on the river Ouse, then over marshy common to Knaresborough, 12 miles away.

Celia stayed at an inn run by a Mrs Mason, who introduced her guest to a floriculturist. This gentleman had a garden where he grew many unusual flowers and plants, and a cherry garden laid out with walks. He had built a tree house from where visitors could sit and admire the views. The gardens, together with the romantic castle ruins and St Robert's Cave, were the tourist attractions in Celia Fiennes' day.

The castle was first built shortly after the Norman invasion, and was enlarged at great expense by King John at the beginning of the thirteenth century. Following the battle of Marston Moor in 1644, it was besieged by the Parliamentarians, and much of it was demolished 4 years later. Following a petition to Parliament by the townsfolk, the Keep was reprieved and used as a local prison, and the Courthouse continued to be used for its original purpose. Its upper storey was only about 50 years old when Celia visited.[2] She would have seen both the Keep and the Courthouse, but she only commented on the ruined state of the walls, the part of the castle which was being used as a prison, and the cellars. The cellars were formerly the dungeons, and Celia went there and drank some strong, clear ale.

Knaresborough Castle 1836.

147

In Knaresborough she commented on the pretty stone buildings and the large market place. The corn and provision market was held on Wednesdays and one can only speculate whether the liquorice, which grew abundantly on the local soil, was sold at the market.[3] The riverside was also an attraction, though Celia commented that the river Nidd was black, possibly the result of pumping from the iron and sulphur mines. Many of Knaresborough's houses were cut into the rocks and a little chapel, dedicated to St Robert, was also cut out of the rock. The chapel was arched and carved with figures, probably of the saints, and an effigy of the devout St Robert was carved at the entrance. There were flowers on the altar, and rushes on the floor for the visitors - Roman Catholics, who continued the tradition of pilgrimage to the resting places of their saints.

Celia also went to the ruins of an abbey where some bones had been exhumed and used as relics. Mrs Mason related the story of a Catholic lady who had once lodged with her. One day, when the lady was visiting the abbey ruins to say her prayers, she found that someone had dug up the bones of a man's arm, with the hand still attached. When the elbow joint was struck it broke open and in the hollow of the bone was a moist, red, jelly-like substance. The woman dipped her handerchief into it and cut off the stained part to make into a relic.

COMMENT

Celia did not mention any medicinal springs in Knaresborough. Her observations on The Dropping Well, which is situated in the environs of Knaresborough, were included amongst those on the Harrogate springs. Despite the local mineralised and healing wells being located at Harrogate and Copgrove, neither place provided suitable accommodation. Like Celia, visitors had to lodge at Knaresborough, which is 2 miles from Harrogate and 6 from Copgrove.

ST ROBERT OF KNARESBOROUGH

St Robert of Knaresborough (1160-1218) was the son of an important townsman from York. Robert became a cleric early in life and, after a short spell at the Cistercian abbey of Newminster, became a hermit. He lived in a cave at Knaresborough with a knight, who was a fugitive from Richard I. On Richard's death in 1199 the knight returned to his wife, and Robert lived here alone for many years. At various times he went to live at Rudfarlington, Spofforth and Hedley, but returned eventually to the cave where he lived out his life. He died in September 1218 and was apparently buried in the chapel beside the cave.[4]

THE CHAPEL OF OUR LADY IN THE CRAG, ALSO KNOWN AS ST ROBERT'S CHAPEL

Celia mentioned *"a little Chapple cut out of the Rock and arch'd and carv'd with figures of Saints I suppose, its called St Robert's Chapple..."* and also that the saint's effigy was carved at the entrance. The chapel, which overlooks the river Nidd, has been variously described down the centuries, though Camden in the late sixteenth century failed to mention either St Robert or the chapel.

When Celia's contemporary the Reverend James Brome visited, he noted that St Robert's chapel was a small vaulted hermitage cut out of the rock and much visited by Roman Catholics.[5] Some stained glass windows depicted two stags yoked together, capturing a legendary incident in St Robert's life. It was said that St Robert begged from King John a piece of land sufficient to plough between 6am and 4pm, using two stags. Knowing stags to be almost untameable, King John envisaged a small piece of land. He was therefore surprised to find that St Robert tamed two stags and used them to plough several acres.

Perhaps the best historical description of the chapel was by Richard Gough.[6] He related how visitors reached St Robert's Chapel by descending a steep hill from the town and crossing the river over a two-arched bridge. The chapel was cut out of solid freestone rock and overhung with trees and moss. Outside the door was a roughly carved figure of an armed knight drawing his sword. The chapel was 10 feet 6 inches long, 9 feet wide and 7 feet 6 inches high. The vaulting was rib and groin. This indicates an Early English Gothic construction of thirteenth century origin. The altar was in the east end and there was a niche behind the altar. On a ledge in front of the altar were three holes for tapers. On the north side was another niche and an arch with a bench in. The bench was said to be St Robert's bed. On the south side, opposite the bench, was another niche above which were three crudely carved heads representing the Trinity. A fourth head depicted the Virgin Mary. A hole in the middle of the floor was referred to as the saint's grave. At the front, or west end of the chapel, was a small, arched, traceried window, and the door.

Kellett's recent history of Knaresborough describes the chapel of Our Lady in the Crag as having been carved into the rock c.1408 by Robert the Mason, almost 200 years after St Robert's death. The measurements are identical to those quoted by Gough.[7] Outside is a life-sized carving of a medieval soldier, most probably a Knight Templar since they had a base at Little Ribston, 3 miles south-east of Knaresborough.

In the nineteenth century Dr Granville commented that the chapel, which was cut out of solid rock, contained fantastic figures, pilasters and niches, and added that there were similar caves in Germany, Salzburg and some other places. This suggests that St Robert was venerated outside England.[8] In the late eighteenth century it was said that that a low entrance from the chapel led into a subterranean passage which in turn led to the market place.[9]

Gough recorded that by the late eighteenth century, access to the chapel was via a set of steps hewn into the rock which led from a nearby cottage, where the tenant kept the key to the chapel. The tenant showed visitors round the chapel with the permission of Sir Thomas Slingsby, lord of the manor.[10] During the seventeenth century a vast tourism industry had grown up, sanctioned by manorial lords such as Slingsby. During the visitor season, local people supplemented their income by offering services to strangers. Examples include Lord Slingsby's tenant showing visitors around the chapel of Our Lady in the Crag; the man who demonstrated the combustible properties of Wigan's Burning Well; the guides to the Wonders at Buxton, and assistants at the baths at Buxton and Copgrove. These freelance activities were not discouraged: the more ways poor people had of making money during the season, the less had to be contributed in poor relief during the winter months.

ST ROBERT'S CAVE

From Knaresborough, St Robert's Cave is approximately one mile down a narrow, tarmaced road which leads past the chapel of Our Lady in the Crag. The road is unsuitable for vehicles. The cave is cut into a limestone rock and faces onto the River Nidd. Inside is a ledge, which may have been used as an altar.

St Robert's Cave and Grave, 1996.

150

The platform outside is all that remains of the chapel and its altar. A rectangle filled with small stones, situated in the centre of the platform, indicates the site of St Robert's original grave. A bench outside the entrance to the cave may have been used as part of the living area. The front would have been of timber construction, similar to the houses which were built into the rocks. The cave was the focal point of many pilgrims until the Dissolution in the 1530s.

Three hundred metres from the cave, in the direction of the chapel, is the site of Knaresborough Priory. Construction began in 1252, and eventually twelve Trinitarian friars were housed here. The priory church was probably built on the site of the church of the Holy Cross, the resting place of St Robert's body after it was taken from the cave. In the Middle Ages, St Robert's relics were visited by pilgrims who came *"in order to perform vigils and burn candles"* and probably continued to do so until the dissolution of the Priory in December 1538.[11] This is most likely the site of the "abbey" where landlady Mason's Catholic lodger found her relic.

TODAY

Visitors can walk round the remains of the castle and its well-kept grounds. A pleasant walk beside the river along the tarmaced road leads to the chapel of Our Lady in the Crag. The chapel is still used for religious worship, but the gate is kept padlocked when the chapel is not being used. Almost a mile past the chapel is St Robert's Cave. On the other side of the main road a short walk leads to Mother Shipton's Cave and the Dropping Well, which is described in detail under Harrogate.

Footnotes:

1   Morris C. (ed.) 1947, *The Journeys of Celia Fiennes*, p.78-9.
2   Kershaw M J. 1987, *Knaresborough Castle*.
3   Brome J. 1700, *Travels over England*, p.214.
4   Farmer H D. 1978, *The Oxford Dictionary of Saints*.
5   Brome J. op.cit. p.214.
6   Camden's *Britannia*, Gough R. (trans.) 1789, Vol.III, p.54.
7   Kellett A. 1991, *Historic Knaresborough*, p.22-23.
8   Granville A B. 1841, *Spas of England: The North*, reprinted 1971, p.92.
9   Camden's *Britannia*, Vol.III, p.54.
10   ibid.
11   Jennings B. (ed.) 1970, *A History of Harrogate & Knaresborough*, p.98.

St. Mungo's Well, Copgrove

Whilst Celia was staying at Knaresborough she took the opportunity to visit St Mungo's Well at Copgrove, 4 miles from Knaresborough and 6 from Harrogate, and much favoured by Roman Catholics.[1]

She recounted the fable of St Mungo's Well. The story was of a new born foundling, abandoned in the cold for the parish to care for. When the church-wardens discovered the child they baptised it with the name Amongust, because they felt that the child should be kept amongst them. Since this was such a tiny parish the event was probably extremely unusual. The Catholic tradition was that Amongust was very clever and devout, and used the spring at Copgrove to wash in. As he became successful he grew rich, and used his earnings to build a wall round the spring. There he cured many diseased people by helping them to bathe. After his death, the constant stream of invalids became an inconvenience to the owners of the ground who forbade visitors and stopped up the well. The spring then burst out in various places around the well and the owners felt obliged to reopen it to the public.

When Celia visited, a high wall still surrounded the well (or bath) which was about 4 or 5 yards square and surrounded by a broad stone pavement. Four or five steps led down to the water which was little more than waist deep although kneeling on a flat stone brought the water up to the chin. The water was exceedingly cold. The spring, which rose in the corner of the well, was very prolific, and the bath was constantly cleansed as the water ran away down the sluice to be replenished at source. Celia liked it immensely. She preferred to bathe in the corner where the spring was, partly because it was coldest there and partly because she was the first to be cleansed by it. She never liked bathing in other people's bath water.

Celia understood that the coldness closed the skin's pores very quickly, causing an immunity to cold. She found that dipping her head in the water cured a repetitive headache she had been suffering from. Despite this welcome immunity, she could not bear to be in the water for more than 2 or 3 minutes because of its coldness. Some of the Catholics, however, appeared particularly hardy, kneeling in prayer for up to 15 minutes. She recorded that it was customary to dip in for a couple of minutes then walk around on the pavement for a time, then dip back in again, repeating this procedure as often as necessary. She used the bath in the same fashion, unaware that this was a Roman Catholic ritual, rather than a mere bathing custom. This prescriptive practise is still used today at Holywell, where the time spent in the water is the length of time it takes to say a prayer - about 2 minutes.

When bathing here she wore a linen garment and changed into her flannel attire at bedtime. Other people bathed in their flannel and slept in the same wet garments, believing it to be very beneficial. This emulated the cold water wrappings practised in the early nineteenth century by Vincent Priessnitz in Gräfenberg, and by the hydropathic doctors of Malvern from the 1840s to the 1870s.

COMMENT

ST MUNGO

Despite the Crown's censure of pilgrimage to holy wells, Catholic resistance was strong, and many holy wells survived the religious upheaval of the sixteenth and seventeenth centuries. Little is known about St Mungo (d.612), but he may have been the illegitimate grandson of a British prince. He was a Scottish saint, though particularly honoured in north-east Yorkshire. Originally named Kentigern his tutor, Servanus, Bishop of Orkney, called him Monagh, an affectionate name which in Norwegian means a dear friend.[2] Mungo was a monk, following the ascetic Irish traditions, and was consecrated as bishop of the Strathclyde area by an Irish bishop. During a period of political disorder he was exiled in Cumbria, but later returned to Scotland. He died in Glasgow and was buried in Glasgow cathedral.[3]

According to William Camden, in about 560 A.D Kentigern, then Bishop of Glasgow, fled to Capgrave in Flintshire, where he established a Bishop's see and erected a monastery, having gathered together 663 brothers.[4] Of these, 300 were uneducated, so turned their hand to cultivating the land and feeding the other brothers, who dedicated their lives to divine service. The monastery apparently survived until the Dissolution in the 1530s.

ST MUNGO'S AS A PLACE OF PILGRIMAGE

Copgrove is an isolated community and has never had a population of more than 150. Its only notable features are St Michael's church and St Mungo's Well. St Mungo's may have been a place of medieval pilgrimage by Roman Catholics, judging by the enthusiasm with which they visited in the seventeenth century. Dr Edmund Deane in 1626 recorded that for a year or two Roman Catholics had flocked to the well on a daily basis, but time had erased any former virtues that the water might have possessed. Deane was a supporter of the Reformation and the new Anglican religion, and went to great lengths to disparage the old religion and St Mungo's. He wrote that it was resorted to by the common sort; that the reports of cures were fiction and lies and that the people who believed the tales of cures were credulous. He scoffed at the idea of cures being effected by water which was barely mineralised, saying that *"the many & severall cures, which have bin attributed unto them in those times, when they were so frequented, were rather fained, and imaginary, than true, and reall."*[5] Camden made no mention of St Mungo's in his late sixteenth century editions. Perhaps this was because it had seen a temporary reduction in popularity following the decline of Roman Catholicism, or he may have been playing down the significance of a Catholic stronghold.

Dr John French in 1652 wrote in *The Yorkshire Spaw* that *"St Mugnos' Well* [sic] *.... hath of late regained its reputation"*.[6] Its period of unpopularity may have been the result of Dr Deane's unfavourable comments 26 years earlier. French could only explain Deane's vitriolic comments as being those of someone who was not a Roman Catholic; if he were of that religion then clearly St Mungo was not his intercessor. French was not a Catholic either, but he still put St Mungo's amongst the four famous wells of Knaresborough.[7] These wells represented the modern scientific world, whilst St Mungo's represented the old world of the Middle Ages, with miracles and saints and gifts of healing. French clearly recognised the value of cold-water bathing in illness. His sentiments were endorsed by Thomas Fuller (1684), who wrote that the well was famous for *"the Sovereign Vertue of the Waters thereof..."*[8]

Roman Catholics were, and still, are superstitious about the number of times some actions must be repeated to be effective. A quotation by Dr Wittie (writing in 1660) regarding St Mungo's, is used as a footnote by the editor of the *Autobiography* of Mrs Alice Thornton, who visited Copgrove Well in 1656. *"It is a quick spring of great repute... [and] they must observe to dip five, seven, or nine times, more or less, according to custom or some think it will not do."*[9] Celia Fiennes visited St Mungo's Well on seven occasions, each time bathing seven times.

HEALING AT ST MUNGO'S WELL

Dr French (1652) described St Mungo's Well as square, with a high wall surrounding it. Adjoining it was a house where people prepared themselves immediately before going into the bath. The water was not mineralised; its effectiveness was due to its temperature, which was 49° F. In 1681 it was chillingly described as *"the coldest of all waters I ever knew"* and a letter from Dr Ellison of Newcastle, on 25 January 1700, said St Mungo's was *"an extream cold spring"*.[10] Invalids with a variety of complaints visited St Mungo's in search of a cure. The earliest writer on the subject, Dr Edmund Deane, suggested that *"both yong and old (especially the female sexe, as ever more apt to bee deluded) halt, lame, blind, deafe, dumbe, yea, almost all, and that for all manner of maladies and diseases, both inward and outward"* went to seek help.[11]

Dr French left a detailed account of the uses of the bath, and much of what he wrote was echoed by Celia Fiennes nearly half a century later. He strongly advised prospective bathers to consult a physician before going to St Mungo's, and adhere to any prescription they were given. He himself advised against such cold baths for youths, old men and thin, cold women. However, he noted that other women in poor health, perhaps who normally dared not even put their hands into water, put their linen on and bathed in St Mungo's despite it being much colder than ordinary water. When they got out they went to one of the nearby houses and went to bed in their wet linen. By early morning they would begin to sweat. This process relieved chronic aches and pains, agues, hard tumours, swellings, and other ailments caused by hot and cold humours. He explained that anyone staying in the water for a quarter of an hour or more would emerge looking very red and feeling very hot. This heat would continue for some time, regardless of their walking about in the cold or not getting dressed. He endorsed the cold water for people like Celia Fiennes who had to wear a cap because of a proneness to head colds. His prescription was to wash the head in the cold water two or three times a day. The coldness closed the pores which both let in the cold and let out the head's natural heat.

For patients who were liable to faint when bathing, he recommended that they should constantly have their mouth full of either cold water or cold beer. For patients who could not bear a complete bath, he advised a hip bath, where they could sit with water only up as far as the navel, a method of bathing he called incession. This method had the same effects as complete immersion, stimulating the appetite and digestion, provoking the bowels into action, repressing a "canine appetite"; staunching bleeding and heavy periods, and curing gonorrhoea, fevers and hydrophobia. A hip bath of warm water acted as a laxative and a diuretic, and eased stone and colic pains. Dr French criticised the English attitude to water curing. He wrote that at the German Spaw (now Spa in Belgium), patients were resigned to drinking the waters for 3 months to a year, depending on the severity of their illness. The English, on the other hand, wrongly believed that a cure could be effected in 2 to 4 weeks.[12]

In 1696 Dr Clayton, a Lancashire physician, first published a book about the well. In the second edition was written *"that people resorted there to be cured of fixed pains, with or without tumour, rheumatism, quartans, strains, bruises, rickets and all weaknesses of the nerves."*[13] Dr Ellison recorded that in June and July, children suffering from rickets were dipped *"in their Shifts and Night-Caps"*. A Dr Thomas Davison wrote that people of all ages, from 6 months to 80 years, were immersed. Children were dipped two or three times, and whilst in the water the *"Officious women"* at the well rubbed their backs and maimed parts. Adults stayed in the water for $\frac{1}{4}$ - $\frac{1}{2}$ an hour. No special diets were needed, but many had a draught of warm ale or sack afterwards. Distempered people went home to bed to sweat for a couple of hours or more. On the other hand healthy people *"go in for Pleasure, put on their Cloaths, and go their Business or Diversion"*. (This was similar to the sequence of bathing and bed at Buxton.)

The Reverend James Brome travelled to Copgrove at about the same time as Celia Fiennes. He reported that Cockgrave [sic] was noted for a well named St Domingo's, which was very effective in curing aches and pains but especially rickets.[14] He noted that large numbers of impotent and decrepit people were there in the summer, when many children were carried to the water and dipped into its icy coldness. He could not understand how people managed to bear the cold, so out of curiosity got into the water. The iciness took away any pleasure there may have been. Upon getting out he felt his body break out into a sweat with the contrast of the water and the summer air. This sweating was part of the curing process.

There are many case studies concerning cures at St Mungo's. Dr Baynard in 1701 reported one Lancashire lady who had distempers, was nervous and hysterical, thin and pale, with a decayed stomach, faint sweats and a low pulse. She had consulted ten or twelve doctors without success and tried every cure. Within a fortnight of being sent to St Mungo's she was restored to health.[15] Dr John Floyer (c.1697) saw a man at the well whose limbs were so numb that he could not feel a pin or needle being stabbed into them. He was very poor and in rags, and to support himself lay at the well side to receive alms from the wealthier visitors. He was helped into the water four or five times a day, and by the time he left Copgrove his skin had become so sensitive that he could feel a fly land on his leg.[16] This example reflects the social scene at that time. Rich and poor suffered bodily afflictions and both believed in the curing ability of the cold water. The lame poor were not ostracised, but received assistance from those who could offer it.

Travelling away from ones native parish was quite acceptable, until the traveller was in danger of being unable to support himself or herself financially. This might be due to sickness, pregnancy or impecunity. In these circumstances the foreign parish would quickly despatch the stranger to his own parish. This changed with the Act of Settlement of 1697, which dictated that travellers could only be returned to their native parish when they actually became chargeable on the parish in which they were temporarily residing. From the time of the Act, travellers were expected to carry a Settlement Certificate, stating who they were and the name of their parish of settlement, usually their native parish. Thus if they became chargeable, their native parish could be sent any bills for expenses. Occasionally a parish would send money to a sick parishioner who had had to move away in search of health. The poor man at the well seen by Dr Floyer was not chargeable to any parish since he was living off charity so was allowed to stay at Copgrove.

Floyer relates a story which he heard from one of the local Justices of the Peace. An old woman had been transported by cripple-cart to Copgrove from Liverpool, almost 100 miles away. After some time she went to the local JP

156

requesting a pass home. He was astounded that not only was she the old woman who had been crippled, but that she had been doing harvest work for a month in order to pay her way home. The pass would establish her as a bona fide traveller, not a vagabond, and enable her to travel unhindered from Copgrove back to Liverpool. Floyer noted that many lame people were transported to the well in cripple-carts.

The lame were taken to healing wells in cripple carts and hand barrows.
Detail from Der Jungbrunnen by Gemälde von Lucas Cranach (d.1546).
Courtesy of Staatliche Museen Preussicher Kulturbesitz, Berlin, Gemäldegalerie.

St Mungo's attracted much attention, from physicians interested in its healing powers and by people of all ages suffering from a wide range of disorders. Being in such a remote spot, news of its efficacy must have been carried by word of mouth. The veracity of the well's healing power would have been difficult to ascertain by those who lived a long way off. But its credibilty was sufficient to encourage many sick people to travel there in the hope of a cure. Visitors were not always lucky; the local parish register shows the following entry: *"A stranger yt came to ye Well and was buried May 29 1710"*.[17]

157

TODAY

An anonymous work published in 1765 noted that St Mungo's Well was no longer used, and it does not appear on Joseph Andrews' map of 1797 which shows over 200 mineral waters and bathing places in England.[18] It is fairly safe to assume that it was defunct, or its use severely curtailed by the second half of the eighteenth century. By 1922 the well appeared to be exactly as it had been in the seventeenth century - surrounded by a high red brick wall dating back to the seventeenth century. The bath was a rectangular cistern approximately 6 feet 4 inches wide, 6 feet 11 inches long, 4 feet deep, with a depth of water not exceeding 3 feet. There were five stone steps leading down into the water. The bath was still open to the elements; Dr Baynard in 1701 had condemned this, suggesting that the bath should be covered. By 1922 it was no longer possible to bathe as the water had apparently been diverted through lead pipes to Copgrove Hall. An inn was later built on the site of the bathing house. This was later replaced by a gamekeeper's lodge built by Henry Duncombe, then a gardener's cottage.

In 1987 the well was shown on the 1:25,000 O.S map SE 3470 6378 and described as St Monagh's Well. It was situated by a public footpath running from Copgrove village through the fields belonging to Copgrove Hall. In 1987 it was said that the well was contained in a large cistern built into a subterranean stream. A padlocked wooden cover prevented close inspection, though water could be heard flowing beneath, and the site was enclosed by a wooden fence.[19] The well-house was also named on the O.S map but no trace of it has survived.

In 1995 the authors visited the site and found that a cistern resembling a bath was situated beneath the patio of a new farm house. Of dressed stone blocks, the cistern measured approximately 6 feet x 6 - 8 feet. The length was difficult to determine because it stretched out of sight under the patio. It was almost certainly the bath which Major described in 1922. Access to the water was by two galvanised manhole covers. When the covers were removed the water was clear, appeared not to be flowing and was 114cm (45 inches) deep. The water is hard, coming off limestone; it is untreated and provides the domestic supply to the farmhouse. In a field adjacent to the house was a padlocked wooden cover resembling a door, set horizontally into the ground. Inside was a small pump house, situated at the bottom of a flight of stone steps. The pump house supplies water to several neighbouring houses, the nearest being a few hundred metres away.[20] Copgrove is still a small, isolated community. The church and manor house still exist, but the once famous well is now built over with farm buildings. It is forgotten by all except a handful of older people who have lived in the village for many years. It would be impossible to guess anything of Copgrove's past from the solitude of the village today.

ANALYSIS - supplied courtesy of Keith and Liz Hogg.

The following is an analysis of St Mungo's Well water. The sample was taken on 20 January 1994 from Wheatlands House, which is about half a mile from the well and privately supplied from St Mungo's.

Determinand	Units	Prescribed Result	Value
Nitrate	mg/l NO3	44.7	50
Chloride	mg/l Cl	37.8	400
Fluoride	ug/l F	374	1500
Sulphate	mg/l SO4	166	250
Sodium Total	mg/l Na	14.4	150
Potassium Total	mg/l K	1.82	12
Magnesium Tota	mg/l Mg	39.5	50
Copper Total	ug/l Cu	<10	3000
Zinc Total	ug/l Zn	21	5000
Aluminium Total	ug/l Al	<10	200
Lead Total	ug/l Pb	<5	50
Manganese Total	ug/l Mn	<1	50
Iron Total	ug/l Fe	<10	200
Temperature	Celcius	5.6	25
pH		7.22	5.5-9.5
Conductivity 20C	uS/cm	883	1500
Colour Filtered	Hazen	<1.2	20
Turbidity	ftu	<0.1	4

Taste : No taste
Smell : No smell

Footnotes:

1　Morris C. (ed.) 1947, *The Journeys of Celia Fiennes*, p.81-2.
2　Camden's *Britannia*, Gough R. (trans.) 1789, Vol.3, p.55.
　　Thomas Fuller in his *Worthies of England*, p.951 says that Mungo's Latin name was
3　Farmer D H. 1978, *The Oxford Dictionary of Saints*.　　　　　　Quentigernus.
4　Camden's *Britannia*, Holland P. (trans.) 1610, p.679.
5　Deane E. 1626, *Spadacrene Anglica*, reprinted 1922, p.73-4.
6　French J. 1652, *The Yorkshire Spaw*, p.1. French noted that the well was sometimes known
　　as St Magnus Well.
7　Today it is accepted that the "Knaresborough" wells are situated in Harrogate.
8　Fuller T. 1684, Worthies of England, p.881.
9　Major H D A. 1922, *Memorials of Copgrove Registers*, p.75; Wittie R. 1660, Scarbrough
　　Spa, p.142-3.
10　Hunter J. (ed.) 1830, *The Diary of Ralph Thoresby* 1677-1724, p.86; Major H D A. op.cit. p.76.
11　Deane E. op.cit. p.73.
12　French J. op.cit. p.1, 46, 49, 86, 121, 122.
13　Major H D A. op.cit. p.75.
14　Brome J. 1700, *Travels over England, Scotland and Wales*, p.213-4.
15　Major H D A. op.cit. p.77.
16　Floyer J. 1722, *The History of Cold Bathing*, p.213.
17　ibid. p.73.
18　Anon. but believed to be T. Short 1765, *A Treatise on the Cold Mineral Waters in England*, p.14.
19　Taylor I. 1987, St Mungo's Well and the Devil's Stone, Copgrove', *Source, The Holy Wells*
20　Information provided by Liz Hogg, owner of Well House, Copgrove.　*Journal*, No.7, p.28.

HARROGATE

Celia Fiennes visited Harrogate on her Northern Journey of 1697. Her journal records several visits to Harrogate over a short period as she explored the neighbouring towns and countryside. Harrogate she found wet and marshy and noted that there were four springs.[1]

1) The "Sulpher" or "Stincking Spaw" she found smelt strongly and was offensive. She likened it to carrion or a jakes (latrine). The water was clear on eruption but produced a white scum. There were two basins and springs and being "quick" springs they quickly cleared any turbidity. The water, she observed, came from the brimstone (sulphur) mines and the ground was bituminous (tarlike hydrocarbons). The water turned silver to the colour of copper. The water was reputed to be good for "scurbutick" humours and some drank a quart or two. Celia drank a quart each morning for 2 days and considered it a good purge. She likened the action to that of Bath water but without the warmth.

2) The "Sweet Spaw" or "Chalibiet" (later known as the St John's chalybeate) spring she found about a quarter of a mile from the "Stincking" Spaw. This water she likened to Tunbridge, the German Spaw (Spa in the Ardennes) or Astrup (Astrop) with its iron content, although it was not as strong as Tunbridge. She found a basin within an arched stone cover.

3) The "Common" water spring lay between the Sweet Spaw or Chalybeate and the Sulphur Springs and this she found good for washing the eyes and pleasant to drink.

We can deduce which spring Celia was referring to when she described the "Common" water. She noted that the Common Well was located between the Sulphur and St John's Chalybeate springs. Inspection of Jennings' modern map of the principal springs suggests that the main route into Harrogate from Knaresborough would mean that the St John's Chalybeate spring was passed before the Tewit Well.[2] Knaresborough is located to the west, beyond Starbeck. The "Common" well of Celia Fiennes was therefore likely the Tewit Well, about three quarters of a mile from the Old Sulphur Well. It was located on the common, later to become The Stray. The expression "Tewit" at the time was used by the vulgar people, which would explain Celia Fiennes' alternative nomenclature.[3] It will be shown that the Tewit Well enjoyed earlier fame but by the end of the seventeenth century was falling out of fashion in favour of the St John's Chalybeate.

4) The "Dropping Well" was the fourth spring that Celia found and this was located about 2 miles away on the outskirts of Knaresborough. She noted that it was a petrifying spring in that it turned things to stone. She observed that

grass, moss and other items were made crisp and stonelike when left in the water. Rising on a bank on a hill, the flow ran along a channel through a moorish area where there were pools of sulphurous smelling water. The clear spring then ran over a brow of a hill where it spread out, cascading over the rock and eventually finding its way into the river at Knaresborough. Where the water poured out there was an arbor where evening supper was taken to the sound of the Dropping Well.

COMMENT

From Celia's journal it is apparent that Harrogate was an established spa although she made little mention of anything other than the springs. The reason is that in 1697 Harrogate was still a small hamlet in the Royal Forest of Knaresborough, a situation which prevailed until about 1775.[4] She lodged at Knaresborough, a few miles from the wells. Knaresborough was where the tourist infrastructure was located in the seventeenth century and the economic focus of the local spa industry. It was not until later that development resulted in Harrogate securing the economic initiative. A visitor season had been established by 1632 and the locality was divided into two - Haregate Head (High Harrogate) was an exposed barren place where the Common and Tewit Springs were discovered whereas the Sulphur Springs were in Low Harrogate where the bogfields were situated. At the time of Celia Fiennes' visit two distinct spa villages were starting to emerge.[5] This situation still prevailed in 1799 when George Carey described the locality as a few scattered houses on a dreary common. The waters came in for similar scorn; Carey described them as tasting like rotten eggs and gunpowder.[6]

EARLY ACCOUNTS

It is necessary to research antiquarian spa texts for a more complete picture of Harrogate at about the time of Celia Fiennes' journey north.

In this respect we are fortunate in having Dr Deane's account of Harrogate available. This predates Celia Fiennes' visit by 70 or so years. Edmund Deane (1572-1640) was an eminent physician from York and he first published *Spadacrene Anglica* in 1626 with several subsequent reprints.[7] From this it is possible to deduce detail of the early establishment of Harrogate as a spa and correct a number of errors that have been perpetuated by later historians.

In *Spadacrene Anglica* Deane identified five springs in the locality justifying attention and these can be matched against those seen by Celia Fiennes. Both authors noted the Dropping Well. Celia's Harrogate Sulphur Well was one of three "stinking-wels" described by Deane. Deane also recorded the "Tuewhit" well, which Celia recorded as the Common water.

Tewit Or Common Spring

In spite of its importance in early Harrogate, Celia Fiennes paid little attention to the Tewit spring.

Deane noted that Harrogate's first celebrated spring, the "Tuewhit" Well (later Tewit) was discovered about 1570 by a Mr William Slingsby (1525/7-1606), not to be confused with his nephew Sir William Slingsby.[8] The spring was designated the "English Spa" c.1596 by Timothy Bright, MD (1551-1615). The name "Tuewhit" was derived from the pewits that once frequented the location to feed on the incrustation around the spring.[9] Stanhope published an account of a visit to the "Tuewhit" Well in 1625 which was recorded in *Newes out of Yorkshire*.[10] A party under the direction of Dr Deane visited the spring and noted that it was similar to the then already well-known and previously visited Spa in Germany. This comparison is confirmed as the Sauvenir and Pouhon springs by Deane[11] thereby establishing that the Spa referred to is the modern day town of Spa in the Belgian Ardennes. The town of Spa developed considerably as a watering place after 1550.[12] The "Tuewhit" spring was contained originally by Slingsby, with a stone surround, albeit requiring some cleaning by Deane's party before they could drink the waters. In comparing the "Tuewhit" well to the Sauvenir spring at Spa, Deane accredited its efficacy to the vitriolum (sulphate salts), otherwise called Chalcanthum (chalcanthite is a sulphate of copper ore $Cu_4SO_4(OH)_6$.[13]) Deane made no mention of chalybeate properties unlike Celia Fiennes when viewing the "Sweet" spaw. The water of the "Tuewhit" spring was particularly suited, according to Deane, for complaints of the internal organs and for cleansing the blood. Other applications included the dropsy, jaundice, dizziness, epilepsy and drying the moist brain; in children worms, gonorrhea, distemper and for ladies, the green sickness.

Deane proposed some caution in the indiscriminate use of the waters, suggesting that opinion from a suitably informed person was essential for the effective amelioration of the complaint. Some discussion was entered into regarding the application of the waters on dog-days. These are days of great heat resulting from Sirius, the dog star, rising with the sun and supposedly adding to its heat. Although the physicians of Classical times concerned themselves with such timings, between July 3rd and August 11th, Deane suggested that such considerations were less applicable in the climate of Yorkshire. He did recommend drinking when the air was pure, hot, clean and dry, the particular season being late June to mid September. This short season was to prevail throughout Harrogate's subsequent spa era. The fountain was avoided after rain until the water had replenished, presumably to allow rain water to be cleared by the mineralised water. Early morning drinking, either at the spring or at ones lodging, was preferred, the daily intake being steadily increased and then decreased over time. Diet recommendations make an interesting catalogue of available foodstuffs of the seventeenth century. The purging effect of the waters was crucial to the basic premise which was cure through a cleansing action.

A temple or gazebo, built over the Sulphur Well as a result of public subscription in 1807/8 was moved to the Tewit Well in 1842 and this is what can be seen today.

The Tewit Well.   *Old Sulphur Well Pump Room*

The Tewit Well or the English Spaw has geochemical similarities but is not the same mineralisation as Celia's "Sweet" spaw.

SWEET SPAW OR ST JOHN'S CHALYBEATE SPRING

Celia Fiennes' "Sweet spaw" was discovered much later than the Tewit, in 1631 by Michael Stanhope[14] who had previously written enthusiastically about the Tewit Well.[15] In 1632 Stanhope brought out *Cures without Care* extolling the virtues of the new-found spring and indicating that its location was on firm ground unlike the Tewit which was marshy.[16] The name St John's Well is a corruption of John's Well. John Hardestie was an attendant at the well for many years during the nineteenth century, living to a ripe age of 96 years. His name has become associated with the well but this is not a name that Celia Fiennes would have been aware of.[17] In 1656 the Sweet Spaw or St John's Chalybeate spring was contained with a walled structure with a low roof over a stone basin. Writing in 1734, Short described the containment as a basin of 18 pints with a pyramidal roof supported by four short pillars, the

whole surmounted by a ball. A surrounding ditch drained the rushy moist ground.[18] After its discovery it eclipsed the sixteenth century Tewit Well which went into decline.[19] The former containment was replaced in 1786 by Lord Loughborough who built an octagonal well house with pinnacled roof. Today's building replaced Loughborough's octagon in 1842.[20]

St John's Chalybeate Spring in the twentieth century.

THE SULPHUR OR STINKING WELL

Jennings (1974) proposed that several ancient holy wells in the locality were reputed as medicinal since the Middle Ages. The Sulphur Wells were frequented by the leprous. Although firm evidence is lacking, the two may have been synonymous.[21]

Deane is also one of the earliest references to the Sulphur Well. His text of 1626 identified the stinking wells. It is interesting to see that he noted that the sulphur springs were linked to the "mynes" and brimstone beneath the earth and that silver was turned the colour of copper by the water. These points are reiterated by Celia Fiennes who may well have learnt these facts from the 1654 third edition of Deane's work. Deane extended the list of complaints suited to the sulphur springs to include itches, scabs, morphewes, tetters and ring-worms. A large number of accounts of seventeenth century cures were also recorded by Grainge, particularly those relating to the relief of sores and ulcers.[22]

George Neale of Leeds was a doctor whose incomplete treatise *Spadacrene Eboracensis* was published in 1734 by Short in his *History of Mineral Waters*. This useful source of information was prepared by Neale about the time of Celia Fiennes' visit.[23] Neale had the upper of the three adjacent springs at the Stinking Wells redug and a substantial basin installed before 1675. He also had to take rapid remedial action when the Sweet Spaw was threatened by misguided landscaping. The success in improving the facilities and flow of mineralised water prompted similar treatment for the other two springs.[24] When Celia Fiennes visited she described two basins which suggests that the work was not completed.

By the mid-seventeenth century, bathing in hot sulphur water was established. Neale claimed credit for introducing the practice although there is evidence to suggest that it was carried out as early as 1652. There were more than twenty bathing houses in Low Harrogate by the time *Spadacrene Eboracensis* was written. The bathing houses were lodgings with tubs available for use. The treatment, which involved hot bathing followed by sweating in blankets, was supposedly good for rheumatism, muscular pains, sciatica and gout. Later Neale's son was to introduce a similar bathing arrangement at the bath house in Cold Bath Road. A century later similar practices were still being employed.[25]

There is evidence of some significant employment of local women in the spa industry around the time of Celia Fiennes' visit. Poor old women maintained the basins of the Sulphur Spaw in a clean condition. In addition to the bathing and lodging houses nearby, there was also a noisy crowd of water women, who would burst into private apartments offering to serve mineral water.[26] In view of the seasonality of the visitor trade, an interesting winter diversion was developed by those dependent on the Sulphur Wells for their livelihood. They would boil the mineralised waters in order to procure the salts which would be sent to all parts of the country, especially London.[27] This practice, as recorded by Neale, is contemporary with the extraction of Epsom Salts from the London spa waters. This controversial practice, it will be shown elsewhere, was to have far reaching implications in the case of Epsom.

The present-day pump room still gives visual access to two of the original well heads in the basement which Celia Fiennes would have seen. These were later covered by a temple or gazebo as a result of a public subscription in 1807/8. When the present day pump room was built in 1842 the temple was moved to the Tewit Well. In 1913 the pump room was provided with an extension. The waters of the Sulphur Well can still be sampled at the museum which now occupies the pump room building.

The growing popularity of Harrogate as a spa in the seventeenth century is evidenced by the accounts that have survived of visitors to the locality. *The Diary of Ralph Thoresby 1677-1724* notes that on 14th June 1681 he went from Leeds, where he lived, "*with cousins and much company to the Spaws, and 15, 16, 17. Drank the sulphur water plentifully;*" he also noted that he walked for health and recreation. Thoresby drank the waters again on the 18th June. On July 8th and 9th he spent both days drinking the waters at the spas, drinking "*at the usual times*" and again on 10th 11th and 12th July. He also visited Knaresborough and gathered some "*remarkable petrified moss*".[28]

POST CELIA FIENNES

There was a steady increase in spa related commerce in Harrogate during the eighteenth century. Improvements in transport and the reliability of the wells were crucial factors in eventually establishing Harrogate as a premier

Northern spa. The town arguably suffered from lack of capital investment and distance from London however. The success of the spa resulted in continual erosion of the common of the forest as more land was required for expansion. An enquiry of 1766 revealed 494 different encroachments since 1708.[29] The Forest of Knaresborough Enclosure Act came about in 1770 with amendments in 1774. As a result a new land owning class was established as land was distributed to local residents. In addition 200 acres of land known as The Stray were set aside near the springs as public open space.[30] This was enlarged in 1789 and remains an important part of Harrogate's townscape. Thereafter, triggered by the release of land and general industrialisation of the north, Harrogate was to prosper as an inland watering place until the general improvements in medicine and chemistry associated with the early nineteenth century resulted in a demise of the old spas and a more scientific approach to the healing properties of mineral springs.

GEOCHEMISTRY

By the late nineteenth century about 80 mineral springs were recognised in the environs of Harrogate.[31] This was recognised in the Borough motto "Arx Celebris Fontibus" on incorporation in 1884. The unique geology in turn gave rise to unusual geochemistry with each spring having its own distinct analysis. Today there are 94 springs within a 3 kilometre radius of Harrogate. Their distribution is closely related to the geological structure, being located along the axis of the asymmetrical Harrogate anticline. Most issue from the Carboniferous Limestone and are abundant in the vicinity of the Harrogate Fault. The more remote springs are less mineralised suggesting dilution by surface water.[32]

Harrogate waters are now generally considered to be meteoric waters, originating from precipitation. The saline content likely results from marine deposits from the Carboniferous Millstone Grit sequence.[33] Harrogate is situated on the eroded node of an anticlinal axis in which older strata emerge at the surface surrounded by younger rocks. This provides a route for deeper waters to percolate to the surface through a variety of rock sequences from the Magnesian Limestone and Millstone Grit beneath. The possibilities for different permutations of efficacy and cure are almost boundless and every combination of ailments responded in different ways to the plethora of variations and treatments available.

By the 1890s the waters were generally grouped as Sulphur or Iron with secondary classifications for various mineralisation within each group. The Old Sulphur Spring, noted by Celia Fiennes, was within the *Sulphur Group* waters under Class 2: the saline sulphur waters, type (a) Strong, with total solids from 30-130 grains. Both the Tewit spring and St John's spring were

166

under *Group 2, Iron Waters,* in class 1: pure chalybeate.[34] The Dropping Well found by Celia Fiennes was, by this time, considered outside of the town and of little importance medically.

ANALYSIS OF THE OLD SULPHUR WELL

	grains/gallon
Sodium sulphydrate	5.215
Sodium sulphide	-
Barium chloride	6.566
Strontium chloride	trace
Calcium chloride	43.635
Magnesium chloride	42.281
Potassium chloride	9.592
Lithium chloride	0.753
Ammonium chloride	1.031
Sodium chloride	893.670
Magnesium bromide	2.283
Magnesium iodide	0.113
Calcium carbonate	29.768
Magnesium carbonate	5.953
Potassium carbonate	-
Sodium carbonate	-
Barium sulphate	-
Strontium sulphate	-
Calcium sulphate	-
Sodium nitrate	-
Silica	0.701
Total	1047.561

gases in cu ins.	
Sulphuretted hydrogen	10.16
Carbon dioxide	40.10
Carburetted hydrogen	-
Nitrogen	-

Source: Morris and Penrose, 1895.

167

Analyses Of Tewit Well (1) And The St John's Well Or Sweet Chalybeate Spaw (2) Of Celia Fiennes.

grains/gallon	(1)	(2)
Ferrous chloride	-	-
Ferrous carbonate	1.358	1.271
Ferrous sulphate	-	-
Ferric sulphate	-	-
Aluminium sulphate	-	-
Calcium sulphate	0.697	0.307
Magnesium sulphate	-	-
Potassium sulphate	-	-
Ammonium sulphate	-	-
Barium sulphate	-	-
Potassium chloride	1.323	-
Sodium chloride	0.280	1.543
Ammonium chloride	trace	trace
Barium chloride	-	-
Strontium chloride	-	-
Calcium chloride	-	-
Manganese chloride	trace	-
Magnesium chloride	-	-
Lithium iodides, bromides, fluorides	traces	-
Barium carbonate	-	-
Calcium carbonate	1.435	2.246
Magnesium carbonate	2.667	3.039
Potassium carbonate	1.057	0.991
Sodium carbonate	-	1.338
Silica	1.041	trace
Organic matter	0.663	trace
Total	10.521	10.753
gases in cu ins		
Carbon hydrogen	11.85	14.95
Carburetted hydrogen	-	0.15
Oxygen	0.40	0.67
Nitrogen	5.53	6.35

Source: Morris and Penrose, 1895.

From the analysis the similarity between the Tewit and St John's Chalybeate waters can be observed in contrast to that of the Old Sulphur Well. The remarkably low ferrous content in the waters is noticeable in spite of classification of the Tewit and St John's as pure chalybeate. The famous chalybeate spring of Tunbridge Wells records a figure of 4.508 grains per gallon for Ferrous carbonate.[35]

168

Jennings published a useful modern day numerical indexing and location guide to the springs of Harrogate. The sources seen by Celia Fiennes can be identified.[36] The Tewit Well and St John's Well are numbers 72 and 73 respectively, both situated at High Harrogate. The "Sulpher" or "Stincking Spaw" is number 1. Jennings goes on to describe some 100 springs in total, some of which have been lost over time.

THE DROPPING WELL

The Dropping Well is outside the town of Harrogate, on the banks of the River Nidd at Knaresborough.

The long-famous Dropping Well at Knaresborough, a petrifying well, has the remarkable ability to deposit limestone calcareous scale over that which it flows. This ability is by no means unique and a similar ability is to be found in the springs of the Teme Valley in Worcestershire.[37] A further petrifying occurrence is recorded by Celia Fiennes at Apsley Guise. An alder tree stake driven into the ground turned to stone after seven years.[38] An early description of the Knaresborough Dropping Well is in Leland's *Itinerary in England 1535-1543*.

" *A little above Marche, but on the further ripe of Nidde, as I cam, is a welle of a wonderful nature, caullid Droping welle. For out of the great rokkes by it distillith water continually into it. This water is so could, and of such a nature, that what thing so ever fallith oute of the rokke and is touchid of this water, growith ynto stone: or els sum sand, or other fine ground that is about the rokkes, cummithe doune with the continualle droping of the springes in the rokkes, and clevith on such thinges as it takith, and so clevith aboute it and givith it by continuance the shape of the stone.* "
Leland then goes on to say that there was once a stone conduit made to convey the water across the river to the Priory of Knaresborough. This conduit fell into disrepair before the Dissolution.[39]

Evidence that the Dropping Well was once considered a healing well comes from Dr Elliot (1789). He considered that 3 or 4 half pints a day was judged a sufficient dose. The dose had previously been several quarts a day - no doubt a petrifying experience.[40] Slightly earlier in 1765 we have a good description of the Dropping Well. It rose up about 12-14 yards below the summit of coarse limestone. After a short cascade it divided over an isthmus of petrified rock generated by the water. The isthmus was 10 yards high and had slipped down from the river bank some 50 years previously. In the chasm so created were many beautiful rock formations. At the time it was not being drunk but deserved attention because of its healing potential which was clearly associated with its ability to solidify all it touched. The water was considered particularly suited to haemorrhages and fluxes. Suggested doses were a quart or 3 pints in a morning. The water should not however be taken with stimulating foods such as onions and peppers and should not be used where thickness of the blood was present or where relaxing, opening, cleansing and stimulating was required.[41]

The Dropping Well is also famous for its cave which was, according to legend, the haunt of an early prophetess. During the fifteenth century Agatha Sontheil lived near the Dropping Well. An encounter with a youth resulted in an amorous rendezvous, eventually followed by betrayal. The couple had become frequent companions and during one encounter the youth announced his immortality and that, in return for her acquiescence, would endow amazing powers, including the ability to foretell the future. The outcome was that Agatha and the youth integrated both on the cosmic and physical levels. As a result of the physical integration, in the summer of 1488, a child Ursula was born to Agatha in the cave at the Dropping Well. The child had considerable physical deformities and was put under the care of the parish. Agatha the mother retired to a convent, there to die. The convent may well have been the Priory of Knaresborough mentioned by Leland, which drew its water from the Dropping Well. This suggests that Agatha was perhaps associated with the Priory is some way before the incident with the youth, maybe as a well attendant.

Ursula was eventually to marry Toby Shipton and thereafter she became known as Mother Shipton. It became apparent that she had inherited the power of prophecy from her mother. Until her death in 1561 she enjoyed the reputation of esteemed oracle of her time. Her extensive prognostications, usually in verse, have been extensively published. Many argue that her prophecies are accurate predictions of events that are still unfolding.[42] Today the mythology is perpetuated in the visitor invocation: *"...when you wish within this Well, give your hand but never tell!"*. Like Ursula Shipton's prophecies, mythology, interwoven with science, continues to evolve in our attempts to

make sense of, and to give us direction, in the reality that we are confronted with. When Celia Fiennes visited the Dropping Well the prophecies of Ursula Sontheil would already have been a century and a half old.

The Dropping Well, Knaresborough, 1996.

170

Early references to the Dropping Well make no references to the cave of Mother Shipton[43] and it is possible that the cave and the prophecies are a later creation. This is borne out by the unlikely hypothesis that the sayings of Mother Shipton were told by one Joan Waller who had listened to the prognostications as a young girl and had relayed them just before her death at the age of 94 years.[44]

The Dropping Well has been a tourist attraction since 1630.[45] Dr Hunter in 1830 gives an analysis of the water as follows.

THE DROPPING WELL - ANALYSIS OF WATER

grains per imp. gallon.

Carbonate of Soda	6
Sulphate of Soda	132
Sulphate of Magnesia	11
Carbonate of Lime	23
Solid Content on Evaporation	172

Source: Hunter 1830.[46]

Modern analyses indicate that the presence of sulphates and carbonates in the water result in part from the dissolution of gypsum ($CaSO_4.2H_2O$) from the Middle Marls. In the catchment zone to the south and west of the spring, subsidence craters exist testifying to this action. In addition, the presence of strontium suggests that small amounts of celestine are dissolved from the Permian sequence.[47]

The petrifying action results from the deposition of calcium carbonate when the water is exposed to air. The action is similar to that which creates stalactites and stalagmites in cave systems. Tufa and Travertine stone are the products of such deposition. The former is of a porous nature whereas Travertine is dense and can be polished. Tufa is historically used for building stone in the Teme Valley in Worcestershire.

TODAY

Apart from the location of the springs, there is very little to see in Harrogate that would have been familiar to Celia Fiennes. Harrogate does however retain much of its nineteenth century spa heritage and this makes it an essential place to explore for the spa enthusiast.

There is a museum of the spa which is located in the Sulphur Well pump rooms and the waters of the Old Sulphur Well water can be consumed at the pump room. Harrogate offers a traditional Turkish Bath facility at the Royal Baths which captures the historic atmosphere of hot bathing. Couples can participate together at selected times otherwise there is segregation. Two hours should be allowed for full enjoyment. The Royal Baths complex is due to be redeveloped and it is hoped that the spa heritage will be a strong theme in the subsequent refurbishment. Harrogate Borough Council offers free Historical Guided Walking Tours of Low Harrogate five days each week during the season.

Footnotes:

1   Morris C. (ed.) 1947, *The Journeys of Celia Fiennes*, p.79-83.
2   Jennings B. 1970, *A History of Harrogate and Knaresborough*, p.284.
3   ibid. p.221.
4   Rutherford J. in "Deane E. 1626, *Spadacrene Anglica or the English Spaw Fountain*, 1922.
5   Jennings B. 1970, op.cit. p.222, 225, 228.
6   Carey G S. 1799, *The Balnea*, p.206-209.
7   Deane E. 1626, *Spadacrene Anglica or the English Spaw Fountain*, John Wright & Sons, reprint, Bristol, 1922.
8   "Tuewhit" is used in this text when discussing the early years of the Well; Tewit is used in a
9   Neesan M G. 1989, *Exclusively Harrogate*, p.3.   modern context.
10 Stanhope M. 1626, *Newes out of Yorkshire*, recorded in Butler A. 1922, p.24-26.
11 Deane E. op.cit. p.76.
12 Crismer L M. 1983, *The Extraordinary History of the Waters of Spa*, p.12.
13 Clarke F W. 1924, *The Data of Geochemistry*, p.678.
14 Hembry P. 1990, *The English Spa 1560-1815*, p.96.
15 Grainge W. 1871, *History and Topography of Harrogate and the Forest of Knaresborough*, Facsimile reprint by M Rigg Ltd. 1988, p.131.
16 Jennings B. 1970, op.cit. p.222.
17 Grainge W. op.cit. p.131 footnote.
18 ibid. p.131/2.
19 Neesan M G. op.cit. p.3.
20 Denbigh K. 1981, *A Hundred British Spas*, p.267,273.
21 Jennings B. 1974, *A History of the Wells and Springs of Harrogate*, p.6.
22 Grainge W. op.cit. p.132-5.
23 Short T. 1734, *The History of the Mineral Waters of Derbyshire, Lincolnshire and Yorkshire*,
24 Jennings B. 1970, op.cit. p.225.   p.286-293.
25 ibid. p.226, 235.
26 ibid. p.226, 228.
27 ibid. p.228.
28 Hunter J. (ed.) 1830, *The Diary of Ralph Thoresby 1677-1724*, p.86.
29 Hembry P. op.cit. p.206.
30 ibid. p.205/6.
31 Smith F W. 1899, *The Natural Mineral Waters of Harrogate*, p.36.
32 Cooper A H. Burgess I C. 1993, *Geology of the country around Harrogate*, p.77.
33 ibid. p.77-80.
34 Morris M. Penrose F. 1895, *The Climates and Baths of Great Britain*, a report by a committee of the Royal Medical and Chirurgical Society of London, Vol.l, p.540-557.
35 Morris M. Penrose F. 1895, Vol.II, p.172.
36 Jennings B. 1974, op.cit. p.21-23.
37 Lees E. 1856, *Pictures of Nature*, p.244-248.
38 Morris C. op.cit. p.341, 351.
39 Smith L T. 1907, *Leyland's Itinerary in England*, 1535-1543, parts 1-3, p.86.
40 Elliot J. 1789, *Nature and Virtues of the Principal Mineral Waters*, p.170/1.
41 Anon. but believed to be Short T. 1765, *A Treatise on the Cold Mineral Waters of England*, p.133-137.
42 Dropping Well Estate, c.1950, *The Life and Prophecies of Ursula Sontheil better known as Mother Shipton*.
43 Short T. 1734, "History of Mineral Waters", quoted in Calvert M. 1844, *A History of*
44 Windsor D. 1990, *Mother Shipton's Prophecy Book*, p.1.   *Knaresborough*, p.255/6.
45 ibid. p.33.
48 Calvert M. op.cit. p.256.
47 Cooper A H. Burgess I C. op.cit. p.79.

172

WIGAN

Celia's account of this part of her 1698 Great Journey gives an insight into the immense difficulties encountered by travellers in the late seventeenth century.[1] Although Liverpool to Wigan was only 14 miles, the journey took 5 hours. The 7 miles from Prescot to Wigan were along narrow lanes, some so stony that the travellers were forced to mount the steep banks at the sides.[2] The length of the miles also seemed to slow the journey. The statute mile of 1760 yards was defined in 1593, but in many parts of the country, particularly in the north, the "old mile" of 2428 yards was used. The old mile was 38% longer than the statute mile; consequently the 14 miles from Liverpool to Wigan would have been nearer 18 miles in the south of England. The party was travelling at about 3 miles per hour; Celia complained that had she been nearer London she could have covered 30 miles in the same length of time, so her anticipated rate was nearer 6 miles per hour.

Celia had nothing to say about Wigan except that it was a pretty market town with stone and brick buildings. Her interest was in the virtues of the "*Channell Coales*".[3] Cannel coal was regarded as the perfect coal. It lit very readily, burned for a long time, and with a brighter flame than other coal. It could also be made into saleable items. Once polished, it resembled jet or ebony, and could be fashioned into decorative and useful objects, such as saltcellars, inkstands and boxes. These were sent to London and often sold in shops selling marble artefacts, because most people could not tell the difference between Cannel coal and black marble. On occasions, when buyers knew of Cannel coal and were aware of a possible deception, they asked for a candle - to test whether they were buying marble or coal.

From Wigan, Celia went 2 miles out of her way to see the renowned Burning Well. The well was sited by a hedge and bank, approximately 100 yards from the Wigan to Warrington road. It was merely a hole in the ground full of dirt and mud. The water appeared to be boiling, and Celia was not sure whether it was one or several springs causing this phenomenon. Despite the boiling appearance, Celia dipped her hand in and found that the water was cold. A man at the well took a dish and scooped out as much of the water as he could. Then, taking the candle from his lantern, he lit a rush and set light to what appeared to be the water in the well. The flame would have been much stronger and higher, completely covering the surface of the well, but a downpour the previous evening had diluted the vapours emanating from the water. The flame was blue in colour, like that given off from burning spirits, and burned for quite a while. Several times the wind blew out the candle, and the man relit it using either the rush, or a spill of wood lighted by the flames in the well.

Celia could not understand what caused the water to burst into flames in this way. Her reasoning was that there was some sort of *"unctious matter"* (oil) in the ground around that area, which gave the springs their igniting property. Her verdict was reinforced when she noticed that when a hole was dug in the clay bank, more of the unctious matter was released, causing the fire to spread and burn more fiercely.

COMMENT

In his *Britannia*, Camden wrote that there was nothing to say about Wigan, which implies that in the late sixteenth century it had yet to develop as a mining area on any notable scale, and the remarkable properties of its coal were yet to be discovered.[4] When Celia Fiennes visited, 100 years later, all this had changed.

There is very little evidence to suggest that the water at the Burning Well was ever used medicinally. Dr John Elliot in 1789 described the water as a clear chalybeate, similar to the water of Islington and Hampstead, both well-known and fashionable spas.[5] This suggests a curative potential but actual use has not been verified.

The man with the candle was probably a local man - making a living from strangers' tips after he had shown them the remarkable properties of the Burning Well. Because of the unpredictable state of the roads, travelling would not have taken place at night. The man at the well had a lantern, however, which suggests that it was there primarily for setting light to the water for the benefit of tourists.

Defoe's natural cynicism is displayed in his short account of this well.[6] Local people, he said, tended to exaggerate the importance and wonder of their natural curiosities. In this case, they did not. Therefore it was of little distinction, so he did not go to see it. His decision may also have been made easier because he had travelled some distance in the wrong direction before he ever heard any mention of the well's existence.

Defoe, however, was impressed with the *"Canell or Candle Coal"*, and noted the mine's location as being on Sir Roger Bradshaw's estate at Haigh Hall, between Wigan and Bolton.[7] Celia passed Haigh Hall a generation earlier, when it was occupied by Sir John Bradshaw. She described the house as standing on a hillside in the middle of a grove of trees, near which were several fine walks and rows of trees. On a bank by a hedge, at the edge of the road, was a tall, carved, stone pillar with a ball on the top, It was a memorial to a cavalry officer who had died and been buried on that spot, and details of the event were inscribed in the stone ball. It seems that during a skirmish, the officer's horse had bolted in fear at the sound of the guns. Whilst jumping the hedge and ditch, the officer's sword was dislodged from its scabbard; when the horse threw its master he plunged onto the point of the sword and died.

THE BURNING WELL

It was observed that the Burning Well was at Ancliff in Lancashire, 3 miles from Wigan, and it was the inhabitants rather than tourists who had given it its name.[8] There was some doubt amongst early writers as to the cause of the well's ability to ignite, but it was generally agreed that even when the well was emptied, the vapour caught light and burned brightly and vigorously. Dr Leigh described the well as sulphurous, but Dr Russel's book said he was mistaken because the water neither smelled of sulphur nor discoloured silver. Russel (1769) believed the vapour to be petrol-based, because there were many coal seams in the immediate vicinity and the well itself was near a coal mine. Monro, writing at about the same time as Russel, credited the phenomenon to the flammability of rising bituminous vapours.[9] The extent of the coal seams in the area, and its concomitant vapours, would explain Celia's comment about the flame spreading when further holes were dug into the nearby bank, releasing more of the easily ignited vapours.

Celia Fiennes did not know what caused the coal to *"give a snap"* when lighted,[10] but modern science shows that the exploding vapours were methane gas. Methane is the simplest hydrocarbon, and is found wherever decomposition of animal and vegetable matter occurs, either under water or in coal mines. Methane is a light carburetted hydrogen (carbon and hydrogen mixed) found especially in coal mines, and when mixed with seven or eight parts air can make a violent explosion. When a lighted candle was held near the well, the vapour sprang alight. Russel likened it to brandy burning on a Christmas cake. He also noted that in calm weather the surface of the water remained completely covered with the flame. Like Celia Fiennes, he found that the water itself was cold, but that eggs and meat could be cooked on the heat of the flame.

Richard Gough (1789), publishing 20 years after Monro and Russel, recorded that the Burning Well lay about one and a half miles from Wigan.[11] The remainder of his text indicates that he studied the others' works before going to Wigan, if indeed he went there at all, and his work was influenced by his reading. Alternatively his work, like that of some other writers, was based to a certain extent on the information he had been supplied with by the man at the well. Gough wrote that when the well was emptied a sulphurous vapour broke out, resulting in the water bubbling, as if boiling. When a candle was applied, it burned like brandy. On a calm day the flame might burn all day, giving off enough heat to boil eggs or even meat; also that the water remained cold, despite the bubbling, and when water was taken out of the well the bubbling ceased.

In the same year that Gough published, Dr John Elliot published his opinion of the mineral well at Wigan.

"It is a clear chalybeate water, resembling those of Hampstead and Islington. From the bottom rises an inflammable vapour, which takes fire at the surface on the approach of a lighted candle."[12]

This does not suggest that people drank the water, as at Hampstead and Islington; merely that the water was ferruginous.

Both this Burning Well and that at Broseley, Shropshire, are now lost; the former deliberately, the latter by neglect.[13]

CANNEL COAL

"Cannel" as a word is probably of Northern origin, and there are several suggestions as to its derivation. In the early eighteeth century the name was thought to be a form of the word candle, or so called because people in the areas where the coal was manufactured did not use candles but worked by the light of the coal, which burned as brightly as a candle. The coal also burned without smoke, like a candle.[14]

It was also known as Scotch coal, though this probably referred particularly to the Cannel coal which was mined at Tyneside. In Scotland it was known as parrot coal. Due to its expense it was chiefly used on special occasions, as Sheridan narrated in *A Trip to Scarborough*. When Sir Tunbelly Clumsy thought his daughter's wealthy suitor was at the door, he ordered the servant to prepare the house for such an important visitor:

"...run in a-doors quickly; get a Scotch coal fire in the parlour, set all the Turkey work chairs in their places, get the brass candlesticks out, and be sure stick the socket full of laurel..."

The Burning Well was clearly situated above or within a seam of this highly flammable Cannel coal. The coal was very cheap in the areas where it was mined, but was also very unusual, and Daniel Defoe knew of no other like it. It burned as soon as a lighted candle was put to it, yet stayed alight as long as regular coals. Evidence of its combustibility is shown by the test for authenticity carried out at the shops in London, where it occasionally masqueraded as marble. It burned regardless of the way the pieces were put into the grate - whether flat or irregular, vertical or horizontal, and because of its versatility

Defoe pronounced it the best sort of coal. It was transported to London, but by the early eighteeth century was so expensive that few could afford it.[15] Like Celia Fiennes, Defoe noted that the coal was as black as jet, and could be used decoratively. When broken open, the faces were smooth and could be polished like alabaster. After being polished, the faces were so clean that the pieces could be put into a lady's cambric handerchief without leaving a mark.

Cannel Coal is a bituminous coal with a high carbon content of 85 - 90%. It is rich in volatile matter including hydrogen, an essential ingredient of animal and vegetable matter, which causes it to burn with a pale blue flame.[16] The origins of Cannel coal are not quite the same as normal coal. Normal coal is the remains of vegetable matter which lived and died either on the soil, or in swamps. Cannel coal was more likely also to contain not only fossilised material, but transported material which originated in lakes. This included fossil fish, which normal coal did not have.[17] It is the fish remains which are the source of nitrogen in the coal, and for this reason Cannel coal is higher in nitrogen than regular coals.[18]

In Britain, Cannel coal was found only in Wigan and Tyneside; the Wigan seams were virtually exhausted by the second half of the twentieth century.[19]

Footnotes:

1 Morris C. (ed.) 1947, *The Journeys of Celia Fiennes*, p.184-5.
2 ibid. p.184-5.
3 Cannel coal is a bituminous coal which is used for making gas and oils and burns with a bright lame.
4 Camden's *Britannia*, Holland P. (trans.) 1610, p.749.
5 Elliot J. 1789, *An Account of the Nature and Medicinal Virtues of the Principal Mineral Waters of England and Ireland*, p.281.
6 Defoe D. 1927, *Tour of the Whole Island of Great Britain*, Vol.II, p.267.
7 By the early nineteenth century, 4 square miles were being mined at Haigh - Marshall W. 1818, *County Reports to the Board of Agriculture*, Vol.1, Northern Department, David & Charles reprint, p.252.
8 Russel R. 1769 (5th edition) *Dissertation on the use of Sea Water* with anonymous supplement *A Treatise on the Nature, Properties and Uses of the Mineral Waters*, p.306.
9 Monro D. 1770, *A Treatise on Mineral Waters*, Vol.I, p.166.
10 Morris C. op.cit. p.185.
11 Camden's *Britannia*, Gough R. (trans.) 1789, p.138.
12 Elliot J. op.cit. p.281.
13 Short T. 1740, *History of the Principal Mineral Waters*, p.39.
14 Defoe D. op.cit. p.266; North R. 1826, *Lives of the Norths*, Vol.1, p.294, from a footnote in Morris C. op.cit. p.185; Scott J. 1973, *Palaeontology an Introduction*, p.33.
15 Defoe D. op.cit. p.267.
16 Hydrogen was formerly known as inflammable air; see *The Oxford English Dictionary*, 1989, 2nd edition.
17 Scott J. op.cit. p.33.
18 Clarke F W. 1924, "The Data of Geochemistry", Bulletin 770, *U.S Geological Survey*, p.769-770.
19 Stamp L D S. Beaver S H. 1964, *The British Isles, A Geographic and Economic Survey*, p.301.

ST WINEFRIDE'S WELL, HOLYWELL

Holywell, in Flintshire, is a most unusual spa. It is renowned not only for the coldness of its water but for its remarkable curing history which has lasted continuously for over 900 years.

Celia Fiennes visited Holywell during her Great Journey of 1698. En route, she stopped in Chester to admire its beautiful medieval buildings. The mayor of Chester, Mr William Allen, was a friend of Celia's brother-in-law, and provided an escort for the rather perilous part of Celia's journey across the Dee sands. This treacherous part of her journey completed, she went to Hawarden to stay with her cousin Ann Fiennes and her husband Dr Percival, the local minister.[1] From Hawarden it was a short journey into Flintshire. The name amused Celia, because there were no flints at all in the county. Instead, she saw an immense number of coal mines, which were reached through "wells" similar to the coal mines she had seen at Chesterfield and the iron ore mines near Buxton. The coal was hauled up through the "wells" in baskets holding about two bushels each. In some areas there were so many mines close to the surface that the roads were in danger of collapsing. Being so close to the sea, the mines needed constant draining and horses were employed to turn the great wheels which drew up the water.

Hawarden was just 8 miles from Holywell - the site of St Winefride's Well, ancient and much visited. Both rich and poor knew of its curative properties but it was the rich, royalty and aristocracy, who had contributed towards the vast and elaborate surroundings which displayed the well's importance. Celia's impression was of a stone construction, supported on pillars, which resembled a triumphal arch or tower. Three sides of the well were paved; the fourth acted as a receptacle for the water which gushed from the well. At the source of issue, several springs bubbled up fiercely into a circle "*which is 8 square walled in*".[2] What she saw was a polygon, surrounded by flagstones which were set in the formation of two squares. One square was superimposed on the other, resembling an eight-pointed star.[3] Lying at the bottom of the well were nine red-tinged stones laid in an oval. The colouring was reputedly the blood of the murdered St Winefride. The water was as clear as crystal, and it was at this walled square well that visitors drank. Celia described the water as being like a good spring water, which would make a delightfully refreshing drink if it were mixed with wine, lemon and sugar.

From the drinking area the water flowed into a rectangular bath, then beneath a bar (stone barrier), before streaming away downhill. Above the drinking and bathing area was the vast stone arch, and beneath it a set of steps where the bathers could descend to the bath. Bathers walked through the bath, emerging at the other side in full view of lookers-on. These were both visitors to the well and passers-by in the street which ran alongside. The bathers' wet costumes had by this stage become transparent, and Celia could only be persuaded to enter the water when some curtains were arranged to shield her from the prying eyes. She liked the clear, cold water, and the fact that it was fast flowing, but it failed as a pleasant summer bathe because it was too shallow to dive and wash in. It was the same depth as the other holy well she visited - St Mungo's at Copgrove.

St Winefride's Well, from R M Zornlin's **World of Waters**, *1855.*

By the time of Celia's visit, St Winefride's Well had been a place of Roman Catholic pilgrimage for centuries. Celia noticed that the pilgrims, unlike her, were not at all perturbed by the transparency of their garments. Most had gone there to be cured of *"lameness's and aches and distempers"* and probably believed that they would be safeguarded by the Saint against all indecencies, privations or illness.[4] Most pilgrims spent much of their time kneeling in prayer, and in a rare mood of cynicism and priggishness Celia described them as *"deluded into an ignorant blind zeale"*, to be pitied by those more educated, such as herself, who knew better. She marvelled also at the Catholics' gullibility in buying useless religious souvenirs from the poor locals, who fished out red-coloured stones from the well and sold them as relicts. Moss grew round the sides of the well, and the locals sold this as well, the pilgrims believing its existence was due in part to the waters of the sacred spring. Each day the locals would gather more moss from the nearby hills and stick it round the sides of the well in readiness for the following day's ingenuous tourists.

Celia was faintly disgusted by the inhabitants of Holywell, who spoke Welsh and walked barefoot and bare legged, a quite unseemly state of affairs to a woman of her proprieties. On the other hand, their food was good: the mutton was sweet, despite the sheep being no bigger than lambs, and the wine and fish, including salmon and eels, were extremely palatable.

COMMENT

ST WINEFRIDE

Winefride (Gwenfrewi in Welsh), was the legendary seventh-century daughter of a local prince, Tewyth, and his wife Gwenlo and her uncle was St Beuno. One day Caradoc, a chieftain from Hawarden, tried to seduce Winefride. When she ran away he pursued her and cut off her head, *"...and after the hede of the Vyrgyne was cut of and touchyd the ground...sprang up a welle of spryngyng water largely endurying unto this day, which heleth al langours and sekenesses as well as in men as in bestes, which welle is named after the name of the Vyrgyne and is called St.Wenefrede's Welle..."*[5] On espying the headless corpse as he was leaving the local church, St Beuno placed the head back onto Winefride's body and after some prayers she returned to life. Following this incident a white scar was always visible round her neck. Caradoc was never seen again. Winefride became a nun and Abbess of the convent at Gwytherin. She died there and was buried in the local churchyard. In 1138 her remains were exhumed and reburied at Shrewsbury Abbey. This legend was not written down for 500 years after her death, but it is a popular Welsh story. The martyrdom of St Winefride is celebrated on 22 June, and her death on 3 November.[6]

EARLY HISTORY OF THE HOLYWELL

The first documented evidence of the existence of a holy well here is in 1093, when a well and chapel at "Haliwel" were granted by the Countess of Chester to the Benedictine monastery of St Werburg in Chester. In 1240, following wars in Wales, the well and chapel were granted by the Welsh Prince Dafydd ap Llewelyn to the Cistercian monks of Basingwerk, who were custodians until the Reformation in 1537.

It is said that by 1115 St Winefride's Well was very famous and much resorted to, notably by royalty. Richard I visited in 1189, and Henry V in 1416 following the Battle of Agincourt. Edward IV also visited, and it is said that afterwards he put some Holywell soil on his crown; Richard III paid 10 marks per annum towards the salary of the priest at the well.[7]

The ceiling bosses are reminders of this early royal patronage. One can still see the emblems of Queen Catherine of Aragon (three pomegranates in a shield surmounted by a crown), and the Tudor arms of the dragon and greyhound, or talbot. Until 1770 the walls of the well were painted with the legend of St Winefride; all that remains is a red colouring in the well's central vaulting.

No exact date survives for the building of the well, its late Gothic surround, and the chapel. The complex was thought to have been erected before 1495 because the arms of the Stanley family, the earls of Chester, were carved into the stonework above the well, and Sir William Stanley was beheaded in 1495. One of the chief benefactors was said to be Lady Margaret Beaufort, Countess of Richmond. Her influence is suspected partly because it was she who paid for the construction of nearby Mold parish church, and partly because her coat of arms is depicted here at Holywell, though there are many coats of arms in the complex. It may also be that her interest was particularly keen through her marriage to the Welshman Edmund Tudor.

Lady Margaret's interest in St Winefride passed to her son, Henry VII, who commissioned a statue of the Saint for his chapel in Westminster Abbey, which was completed in 1512. The polygonal "star" shape of the well resembles the star in Henry VII's Abbey chapel. The Westminster chapel and the early sixteenth-century restoration of Bath Abbey were the work of Robert and William Vertue, masons to Henry VII and masters of fan vaulting. Following Robert's death, William built St George's Chapel, Windsor. If the Vertues also designed the star here at Holywell, it would date the well at 1503-19.[8]

FFYNNON FAIR (ST MARY'S SPRING)

There is also a polygonal star at Ffynnon Fair in Cefn, near St Asaph. The earliest mention of this spring is on a map of the 1570s, though following archaeological excavations in the 1960s it was established that a building had existed on the site since the thirteenth century. Phase two of the complex was completed at the end of the fifteenth century, and the star could be either late fifteenth or early sixteenth century - contemporaneous with the Holywell star. Ffynnon Fair and its adjacent chapel were extensively visited by pilgrims until the Reformation. Recusant Catholics continued to visit until the Commonwealth, when the chapel was defaced and the roof stripped. Pilgrimages were reintroduced during the reign of James II whose wife, Mary of Modena, was most generous to the Catholic priests at Holywell. Most pilgrims visited both Ffynnon Fair and Holywell.[9]

THE HOLYWELL CHAPEL

The chapel, which measures 52 feet by 20 feet, is situated above the well. In the 1480s or 1490s an earlier chapel was replaced with the present Perpendicular Gothic chapel, possibly by Lady Margaret Beaufort. Today the stained windows in the chancel display the arms of Sir William Stanley, Earl of Chester and Knight of the Garter. His badges are the eagle's leg and the three legs of the Isle of Man. Also shown are the talbot and red dragon, the arms of England during the reign of Henry VII. Royal patronage was maintained when, in 1686, the Catholic James II and his wife Mary of Modena came here to beg St Winefride to bless them with a son. Their prayers were answered two years later. Following their visit Queen Mary made a gift of the well to the Jesuits and a commemorative stone inscribed with the date 1687 can be seen in the side of the well.

Twenty five years before Celia Fiennes' visit Richard Blome commented that the chapel above the well was of freestone. In the chancel was some glass depicting aspects of St Winefride's life, her savage death and her timely resuscitation.[10] This glass has gone, but visitors to Holywell can still see St Winefride's legend depicted in stained glass in the nineteenth century Roman Catholic church, which is situated between the well complex and the Beaufort Arms inn. In 1723 the well chapel was taken over by Protestants and used as a schoolroom, and the Star and the Cross Keys inns were used as chapels by the local Roman Catholics.

A PLACE OF PILGRIMAGE

Miracle cures took place here; it was a holy well rather than a popular health resort such as Bristol, Tunbridge and Bath. In 1703 the Roman Catholic Nicholas Blundell and his wife, plus his man and her maid, made a five-day pilgrimage to Holywell. The first two days were spent travelling, the third day spent in prayer and bathing, and the last two days on the return journey. Mrs Blundell visited again in 1710 after a bad attack of the gravel. She drove as far as Liverpool and hoped to walk the last few miles, which would have meant negotiating the Dee sands, as Celia had done. This was very much in the spirit of a pilgrimage.[11] Blundell's diary refers to several three-day pilgrimages to Holywell by his servants and labourers.

Numerous writers have commented on Holywell's attraction to Roman Catholics. Thomas Fuller in the 1680s wrote that superstitious pilgrimages were still made to the well by people who lived in the county, adding that perhaps the Welsh proverb "*Goreu Pererindod Cyrchu offeren sull*" (the best sort of pilgrimage is to undertake regularly ones divine duties on the Sabbath) might be more appropriate.[12] Daniel Defoe, writing in the 1720s, detected vast numbers of visiting Roman Catholic priests.[13] One must be wary of the tone of such comments. Most were about adherents to the old, disgraced Catholic religion, written by Anglicans or Nonconformists who were in their own ways just as superstitious. For example, in the 1660s Samuel Pepys wore a hare's foot round his neck to ward off illness, and in March 1791 James Woodforde, a country parson, tried to cure a stye by rubbing it with the tail of his black tom-cat.

Holywell remained a place of pilgrimage, despite the Reformation and conflicts with Protestant authority particularly under Elizabeth I. Attempts had been made by Henry VIII's ministers to curb the perennial flow of pilgrims to holy wells, notably to Buxton. In 1579 Queen Elizabeth instructed the Council of the Marches "*To discover all Papist activities and recommend measures for suppressing them...to pay particular attention to St. Winefride's Well and in view of the claim that the water is medicinal to appoint two men to test its properties; if not medicinal the Well should be destroyed...*"[14] Despite these threats to its existence, the well and chapel continued to be maintained by the Jesuits, and to this day remain a centre for Roman Catholics.

Although Holywell was a popular place of pilgrimage, its facilities remained primitive. During the seventeenth century the only places to stay were the Star and Cross Keys inns. It was in the latter that Nicholas Blundell, his wife and their servants, stayed during their pilgrimage in 1703. Celia did not record an overnight stay, so we must assume that she did not take advantage of these lodgings.

Daniel Defoe noted that the majority of buildings in the town were either public houses or houses used as lodgings.[15] It may have been the lack of aristocratic lodgings which deterred the gentry from further afield, and ensured that Holywell was chiefly frequented by less demanding visitors from North Wales. By the 1780s the sparse accommodation would not have been such an inconvenience, since Thomas Pennant wrote that visitor numbers had greatly decreased and that the majority of pilgrims were from neighbouring Lancashire.[16]

Another likely reason for Holywell's attraction to pilgrims and the sick, rather than to the aristocracy, may have been its lack of entertainment. From the mid-seventeenth century to the late eighteenth century many spas provided facilities for dancing, gaming, debauching, music, souvenir shopping, eating and drinking. None of these diversions were provided at Holywell. The souvenirs were of a religious quality; relaxation time was spent, according to Elizabeth Blundell, in reading the Bible and discussing theological matters, and exercise was walking in the shade of the trees which were laid out in irregular groves.[17]

THE WATER

The well water was remarkably clear, pure and pleasant-tasting, and was used by the local inhabitants for all their domestic purposes. This was the advantage of the low mineral content. At other spas the high mineral content meant that, taken internally, the waters would have a major effect on the constitution, as in the case of Epsom water. Despite Holywell's purity, there was no reason to doubt the medicinal efficacy of its water in certain disorders. These were precisely those for which Malvern's Holy Well spring was frequented at the same time, and where eye complaints, cancers, old ulcers, skin conditions, kidney complaints and glandular obstructions were all being successfully cured.

William Saunders in 1805 described St Winefride's Well as rising out of limestone, and one of the finest and most copious springs in the kingdom.[18] One traveller, who visited Holywell 25 years before Celia, observed that the flow of the spring was sufficient to drive a mill.[19] Another traveller, writing shortly after Celia's visit, reiterated that the mill was driven by the flow.[20] Thus we know for certain that Celia Fiennes was also aware of the utilitarian function of the water apart from curing.

From the 1830s there were nineteen major factories sited between the well and the sea, all relying on the Holywell water for power. Prior to 1917 one source gauged the flow at 21 tons per minute, another at 100,000 gallons per minute and Dr Johnson's estimate in 1774 was 100 tons per minute. It is widely acknowledged that if the huge stones were not placed over the source, the artesian force would cause the water to hit the ceiling.[21] In January 1917 tunnelling in the vicinity staunched the flow, and work ceased at the factories. Nine months later the flow was reinstated but was weaker than previously. The factories in Greenfield, below the well, never recovered from the hiatus in production.[22] Today the flow is estimated at 10 million litres per annum; Greenfield is a sad reminder of the area's industrial heritage.

The factory nearest to the well was St Winefride's Brewery, which closed in the 1920s. In the 1930s the land was bought by the Catholic church and the buildings demolished to make way for the green which now fronts Holywell.

BATHING

Access to the well was from the road via a doorway which is now kept locked except on special occasions. The door is situated opposite the statue of St Winefride which nestles in its Gothic niche. Once at the well-side it was the custom for pilgrims to descend the four steps into the water of the narrow bath, walk through the water and up the steps at the other side; then walk in a clockwise direction round the back of the walled star shape. This was performed three times. Finally, the pilgrim bathers would walk under the bridge and complete their ritual by kneeling on St Bueno's Stone from which, it is said, the saint had instructed St Winefride.[23] This stone is now cemented to the bottom of the bathing area, to the right of the steps. Celia mentioned Catholics kneeling in the water, but did not indicate that there was anything ritualistic about the procedure. Another seventeenth century traveller remarked that pilgrims visited out of blind devotion, some for the good of their soul, others for the good of their bodies.[24] However, Thomas Pennant pointed out that this over-zealousness had cost a few lives; possibly the great coldness of the water had induced fatal hypothermia.[25] Some pilgrims knelt around the well mumbling over their beads and kissing the stones reverentially, crossing themselves with the holy water to drive evil spirits away.

The ritual attached to bathing dates back to that part of the legend when St Bueno was instructing Winefride. He advised that anyone who came to the well and asked for cures by invoking her name should have to ask at least three times before receiving an answer. This was interpreted as meaning that those making requests for help would have to bathe three times before their prayers were answered.[26] The Reverend Christopher David in his history and guide to St Winefride's, says the custom probably originates from the Celtic custom of triple immersion. Trine immersion was also advocated by the fathers of the early Christian church. St John Chrysostom (A.D c.347-407), one of the Greek doctors of the church, interpreted the word baptize as *"Trina mersione baptisma cuique tribuere"*. The trine immersion is perhaps best described in *de Sacramentis* by St Ambrose (A.D c.334-397), one of the Latin doctors of the church. He wrote that those about to be baptized were asked *"Dost thou believe in God the Father?"* and on answering *"I do believe"* were dipped into the water; on answering *"I do believe"* to the second question, *"Dost thou believe in the Lord Jesus Christ?"* they were dipped again. The same answer would be given to the third question, *"Dost thou believe in the Holy Ghost?"*, at which the third immersion took place. This custom signified faith in the Trinity and recognition of the three days which Christ spent in the tomb. Desiderius Erasmus (1467-1536), the German scholar and theologian, noted that the practise of triple immersion was retained in England long after it had died out in other parts of Europe.[27]

BATHING COSTUMES

Visitors to the early healing wells - Bath, Buxton and St Winefride's - could never be sure in advance what type of bathing costume would be available. Buxton apparently did not have costumes for hire or sale at all, because John Floyer noted disapprovingly in 1697 that the bathers were naked. Celia did not mention naked bathing at Buxton, because the sexes bathed separately and so did not cause embarrassment. From Celia's accounts, it appears that Bath offered the best quality linen garments - matching drawers and waist-coats for the gentlemen and stiff yellow canvas gowns for the ladies. These billowed out as they filled with water, disguising the shape of the body. At Holywell, where mixed bathing was the custom, the poor were not so lucky. Attempts to hide their nakedness were thwarted as the water caused cheap, thin, linen garments to cling exposingly to their bodies.[28] As late as 1774 Dr Johnson wrote of St Winefride's that *"...the bath is completely and indecently open: a woman bathed while we all looked on*".[29] Originally the road leading past the well was much lower, and from the road passers-by could walk into the gallery above the bathing area and watch the bathers. Bath also had viewing galleries. It was not until 1875 that the Jesuit fathers at Holywell built bathing cubicles and installed screens to protect the bathers from public eyes.

SOUVENIRS - SWEET MOSS AND RED STONES

Camden, in the late sixteenth century, recorded that Holywell was renowned for the sweet, pleasant-smelling moss which grew there.[30] Richard Blome mentioned that the country people believed that the sweet moss was St Winefride's hair.[31] James Brome also noted that the fragrant moss growing at the well-sides was supposedly produced from St Winefride's hair. He found that shortly after gathering the moss the sweet smell dissipated. Celia Fiennes mentioned the moss, but not the fragrance. During the seventeenth century the moss was dried and woven into wreaths which were sold for their healing properties. It is also said to have been taken away and dried before being made into hair poultices. Thus it appears that the "hair" was taken for healing purposes rather than as souvenirs, which Celia Fiennes suggested. Thomas Pennant, a naturalist and historian, identified the moss as *Jungermannia asplenoides*, which is found in other holy wells.[32] He also examined the red stones, and found that the colouring was caused by a velvet-like growth, *Byssus Jolithus*. Brome also noted the "blood-stained" stones, and saw pilgrims collecting both stones and holy moss as relics; today neither are found at the well.

Crutches left at the well-side. The display of such relics is no longer fashionable.

Holywell's miraculous ability to cure lameness was manifested by the number of crutches which visitors left behind them, and which filled the crypt until the 1960s. The majority of cures seem to have been connected with lameness. For example, in 1918 an incurable consumptive patient was discharged from a hospital in Liverpool. After bathing once at the Holywell she could walk unassisted; a second immersion caused an excretion of phlegm, following which she was never again troubled. Other types of cure were effected. Coverage in the Liverpool *Courier* of 6 August

186

1623 relates the story of a baby being cured of blindness after being immersed in the cold water. Many letters survive, written by former invalids, which detail the various successful cures.

FFYNNON BEUNO (ST BEUNO'S WELL)

In a depression in a field on the hillside above St Winefride's Well is St Beuno's Well. It is said that it was here that the virgin was martyred. Her decapitated head rolled down the hill and rested on the spot from which the Holywell spring now issues.

TODAY

The healing rituals continue today. On Sunday 14 May 1995 the authors visited St Winefride's Well and found a man whose paralysis had been cured by bathing there. An elderly Roman Catholic from North Wales, he had been paralysed down one side following an accident. He was confined to a wheelchair, and doctors confirmed that he would never walk again. The invalid had bathed ritually at the well twice a week for the past 18 months. His ritual was to roll his trousers above the knee and stand in the motionless water of the bathing chamber between the stone screen and the bridge for the 2 to 3 minutes it took to say a prayer. He then got out and sat on the stone seat nearby for a further 2 to 3 minutes before going back into the water. This procedure was carried out three times. The man could walk unaided, although very slowly, which is not unexpected at 84 years of age.

Today, pilgrims of all denominations are welcomed at Holywell. The well is open at most times of the year and visitors can change in the cubicles at the pool side. The Roman Catholic church is open, and Father Bernard Lordan will guide visitors round the Roman Catholic church by prior appointment. The well is very much as Celia Fiennes would have seen it, though bathers are rare. One cannot be insensible to the saintliness and spiritual atmosphere of the place; perhaps, to a degree, this is sustained by the annual remembrance, on 3rd November, of St Winefride's death.

Processional banner of St Winefride.

Footnotes:

1   Sir Edmund Harrison.
2   Morris C. (ed.) 1947, *The Journeys of Celia Fiennes*, p.180.
3   Ffynnon Fair near St Asaph, Clwyd, also has a star well.
4   Morris C. op.cit. p.180.
5   From the first printed version of the *Life of St Winefride* by William Caxton.
6   David C. 1971, *St Winefride's Well, a history and guide* (no page numbers)
7   ibid.
8   Fox A. 1971, *The Pictorial History of Westminster Abbey*, p.18; Cunliffe B. 1986, *The City of Bath*, p.92.
9   Information courtesy of Tristan Gray Hulse, 1995.
10   Blome R. 1673, *Britannia*, p.285.
11   Margaret Blundell (ed.) 1952, *Blundell's Diary and Letter Book 1702-1728*, p.19/62-3.
12   Fuller T. 1684, *Worthies of England*, p.954.
13   Everyman, 1927, p.66.
14   P.R.O, Patent Rolls 21. Eliz. Part 7. quoted by Rev Christopher David, 1971.
15   *A Tour Through England and Wales by Daniel Defoe*, p.66.
16   Pennant T. 1784, *A Tour in Wales*, Vol.1, p.39, noted by Edwards N. 1994, "Holy Wells in Wales and Early Christian Archaeology", *Source, The Holy Wells Journal*, New Series No.1, Autumn, p.230.
17   Morris C. op.cit. p.180.
18   Saunders W. 1805, *Mineral Waters*, p.110.
19   Blome R. op.cit. p.285.
20   Brome J. 1700, *Travels over England*, p.223.
21   Dugdale J. 1819, *The British Traveller*, Vol. IV, p.650; Tristan Gray Hulse, 1995.
22   Davies K. 1977, *The Greenfield Valley*, p.19. See Wilkes D R. 1985, *Holywell and Greenfield*, p.18-19.
23   Saunders W. op.cit. p.110.
24   Brome J. op.cit. p.223.
25   Pennant T. op.cit p.230; The temperature of the water is said to be 42-43° F but a reading in October 1995 was 50° F. The water never freezes.
26   Edwards N. op.cit. p.13.
27   For further information see Floyer J. 1722, *History of Cold Bathing*.
28   Morris C. op.cit. p.181.
29   Quoted by David C. 1971 in *St Winefride's Well, a history and guide*.
30   Camden's *Britannia*, Holland P. (trans.) 1610, p.680.
31   Blome R. op.cit. p.285.
32   Pennant T. op.cit. p.14.

NANTWICH AND NORTHWICH

Celia arrived in Nantwich from the east having journeyed from Newcastle-Under-Lyme, near Stoke, via Betley. This was part of her Great Journey of 1698.[1]

Nantwich she described as a well built, pretty, large town. Here she recorded *"salt springs of which they make salt and many salterns which were a boyling the salt"*. From Nantwich she travelled to Chester along a causeway. She also visited Northwich, 20 kilometres to the north of Nantwich, later in the same Great Journey and again she observed the salt industry. She noted the similarities between the three wiches where salt was produced, Droitwich, Nantwich and Northwich. It is in her description of Northwich that the best impression can be gained of the industry in the late seventeenth century.

She found Northwich to be a small town full of salt works. She observed numerous brine pits and the town was full of smoke from the fires of the salterns or salt pans being used to evaporate the brine. In the brine pits they had recently discovered rock salt, a clear crystalline salt that looked like sugar candy. The rock salt made good brine when mixed with fresh water and was being shipped to Wales. By boiling the rock salt in salt water a good quality commercial salt resulted.[2]

COMMENT

Rock salt is known to have been mined in Austria as long ago as the fifteenth century B.C. Solid geological deposits of sodium chloride (NaCl) originate from ancient marine or salt lake evaporation. Sea water is the greatest potential source of rock salt but mining in solid form avoids the evaporation process.[3] Pliny (77 AD.) recorded that sea water had curative properties and recommended it for such maladies as the swelling of the breasts. One sextarius of salt, when added to four sextarii of water, gave a good artificial sea water. It is apparent from Pliny's text that salt was commercially exploited throughout the known world at the time, from India to Africa to Germany and Spain.[4]

Nantwich was once the centre of the Cheshire salt industry and is known to have been an important source of salt in Roman times. In the mid-nineteenth century the Northwich and Winsford centres supplanted Nantwich. The last salt to be manufactured in Nantwich was in 1847.[5] The Nantwich exploitation had always been through the extraction of groundwater rich in brine, either through springs or wells sunk for that purpose. Mining for rocksalt and the more modern technique of controlled solution cavities was not used in Nantwich.[6]

When Celia Fiennes was in Nantwich, one brine-shaft that was being worked was "Old Biot". Legend has it that this was the oldest saline spring in the town and was worked before the Roman occupation.[7] The spring, situated on the east side of the River Weaver, continued to produce until 1818.[8] The new Medicinal Baths of 1883 occupied the site of "Old Biot". The shaft had previously been traditionally decked out with ribbons and flowers on Ascension Day.[9] This practice is described by Hope, 1893, who records that the old inhabitants also sang a hymn of thanksgiving for the blessing of the brine. Young people meanwhile celebrated the day with song and dance around the well.[10]

The rock salt that Celia Fiennes noted was from the Marbury Estate at Marston, Northwich, upon which she held a mortgage. Northwich salt was the first rock salt to be discovered in England. Rock salt was first discovered in 1670 by one John Jackson searching for coal on the Marbury estate.[11] The Royal Society announced the important discovery in *Philosophical Transactions* of 12 December of that year. In the announcement it was revealed that the *"Rock of Natural Salt"* occurred 33 and 34 yards from the surface, as revealed by an auger. A shaft was being sunk to reach it.[12]

Commercial exploitation started in 1682 and Morris indicates that in 1694 a company was formed to mine the deposits. Exploitation lasted for 38 years until the mine was flooded. When flooding occurred, new pits were dug, about 150 feet deep and often up to 100 feet in diameter. After 1781 deeper deposits were sought where the salt was more pure. Meteoric water inundated the workings resulting in the salt going into solution. When the workings caved in they became reservoirs of brine which was then pumped. Such mining had a catastrophic effect on the landscape.[13] Unfortunately by 1883 the town itself was reported as tumbling down as a result of being undermined.[14] Inundation by fresh water had the effect of diluting the springs thereby increasing the evaporation costs. The occurrence of dry rock salt avoided the necessity of boiling brine in pans and Morris proposes that Celia was attracted to new technology and innovation, hence her willingness to invest finance in the enterprise.[15] By 1808 the mines to the south of the town were being described as extending over several acres to great depth. The crystal roof was supported on pillars giving a beautiful appearance in the light of the workmen's candles.[16]

The fishing industry provided a ready market for salt.

GEOLOGY

The origin of strata rich in salt is generally recognised to be from evaporation of highly mineralised waters, usually sea water. From the table of principal ionic constituents of sea water in parts per million, it can be observed that sodium chloride or common salt (NaCl) ions are the most prolific.

Cl^-	19011
Na^+	10570
Mg^{2+}	1271
SO_4^{2-}	2664
Ca^{2+}	406
K^+	380
HCO_3^-	121
Br^-	66
CO_3^2	18

Source[17]

On evaporation sea water precipitates the least soluble material first. As evaporation continues the sequence of deposition is in order of solubility as follows:

First	Calcite	$CaCO_3$
	Dolomite	$CaMg(CO_3)_2$
then	Gypsum	$CaSO_4.2H_2O$
or	Anhydrite	$CaSO_4$
at 10% volume	Halite	NaCl

followed by rarer compounds such as

	Epsom Salts	$MgSO_4.7H_2O$.

An imaginary column of 1000 metres of sea water would give 11.8 metres of rock salt or halite.

In Cheshire it is believed that the deposits resulted from prolonged marine inundation and evaporation, by saltwater, of a shallow basin. At the time the climate was considerably hotter, being comparable with that of the Sahara today. The water originated not from the open sea but from a subsiding structural depression around Byley where the calcium compounds were precipitated. After deposition of substantial amounts of Halite, the bottom currents returned the water to the open ocean before deposition of the rarer compounds. Such theories raise more questions than they answer and earth scientists are some way from resolving the explanation for the depositional processes.[18]

There are two saliferous strata groups in the Nantwich locality, the Upper Keuper Saliferous beds and the Lower Keuper Saliferous beds. Both are of

Triassic origin (225-190 million years ago). Together these total in excess of 2,000 feet in thickness separated by about 1,000 feet of mudstone of the Middle Keuper Marl.[19] A modern alternative name for the Keuper Marls is the Mercia Mudstone Group.

NANTWICH MINERAL WATER SPA

Although the curative potential for brine was long known it was not until 1883 that brine baths were eventually opened in Nantwich, almost two centuries after Celia's visit. Henry Tollemache, M.P., gave the opening address, noting that the new baths would hopefully be patronised by two local dignitaries, Lord Combermere and Captain Massey, presumably two individuals who particularly needed the cure.[20] When first opened the baths provided private hot brine baths and a large swimming pool. The health restoring powers were apparently particularly appropriate for those countrymen who, in early life, injured their health through dissipation and sin. So much for Henry Tollemache's first customers! A visit to Nantwich avoided the long journey to Carlsbad or similar German spas. Brine could also be dispatched in casks to private houses or to any railway station in England.[21] The Old Baths were supplied directly from a spring which proved to be not as strong as Droitwich brine.

ANALYSIS OF NANTWICH MINERAL WATER

according to Frankland.

grains per gallon

Chloride of sodium	14,697.01
Chloride of potassium	135.28
Bromide of potassium	1.67
Carbonate of lime	15.49
Carbonate of soda	6.95
Sulphate of lime	455.99
Chloride of magnesium	157.90
Sulphate of soda	353.09
Alumina and peroxide of iron	2.53
Silica	0.47
Nitrate of soda	0.47
Total	15,826.85

Specific gravity 1142.76.

Source: Garrod, 1895.[22]

The therapeutic qualities of Nantwich brine are similar to those of Droitwich.

TODAY

Nantwich is a pleasant country town, once a market town, with only indirect evidence of a former salt industry. It was destroyed by fire in 1583 and rebuilt to a rich Elizabethan style. Much of the built environment reflects this important stage in the town's evolution. Old Biot is commemorated by a plaque in the gardens by the river bridge at one end of the High Street. Nearby is an ornamental fountain feature.

Northwich has suffered the most from the salt industry. Over 250 shafts and mines have been identified by the Brine Compensation Board, set up in 1891 and still making payments. The town retains a number of traditional framed buildings. Modern development, typical of twentieth century urbanisation, has resulted in the town's unique building heritage being tastelessly diluted. There is a Salt Museum near Northwich and the Lion Salt Works is being restored.[23]

Marbury Estate is now a country park managed by Cheshire County Council. The Hall, which post-dated Celia Fiennes, was demolished in 1968 and the site remains open.

Footnotes:

1   Morris C. 1947, *The Journeys of Celia Fiennes*, p.177.
2   ibid. p.224/5.
3   Kourimsky J. 1977, *Minerals and Rocks*, p.88.
4   Pliny, A.D.77, *The Natural History*, Bostock J. (trans), 1861, Chapter 33, p.496-512.
5   Davies D C. 1892, *Earthy and other Minerals and Mining*, p.65.
6   Poole E G. Whiteman A J. 1966, *Geology of the Country around Nantwich and Whitchurch*, Geological Survey of Great Britain, p.100/101.
7   "The Nantwich Brine and Medical Baths", *Nantwich Guardian*, 1883, booklet printed by the Guardian, Part 2, p.1.
8   Poole E G. Whiteman A J. op.cit. p.101.
9   Nantwich Guardian, 1883, Part 2, p.1,6.
10 Hope R C. 1893, *Holy Wells of England*, p.7.
11 Davies D C. op.cit. p.67/8.
12 Rochester M. c.1990, *Rock Salt Mining in Cheshire*, p.1.
13 Hopkinson B. 1984, "The British Salt Industry and Droitwich", *Industrial Heritage*, Vol.2, No.4, Winter, p.9.
14 Nantwich Guardian, 1883, part 2, p.5.
15 Morris C. op.cit. p.224, footnote and xxi.
16 Capper B. 1808, *A Topographical Dictionary of the United Kingdom*, see "Northwich".
17 Gill R. 1989, *Chemical Fundamentals in Geology*, p.95.
18 Rochester M. op.cit. p.1, 2.
19 Poole E G. Whiteman A J. op.cit. p.12/13.
20 Nantwich Guardian, 1883, part 2, p.1-5.
21 ibid. part 1, p.3-6.
22 Ord W M. Garrod A E. 1895, "Nantwich" in *The Climates and Baths of Great Britain*, Royal Medical and Chirurgical Society, p.568.
23 Fairley R. 13 January 1996, "Exploring the Crystal Maze", *Weekend Telegraph*, p.11.

DROITWICH

Also on her Great Journey of 1698 Celia Fiennes passed through Droitwich.[1] The town had not developed as a spa in the seventeenth century but what was apparent to Celia were the salt springs that were to lead subsequently to an era of prosperity for Droitwich as a health resort.

She was on her way to Worcester when she passed on her left Sir John Pakington's house at Westwood near Droitwich. It appears from her journal that she did not go into Droitwich having baited (eaten) at the Seven Stars earlier. Her route passed through Ombersley, to the west of Droitwich as she headed south to Worcester. She noted that Droitwich had three salt springs divided by a fresh water spring nearby. Earlier she had noted that there were salt hills near the brine pits. The salt water was boiled to good account. She found accommodation difficult due to the parliamentary election, the conclusion of which coincided with her arrival at Worcester the following day. Sir John Pakington and Mr Walsh secured the seats. She likely stayed at Ombersley overnight.

COMMENT

Droitwich lies on the River Salwarpe, a tributary of the River Severn, in Worcestershire. Travelling south to Worcester it was perhaps the Seven Stars at Redditch where the party rested. As they proceeded it is possible to gain a good appreciation of the election fever that was sweeping the county from the following contemporary account. *"I am but just come back from the election at Worcester for the Kts of the Shire, where we had so much crowd and noise I scarce know where I am yet....The candidates were Sir John Pack; Mr Walsh, an ancient gentleman of the county, a well bred man, a great poet, but his estate reduced to about 300£ a yeare, of which his mother has the great part; and Mr Foley that has neare 10,000 but none of the other qualities."*[2]

Sir John was elected and a period of service continued to his death in 1727. He was born in 1671, only child of Sir John and Lady Margaret and was first elected as a Knight of the Shire at the age of 19.[3] His bust can be seen in the Droitwich Heritage Centre.

Westwood House and Park, mentioned by Celia Fiennes, was the seat of the Pakingtons. The estate came into the family's hands in 1539 with the dissolution of a nunnery. The house itself dates back to the time of Elizabeth I.[4] It has been described as one of the finest, most perfect and interesting Elizabethan mansions in England. The building is three storied with projecting wings and countless mullioned windows. The grounds include substantial areas of lake.[5] There is no formal public access and the house is now divided into a series of private apartments.

Celia Fiennes also recorded three salt springs at Droitwich and these may have been a reference to the three areas where salt was extracted, Upwich, Middlewich and Netherwich; the latter comprised two separate pits. "Wich" was an early suffix indicating salt. The medieval map of Droitwich identifies the three sources in the vicinity of the River Salwarpe, about 300 metres apart, in an east-west configuration.[6] The Upwich pit, the greatest of the brine pits in Droitwich, was originally on the north side of the River Salwarpe. Today all three of the salt extraction locations are on the south side as a result of Brindley realigning the river between 1768 and 1771 when the Droitwich Canal was dug.

During the Middle Ages the Upwich pit was known as Saint Richard's pit. Writing in 1680, Dr Ravel, in *A Survey of Geography* gives an account of the Upwich pit at about the time of Celia Fiennes' visit. *"The Great Pit which is call Upwich is three foot drop in which there are three distinct springs rising in the bottom, one spring into the pit North-West, another North-East, the third South-East which is the* [strongest?] *both in quantity and quality. They all differ in saltiness which* [I] *can give no exact account of, it being impossible to separate them but there will be some mixture. The Pit is about ten foot square. The sides are made of square elm jointed in at the full length which purpose is occasioned by the Saltiness of the ground, which appears to me to have been a bog, the surface of it is made of ashes....The quality of the brine that the pit yields every twenty-four Hours is as much as will make 450 bushels of Salt which is drawn out twice or three times a day etc."*[7] The three springs within the pit may have been the three springs referred to by Celia Fiennes rather than the three areas where salt was extracted. Mackinlay (1893) records that St Richard's salt spring was annually adorned with flowers although no date is given when this took place.[8] This was a similar practice to that at "Old Biot" shaft in Nantwich.

After a pump was installed at St Richard's or Upwich pit c.1420, over 15,000 gallons of brine a day were being extracted. This prolific pit at one time produced 92 percent of the brine for boiling.[9]

Celia visited the Droitwich area at a particularly important point in its development. She recorded a salt industry which was as it had been for hundreds of years but had recently been freed of a Borough monopoly. She was not to know that improved methods and technology would transform the industry within a few years of her visit.

THE DROITWICH SALT INDUSTRY

First firm evidence of organised salt production at Droitwich can be dated to the Iron Age, about 3rd-2nd century BC. Archaeological remains of the "briquetage" brine vessels indicate a distribution network throughout

Herefordshire and Worcestershire and down the Severn estuary. Later, a major Roman settlement, known as Salinae, and salt extraction industry, was based at Droitwich. *Historia Britonum*, ninth century, describes the Droitwich springs as Quarium Miraculum, the eighth miracle.[10] The *Domesday Survey* of 1086 records that William held in demesne all salts, wells and pits which were worth £65 per annum. There were eight pits which included Upwic, Midelwic and Helperic.[11]

By the tenth/eleventh centuries there was an extensive network of salt ways extending from Droitwich into neighbouring counties. King John's charter of 1215 conferred the rights to brine and salt dues on the Burgesses of Droitwich in return for an annual payment of £100. As a result there was a Borough monopoly from 1215-1695.

Camden's *Britannia*, first edition 1586, describes Droitwich as follows:

"Then runneth Salwarp downe to Droitwich (Durt-wich) some term it, of the salt pits and the wettish ground on which it standeth.....where three fountains yeelding plenty of water to make salt of, divided asunder by a little brooke of fresh water passing betweene, by a peculiar gift of nature, to wit, from Midsommer to Midwinter, in many set fornaces round about. Wherewith what a might deale of wood is consumed, Feckenham forest (where trees grow sometime thicker)...."

Camden then goes on to describe Richard de la Wich, Bishop of Chichester and the comments of Gervase of Tilbury:

"In the Bishopricke of Worcester there is a country towne not farre from the City named Wich, in which at the foot of a certaine little hill, there runneth a most fresh water: in the banks whereof are seene few pits or wels, of a resonable depth, and their water is most salt. When the water is boiled in Caudrons, it becommeth thick and turneth into passing white salt, and all province fetcheth and carrieth it, for that betweene Christmas and the feast of S. John Baptists Nativity, the water floweth most salt....."

The Middlewich pit, which had been abandoned about 1477, was re-established on his land by one Robert Steynor in 1689, just prior to Celia's visit in 1698. Steynor had successfully challenged the Borough monopoly and the ancient customs and traditions came to an end in 1695.[12]

After 1695, new wells were sunk into the brine strata and extraction started on a massive scale compared with earlier workings. This was aided by improved technology and production soared to 15,000 tons per annum in 1772 and 132,000 tons per annum by 1873.[13] One particular innovation was the sinking of a 4 inch bore through the bottom of a pit. This technique, dating from 1725, considerably enhanced the yield, tapping deeper reservoirs of brine.[14] The old Upwich pit went into decline in the early eighteenth century and subsequent developments resulted in the locality becoming a canal wharf.[15] In the nineteenth century, one salt entrepreneur in particular secured, through a process of buy-outs, a monopoly on Droitwich salt. John Corbett then relocated the industry at Stoke Prior, just over 5 kilometers to the west.

The town remained an important source of salt until the 1920s. Salt has a variety of long established uses. These include flavouring and preserving food, leather curing and glazing in the pottery industry. The naturally occurring salt springs at Droitwich therefore have been a valuable economic asset to the town for at least 2000 years.[16]

At one point the springs supplied about one third of Britain's salt requirements. Droitwich salt was particularly pure; the springs contained few minerals other than sodium chloride. In addition the springs were not diluted by fresh water seepage. The absence of contaminates made the Droitwich springs particularly attractive to commercial exploiters. The Upwich pit was consistently the most prolific. Close by was Feckenham forest, a ready source of timber for firing the brine vats.

The brine springs emerge at the surface by natural artesian pressure. The mineralised water was transferred to pans where it was evaporated with the aid of a fire beneath. Wet crystals were then removed and dried to form a solid block. The Upwich brine pit was excavated in the 1980s and substantial evidence obtained of successive eras of exploitation from Roman times based on variations of the evaporation pan principal. Evidence of considerable construction work and equipment came to light during the excavations, with the technology changing as time progressed. Wood was the principal fuel up until the fourteenth century when coal became available.

When Celia Fiennes was in the locality, iron pans had just come into use and coal was the main fuel. Some salt makers still used lead pans made from a single sheet measuring 5 feet 7 inches x 3 feet (1.7 x 0.9 metres). By the second half of the seventeenth century 3,000 tons of salt were being produced annually. In 1678 the Upwich pit could produce 10 tons of salt per day. Various types of salt were produced which included "white salt", made as loaves in baskets, "clod salt" which was scraped off the pan and "knockings", formed on the outside of the baskets. The baskets were used for drying and draining the salt. Salt making buildings were clustered around the pits. Improvements in transport meant that Droitwich salt could be shipped to the West Country and Ireland. The Middlewich pit closed in the late seventeenth century but otherwise the industry was basically unchanged since medieval times.[17] It was noted in 1669 that the finer grained pure salt made in moulds travelled better, a significant factor for the Droitwich trade at the time. Impurities, such as calcium and magnesium chloride, are hygroscopic, absorbing atmospheric water and despoiling the salt. Magnesium chloride also turns fat rancid rendering the salts unsuitable for preserving meat. Salts from elsewhere in England also contained sand and other solid impurities rendering them less desirable than Droitwich salt. Merchant salters existed by the seventeenth century who acted as wholesale agents for the more distant markets.[18]

THE SALWARPE

The river that runs through Droitwich, around which the salt springs are located, may well have been navigable in medieval times. When Celia Fiennes toured in 1698 the river had been the subject of much investment in order to improve the navigation. The role of rivers as arteries of trade before the canal era is often underestimated. The need to transport salt along the trade routes of the Severn and the benefits to be had from the importation of coal prompted men like Andrew Yarrington to propose a navigation scheme in 1655. Nothing was done until 1662 when an Act was secured which provided £2,000 contribution from the salt works at Droitwich towards the expenses of a navigation works on the river Salwarpe. Sir Timothy and Charles Baldwin were among others who each spent thousands of pounds on the river. Lord Windsor eventually completed five of the proposed six locks but the scheme remained unfinished. Further Acts in 1693 and 1747 failed to result in an effective navigation and it was the canal by Brindley in 1771 that eventually located Droitwich on a navigable waterway.[19]

THE SPA

The town was developed as a health spa in the nineteenth century by John Corbett, who relocated the extractive industry at Stoke Prior. Corbett provided a number of public and commercial buildings.[20]

Brine as a therapeutic treatment started to be recognised about 1830 and by 1836 the Royal Brine Baths were opened in Queen Street. Luke cites an outbreak of cholera that was successfully treated in 1852 as being instrumental in the development of the spa.[21] The spa industry flourished thereafter and today Droitwich has a modern brine baths in which visitors can relax and bathe.[22]

THE MINERAL WATERS

The salt content of the waters is derived from extensive Triassic rock salt beds which lie beneath the surface at a depth of 200 feet or thereabouts. The salt geologically originates from marine evaporation and is a source of particularly pure sodium chloride, 96.48 percent or thereabouts of all mineral solids in the water so being. The geology of the district results in an artesian aquifer which surfaces through fissures and localised discontinuities. Fresh water supplying the aquifer constantly takes the sodium chloride into solution enabling brine to be extracted at the surface.[23]

A typical analysis is given by Herapath:

ANALYSIS OF DROITWICH MINERAL WATER

	grains per gallon
Sodium chloride	21,761.872
Magnesium chloride	2.560
Calcium sulphate	91.120
Aluminium sulphate	14.400
Sodium sulphate	342.720
Sodium iodide	0.208
Total	22,212.880

Comparison amounts of sodium chloride

Droitwich by Horner	21,585.50
Daubeny	16,910.00
Northcote	19,392.57
D T. Taylor	21,509.77
Channel sea water by Schweitzer	1,946.09
Nantwich by Frankland[24]	14,697.01

Source: Garrod, 1895.[25]

Bathing in the water, which would be heated for the purpose, would be a treatment for muscular rheumatism and sciatica. Gout and osteoarthritis were also treated in a similar manner. Other ailments treated included gonorrheal arthritis and general debility. Cardiac disease patients should avoid the brine baths. For those who wished, nearby Malvern Spa offered a Droitwich brine facility at the end of the nineteenth century.[26] Although normal treatment was external by bathing, small quantities could be drunk to good effect, acting as a solvent to mucus of the stomach and as a liver stimulant.

TODAY

The Spa: Droitwich has one of the most modern spa bathing facilities in England. The Droitwich Spa Brine Baths is located in St Andrews Road and is available for public use. A range of health and beauty treatments are available as well as the brine bath. Booking is desirable during peak demand periods. The buoyancy that results from the brine is a most interesting experience for those bathing in it for the first time. Light luncheons are served by arrangement

The Chateau Impney: The Chateau is now a hotel. It was built by John Corbett as a home in the nineteenth century, after he had gained a monopoly of the local salt interests. It is testimony to the wealth that was to be had from the salt industry.

Westwood House: This brick-built Elizabethan House survives and is noted for its stone mullions and gatehouse.

The Museum: There is a local Heritage Centre in the spa area of the town. The building was once the brine baths and is located adjacent to the modern spa establishment.

The Church of the Sacred Heart and Catherine: The walls and ceiling of this church are covered in mosaics depicting the life of St Richard who gave his name to the Upwich pit.

The brine pits: The brine pits are no longer visible. Saint Richard's pit, the Upwich pit, was re-interred when archaeological excavations in the 1980s were completed. In due course it is hoped to reopen the pit and mount a permanent exhibition.

The medieval timbers of St. Richard's or the Upwich brine pit revealed during excavations in the 1980s.

200

Footnotes:

1   Morris C. (ed.) 1947, *The Journeys of Celia Fiennes*, p.225, 231.
2   Pakington H & R. 1975, *The Pakingtons of Westwood*, p.48.
3   Barnard E A B. 1936, *The Pakingtons of Westwood*, p.47.
4   Middlemas B. Hunt J. 1985, *John Corbett, Pillar of Salt, 1817-1901*, p.17.
5   Hall S C. LLewellynn J. c.1890, *The Stately Homes of England*.
6   Hurst J D. 1992, *Savouring the Past, The Droitwich Salt Industry*.
7   From an unidentified published manuscript, "St Richard of Droitwich", p.6.
8   Mackinlay J M. 1893, *Folklore of the Scottish Lochs and Springs*, p.207.
9   Hopkinson B. 1994, *Salt and Domesday Salinae at Droitwich A.D. 674 to 1690*, p.20.
10 Hopkinson B. 1984, "The British Salt Industry and Droitwich", *Industrial Heritage*, Vol.2, No.4. p.5/6.
11 Middlemas B. Hunt J. op.cit. p.16.
12 Hopkinson B. 1984, op.cit. p.12.
13 ibid. p.12/13.
14 ibid. p.12.
15 Hurst J D. op.cit. p.28.
16 ibid. p.2-13.
17 ibid. 1992, p.23-28.
18 Hopkinson B. 1984, op.cit. p.13-15.
19 Paget-Tomlinson E W. 1978, *Canal and River Navigations*, p.209/210; Willan T S. 1936 (new edition 1964), *River Navigation in England 1600-1750*, p.66.
20 Hurst J D. op.cit. p.30-31.
21 Luke T D. 1919, *Spas and Health Resorts of the British Isles*, p.112.
22 Hurst J D. op.cit. p.31.
23 Garrod A E. "Droitwich", in Ord W M. Garrod A E. 1895, *The Climates and Baths of Great Britain*, Vol.1, p.561/2.
24 Garrod A E. "Nantwich" 1895, in Ord W M. Garrod A E. *The Climates and Baths of Great Britain*, Vol.1, p.568.
25 Garrod A E. op.cit. p.562/3.
26 ibid. p.562-6.

RICHARD'S CASTLE

Celia was on her way home to Newton Toney when she commented on the Bone Well at Richard's Castle, near Ludlow. She had visited the Foley's at Stoke Edith and was to cross the Malvern Hills on her way to Upton. This late journey probably took place after 1701 because Stoke Edith was finished by then. The fountain was always full of fish and frogs bones *"tho' often cleared, yet still renewed"* according to our inveterate traveller.[1]

COMMENT

Although not a healing spa, the Bone Well was one of many wonderments that Celia Fiennes observed of mineral water springs and nature.

The Bony Well, as it is now called, is near Richard's Castle in south Shropshire. The well lies beneath the ruined earthworks of the castle of Richard Fitz Scrob[2] or Scrope, built in the time of Edward the Confessor. At the time of the Domesday survey it was held by Osborn Fitz-Richard, a family which was later to assume the name of Say. The place was anciently known as Gaytor or Boytanc and was a place of considerable importance until the reign of Henry III (1216-1272). It was granted a charter for a market and fair by King John. Today the castle is in the hands of the Salwey family who have held the manor since the fifteenth century.[3] Small bones found in the well were alleged to be those of victims of an ancient battle. The battle to which the bones were attributed was probably the 1645 defeat of Sir Thomas Lundesford's 2,000 Royalists near the castle by Colonel Birch.[4]

The alternative view is that the bones are those of small fish and frogs. Camden noted the spring observing, like Celia Fiennes, that it contained fish or small frog bones which gave rise to the name Bone-well. Apparently the bones were not evident in winter.[5] The Bone Well was something of a tourist attraction at the time of Celia Fiennes as we can deduce from contemporary accounts. The Rev. James Brome (1700) said of the Bone Well, near Richard's Castle, that it presented them with a great rarity. *"... 'tis a Well called Bone Well, upon the Surface of which are still bubbling up several little bones of Fishes, and when those which appear are taken away, others do immediately succeed in their room."*[6] Slightly earlier, Richard Blome (1673) said of the Bone Well that it was *"a Spring wherein are always found the bones of small fishes but not so much as a finn to be seen."*[7] Yet another description comes from a contemporary of Celia Fiennes, Thomas Fuller. In 1684 he stated that *"As for Wonders, Bone-Well, near Richard's Castle, is always full of Bones of little Fishes of which it can never be emptied, but that they return again."*[8]

The spring is located at Green Farm which is private property and it is necessary to secure the lord of the manor's permission to view. To find the well, proceed from the village up the road by the side of the "Castle" public house to Hanway Common, keeping left past the church on the left, to the top of the hill where there is a cattle grid. On the left there is a steep valley accessible through a gate. Walk down the valley until a gate is seen. The well is immediately on the left by the gate and is one of a number of springs in the locality. The well has been used for sheep dipping in the past but is now used as a local water supply.

Richard's Castle lies on the north-eastern rim of a plunging anticline of Silurian limestones, rich in fossils. To the south-east lies the more recent Old Red Sandstone series. Although the Silurian limestone provides a limited aquifer for water supplies to towns such as Ledbury, the water is generally rather hard.[9] The Bony Well spring erupts from a bed of grey limestone which contains numerous small fossils and this explains the phenomenon of bones appearing. Celia Fiennes would have had little understanding of geological time scales and therefore would have adopted one of the local legends to explain matters.

Footnotes:

1   Morris C. (ed.) 1982, *The Illustrated Journeys of Celia Fiennes*, p.16, 230.
2   Hughes J. 1977, *Shropshire Folklore, Ghosts and Witchcraft*, p.62-63.
3   Wright T. 1826, *The History and Antiquities of Ludlow*, p.215-216.
4   ibid. p.217.
5   ibid. p.216-217.
6   Brome J. 1700, *Travels over England, Scotland and Wales*, p.102.
7   Blome R. 1673, *Britannia: or, A geographical description of the kingdoms of England, Scotland and Ireland*, p.118.
8   Fuller T. 1684, *Worthies of England*, p.377.
9   Earp J R. Haines B A. 1971, *The Welsh Borderland*, British Regional Geology, p.5, 104.

MALVERN

Malvern was a locality through which Celia Fiennes passed on several occasions between 1696 and some time after 1701. The last recorded occasion was after noting the Bone Well at Richards Castle.[1]

Celia Fiennes mentioned the Malvern Hills on her Great Journey of 1698, comparing them with the Wrekin which she considered not as high, in spite of local legend that the Wrekin was the highest ground in England.[2]

Earlier in 1696 she had made a visit to her uncle Richard Fiennes' widow in Gloucestershire and later to John Fiennes, another uncle who lived at New House, Stretton Grandison, in Herefordshire. It was as a result of this journey that we learn most from her about Malvern. Crossing the River Severn at Upton on the old stone bridge, she began her ascent to the Malvern Hills. These, she said, were also known as the English Alps[3] and had once been accepted as the natural division between England and Wales. She described them as being two or three miles high[4] and a pyramid shape at the top. By this she must have meant that the hills formed a narrow ridge along which people could walk with views across the plains to both east and west. She rode to the top of one of the highest hills and could see the countryside for 40 miles around, and the city of Worcester in the distance. If she could see Worcester than it was probably either North Hill or the Worcestershire Beacon which she climbed. From the Herefordshire Beacon she would not have been able to see Worcester.

COMMENT

Celia's journal introduces the reader to a period of some mystery with regard to the Malvern waters. There is a dearth of early research material relating to the springs although it is apparent that they were in existence. This chapter explores the few early references in order to provide a framework for scholarly work of later centuries. In a way Celia acts as an unwitting guide.

The route from the bridge at Upton into Herefordshire would have taken Celia along the old coach road past Little Malvern Priory. Near the Priory she would have passed a spring now known as Ditchford's Well, one of the early distinguished sources, as she started to climb the Malvern Hills. Recent investigation has unearthed in excess of sixty celebrated water sources in the Malverns[5], only a few of which were mentioned in pre-nineteenth century literature. Those which were mentioned in early literature were notable for their healing properties; the sources which became renowned latterly were those which provided water for domestic and hydropathic purposes following Malvern's nineteenth century rise to fame as England's foremost inland spa.

When Celia Fiennes visited the area in the late seventeenth century, the wells now known as Holy Well, the Chalybeate Spring, the Hay Well and St Ann's Well would have been amongst the most notable springs. However, seventeenth and eighteenth century publications present a number of problems when attempting to unravel the history of these early famed water sources. This in turn raises questions as to the identification and location of particular springs which, it will be shown, are not necessarily as exact as modern designations suggest.

The modern day Holy Well is situated some 3.5km south of Great Malvern town, on a bend along Holywell Road, the old main road between Worcestershire and Herefordshire. Coaches would have had difficulty negotiating this point, partly due to the narrowness of the road and the sharp bend, and partly because of the frightful state of the road surface which Celia Fiennes described as "*deep and difficult*" and "*the worst way I ever went in Worcester and Herrifordshire - its allways a deep sand and soe in the winter and with muck is bad way, but this being August it was strange and being so stony made it more difficult to travell.*"[6]

One can speculate that Holy Well had formerly been part of a monastic hospital in the medieval period, linked to Little Malvern Priory. In 1559, following the dissolution of the monasteries, the lordship of the Manor of Hanley Castle, in which the Holy Well is situated, was granted to John Hornyold. Hornyold may have authorised the clearance of undergrowth around this constant spring for the general use of the tenants and freeholders, making the spring more visible to passing travellers.

The Chalybeate Spring is about 0.3km to the east of the main road through Great Malvern and near the modern town centre. The issue was in the grounds of Great Malvern Priory. The water was renowned for curing blood ailments and differs from most other Malvern springs because of its mild iron impregnation.

St Ann's Well is located on the hillside above and to the west of Great Malvern. Its water flowed through the grounds of Great Malvern Priory.

The Eye Well is generally accepted to lie about 200m above and to the west of the modern Holy Well. It has been suggested that there may be some confusion with the Hay Well and that this Great Malvern town centre well is the likely original claimant to the name.[7] The Hay Well was undoubtedly a principal source of water for Great Malvern Priory and fed the Subpriors Orchard pool.

MALVERN BATH.

The recently discovered illustration shown opposite is dated c.1750 and is the earliest known view of any of the Malvern springs and wells. The location is the modern day Holy Well. The bath house is situated beside the road, later (1843) to be relocated further back to allow for carriages pulling up. The stairs at the side probably led to an upstairs toilet, similar to that at Scarborough Spa. The wooden hut to the left of the bath house accommodated the poor. It is probably the hospital which Thomas Short noted was endowed by a Bishop of Hereford for the reception of travellers from Herefordshire.[8] The building to the right of the bath is the present day Holy Well Cottage. On the hill behind, the faint outline of a building suggests that the higher issue of Holy Well, now known as the Eye Well, was used by walkers on the laid-out paths. Today the area around Holy Well is densely wooded, reflecting the demise of sheep grazing.

Having identified the principal springs it is possible to review the early literature. However examination of this literature throws into doubt two currently accepted assumptions. Firstly, that the true Eye Well is the spring which is now situated above the modern Holy Well; secondly, that early references to a "holy well" pertain to the spring which we now know as the Holy Well and not to some other spring.

THE EYE WELL

Possibly the earliest known documentary evidence of a healing well at Malvern is in Banister's *Breviary of Eyes* of 1622:

> *"A little more Ile of their curing tell,*
> *How they helpe sore Eyes with a new found Well:*
> *Great speech of Malourne hills was late reported,*
> *Unto which Spring, people in troupes resorted."*[9]

Modern scholars generally accept that Banister is referring to the Eye Well above modern Holy Well, a point which, on investigation, proves to be not so. The original text does not elucidate exactly which well Banister was referring to and any association with what we now call the Eye Well is not confirmed. These doggerel lines merely confirm that a new spring had been found, the water of which cured eye complaints. A search of other eighteenth and nineteenth century publications helps to identify which spring Banister was referring to.

In 1743 a local physician, Dr John Wall, became the first person to analyse the mineral content of Malvern's spring waters. Shortly after Dr Wall's analysis the following doggerel was penned.

> *"The Malvern water, says Dr John Wall,*
> *Is famed for containing just nothing at all."*

These lines misleadingly suggest that the water contains no minerals, a fact not in keeping with Wall's analysis. He published the results of two springs that he analysed - the Chalybeate Spring and Holy Well - indicating that they had remarkable purity. One can conclude, therefore, that these were the most notable springs at the time, a point confirmed by Dr Russel in 1760 who reiterated Dr Wall's treatise in a supplement to his own *Dissertation on the use of Sea Water* (4th edition). William Owen, the publisher of Dr Russel's book, was by this time selling Malvern Water at his mineral water warehouse in London. The Chalybeate Well is described as one quarter of a mile below Great Malvern and the Holy Well midway between Great and Little Malvern thereby confirming the location of these two springs.[10]

Dr Wall's treatise was first published in 1756 and subsequently updated.[11] In the second paragraph of a footnote in the third and final edition of 1763, Wall refers to a third well, situated above Holy Well. The same reference quotes Banister's doggerel, mentioning the curing of eye diseases. Dr Wall also republished an undated Addenda from Camden's *Britannia*[12] which noted that there was a spring beside Holy Well, known as the Eye Well. This footnote has been used by many as an indication of the whereabouts of the modern day Eye Well.

The footnote in Dr Wall's *Experiments and Observations on the Malvern Waters*, 1763, page 2.

Besides these two springs there is also a third, which flows about a hundred yards higher up the Hill than the Holy-Well: this has been thought more appropriated to diseases of the eyes: but it does not seem (upon any trials) to differ from the Holy-Well, I therefore did not think it necessary to take any particular notice of it.

Mention is made of these Springs in Bannister's "Breviary of the Eyes", printed A.D. 1622 in these lines:

.......(Breviary as previously quoted).........

In the Addenda to "Camden's Britannia" are the following words; "Near the division (betwixt Worcestershire and Herefordshire) is a Spring that has long been famed for the virtue of healing eyes, and other parts of the head, called therefore Eye-Well. And beside this is another spring called Holy-Well heretofore, much resorted to for curing all scorbutic humours and external ulcers, by bathing and drinking of the Waters" And in "Geography Reformed" these Wells are taken notice of in these words; "There are two medicinal Springs (in Malvern Hills) called Holy-Wells, one of which is good for the eyes, and putrid foetid livers; the other for cancers" J.W.

A detailed study of the footnote produces some vexing observations about the location of the Eye Well and the designation of individual wells.

Firstly, Dr Wall dismissed the well above Holy Well as the water was the same as that from Holy Well albeit supposedly good for eyes.

Secondly, Dr Wall believed that Banister referred to *"these springs"*. To Dr Wall, these were likely the *"two springs"* referred to earlier in the footnote and main text, that is the Chalybeate and Holy Well, as discussed in the paragraph to which the footnote applies. There is no indication that Dr Wall was referring to the spring above Holy Well. Therefore, based on Dr Wall's text so far, any conclusion that this is the Eye Well is unfounded. Furthermore, Banister's full original text, as indicated previously, gave no clue as to which spring it refers.

Thirdly, Dr Wall then cites *Britannia* which indicated that there was a spring called Eye-Well and *"beside this"* Holy-Well. Modern use of the preposition *"beside"* suggests "next to". This therefore identifies two adjacent springs but *"beside"* gives little indication of the distance apart, if modern rendering is used. However, this would be a likely misinterpretation of the word *"beside"*. Kahn et al propose that *"beside"* was historically used to indicate "as well as" and cite the case of Irving.[13] Today we would use the word "besides". A modern day reader should therefore consider that Camden's *Britannia* was suggesting an Eye-Well in addition to Holy Well rather than an Eye-Well next to Holy Well. The Eye Well could therefore be some distance from Holy Well. The *Britannia* Eye-Well, it will be suggested later, could be the Hay Well mentioned earlier.

Fourthly, Dr Wall then quoted *Geography Reformed* which stated that there were two medicinal springs called Holy-Well. This now complicates any interpretation of where these springs might be by indicating that more than one spring was called Holy-Well, one of which may be the Eye Well.

Summarising the debate so far, it would be easy to conclude that the spring in Banister's *Breviary* is the same spring that Wall mentioned cured eye diseases, that is the one above Holy-Well. This hypothesis is supported by Camden's *Britannia*, if *"beside"* is incorrectly used in the modern idiom. The notion that the Eye Well issues immediately above Holy Well also arises from the interrelationship of the various texts in Wall's footnote. On careful analysis of the footnote it can be seen that there is actually no firm evidence to suggest that this is so. In spite of this, the unfounded conclusion - that the *Breviary* refers to the spring above Holy-Well - has been perpetuated by historians ever since.

The question which now arises is whether there is any further evidence which supports, or refutes, this unfounded conclusion?

Dr Granville on his 1837 visit to Malvern[14] noted that the Holy Well was not a spring but merely a streamlet, suggesting that it was fed from the spring above i.e the modern day Eye Well. Dr Wall saw no difference in the mineral content of the two springs. Together, these two facts imply that they were one and the same source. If this were the case, then one might predict that the great *"troupes"* to which Banister referred would resort to the easily accessible Holy Well rather than make the tedious ascent to the source in the thicket above. Of the Holy Well, Dr Wall in his 1763 edition, gave many *"...Instances of Persons who have come to Malvern for Disorders of the Eyes and Eyelids and received Cures..."*[15] This supports the argument that Banister was actually describing Malvern's modern day Holy Well. This well, at the time, was likely a series of springs with several issues before nineteenth century containment.

Further doubt over whether Banister's eye-curing well is the same as the present day Eye Well emerges in Australia. There, common parlance is to refer to the point where the water issues from the ground as the "eye" of the spring. Wishart's *Field Guide to the Mineral Springs of the Central Highlands of Victoria* refers several times to such "eyes".[16] In England *The Miners Dictionary* of 1747[17] uses the expression "eye" to describe where the underground workings come to the surface. These examples give credence to the suggestion that the modern day Eye Well at Malvern resulted from the misapplication of the description the "eye" of the Holy Well.

There is a theory that Eye Wells were not originally regarded as healing wells at all: that there is a mythological belief that such wells gave perception and vision. This possibility has been expressed on numerous occasions.[18] The view is comprehensively developed by Bord in 1985, who observed that Eye Wells were seen by pilgrims as the eye of God.[19] To look into running water was to look into God's eye. In Welsh, Llygad means source of a stream as well as eye.

In *The Waters of the Gap* (1981)[20] Stewart explained that in Welsh and Old Irish "suil" or "sulis" means a gap, orifice or eye. He says that this native Celtic word became Romanised in Aquae Sulis (Bath) and translates as *"waters of the gap"*. Sulis became the name of a goddess at Bath and the link between the Celtic and Roman mythology established.

An alternative interpretation to Stewart's, using "eye" rather than "gap" as the meaning of Sulis, is that Aquae Sulis means *"the waters of God's eye"*. This description would be sympathetic to Celtic beliefs that water sources were generally sacred, and the religious concept that life was created from within a boiling cauldron. The spring at Bath was possibly a Celtic Eye Well, but named Aquae Sulis with the merging of the Celtic and Roman religions. This therefore gives a further alternative meaning to the description Eye Well.

THE HOLY WELL

In Malvern, not only is there confusion over the meaning of the term Eye Well and its site, but there is also some doubt about the meaning of the term "Holy Well".

As has been indicated, in the 1763 edition of his treatise, Dr Wall made the footnote reference to "*these two springs*" by which he likely meant the Holy Well and the Chalybeate springs. He also reiterated the information from *Geography Reformed* that there were two medicinal springs in Malvern called "*Holy-Wells*". One was good for the eyes, the other good for the putrid foetid livers.[21] There was thus more than one holy well in Malvern!

This generic application of the epithet "holy" is perpetuated by Drs Wilson and Gully, Malvern's great nineteenth century hydropathic practitioners. In their 1843 prospectus they observed that the Malvern springs came to be known as holy for the same reason as St Winefride's Well at Holywell, Flintshire.[22]

St Winefride's Well became "holy" for two reasons. Firstly, because a mighty spring of water miraculously emerged from the spot where the saint's decapitated head hit the ground. No such martyrdom occurred at Malvern. Secondly, St Winefride's Well was holy because of its curative properties. This indicates that Wilson and Gully were referring to the curative properties of the waters when they compared St Winefride's with Malvern.

The Dr Wall treatise mentioned two holy wells, and named Holy Well and the Chalybeate Spring. Both were renowned for curative properties and both had historic monastic associations. The suggestion is that a healing well with religious associations could be deemed a holy well. The application of the term Holy Well in this manner echoes medieval circumstances when religious orders maintained the healing wells and hospitals. The thesis that a Holy Well and healing well are synonymous, is sustained by the diarist John Evelyn who, in 1654, recorded how he "*...deviated to the Holy Wells* (plural), *trickling out of a vally thro' a steepe declivity towards the foot of the greate Mauvern Hill; they are said to heale many infirmities, as king's evil, leaprosie, sore eyes &c.*"[23] Unfortunately Evelyn does not record their precise locations. A similar use of the plural "Holy Wells" occurs in the *Philosophical Transactions of the Royal Society* in 1666. In spite of Malvern being the location of a spring famed for curing eye complaints, the use of the plural confirms more than one spring being referred to with uncertain locations.[24]

ST ANN'S WELL

It is now possible to examine the modern day St Ann's Well to ascertain whether the confusions apply to this source. The name "St Ann's Well" was used in very

211

few Malvern texts in the eighteenth century. Probably the first mention was the Foley Estate map of 1744 which identified St Ann's Well. Evidence that Dr John Wall knew of and analysed St Ann's spring comes from Weaver and Osborne who published a recently discovered hand written document by John Wall which included a simple analysis.[25] This important document, which was not formally published by John Wall, likely dates from the mid-eighteenth century.

Dr John Wall is generally accredited with the first analysis of Malvern waters but his experiments lacked the sophistication and knowledge of the later work of Philips Wilson. Dr Philips Wilson, in 1805, published the first detailed analysis of St Ann's and Holy Well waters.[26] His analysis is one of the first allusions to St Ann's Spring as a named spring in formal documentation.

There is evidence therefore that St Ann's Well was of sufficient importance during the eighteenth century to be plotted on maps and analysed by Dr John Wall. These are the first uses of the name but it is inconceivable that the spring was not referred to prior to this. It was a substantial issue flowing through a medieval settlement. The conclusion must be that a different name was used. As the waters of St Ann's Well flowed through the Great Malvern Priory there was a religious association. Was St Ann's Well also one of Malvern's Holy Wells? The answer would appear to be affirmative although speculative.

The alternative argument, on the basis that Holy Wells were healing wells, is that St Ann's Well would not have been considered a holy well, since there were apparently no accounts of it having any curative properties under the St Ann's name. There may of course be mention under an alternative name such as Holy Well. In addition St Ann's Well could also be geologically considered the "eye" of the Chalybeate and Hay Wells. Any mention of the Chalybeate could therefore imply the modern St Ann's Well in a similar scenario to the well above the modern Holy Well being part of the same issue. The St Ann's Well was probably named in the eighteenth century, after a saint, to give it respectability, in the same way that the Restoration spa at Astrop was named after St Rumbold - Astrop's was a healing spring.

If St Ann's Well was one of Malvern's Holy Wells, this raises questions regarding how the key springs of Malvern were referred to and in particular, which ones were early authors considering. Was St Ann's the well referred to in various early seventeenth century writings?

It is recorded that Gervase Markham visited Holy Well a little earlier than 1622, possibly around 1612/13.[27] The question that such text raises is where was this Holy Well? Was this the modern day Holy Well or one of the healing wells in the vicinity? Weaver and Osborne certainly identify a second modern day Holy Well but this is some distance away.[28]

What is apparent is that Holy Well, as a generic description for all the healing wells, may have even included St Ann's Well. This would have been before the naming of the spring after a saint in the mid-eighteenth century. Other Holy Wells may have included Ditchfords Well, mentioned earlier. It also possibly included the Hay Well which was once located within the grounds of Great Malvern Priory and thus had religious associations. This would give credence to the view expressed earlier that the Hay Well was in fact the original Eye Well. This view was expressed as long ago as 1883 in an advertisement for the Hay Well Baths.[29] Confusion could also result from "Hay" and "Eye" sounding remarkably similar in traditional Worcestershire dialect.

Other springs which may have been designated Holy Well occur on the western side of the Malvern Hills. Walm's Well, beneath the Herefordshire Beacon, is mentioned as early as 1631.[30] Its slightly sulphurous water was said to have been applied internally and externally by local people and was known for curing eye diseases.[31] The water at Moorall's Well was also applied externally and a brick-lined bath was provided in a nearby cottage. It also had a reputation for curing eye complaints.[32] Both of these springs are said to have been named after saints.

Nash quotes an old song saluting the healing properties of an unnamed spring in Malvern. It was written pre 1628 because it was in that year that the deer were removed from the Chase prior to its disafforestation.

"A chase for royal deere
Rounde doth besette thee,..."

The verse also notes what a nuisance the deer were and goes on:

"Out of that famous hill
There dailie springeth,
A water, passynge stille,
That always bringyeth
Grete comfort to alle them
That are diseased men,
And makes them well again...

Haste thou a wound to heale,
The whyche doth greve thee;
Come thenn unto this Welle,
It wille releive thee,
"Noli me tangeries",
And other maladies,
Have theyre theyr remedies,...

A thousande bottles there,
Were filled weeklie,
And manye costryls rare
For stomachs sicklie;
Some of theme into Kent,
Some were to London sente,
Others to Berwick wente... "[33]

This song demonstrates that a celebrated well was in the locality without identifying it by name. As this was also the first evidence of water bottling in The Malverns it would be valuable for historians to be able to identify the precise location. Even if the spring referred to had been called the Holy Well it could not be relied on as a positive identification of the present day Holy Well location.

Scholars clearly need to be wary of generic terms being misinterpreted. One can be fairly sure that Malvern's modern day Eye Well is not the eye well mentioned by Banister in 1622, although some doubt must remain. The practise in earlier centuries of all nouns beginning with capital letters gives an added difficulty to the interpretation of some documents. Thus Holy Well as a generic term could be easily misinterpreted as a specific Holy Well, and vice versa. An Eye Well could also be generic or specific and was not necessarily named after its efficacy in curing eyes. These considerations particularly apply before the close of the eighteenth century; after that time most wells were individually named.

In conclusion, it is apparent that most of the current names for springs and wells emanate from post medieval times. The absence of early text using modern names does not mean that the particular well was undiscovered. It is likely that it was being referred to under a generic Holy Well description. Celia Fiennes would no doubt have been aware that there were Holy Wells in the Malvern Hills in the late seventeenth century. The absence of unique designations suggest that they were very much matter of fact rather than venues for a pilgrimage of healing.

TODAY

The tiny twelfth century Benedictine Priory at Little Malvern Priory, which Celia Fiennes rode past, can still be seen today. In addition, St Ann's Well and Holy Well are easily located and the water freely drunk in their well houses. There are no visible signs of Ditchford's Well; some years ago it was contained to supply a nearby farm.

It is unlikely that Celia visited Great Malvern Priory since she entered the Malvern area from the south. It was originally an eleventh century Benedictine monastery attached to Westminster Abbey and is now considered amongst the finest parish churches in the country. The former gatehouse accommodates the museum of local history and is well worth a visit.

Holywell Road is still gas lit.

On the hill above Great Malvern, St Ann's Well supplies delicious home-cooked vegetarian meals and teas. From October to April it is best to telephone to ensure opening times.

Footnotes:

1   Morris C. (ed.) 1947, *The Journeys of Celia Fiennes*, p.336/7.
2   ibid. p.227/8.
3   ibid. p.43.
4   The highest peak on the Worcestershire Beacon is 1395 feet.
5   Weaver C. Osborne B. 1994, *Aquae Malvernensis*.
6   Morris C. op.cit. p.337, 233.
7   Weaver C. Osborne B. op.cit. p.137/8.
8   Short T. 1734, *Natural Mineral Waters*, p.88.
9   Banister R. 1622, 2nd edition, *A Treatise of One Hundred and Thirteen Diseases of the Eyes, and Eye-Liddes*. See the heading "Of Curing Eyes with Well Water".
10 Russel R. 1760 (4th edition) *Dissertation on the use of Sea Water* with anonymous supplement *A Treatise on the Nature, Properties and Uses of the Mineral Waters*, p.22-32.
11 Wall J. 1763, "Experiments and Observations on the Malvern Waters" in Wall M. 1806, *Malvern Waters*, p.1/2.
12 first edition 1586, second edition 1594
13 Kahn J E. (ed.) 1985, *The Right Word at the Right Time*, p.93.
14 Granville A B. 1841, *Spas of England, The Midlands and South*, p.268/9.
15 Wall J. 1763, *Experiments and Observations on the Malvern Waters*, 3rd edition, p.120 and passim.
16 Wishart E & M. 1990, *The Spa Country*, Spa Publishing, p.80, 163 and passim.
17 Hooson W. 1747, *The Miners Dictionary*, reprint 1979 by the Institution of Mining and Metallurgy, London, see "eye".
18 Weaver C. Osborne B. op.cit. p.102.
19 Bord J & C. 1985, *Sacred Waters*, p.35/6.
20 Stewart B. 1981, *The Waters of the Gap*, p.25.
21 Wall J. 1763, op.cit. p.2.
22 Wilson J. Gully J M. 1843, *Prospectus of the Water Cure Establishment*, p.21.
23 Bray W. (ed.) 1891, *The Diary of John Evelyn*, p.234.
24 Royal Society, 1666, *Philosophical Transactions*, No. 20, vol.i, p.358/9, see Lennard R. 1931, *Englishmen at Rest and Play*, Clarendon Press, Oxford, p.32, 235.
25 Weaver C. Osborne B. op.cit. p.93.
26 Wilson A P. 1805, *An Analysis of Malvern Waters*, p.42, 58.
27 Smith B. 1978, *A History of Malvern*, p.286.
28 Weaver C. Osborne B. op.cit. p.101.
29 ibid. p.137.
30 Smith B. 1964, *A History of Malvern*, p.173.
31 Weaver C. Osborne B. op.cit. p.81.
32 ibid. p.69.
33 Nash R. 1782, *Collections for the History of Worcester*, Vol.2, p.125; Nott J. 1885, *Some of the Antiquities of Moche Malverne*, p.145/7.

BRISTOL

It was during the Great Journey of 1698 that Celia Fiennes visited Bristol.[1] She was on her way south via Gloucester and called in briefly to Bath where she updated the information given as a result of her first visit. Bristol at the time was a particularly important town and had superceded Norwich as the second town of England.

The prosperity of Bristol was based not on its attributes as a spa, but on its merits as a port. The river Avon flows into the Severn estuary in the vicinity of Bristol. Water transport, being the principal bulk carrier of goods, meant that Bristol was geographically convenient to the trade routes along the coast lines of south-west England and south Wales, as well as having access inland through the river network. Celia noted in her journal that tin and copper was shipped to Bristol from Redruth in Cornwall. Sea coal from Bristol was being distributed through Taunton by packhorse after being transferred from barges at Bridgwater. The cost in Taunton for two bushels was two shillings.[2] At the docks, Celia came across loaded ships and wherries. There was also a substantial bridge with houses on, similar to London Bridge.

The streets of Bristol were found to be *"well pitch'd"* and the buildings, principally of timber, were high and jettied. This made the streets narrow and dark. Goods were moved about on sleds to protect the street surface. In the market place Celia found a magnificent cross, similar to Coventry cross in style. Built in a series of tiers, it was richly ornamented with effigies of kings and was topped by a spire.

Bristol castle had disappeared before Celia's visit but the layout of the city still bore traces of a fortified settlement with twelve entrance gates. Celia observed only one church, likely St Mary Redcliffe, and the cathedral, although she noted that there were nineteen parish churches. William Schellinks, touring in 1662, recorded nineteen churches also but only five gates.[3] Such accounts are suggestive of organised early tourist information. Celia also observed some noble almshouses. In one she recorded that there was accommodation for six men and six women. Another, built by Mr Coleson (Colston), was a house built of stone around a handsome court, with gates and a palisade with four grass plots divided by walks. One side was for men and the other for women whilst in the centre she found a chapel, two kitchens, a room for washing and brewing and gardens behind. Inmates were allowed 3 shillings (15 new pence) a week and coal to maintain them.

There was a large conduit of carved stone by the quay. It conveyed water about the town but the taste was somewhat brackish. This did not compare with the hot spring that she visited at St Vincent's Rock where the water was clear and sweet and as warm as new milk. The spa was located in the Avon gorge about 2 miles from the city centre. Visiting the Hotwells, as the area was known, was only one of the pastimes associated with the area. The other was searching for Bristol diamonds in the Avon gorge. Although not as hard as real diamonds, the Bristol diamond was made into jewellery.

Having visited the Hotwells, Celia proceeded next to Wookey Hole via Aston (Ashton Court). This involved taking a ferry across the Avon. Ashton Court was located a mile from the water side on the far side and she particularly commented on the fine park and, what was even then, a large old house.

COMMENT

Celia Fiennes found Bristol a large, prosperous city and port. Jacobus Millerd's plan of Bristol, dated 1673, gives a detailed view of the city at about

the time of her visit and is invaluable for under- standing the town- scape.[4]

Part of Jacobus Millerd's plan of Bristol, dated 1673, showing the bridge and High Cross.

217

It is possible to retrace Celia's footsteps with ease although the urban land-scape has changed considerably in the intervening 300 years. For example, Celia Fiennes remarked on the bridge with houses on. This was similar to London Bridge and was built in 1247 and demolished in 1761.[5] There were a number of distinct differences between the Bristol and London bridges. Bristol Bridge was considerably shorter and a feature of the bridge was that the houses were built with the intention of pleasing the eye when viewed from the river. In 1662 William Schellinks commented in his journal that the bridge was closely built on both sides with handsome houses and shops.[6] On London Bridge, by contrast, the outward appearance of the buildings was considerably less attractive. Pope, who took the Hotwells waters in 1739, confirmed that, like London Bridge, the bridge at Bristol was built up on both sides and just as crowded.[7]

The Bristol bridge connected what was seen historically as two distinct and separate towns, one side being in Gloucestershire and the other in Somerset. The towns were merged in the time of Henry III and the bridge built. It incorporated buildings which included a chapel in the centre and shops from where considerable trade was conducted.

John Ogilby in his *Britannia* (1698) recorded that Bristol held markets on Wednesdays and Saturdays which were plentifully provided. Fairs were held on St James' Day and St Paul's Day and were well frequented. St James the Great's Feast day is 25 July and St Paul's Feast day is 29 June.[8] The magnificent market cross that Celia saw marked the place where goods from both sides should be traded after the merging of the two communities. It was located at the junction of High, Wine, Broad and Corn Streets but was removed in 1736, being an obstruction. Initially resited at College Green it was then relocated at Stourhead by the Hoare family.[9]

Celia's comment regarding the well pitched streets refers to the practice of the time of sloping the surface to the middle. The centre then effectively became an open sewer. This in turn led to the custom of men walking on the outside of the lady to protect her skirts from the debris thrown up by passing traffic.

BRISTOL DIAMONDS - LAPIS CALAMINARIS

There are several schools of thought on the identity of the Bristol diamonds, Lapis Calaminaris, that Celia Fiennes searched for in small crevices in the rock of the Avon Gorge. Some were clear, colourless and brilliant and were of sufficient quality to make into jewellery. They were hard enough to cut glass and some, tinged with yellow and purple, were called Bristol topazes and amethysts. A local industry grew up supplying the demand for Bristol diamonds to visitors but shops were reputed to be selling "spar crystals" rather than the genuine specimens.[10] Earlier visitors to the city recorded the search for the diamonds. In 1634 three worthy gentlemen visited Bristol as part of a survey of 26 counties. They inspected the strange hot well that gushed from the rocks when the tide was out, finding that people washed in and drank the medicinal waters. They also marvelled at the copious cold spring that fell from the rocks opposite the hot well. Having seen the wells they retraced their path up the 200 slippery steps seeking on the way the *"glittering bastard diamond stones"*.[11] The State Papers of James I mention that Bristol diamonds were used to decorate the King's palace, Theobalds.[12]

Bristol historian Helen Reid (1992) identifies the diamonds as quartz of magnesian conglomerate and this is possibly a reference to the Dolomitic conglomerate found in the Bristol area derived from Triassic times.[13] A more detailed explanation is that Bristol diamonds occur as Celestite crystals found in the Triassic Keuper Marls. These are orthorhombic, strontium sulphate crystals, $SrSO_4$. They have a specific gravity of 3.9-4.0 with a hardness of 3.0-3.5. The crystals can vary in colour from blue, colourless, yellow or reddish, often with a pearly lustre. Commonly found in sedimentary rocks, hydrothermal veins and in cavities in igneous rocks, important deposits are located at Yate near Bristol. Often the crystaline deposits are the result of secondary leaching from the primary deposits. These can fill joints or fissures in the underlying rock or extend downwards as veins and stringers.[14] Commercial exploitation is carried out for a variety of uses in the food, chemical, surgical and pyrotechnical industries. When the mineral is added to fire the flames become crimson. This special effect was used by Bengalese priests to impress believers.[15]

Marshall in 1818 observed that Mr Billingsley, reviewing the economy of North Somerset 1794/8, found Lapis Calaminaris being worked as a mineral deposit in several villages. The worked deposits were all near the surface and occurred in "chasms" or dykes between solid rock. This industry employed 400-500 miners and the average price was about £5 per ton. Mined to a depth of up to 30 fathoms, a hazel divining rod was reliably used to ascertain where the ore lay before a shaft was sunk.[16]

Geodes or potato stones of banded agate lined with quartz crystals occur sometimes in association with Celestite. They have been shown to be on occasions pseudomorphs, that is replicating the crystal structure of Celestite. The geodes particularly occur in the Triassic (Keuper) Dolomitic Conglomerate and likely originated from the alteration of either reworked anhydrite nodules or anhydrite replaced pebbles of Carboniferous rocks. There is a further source of quartz crystals in the St Vincent's Rocks. Fissures lined with red, yellow and colourless quartz extend to at least 200-300 feet below the base of the overlaying Triassic rocks into the Carboniferous.[17]

Dr Russel (1755) of Brighton and Epsom fame expressed another view. Lapis Calaminaris to him was the grey calamine found in England near copper mines. Calamine is the now obsolete term for Smithsonite ($ZnCO_3$). It was used in brass making. Relying on the ancient classical texts, Dr Russel believed that it *"can be taken internally for fluxes of the belly"*. Called Golden Powder, adults would start at 5-10 grams daily, thereafter increasing the dose as necessary. In this way it would remove the most stubborn obstructions of the bowel and consume viscous humours.[18]

It can be seen that there were several possibilities with regard to what Celia Fiennes described as Bristol diamonds. The geode is likely the true Bristol diamond and this conforms with the views expressed by Kellaway and Welch (1993) detailed above. The occurrence of quartz no doubt gave rise to confusion and possibly deception. Examples can be seen at the Bristol Museum and Art Gallery and Goldney Grotto in Bristol.

THE CONDUITS

The abundance of spring water was a key element in the determination of the founding and subsequent development of the city. The first water engineers were the medieval monks and friars. They were able to tap springs outside the city walls and convey the water through pipes made of lead and wood to conduit houses. From there water bearers would distribute the spring water to individual locations. A guild of water bearers was formed.[19]

By the fifteenth century St John's Pipe, All Saint's Pipe, Jacob's Well Pipe, Temple Pipe and Redcliffe Pipe existed together with ancillary "feathers" which distributed water to key points throughout the city. St John's Pipe still functions and there is a running conduit in Nelson Street. In addition, a Friary pipe belonging to the Dominican Order at Quaker Friars and rising at Ashley Vale Penny Well was appropriated by the city Mayor and Corporation and became known as Quay (Key) Pipe. This was used for supplying ships and was reputed to be good for scurvy. It was used to furnish water for Cabot's voyage of discovery to America in 1479 and was the large conduit noted by Celia Fiennes.[20] The public outlet in 1717 was by Clare Street but it was moved several times during the eighteenth century.

An anonymous paper, attributed to one Joseph Leech, and published in the 1850s, gives a more detailed picture of the Key Pipe. It is described as a miniature waterworks which was constructed in the fourteenth century. It may be earlier but records exist confirming that maintenance was carried out after 1376.[21] Celia observed a finely carved stone conduit and this is what caught the eye of John Leland when he visited Bristol in 1534 and which he described as a "faire castellette". The chief decoration was a head of Momus, the god of laughter, suggesting that the water of the conduit was conducive to enjoyment and good health. Such enjoyment of the conduit was not limited to the water therein. During the seventeenth century, about the time when Celia Fiennes visited Bristol, it was practice to fill the lead cistern under the Quay with alcoholic beverage as part of a public celebration. An officer of the Corporation dispensed the liquor during such occasions.[22] The castellette was demolished in 1770 although the cistern was rediscovered in St Stephen's Street in 1880 [23].

The Ashley Vale source of the Key Pipe was the "Penny" or "Beggars Well", a withy bed between Ashley Court and the Mill Stream, the latter flowing from the Boiling Well located towards Stoke House. Key Pipe was formerly a friary pipe belonging to the Dominicans at Quakers Priors. Ashley Vale is about 2 kilometres north of the city centre and is now extensively developed as housing estates. The stream can still be identified but little remains that Celia Fiennes would have recognised. At the withy bed there were two springs overflowing into a lead cistern and conduit house. From there the pipe ran along the north bank of Mill Stream to Lower Ashley House where it turned under the brook and headed towards the hamlet known as Botany Bay. There a conduit then supplied the further pipe which ran under Newfoundland Street, then passing the White Horse Inn in Milk Street, through Horsefair, over Bridewell Bridge, where a feather once supplied the Bridewell, along the north side of Nelson Street, crossing the pavement flanking St John's Church, along Quay Street to the cistern under the Quay where there were two cocks for the use of shipping. As such it was considered the greatest of all Bristol pipes and conduits.[24]

Another pump with a castellette over was St Peter's Pump. It was surmounted by an imposing pillared pinnacle constructed in 1474 by William Spencer. This was also known as St Edith's Well and was located in Peter Street near St Peter's Church. It was removed by Act of Parliament in 1766.[25] Like the old High Cross, it was removed to Stourhead in Wiltshire by the Hoare family where it stands at the head of the river at Six Wells Bottom. Sir Richard C. Hoare, Bart. has been described as the Lord Elgin of Bristol, having carried off a variety of sculptured monuments from our British Athens.[26] This is an unfair description on two counts. It was Henry Hoare "The Magnificent" (1705-1785) who secured the Bristol Cross for Stourhead in 1764. Richard C. Hoare was the son of Henry's nephew. Following riots in London in 1780, which Henry envisaged would jeopardise his banking business and personal assets, he passed Stourhead to Richard. It was thus Henry "The Magnificent" who perhaps should have been described as the Elgin of Bristol. Woodbridge records however that Henry Hoare rescued the Bristol Cross from the grounds of the cathedral where it lay in many pieces. It had previously been dismantled at the request of the Bristol people because of its ruinous state and because it was seen as a superstitious relic.[27] After removal from the crossroads in 1736 as an obstruction, the Cross was initially resited at College Green but became the loitering spot for the disorderly.[28] With such an inglorious history to the Cross, the Hoares were conservationists rather than pirates of Bristol treasures.

THE HOTWELLS

When Celia visited in 1698 she would have travelled from the city centre to Clifton and the Avon Gorge to take the waters, a distance of about 2 miles. The area became known as Hotwells after the thermal springs that erupt at the foot of St Vincent's Rock. The rock was originally surmounted by a chapel dedicated to the saint, a native of Spain and martyred in AD 305. His name was applied to the springs as St Vincent's Well. A cave, which still exists in the cliff, is reputed to be the old hermitage, once connecting with the chapel of St Mary and St Vincent.[29]

At Clifton, Celia would have found the newly built Hotwell House (1696) which provided a pump room and lodgings. By 1702 a second New Hotwell had been established some 200 yards further along the river bank. Being more remote and within sight of the gibbeted remains of murderers, this secondary spa survived less than 100 years. To Celia therefore, Bristol was an adolescent spa at the end of the seventeenth century. It was during the eighteenth century that Bristol was to develop as an important social centre and mature spa. About the time of Celia's visit the bottled mineral water trade was starting to develop also and in 1701 baskets of Bristol water are recorded as going to Gloucester and Chester. The port facilities and Bristol's extensive glass bottle industry greatly enhanced the potential for the subsequent development of this trade.[30] By the mid-eighteenth century the Quay was reckoned to be the longest in England.[31]

The faid *John Fiddes* has fettled fuch a Correfpondence for the *Pyrmont*, *Bath*, and *Briftol* Hot Well-Waters, that he has them fent him frefh and in their greateft Perfeɛtion ; which are fealed with their proper Seals, as in the Margin.

The Prices of the WATERS *in* London, *delivered to any Part thereof, free of all Charges* ; viz.

German, *Spa*, and *Pyrmont*, at 14 *s. per* Doz.
Spa, Half-Flafks, at 10 *s. per* Doz.
Scarborough and *Bath*, at 7 *s.* 6 *d. per* Doz. and 4 *s. per* Half-Doz.
Briftol, at 6 *s. per* Doz.

Seal on Mineral Waters sold by John Fiddes of Covent Garden, 1734.[32]

Little is known about the first discovery of St Vincent's Well. In a 1640 account, by a physician, of the healing properties of the well, the discovery is dated about 1340. The physician is not identified in the manuscript which is deposited in the British Library.[33] One of the earliest mentions of the Hotwells spring is by the fifteenth century topographer William of Wyrecester

222

(Worcester) when sailors said that it cured leprosy.[34] William made his perambulations between 1477 and 1480. He was born in Bristol and retired to the city also. His extensive descriptions of Bristol and other towns are an important chronicle of England at that time.

St Vincent's spring at Hotwells first came to the wider public notice in the mid-sixteenth century when many new springs were being discovered and recognised as potentially of medicinal value.[35] William Harrison, whose *Description of England* was published in 1577 and 1587, dismissed the miraculous wells and cures associated with earlier religious beliefs. Instead he advocated a more down to earth approach integrating the idea of religious sanction with medical benefit. Harrison specifically mentioned the St Vincent's Rock and spring.[36] Early visitors included Lord Paulet's wife who drank the waters in 1629. John Evelyn, the diarist, whose brother Richard was later lord of the manor at Epsom Wells, visited St Vincent's Rock on 30 May 1654. Like Celia Fiennes he visited the Hotwells and searched for Bristol diamonds.[37] Evelyn was closely followed by William Schellinks in July 1662. There were two abundant springs, one hot and one cold. He drank the waters which were milk-warm and was shown Bristol diamonds by his landlord. The ale, brewed from the waters, commanded greater praise than the waters themselves.[38]

In 1630 John Bruckshaw was licensed by Charles I to exploit the water and mineral wealth, including containing the spring and building a bath, for a period of 40 years. He supplemented the commercial opportunity with numerous extravagant claims as to the efficacy of the waters as well as claiming to be the original discoverer of the thermal waters.

Other early testimony to the St Vincent's spring include the writings of Tobias Venner MD. He described it as a hot water suited to treatment for the stone. Venner published a treatise on the Baths of Bath in 1628. He included a substantial criticism and censure of Bristol mineral waters, later described as pompous drivel.[39] He had a practice at Bath and no doubt felt patients' best interests were served by patronising that city and his practice. He died in 1660, when a memorial monument to him was sited in Bath Abbey.[40] Bath and Bristol at this time were clearly developing in tandem and some rivalry existed between the two.[41]

In 1676 the Bristol Society of Merchant Venturers bought the moiety of the Manor of Clifton which included 200 steps down the cliff side at St Vincent's Rock. The following year the Queen, Catherine of Braganza, wife of Charles II, visited the spring although the occasion was not overtly supported by the civic authorities for political reasons. By 1680 the efficacy of the waters had been extended to the cure of diabetes. James Gagg, a baker, suffering from the ailment, successfully used the thermal waters as a cure to everyone's great surprise.[42]

Until the 1690s the facilities were undeveloped to any great extent and the Society of Merchant Venturers rented out the Hotwell in 1687 for £2 a year. Contamination by the tide was a recurring problem. In 1691 it was necessary to build a substantial wall around the enclosure. Unfortunately this threatened to stop the spring outfall and the entire spa was endangered. This potentially disastrous event was followed by a major initiative to develop the Hotwells by a group of Bristol business persons in 1695. They took a lease of 90 years from the Merchant Venturers and this committed them to substantial capital investment. Robert Yate was one of the principal entrepreneurs at the time. He was a former mayor (1693) and Master of the Merchant Venturers in 1692.[43] The result was Hotwells House, built in 1696, which Celia Fiennes would have seen as a new development in Clifton.[44]

The Hotwells House was a somewhat austere building perched on a rocky ledge over the water. Some saw it as a romantic place with enchanting views, others were less impressed, particularly because of the stink of the river mud when the tide went out. The pump room at the house required a lift of 30 feet to raise the water for use. The tides rose and fell by a similar amount. There was a system of valves which prevented the ingress of tidal water at high tide but the technology was suspect.[45] Although access to the Hotwells and the surrounding Clifton area remained difficult throughout the eighteenth century, the capital investment led to a period of spa prosperity for Bristol which was to last for 100 years.

After over a century as a spa centre the Hotwells House was demolished in 1822 to make way for road improvements. This coincided with a general decline of the spa although there was subsequently a minor revival in the early nineteenth century with a new pump room being built. It enjoyed the grandiose title of "The Royal Clifton Spa Pump Room, Baths and Mineral Aerated Water Manufactory, Hotwell".[46] Mr James Bolton was the energetic entrepreneur behind the scheme. In 1867 the later pump room was demolished and a public fountain provided. Contamination by the river water could not be ignored and a Dr Griffin queried the authenticity of the fountain water. In spite of this the pump continued in use until 1913 when it was sought to replace the supply with an uncontaminated source achieved by borings. The attempt was not successful.[47]

A further pump room, known as the Clifton Spa, was opened in 1894. This was located in Prince's Buildings above the Colonnade. A substantial building with magnificent interior it was convenient to the underground railway that once scaled the cliffs of the Gorge. The pump room was awaiting demolition some years ago.[48] So the sun eventually set on Bristol's spa industry.

Geochemistry

Dr Granville, writing in 1841, described the St Vincent Well as a "sub-tepid" spring. He found that the water temperature was around 73° F and this, he said, was certainly not hot.[49] The geological background to the emergence of thermal waters at Clifton is similar to that of Bath, both believed to be from a common aquifer. This is covered in detail under the section on Bath. Dr Granville gave an analysis of the waters.

Analysis Of Clifton Wells Thermal Waters.

The comparable analysis for Bath waters is given to illustrate the similarities.

grains per pint.

	Clifton	Bath
Soda with Muriatic acid	-	1.89
Soda with Sulphuric Acid	2.02	2.42
Soda with Carbonic acid	-	-
Lime with Muriatic acid	0.47	-
Lime with Sulphuric Acid	0.93	10.20
Lime with Carbonic acid	1.68	1.33
Magnesia with Muriatic acid	0.90	1.67
Magnesia with Sulphuric acid	-	-
Magnesia with Carbonic acid	-	-
Alumine	-	0.01
Silica	-	0.41
Oxide of Iron pure	-	-
Oxide of Iron with Carbonic acid	-	Pr.Ox.0.03
Iodine	-	-
Bromine	-	-
Sulph.Hydr.gas cu. ins.	-	-
Carburetted Hydrg. in cu. ins.	-	-
Azote in cu.ins.	-	-
Free Carb.gas in cu.ins.	3.75	0.20
Authority	Dr Carrick	Walcker
Date	1819	1829

Source: Granville 1841.

The Waters

The Hotwells water was described in 1769 as sometimes of a whitish colour which disappeared as it cooled. Many small bubbles were thrown off when first taken from the pump. The taste was milky, soft and pleasantly agreeable to the stomach. The water was without smell and lukewarm to the touch. Bristol water supposedly thickened the humours and was successfully prescribed for internal inflammations, hectic fevers, coughs and the scurvy.

As noted previously, following the cure of James Gagg, it was recommended for diabetes. It also was used for obstructions of the urinary passages and was most efficacious when drunk warm. In spite of this it was available from Owen's Original Mineral Water Warehouse in London by the mid-eighteenth century. For those purchasing bottled Bristol water it was recommended that the bottle be placed in boiling water to raise the temperature before use, thereby restoring its virtues.[50]

It was also used in treating ulcers of the eyes and the promotion of appetite and digestion. Scrophulous and cancerous ulcers were relieved, either by washing or by application with linen dipped into the water. Further claims included the stopping of bleeding, curing of windiness and generally strengthening the stomach.

The recommended method of drinking the water was, on the first day, a glass or two before breakfast followed by similar about 5pm. Thereafter three glasses before breakfast and three in the afternoon. Some cures could be effected in weeks, others took months. At the pump house, high tides meant a cessation of use until the water had flushed through any seawater inundation. Many preferred to supplement their intake by taking the waters at their lodgings instead of ordinary water, when it could be made into tea if so wished.

THE ALMSHOUSES

Celia Fiennes saw two almshouses during her visit. The first, which housed six men and six women, was almost certainly White's almshouses, shown on Millerd's plan of Bristol, 1673, as in Bearlane. They were completed in 1613 by Dr Thomas White for six men and six women. Thomas White was born in Temple Street, the son of John White and enjoyed various high offices in the church during the sixteenth century.[51]

Colston's Almshouses, built in 1691.

The second almshouses, which survive today, were those of Mr Edward Colston. In 1690, Colston negotiated with the Corporation for 3 acres of land on St Michael's Hill for almshouses and a chapel.

The almshouses were built in 1691, accommodating twelve men and twelve women. The overall cost of building was about £2,500 including £100 for the land. When Celia Fiennes visited, the almshouses would have been a new development on the fringe of the city. In 1696 a management body was formed, comprising mainly members of the Merchant Venturers Society. Colston endowed the almshouses with rents from fee-farms and conveyed the property to the management body in perpetuity.[52]

Colston's business interests in Bristol included sugar refining.[53] He traded with the West Indies, was a governor of Christ's Hospital in London, a Royalist, Tory and confirmed Anglican. He founded the Colston School, provided funds for enlarging the Seamen's Almshouses and shared the costs of the cathedral restoration in the seventeenth century.[54] He died in 1721 in Mortlake and there is a statue to his memory in Bristol's Broad Quay.

ASHTON COURT

Celia Fiennes visited Ashton Court when she left Bristol having taken the ferry across the river. Today it is readily accessible by crossing the Avon suspension bridge at Clifton from where the entrance is a 5 minute walk. The estate was purchased for the people of Bristol in 1972 and the extensive parkland and deer park remain open to the public for recreation.

The Domesday Book records the Manor of Ashton, when it was clearly a wealthy estate. William de Lyons acquired Long Ashton in the late thirteenth century, including the manor house on the present site of Ashton Court. The family was granted a licence to enclose the Park in 1392 by Richard II. In 1545 it was purchased by the Smyth family in whose hands it remained for 400 years. The Smyths were Bristol merchants and Thomas Smyth built a new south facade in 1632/3.[55] Celia Fiennes therefore saw this facade which survivies today.

Ashton Court, Bristol.

When Celia Fiennes visited the house it would have been in the hands of John Smyth who married Elizabeth Astry in 1692. They had their third daughter the year Celia journeyed to Bristol. Although they subsequently went on to have three sons, all died without issue and the male line became extinct. Succession was through the female line: Jarrit Smith, who married Florence, born 1701, changing his name to ensure continuity.[56]

TODAY

The Hotwells have all but disappeared into obscurity. The Colonnade is the most striking remaining architectural feature in the Gorge. This once adjoined Hotwell House and formed part of the complex of eighteenth century spa buildings. Later it abutted Bolton's Royal Clifton Spa. The New Hotwells site is still identifiable by a public fountain which once pumped water for public use, located alongside the busy Portway road. This was built by the Corporation in 1894 but no longer functions.[57] The remains of the spa can best be viewed from the Avon suspension bridge, opened in 1864.

The cathedral and College Green, mentioned by Celia Fiennes, remain in the centre of Bristol. The Green provides ready access to the key elements of the city. Ashton Court and Colston's Almshouses are also buildings that Celia Fiennes saw and which survive today.

Bristol is a most fascinating city and there are many interesting sites to visit in addition to those frequented by Celia Fiennes. The SS Great Britain and the reproduction of John Cabot's "Matthew" on Redcliffe Quay, in which he discovered Newfoundland, and arguably America in 1497, testify to Bristol's maritime history.

Footnotes:

1   Morris C. (ed.) 1947, *The Journeys of Celia Fiennes*, p.237-9.
2   ibid. p.243, 261.
3   Exwood M. Lehmann H L. (trans.) 1993, *The Journal of William Schellinks' Travels in England, 1661-1663*, p.102/3.
4   *Jacobus Millerd's plan of Bristol*, 1673, republished 1952, Waterlow and Sons, Bristol Reference Library, ref. B2S831.
5   Morris C. (ed.) 1982, *The Illustrated Journeys of Celia Fiennes*, p.193.
6   Exwood M. Lehmann H L. op.cit. p.102.
7   Home G. 1931, *Old London Bridge*, p.255, 256.
8   Farmer D H. 1978, *The Oxford Dictionary of Saints*.
9   Shiercliff E. 1793, *The Bristol and Hotwell Guide*, p.6/7.
10 ibid. p.65.
11 Latimer J. 1970, *The Annals of Bristol in the Sixteenth Century*, p.129/30.
12 Happerfield L. Hutton S. 1915, *Bath and Bristol*, p.55.
13 Reid H. 1992, *A Chronicle of Clifton and Hotwells*, Redcliffe, p.9.
14 Kellaway G A. Welch F B A. 1993, *The Geology of the Bristol District*, p.155.
15 Kourimsky J. 1977, *Minerals and Rocks*, p.202.
16 Marshall W. 1818, *The Review and Abstracts of the County Reports of the Board of Agriculture*, Vol.2, p.494/5.

17 Kellaway G A. Welch F B A. op.cit. p.143.
18 Russel R. 1755, *Oeconomy of Nature*, p.192-198.
19 Bristol Waterworks, 1949, *The Water Supply of Bristol*, p.1.
20 ibid. p.1.
21 Nickolls J F. Taylor J. 1881, *Bristol Past and Present*, Vol.1, p.139.
22 Anon. c.1850, *The Pipes, Pumps, and Conduits of Bristol*, p.8/9.
23 Nickolls J F. Taylor J. op.cit. p.139.
24 Anon. c.1850, op.cit. p.9.
25 Woodbridge K. 1995, *The Stourhead Landscape*, p.59/60.
26 Anon. c.1850, *The Pipes, Pumps, and Conduits of Bristol*, p.6/7; Rattue J. 1994, "Wells at the Bottom of the Garden", *Source, The Holy Well Journal*, new series, No.2, winter, p.24. note: there may be confusion between the High Cross and St Edith's Well in Rattue.
27 Woodbridge K. op.cit. p.25, 28.
28 Shiercliff E. op.cit. p.6/7.
29 ibid. p.63.
30 Hembry P. 1990, *The English Spa, 1560-1815*, p. 245.
31 Boddely T. 1755, 3rd edition, *The Bath and Bristol Guide*, p.44.
32 Taken from Shaw P. 1734, *An Enquiry into Scarborough Spaw Waters*, endpiece.
33 Anon. 1640, *Accounts of Hotwells by a physician*, British Library, Sl. 640 ff.340-351.
34 Reid H. op.cit. p.9.
35 Hembry P. op.cit. p.15.
36 ibid. p.18/19.
37 Bray W. (ed.) c.1946, *The Diary of John Evelyn*, 1641-1705/6, p.229.
38 Exwood M. Lehmann H L. op.cit. p.104/5.
39 Latimer J. op.cit. p.106.
40 Freeman H W. 1888, *The Thermal Baths of Bath*, p.102/3.
41 Hembry P. op.cit. p.55.
42 Waite V. 1960, *The Bristol Hotwell*, p.6.
43 Latimer J. op.cit. p.472, 499, 500.
44 Hembry P. op.cit. p.97.
45 Waite V. op.cit. p.6/7.
46 Bolton J. c.1854, *Visitor Guide to Clifton, Bristol, Hotwells, and Neighbourhood*, frontispiece.
47 Waite V. op.cit. p.13-15.
48 Tydesley B. c.1975, *Save the Clifton Spa Pump Room. Built 1894*, undated typescript.
49 Granville A B. 1841, *Spas of England, Southern Spas*, p.352.
50 Russel R. 1769 (5th edition), *Dissertation on the use of Sea Water* with anonymous supplement *A Treatise on the Nature, Properties and Uses of the Mineral Waters* p.178-185.
51 Nickolls J F. Taylor J. op.cit. p.275.
52 Latimer J. op.cit. p.457.
53 Pryce G. 1861, *A Popular History of Bristol*, p.225.
54 Edwards T. 1951, *British Cities, Bristol*, p.27/8.
55 Bristol City Council, c.1994, *Ashton Court Mansion and Estate*, publicity leaflet.
56 Bantok A. *The Smyths of Ashton Court*, 1980, p.7.
57 Waite V. op.cit. p.4.

BATH

Celia Fiennes first came to Bath from Newton Toney via Warminster and this was likely one of her first recorded travels. After her mother's death Celia's journeys began in London. The Manor House at Newton Toney was where Celia was likely born in 1662 and where her mother lived until her death in 1691. Celia was probably about 25 years old when she embarked on this early visit in the late 1680s. Her record was to set the pattern for her later journals. The packhorse trail was particularly difficult for her carriage which got stuck in stones and marsh. The way into "the Bath", as she describes the town, was steep and stony.

The dates that Celia Fiennes visited Bath are difficult to establish with confidence. Morris suggests that it was before 1687 based on her failure to mention additions to the Cross Bath made in that year in honour of the visit of Queen Mary of Modena. In fact Morris hints that the date may even be before 1684 when her sister who accompanied her was married.[1] Smith suggests a much later date of 1695.[2] She certainly visited Bath a second time on her Great Journey of 1698 and used this as an opportunity to update the information from her earlier visit which included the new adornments to the Cross Street Bath cross.[3] This places her first visit either before its erection in 1688 or in 1689 or thereabouts when it appears to have been temporarily removed. The fact that her main account of Bath had been updated since first drafting is also apparent from Morris's 1947 text in which the description of the baths was followed by an account of Queen Anne's Coronation in 1702.[4] We are likely dealing with a conglomeration of recorded experiences from several dates.

Celia's first impressions of Bath were unfavourable. She noted the indifferent houses, the low lying situation and she disliked the steamy atmosphere caused by the baths. She commented on several good aspects, houses built as lodging adorned with furniture and the size of the streets. In 1698 she was somewhat more enthusiastic about Bath, recording it as a pretty place and noting new features.[5]

In her main account Celia recorded that there were five baths and it is in her descriptions that we are given an insight into the spa ethos of late seventeenth century Bath. The first was the **Hot Bath**, small and enclosed, with water straight from the springs and therefore at its hottest. From the Hot Bath the water flowed into the **Lepers Bath**. Next Celia noted the **Cross Bath**, which was larger than the Hot Bath and not so hot. When bathing the gentlemen sat on seats around the cross in the middle of the bath and the ladies in arches with seats around the walls. All was in stone and a stone cushion could be supplied if the seating was too low. It was customary to sit in the water up to the neck. Being cooler, this bath was generally used in summer. There was a gallery around the bath where those not bathing could walk and view the bathers. Besides bathing attendants there was a Sergeant who kept order. Often those of fashion made the acquaintance of the Sergeant when they began to bathe in order that he could look after their interests during the season.

When bathers walked about in the bath they were escorted by attendants to ensure that they did not overbalance, the way being cleared by other attendants. In the arches there were rings which could be used to steady oneself. The hot spring water bubbled up so rapidly from the bottom of the bath that it scalded the feet. This particularly applied in the **Kings Bath** where the centre cross and seating was appropriately known as the Kitchen. The Kings Bath comprised a great cross with seats in the middle. It was the largest of the baths. There was also a pump where scalding water could be directed at particular parts of the body depending on the ailment. One hundred pumps cost two pence, so Celia thought.

Ladies wore a yellow canvas robe for bathing which was stiff and large, rather like a parson's gown. The men had drawers and waistcoats of similar material. The garments filled and did not cling to the body as inferior linen did. This suggests that Celia was modest and approved of this arrangement. She also noted that the water would turn linen yellow which accounted for the colour of the bathing apparel. When bathing was completed, a partially submerged door led to stairs out of the water. Once the door was closed behind, bathers ascended the stairs discarding the bathing robe. The attendant then replaced the robe with a flannel garment like a nightgown with great sleeves. Slippers were provided and bathers would be seated on a chair in a slip room, possibly in front of a fire. The chairs were with a low seat, with red baize, and enclosed by a frame over the head. Curtains enabled bathers to enclose themselves and keep warm. Attendants then transported the bather to their lodgings where they would transfer to bed and sweat as they pleased. Maids in the lodgings then attended until the subject had completed the treatment.

This arrangement existed for all the baths including the **Queens Bath**, the second largest bath after the Kings Bath. The Queens Bath was directly fed from the Kings Bath and was hotter than the Cross Bath although cooler that the Kings Bath. Each bath had a gallery surrounding it and from a gallery at the Kings Bath water from a pump could be drunk. The water was observed to be hot and smelling like boiled eggs; the nearer the pump, the less offensive.

The baths were emptied after the morning bathing at about 10-11 o'clock. Sluices enabled the bath to be refilled by the springs that bubbled up out of the gravel floor. This could be completed by the evening should bathers wish to return to the bath. A white scum appeared on the surface of the water when refilling had taken place. This was removed by attendants. Failure to remove the scum resulted in what was known as bath mantle, giving rise to pimples and heat rash. A similar effect was noted if bathers failed to purge before bathing.

Outside the baths, the town was organised for pedestrians and chairs but not for coaches and carriages. There was pleasant walking around the cathedral cloisters and the Meads. The surrounding hills were not resorted to. Celia later noted many places where there were green walks. Near the cathedral there was the priory with rows of trees and a green surrounded by the houses of deans, prebends and doctors. In the Kings Mead there were Cake-houses where visitors could enjoy "*sulibubs and liqueurs*". There was also a produce market where goods could be secured for reasonable prices. The principal cost in visiting Bath was the lodging and fires, although she acknowledged that the service was good.

At this point Celia diverted from her topographical description of the town to outline the celebration details and parade associated with the Queen's coronation in 1702, the year that she wrote up her journals. This suggests a further visit in that year. Princess Anne was a frequent visitor to Tunbridge Wells before her coronation on the 23 April. The parade, which Celia described in some detail, ended up in the abbey or cathedral for a sermon. Following this there was music and bonfires with feasting and dancing. Confusion exists to this day regarding whether Bath has an abbey or cathedral.

Illustration: Bath Abbey or Cathedral as seen today, the facade having changed little since Celia Fiennes walked around the precincts.

COMMENT

When Celia Fiennes visited Bath she found a city of about 300+ houses with the old city walls still largely intact. The survey of 1641 showed that there were about this number of houses and there had been little development since that date. Given an average number of persons to each house of between 3 and 5, the main city population would have been about 1,200.[6] Allowing for visitors, servants etc. the population was probably about 2,000 when Celia visited.[7] Woollen manufacture had been the city's staple industry but by the latter part of the seventeenth century Bath was in financial difficulties. It did not even possess a goldsmith, a situation which the council proposed rectifying by offering the freedom of the city to lure such talent.[8]

The main tourist attraction were the hot baths and Celia noted the Hot, Lepers, Cross, Kings and Queens Baths. Bath had a reputation for its hot mineral springs dating back to time immemorial and yet it had failed to keep pace with the developments that were taking place at the new spas such as Tunbridge and Epsom and the town of Spa, then in Germany. Richard Nash, later to become the famous Master of Ceremonies, first visited Bath in 1705, finding it an uninteresting little spa.[9] In fact seventeenth century Bath has been likened to the work of savages when compared to the Roman city which is only now being fully appreciated.[10] Why might this be?

From Celia's own account it is apparent that travel was difficult. She had personal ties with the area but for the traveller from London, Epsom and Tunbridge Wells were much more convenient. There were also few local amenities although similar could be argued for Tunbridge and Epsom at that time. What is noticeable at both Tunbridge and Epsom is that there was a distinct social scene into which Celia involved herself. She mentioned the seats of the aristocracy and gentry in the localities. These formed a permanent facility for socialising and hospitality not available to the common people. Such social intercourse is less significant in her visit to Bath, which was clearly more isolated from the capital.

Bath was destined to prosper in the eighteenth century and the facilities, as recorded by Celia Fiennes, changed considerably in the ensuing years. Improvers such as John Wood, the architect, were to remodel the city while Beau Nash remodelled the social round. The medieval relic was to be replaced by a Georgian city.[11] With Celia's account therefore we have a valuable record of a premier spa on the verge of major expansion. What Celia wrote about was to prove the legacy which would pave the way for that future development of the city that can be seen today. In order to understand that legacy and the difficulties that Bath was faced with, it is necessary to investigate seventeenth century Bath in greater detail.

The Kings Bath looking very much as Celia Fiennes would have found it -
a sketch by William Schellinks 1662.
Courtesy of: the Austrian National Library and Picture Archive, Vienna.
Negativ aus dem Bildarchiv der Österreichschen Nationalbibliothek, Wien.

SEVENTEENTH CENTURY BATH

The latter part of the seventeenth century found Bath in disarray after the Civil War and Restoration. Traumatic fighting and shifting political allegiance led to disputes over parliamentary representation and appointment of a mayor in the 1660s. Later there was further disharmony during the Exclusion Crisis of 1680. The possible succession of the Popish King James was seen by the Whigs as undermining the constitution and religion of the state. The Tories however considered that James had the right from God to wear the Crown.[12] The city council had declared a pro Yorkist position in May but, fearful of losing their charter, had to do a speedy backtrack when Monmouth, with Tory inclinations, arrived in August.[13] In spite of this Bath was securing a tourist trade. As early as 1628 Dr Venner appeared to have sufficient trade to occupy him sufficiently in Bath for a whole year, having previously practised there in the spring and autumn. By the summer of 1653 there were three resident physicians at Bath. Although the baths lacked amenities such as roofs, making them impractical in cold weather, for treatments such as bucketing and pumping.[14]

Probably the greatest curb on development was the geography of the city. The 1379 poll tax suggested that there was limited suburban growth during medieval times.[15] The delineation of the city was essentially the ancient city walls. In 1660 Bath was still a small town with fifteen streets in 32 acres. The River Avon encircled the city on two sides and building to the west was blocked by 92 acres of common lands owned by the Corporation and farmed out. Although Bath stood at the junction of four great routeways, to Bristol, London, Exeter and South Wales, the state of the roads was such that trade was severely hindered by inadequate transport. The Corporation, which owned four-fifths of city property was disorganised and reluctant to embark on change, thereby stifling initiative.

Dr William Turner, in 1562, published the first major treatise on an English spa as part of a review of European Baths. Bath was the only English resort discussed; he considered it grossly underutilised to the detriment of the populace at large, especially in the North. His text was a damning indictment of the state of Bath. He recommended that baths should be drained and cleaned every 24 hours, that there should be separate baths for individual treatment and that the baths should be covered. He suggested vapour treatment facilities. He further proposed that there should be a bath where horses could be treated.[16] Turner's critique was not in vain. A century later William Schellinks was to observe a horse bath, indicating that some modernisation was taking place. In spite of this by the late seventeenth century development was not keeping apace with spas elsewhere in England. Bath traditionally had two seasons - spring and autumn - which were first determined by Dr Turner in the 1560s. The seasons were not dictated by the whim of the aristocracy to fit in with the summer seasons at Tunbridge and Epsom, but by geography and the nature of the waters. Bath, a low-lying township with a steamy atmosphere, would have been quite unbearable for invalids during the summer, whereas the chalybeate and saline waters of Tunbridge and Epsom respectively were recommended to be drunk during the summer months.

Celia Fiennes disliked the confined atmosphere of Bath and would have been aware that the city was blighted by outbreaks of sickness, smallpox and fever between 1665 and 1690.[17] Joan Sheppard gives a general retrospective description of the town which illustrates the general ambiance in the early years of the eighteenth century. *"The rooms where the balls were held were dirty, untidy and badly lighted: there was no regular band or caretaker. The streets were muddy in winter and dusty in summer, because they were not paved. Lodgings for visitors were expensive, dirty and poorly furnished; the floors, wrote John Wood, were stained brown with soot and small beer to hide the dirt! Worse still, many of the people in Bath behaved in a rude and quarrelsome way."*[18] It was not until 1755 that the *Bath and Bristol Guide* reported that the roads had been lately repaired.[19]

Given the conditions outlined, Bath was in no position to entertain tourists in any great number during the seventeenth century, even if they could be squeezed into the infrastructure which still nestled within the old town walls. A military survey of 1686 revealed that there were 324 available beds in inns and alehouses with stabling for 451 horses. This was less than the nearby city of Wells.[20]

One tourist who visited Bath in the seventeenth century was William Schellinks in 1662. His journal noted a very good inn, the Bear, and the same baths as later visited by Celia Fiennes. Outside the Southgate there was also a horse bath. Schellinks recorded the custom of visiting the baths early in the morning and at 5am he saw a lot of people at the Kings and Queens Baths. He described how bathers donned special underpants and shifts for the men and women respectively. Hot wine boiled with sugar and herbs helped to prevent fainting once in the water. Attendants helped strangers to the seats located in the bath. People often remained in the water for several hours and hot water could be pumped over afflicted parts of the body as well. Some people had as many as 1,800 pump strokes. A personal manicuring service was also to be had. Retiring from the water, the bather sweated in a warm bed for one or two hours, possibly being entertained by musicians and drinking mulled wine.[21] Schellinks' experience was very similar to that of Celia Fiennes some years later.

The essential ingredient for the successful spa in the latter part of the seventeenth century was the patronage of the nobility and gentry. Such patronage followed the Royal Court. In 1663 Bath's loyalty to the crown was displayed when Charles II and Catherine of Braganza visited the city with the Duke and Duchess of York, albeit after a visit to Tunbridge Wells. Dr Alexander Fraizer, the king's physician and political agent, was particularly enthusiastic about the mineral waters and likened them to Bourbon, where he had treated Queen Henrietta Maria.[22] The mineral water at Bourbonne-les-bains was classified later as a muriated saline thermal spring.[23] Fraizer also advocated drinking the waters and the Mayor of Bath responded by erecting a drinking pump in the middle of the Kings Bath as part of the new cross in 1664.

After the Restoration, Bath had a steady stream of visits by the nobility but was clearly in competition with the more convenient Tunbridge Wells and to a lesser extent Epsom, the latter being of particular appeal to the commuting gentry of London. It is also apparent that, as the century progressed, some new building was taking place and visitors like Celia Fiennes noted the better appointed premises particularly on her later visit. In 1690 there was a newly built coach house and another in 1692. The streets in the city centre however remained narrow and although today we would welcome such a layout as a walking precinct, at the time it caused congestion. Municipal services were a problem throughout this era. The water supply conduit was over-used and rubbish littered the streets of the overcrowded city. The baths themselves enjoyed only minor improvement; for example the Cross Bath was given a pump and cistern in 1665.[24]

Eventually James II was deposed in 1689 and this led to Bath celebrating the onset of the reign of William and Mary with enthusiasm. The cross in the Cross Baths was removed as a conciliatory gesture. As the uncertainty was replaced by optimism, Bath entered an era of city development. Premises were extended, often downward as cellars were enlarged. Ribbon development took place to the north-east and landscaping was carried out. New enterprises were established including bookshops and bowling greens.[25]

Princess Anne had resorted to Bath in 1688 when the birth of her son and intrigues at Tunbridge Wells had put her in an equivocal position. She subsequently returned to Tunbridge until the affair of the pantiles in 1687/8 which is detailed in the chapter on Tunbridge Wells. Severing her allegiance completely with Tunbridge she had visited Bath four times by 1703, three times as Queen. This put Bath firmly on the Court map and prosperity followed in spite of the fact that it was to be the last visit of a reigning sovereign until 1917.[26]

Perhaps sensing the forthcoming social revolution at the spa or aware of the undercurrent of immoral behaviour, the Bishop of Bath and Wells from 1685-1690 was advocating invalids to take all care and not to abuse the bath by lasciviousness and impurity. Only God's immediate blessing ensured that the waters would in turn heal the sufferer. This theme was taken up by Dr Peirce in *Bath Memoirs* (1697); patients should pray to the Great Physician of Soul and Body.[27] The origins of this supposed divine intervention originated from Turner's publication of 1568 *"and by the help of almighty God be healed there"*.[28]

The seventeenth century was one of dormancy for Bath's mineral water springs and their development. Celia Fiennes came at the end of this era, preempting the period of growth as the premier spa by a few years. In her journal we have a valuable record of the late medieval city before it embarked on the social and economic era of Beau Nash. In the eighteenth century, Bath was to be at the forefront of English spas as they enjoyed the zenith of their development.

BATH THE ANCIENT SPA

Evidence suggesting Mesolithic use of the springs has enabled the utilisation of the hot springs to be determined back to about 7,000 BP. Neolithic and Bronze age evidence is peculiarly absent but iron age archaeological evidence confirms human activity in the area from about 2,600 BP to the Roman occupation.[29]

Kellaway has provided an insight into pre-Roman Bath using subterranean evidence. Two small knolls were encircled on three sides by the extensive alluvial floor of the river valley. The Cross and Hetling springs issued from the summit of the western knoll and the Kings Spring issued in the centre of the area. The outfall of the Kings Spring flowed south between the knolls to the river. The Kings Spring, the largest, would have been surrounded by a substantial area of treacherous ground, between 20 and 30 metres in diameter, resulting from the infilling of the geological spring pipe (see also Geochemistry).[30] Celtic reverence for the springs lends support to the notion that until Roman times the area was left very much in its natural state.

It was the Romans who contained the springs with the construction of a thermae about the time of Claudius. The Kings Spring was contained in a stone and lead lined reservoir and water flowed first into the Great Bath and then to the Roman drain. The two smaller springs just to the west were also utilised and other smaller baths were incorporated in the general arrangements. The Temple of Sulis Minerva flanked the reservoir and it is generally recognised that the temple and thermae formed an integrated complex. Over a period of three centuries, modifications and improvements resulted in a sophisticated complex offering a wide variety of treatments. Twentieth century excavation has enabled a much clearer picture of the remarkable Roman engineering to be gained. Much of this engineering continues to function and has had a major impact on the cityscape today.

During the Roman period the infrastructure at Bath positioned it as a primary facility both for bathing and recreation as well as religious purposes. The symbolism of Aquae Sulis was a blend of Roman and Celtic mythology deliberately absorbing the local cult as a means of Romanising the custom and use of the site. Sulis and Minerva were goddesses with similar attributes, one however was Celtic and the other Roman.[31] Nielsen proposes that Roman baths were secular.[32] The application of mythological and religious symbolism may well have been to provide a themed experience rather than for serious religious worship. The merging of such deities at Bath is discussed further under Malvern.

When the Kings Bath was investigated in the late 1970s, large quantities of inscribed lead and tin tablets of Roman origin were discovered. Most of these were requesting retribution as a result of theft, seeking the gods' assistance to punish the offender.[33] Such curse tablets are indicative of the wide variety of applications to which the thermal waters were put.

Sometime shortly after AD 300 the city wall was erected. This was almost certainly as a defensive measure during the final stages of the Roman occupation.[34] Aquae Sulis remained in Romano-British hands until the Saxon incursion. A Saxon poem of the time records the thermal waters running freely from the remains of the abandoned Roman buildings. The city became known as Akemanceaster and there is evidence to indicate that the waters continued to be used at the time although water ducts were largely buried under debris and flood silt. This gave rise to numerous outlets for the water. Cunliffe points out that it would be wrong to assume that the buildings were reduced to a marshy rubble. Some of the substantial buildings continued to stand into the eighth and ninth centuries. In addition repaving took place, often utilising the remnants of the Roman buildings.[35]

A monastery was founded at Bath around AD 670. A Charter of 675 by Osric, King of the Hwicce, enabled a convent of the Holy Virgins to be established with founding nuns from near Paris. Later in 757-8 a grant of land was made to the monastic brothers of St Peter. This foundation was being described as most famous by 781.[36] The religious establishment increased over the centuries culminating in AD 973 when Edgar, first King of England, was crowned in the Saxon church.[37]

By the tenth century Bath was a small prosperous town with a monastery of national repute. About this time the religious establishment became Benedictine.[38] In Norman times the abbey was remodelled as the great cathedral church, subsequently destroyed to make way for the smaller abbey church in the sixteenth century which can be seen today. John of Tours and others carried out considerable improvements to the town and its bathing facilities. The *Gesta Stephani*, compiled in 1138, confirms that the hot springs were resorted to by people from all over England for healing.[39] The Benedictine monastery would have used the waters as part of their programme for the caring of the sick. In addition to the Kings Bath two other baths are reputed to have been built, the Prior's Bath and the Abbot's Bath. There was also an infirmary.[40] St John's Hospital was founded 1174 as a charity by Bishop Reginald Fitz Josceline and the Hospital of St Katharine in 1444. Other hospitals included that of St Mary Magdalen.[41] For nearly 400 years the religious establishment controlled the hot springs and baths.[42] The Black Death, in the early part of the fourteenth century, devastated the religious institutions and secular community. This led to a period of declining moral standards in monastic life eventually to be overtaken by the Dissolution.

In the Middle Ages usage continued and Henry VI visited the city about 1400, only to be affronted by the naked men in the communal bath. The abbey monks built up a reputation for sexual excesses, both hetero and homo sexual; some were reputed to have as many as ten women at the time.[43] Following the suppression of the monasteries in 1539, the springs passed out of the control of the church. Elizabeth I granted the city a second charter in 1590 and the springs were entrusted to the Corporation.[44]

In Elizabethan times the city was dominated by the shell of the abbey which was commenced in 1499. The adjacent priory ruins were mined for building stone. Elsewhere the medieval street layout remained. The Corporation steadily acquired not only the former powers but also the lands of the priory, with the exception of the Abbey House estate which remained in controversial private hands until 1572. Visitors to the city were encouraged and the Queen eventually arrived in 1574. Elizabeth's concern about the state of the city is indicated by her initiative to consolidate the various parish churches into a single parish and to promote the restoration of the abbey. Letters Patent authorised countrywide collections to fund the restoration although the abbey still remained roofless until the early seventeenth century. In due course Elizabeth was followed by the nobility and gentry, thereby ensuring Bath's recognition as an important spa centre.[45] When Celia Fiennes visited, she observed that the abbey and grounds had become the congregating point for the visitors to the hot springs, later to be superceded by the more formal pump room and other facilities.[46]

GEOCHEMISTRY

Bath has three thermal springs with temperatures varying between 117 and 120° F (47 and 49° C).[47] These are the Kings spring, the Cross Bath spring and the Hetling spring. Of the three, the Kings spring is the greater. In the geological time scale, the present configuration of the springs is of very recent origin. The issues originate from a deep source by way of a geological, conical spring pipe transferring the water to the surface. The geological spring pipe was filled with mid-late quaternary gravel, dating it to possibly 80,000 BP. Since that time the Bath mineral springs have probably been diminishing in volume. The Roman installations could accommodate a larger flow than that of today, but in the absence of quantitative evidence, any judgement on flow changes are speculative.[48] Variations in the artesian head of the waters in the various baths may explain the volume changes between sources from time to time as baths and buildings were altered. Recent monitoring has not identified any material changes in volume.[49]

The thermal springs likely originate as a result of tectonic rifts associated with the realignment of early surface drainage from east to west. Such hydrodynamic processes also gave rise to the Avon Gorge and the emergence of thermal springs at Bristol. The bedrock from which the springs emerge is Lower Lias Clay which forms the floor of the Avon Valley. The springs at Bath and Bristol both emerge near the margin of the concealed Carboniferous rocks of the Bristol and Somerset coalfield. Current theory suggests that the thermal water is circulating in the fissure system at depths of between 2,700 and 4,000 metres.[50] Heating of the thermal waters is as a result of the depth of travel within the earth's core.[51] The underlying Carboniferous Limestone beds are the likely transmission zones. Groundwater in the north-eastern Mendips may be therefore migrating north through the synclinorium and then emerging as a result of the tectonic belt extending between the Avon and the Wick thrust lines. Isotopic evidence confirms that the water is derived from relatively recent rainwater and is thousands rather than tens of thousands of years old. Burgess et al propose an age of 4,000 years since precipitation.[52]

Explanations for the phenomenon of Bath mineral waters, contemporary with Celia Fiennes, are extraordinary compared with modern scientific understanding. Rice Charleton, in 1754, considered that the waters comprised *"Elementary Fire, Elastic Air, an Alcaline Earth, a Neutral Salt, Common Marine Salt, Iron, and a fine Aromatic Balsam, mixed together and dissolved in pure water."* The heat he attributed to *"fui generis"* an Elementary Fire which existed in all bodies. Laboratory experiments to release this Elementary Fire read like a thermonuclear incident as Rice Charleton endeavoured to progress scientific understanding.[53] He also observed strange black cakes floating on the surface of the springs in spring and summer. These he identified, not as bituminous matter, as had previously been supposed, but as a jelly moss, Conferva Gelatinofa.[54]

The modern chemical analysis of each of the three Bath springs is similar and the following, showing elements combined, is typical.

Analysis of Bath Thermal Waters by Mr Attfield, 1895.[55]

grains per imperial gallon

Calcium carbonate	7.84
Calcium sulphate	94.11
Calcium nitrate	0.56
Magnesium carbonate	0.56
Magnesium chloride	15.24
Sodium chloride	15.19
Sodium sulphate	23.16
Potassium sulphate	6.70
Ammonium nitrate	1.06
Ferrous carbonate	1.22
Silica	2.71
	168.35

Traces of rubidium, lithium and strontium

dissolved gas per imperial gallon

| Oxygen | 0.74 |
| Nitrogen | 4.60 |

A flow of water coming directly from the spring beneath the Kings Bath was drunk and once supplied the Grand Pump Room, erected in 1796, well after Celia Fiennes' visit. Discovery of a pathogenic amoeba in the waters resulted in closure of the Pump Room in 1978. Subsequent boring has enabled the source water to be tapped prior to contamination. The amoeba requires oxygen to survive and the bores have tapped ground water before exposure to atmospheric oxygen. This water is then fed to the Pump Room fountain where drinking can once again resume.[56]

THE HISTORY OF THE FIVE BATHS

CROSS BATH AND SPRING

The Cross Bath or balneum crucis is the site of one of the original springs of Bath. The name is traceable to 1302 when it was likely a holy well surmounted by a Christian cross. Tradition suggests that it was a pre-Christian sacred spring. Its utilisation is therefore very ancient. A bath was in existence from Roman times and a carved stone supposedly representing Aesculapius has been found nearby.[57] It was likely refurbished in medieval times to be recorded by Leland in the early years of the sixteenth century.[58] There was a stone construction in the centre, shown on Speed's map of 1610, topped by a human figure. This was restored in 1674 and a new gallery added with a pump at the north end by Robert Lord Brook. He had recovered from diabetes apparently as a result of imbibing the water.[59] Samuel Pepys arose at 4am one morning in 1668 to bathe in the Cross Bath.[60]

The Cross Bath was given a new central umbrella-shaped pump and cistern in 1665 and temporarily renamed Queen Catherine's Bath after Queen Catherine of Braganza's visit in 1663.[61] This was replaced by a new cross in 1688, an elaborate affair comprising four columns surmounted by angels around a dome with a cross at the highest point. The structure was erected by John Drummond, Earl of Melfort, in commemoration of Queen Mary of Modena having used the bath with good results in 1688.[62] She was the second wife of James II and of Catholic disposition. James II lost the throne due to his son and heir, by his second wife, being brought up to the Catholic tradition. In the year 1689, with the onset of the reign of William and Mary, who were Protestant by faith, the cross in the Cross Baths was removed as a conciliatory gesture.[63]

Reiterating the earlier discussion, the cross assists in dating Celia's visits. Celia Fiennes failed to mention this elaborate cross indicating that her first visit was perhaps unlikely when it was standing. As Celia mentioned the cross in her second visit in 1698, this places her first visit before its erection in 1688 or in 1689 or thereabouts before the cross was reinstated.[64] The cross appears to have been reinstated before Celia's second visit in 1698; Fayram's print of 1739 clearly shows this magnificent structure dominating the Cross Bath.[65] The cross was eventually demolished in 1783.[66]

Wood reported that in 1693 the bath could be filled for bathers in eleven and a half hours.[67] The temperature of the Cross Street spring at 41-42° C was lower than that of the other two springs suggesting that there was an intrusion of low temperature water in the source.[68] The spring that supplies the Cross Bath lies 14 feet below the flooring of the bath and flows at a rate of half a hogshead per minute (about 25 gallons).[69]

The Cross Bath and Bath's oldest charity and proprietor of the Baths, the Hospital of St John, have had an unenviable record of misappropriation of funds over the centuries. When Elizabeth I gave the Corporation power to appoint a master and clergy to the well with endowed living, it was decided to appoint the mayor as master of the Hospital and the paupers were ejected. Subsequent misuse of the charity assets included fraudulent land assignment with the proceeds disappearing into the pockets of the Chapman families.[70]

We are able to gain an appreciation of what the Cross Bath was like at the time of Celia's visit from a mid seventeenth century description by Thomas Johnson. *"almost triangular, twenty five feet long and of equal breddth at the widest part. It has arched seats on all sides, three dressing rooms and as many flights of steps. It is surrounded by a wall. The springs here are smaller than in the Kings and Hot and it is therefore not so hot."* A plan is given by Guidott in *De Thermis* 1691.[71] The arches that Celia mentioned probably dated from the Norman refurbishment, similar to the Kings Bath.

The building that Celia Fiennes saw was modified in 1784 and restyled again in 1791 by Thomas Baldwin and John Palmer.[72] The interior was again

redesigned, this time as a swimming pool in 1885. The present building is managed by The Springs Foundation.[73]

The Cross Bath in 1996 showing the spring rising in the centre.

THE HOT BATH

The Hot Bath was probably fitted out with arched recesses during Norman times, similar to the Cross and Kings Baths. It was enlarged at the end of the sixteenth century resulting in a drop in water temperature. A contemporary plan shows recesses on opposite sides and three street entrances. Like the other major baths it had a cross or tower in the centre. Originally open to all, the Bath was "gentrified" before Celia Fiennes' visit.[74]

The Hot Bath, which was supplied by the Hetling Spring, was filled in a similar time to the Cross Bath, eleven and a half hours. The temperature is the highest of the three springs, at 48° C. The bath facility that Celia Fiennes observed is now gone.

The Hetling spring was improved with the installation of an 8 foot stone cylindrical containment in 1772 and the old Bath House pulled down a year later to be remodelled by Wood. This remedial work was carried out because it was suspected that the water was leaking away. The containment was exposed during restoration work in 1986 and remains beneath the pavement immediately outside the present Hot Bath building entrance in Stall Street.[75]

Wood's remodelling of the Hot Baths 1775-78 produced an attractive building with semi-enclosed pool. This building survives today though heavily modified.[76] The Hot Bath was also known as the old Royal Baths and was located, open to the sky, in the centre of the Royal Private Baths complex. A tepid bath was added in 1830 by G P. Manners. This considerably enhanced the facilities and made the Hot Baths complex a serious rival to the Kings Bath.[77]

The spring was estimated to run at 1.5 hogsheads per minute (75 gallons) at a temperature of 102° F (39° C) by Freeman in 1888. At the time it also supplied a bath at the Royal United Hospital.[78]

THE KINGS BATH

The Kings Bath was sited immediately over the main thermal spring. This was the site of the original Roman reservoir containment which was built around the perimeter of the conical depression or geological spring pipe. The reservoir was enclosed with a substantial barrel-vaulted masonry roof in the late Roman period.

It was located within the grounds of the original monastery and although unlikely used by the healthy monks, the Rule of St Benedict would have deemed it suitable for the sick, young, aged and guests. Other baths during medieval times included the Abbot's and Prior's Baths. These had disappeared before Celia Fiennes' visit.[79]

The hot springs gained reputation for their healing qualities and this prompted a development programme. A new monastic infrastructure started by the Norman bishop, John of Tours (reigned 1088-1122) and continued by Bishop Robert (reigned 1136-1166) is the basis of the Kings Bath that Celia Fiennes found. This development resulted in the Kings Bath being superimposed over the Roman reservoir which was filled with debris, some of which was the remains of collapsed Roman buildings. Arched niches were provided for the bathers. The Kings Bath is described in some detail in the *Gesta Stephani* of 1138.[80]

The medieval bath was modified in 1624 with the addition of the balustraded gallery from which onlookers could peer down on the bathers, a custom noted by Celia Fiennes. The balustrade was donated by Sir Francis Stonor after being cured of the gout.[81] Further modifications took place as a result of the Improvement Act of 1789.[82]

In the centre of the Kings Bath was a fanciful tower or cross with niches for bathers. A new pump and the cross had been installed in 1664 celebrating the endorsement of Dr. Alexander Fraizer, the Kings physician.[83] Pumps had existed previously, together with separate pump rooms, and Hembry records a pump as early as 1587. The 1664 edifice was nicknamed "The Kitchen" because of the excessive heat that arose from the source beneath. Celia examined this. It was rebuilt in the 1780s when Baldwin restored the Bath and further replaced by a mock-Jacobean structure in the nineteenth century.[84]

The spring rose through the floor of the Kings Bath from where it overflowed to the Roman drain via the Queens Bath. The Victorians reconstructed the floor over the spring but this was removed in the 1978-80 period. At the time of the Victorian improvements the spring was estimated to be flowing at about 2.5 hogsheads per minute (125 gallons). The temperature of the spring, which is the principal source of thermal water at Bath, is 46° C. Excavations carried out in the 1880s removed debris from this area and at the same time possibly damaged the foundations of the eighteenth century Pump Room through erosion by spring water.[85] Freeman bemoans the removal of the Roman lead lining by the Victorians.[86] Further excavation in the 1980s of the original underlying Roman reservoir and spring containment yielded much valuable archaeological evidence.

The Kings Bath today with part of the Victorian floor removed to show the original spring. The steps, balustrade and rings observed by Celia Fiennes can be seen. The 1624 balustrade is now built into the wall.

There is an effigy of King Bladud in the Kings Bath. Bladud was the legendary ancient discoverer of the thermal waters, having been banished from his father's court with leprosy. Whilst caring for a herd of swine, also with leprosy, he noted the beasts wallowing in the mud of the springs thereby receiving some benefit. He followed in their footsteps and supposedly also received benefit. There is little historical evidence for this tale other than the writings of the Welsh chronicler Geoffrey of Monmouth. His twelfth century account proposes that Bladud built Kaerbadus, now Bath, at the time of Elias the prophet. Bladud later died while attempting to fly. From this the later legend was elaborated.[87] The statue was set up in 1699, about the time that Celia was visiting Bath.[88] The effigy likely comprises two previously separate remnants of other statuary from elsewhere, possibly the town gates.[89] The much reproduced illustration by Johnson, c.1670, shows the bath as Celia Fiennes would have found it. It is open to the sky and the promenade area for observers is apparent. Celia noted the rings for bathers to grasp. These were bronze rings donated by those grateful for the cure in the seventeenth century. Legends on some rings give testimony to the cure.

The smaller Queens Bath was immediately adjacent, also open to the sky. It was not until 1706, after Celia's visits, that the Pump Room was added immediately alongside opposite the Queens Bath.[90]

THE QUEENS BATH

This bath no longer exists but it was located over the Roman circular bath which can be seen today. Freeman (1888) proposed that it was originally constructed in 1597 by Mr Bellott, founder of Bellott's Hospital. Cunliffe suggests an earlier date of 1575.[91] Queen Anne of Denmark, wife of James I, visited the city in 1613 and later in 1615. During the second visit she declined to use the Kings Bath as had been her custom due to a circle of light which came as a flame from the bottom of the bath. This may well have been a spectacular methane ignition which no doubt was frightening to those in the bath at the time.[92] Removing to the New Bath as it was then known, the bath took its name from her thereafter. A cross was erected in the bath to commemorate her usage and the bath enlarged. The cross, which was located in the bath centre, was surmounted by crown with the motto "Annae Reginae Sacrum" inscribed in gold. The cross was eventually removed about 1732 and would therefore have been observed by Celia Fiennes.[93] She does not mention this cross and this casts into doubt any reliance on her failure to mention features as a means of dating her recordings.

Celia does note that the Queens Bath was located next to the Kings Bath and that the latter flowed into the former. After about 1598 the overflow from the Queens Bath in turn fed the Horse Bath observed by William Schellinks. This was a large pond outside the city walls and was used for clearing congestion of the lungs, a complaint common in horses.[94] It was in use for approximately 70 years. The Queens Bath was eventually removed in the 1880s at the time of major reconstruction by the Victorians. The removal exposed the circular Roman bath beneath.

THE LEPERS BATH

Also known as the Lazars Bath, the Lepers Bath was built probably as a result of the demise of the monastic hospitals. It was likely constructed in 1576 by John de Feckenham, last Abbot of Westminster, together with a *"leper howse"*. John Wood, the architect who was responsible for its demolition in 1776, described it as mean, obscure and small.[95] The facility seen by Celia Fiennes replaced a much earlier house for lepers built in 1138 by Bishop Robert of Lewes. Close to the Cross and Hot Baths, it was demolished in Elizabethan times.[96] It was dedicated to St Lazarus, who traditionally died of leprosy, which gives rise to the name Lazars Bath.[97]

Celia Fiennes noted this bath but gave little detail. It was a minor bathing facility set aside from the main baths for the treatment of those unfortunates who contracted the ailment. In this way their presence would not have deterred usage of the Hot Bath. Although leprosy as we know it died out during Tudor times, the term continued to be used for chronic skin complaints.[98] It was fed by the waters of the Hot Bath. The Lepers Bath is shown on Gilmore's 1694 map as adjacent to the Hot Bath where it is described as *"Beggers or Lazors Bath"*. Further reference to the Lepers Bath comes in the *Bath and Bristol Guide* of 1755 which mentions a Lepers Hospital alongside a bath of the same name.[99] The bath was eventually converted to an underground tank by Wood during his 1776-7 remodelling of the Hot Bath. The little hospital building which accompanied it was removed a few years later.[100]

EFFICACY OF BATH WATER

The curing properties of Bath water have come under extensive scrutiny over the years. Celia Fiennes made little comment on the ailments that Bath waters were supposed to have been suitable for. This subject has been extensively covered by a multitude of doctors, some of great repute and some controversial, since William Turner's original treatise of 1562.

Typically, Dr D. Monro (1770) tells us that Bath water acted powerfully on the urine, sometimes purged and caused a propensity to sleep. They stimulated the nerves and fibres and increased the tone of the stomach and bowels. The waters increased the action of the vascular system, removing obstructions and promoting circulation. They were particularly suited to complaints that manifest such symptoms. The doctor recommended Bath waters for gouty and rheumatic complaints, hysteric and hypochondrical disorders and scrophulous cases. For females they could cure barrenness. Bathing in the waters could be beneficial in some of the cases and pumping on paralytic members restored the natural vigour! Dr Monro noted that once people drank the waters in considerable quantities, up to 8 or 10 pints in a day. Eighteenth century practice was to reduce this to a half or a quarter of earlier doses, depending on the circumstances. Other recommendations included retiring to bed at 10 or 11 o'clock at night, evacuating before bathing and possibly adding soap and milk to the waters for drinking.[101]

The twentieth century has seen a more scientific approach to evaluating the waters and radioactivity was promoted in the 1920s as a valuable property possessed by Bath waters. This came at a time of competition between the major UK spas which were in the final death throes as medical centres. Dr J. Munro (1928), a member of the Scientific Committee of the British Spas Federation, published a detailed paper on the Radon content of Bath water.[102] This was subsequently developed in the Spas Federation guides as an outstanding feature of the waters which was taken as the factor to explain the physiological properties.[103] A subsequent greater understanding of radioactivity and its dangers led to a reappraisal of such a cure as part of the marketing proposition for Bath.

Although the more outlandish claims for Bath water cure were perhaps a combination of placebo effect and wishful thinking, modern medicine has identified one particular ailment, "Colica Pictonum", which the water alleviates.[104] It is this complaint that perhaps made Bath so attractive to the Romans. "Colica Pictonum" is a condition typified by severe abdominal colic and constipation followed by loss of function of the limbs. The condition arises as a result of lead poisoning. Evidence suggests that the Romans unwittingly were dependent on extended hot bathing to remain healthy. Lead poisoning was a widespread, severe, undiagnosed problem in Roman times. Lead water pipes, lead eating utensils, pewter ware, lead-glazed earthenware, food colourants and wine additives, cosmetics and many other household items all contributed to the accumulation of lead in the body. Mild symptoms include tiredness and headaches, more chronic symptoms were wasting, convulsions and death. Gout and reduced fertility may also result from lead intoxification. By the sixteenth century Bath had a well-established reputation for curing such ills although the diagnosis remained obscure. A pattern of drinking and bathing evolved, especially after 1650 when a clean, direct supply of spring water was available for drinking.

Twentieth century space research gives a clue to how such a cure was effected. It centres on the near total submersion of the body in water for a prolonged period, a technique used by NASA for astronaut training. The body, when immersed, incorrectly diagnoses the condition, when responding to the increased external water pressure. The pressure on the lower limbs results in a redistribution of body fluid to the central zone. The body assumes an increase in total body fluid, resulting in a discharge of water, sodium and calcium. As the body handles lead and calcium in similar ways, lead is also expelled. A prolonged course of treatment would result in significant expulsion of residual lead. Supplementing this is the drinking intake which provides iron and calcium. Both of these elements are believed to deter lead absorption in the body. Although the diagnosis was not understood, the cure would have been of major importance to the Romans. In addition however we also have an insight as to why Bath was to become the premier English spa in the eighteenth and nineteenth centuries.

The rich and the poor suffered lead and other heavy metal poisoning. The poor were afflicted often due to working in lead based industries. Water supplies were often reliant on lead plumbing. Fortified wines in the eighteenth and nineteenth centuries have also proved to have been heavily contaminated with lead. The rich suffered the toxic effect on the kidneys. This led to the retention of uric acid, which in turn promoted gout and other associated maladies. Gout was also caused through meat eating, the principal source of uric acid. The rich became victims of their own affluence.[105] As a result the rich and poor alike flocked to the unique waters of Bath to secure relief. Here we have the underlying reason why Bath prospered. The manufactured social climate created by Beau Nash and the built environment of John Wood were not the raison d'etre for Bath's rise to the premier position in the 200 years following Celia Fiennes. They were merely the result of the pursuit of health, as the prosperous sought the trappings of their normal lifestyle during a prolonged stay.

TODAY

Bath is a major tourist resort with much of its appeal based on its spa heritage. The waters can be sampled in the Pump Rooms by the Kings Bath but cannot be bathed in.

The Springs Foundation is responsible for the Cross Bath which retains a character of peace and tranquility in the bustling tourist area. The Cross Bath can be viewed occasionally.

Archaeological excavation has yielded outstanding remains of Roman Bath. These can be viewed as part of the Kings Bath and Pump Rooms complex. Bath City Council have a hand held audio guide to the Roman Baths Museum. The Kings Bath is a building that Celia Fiennes may recognise some parts of, if she were alive today. The Hot Baths are closed and derelict but still retain their eighteenth century bath and general layout. New uses are being considered which include a Museum of Spa Heritage and Mineral Waters or a modern spa treatment centre. The abbey/cathedral can be also be inspected, again a building which Celia Fiennes would recognise.

Footnotes:

1 Morris C. (ed.) 1947, *The Journeys of Celia Fiennes*, p.xxii.
2 Smith R A L. 1944, *Bath*, p.47.
3 Morris C. (ed.) 1982, *The Illustrated Journeys of Celia Fiennes*, p.191.
4 Morris C. 1947, op.cit. p.19-23.
5 ibid. p.236.
6 James P R. 1938, *The Baths of Bath in the Sixteenth and Early Seventeenth Centuries*, p.12, 13.
7 Cunliffe B. 1986, *The City of Bath*, p.110.
8 Hembry P. 1990, *The English Spa 1560-1815*, p.113.
9 Hamilton M. 1978, *Bath before Beau Nash*, p.1.
10 Hinde T. 1988, *Tales from the Pump Room*, p.9.
11 Hamilton M. op.cit. p.10.
12 Canning J. (ed.) 1988, *Macaulay's History of England*, first pub. 1848-1861, p.103-3.
13 Hembry P. op.cit. p.85-86, 90.
14 Lennard R. 1931, *Englishmen at Rest and Play*, p.25/6, 31.
15 Cunliffe B. 1986, op.cit. p.88.
16 Turner W. 1568, *A Booke of the natures and properties as well as the bathes in Germanye and Italye.*
17 Hembry P. op.cit. p.86-87.
18 Sheppard E J. 1962, *Bath in the Eighteenth Century*, p.3.
19 Boddely T. 1755, *The Bath and Bristol Guide*, p.25.
20 Hembry P. op.cit. p.87.
21 Exwood M. Lehmann H L. (trans.) 1993, *The Journal of William Schellinks' Travels in England, 1661-1663*, p.105-6.
22 Hembry P. op.cit. p.88.
23 Madden T M. 1874, *The Spas of Germany, France and Italy and their Uses*, p.9, 10.
24 Hembry P. op.cit. p.88, 89.
25 ibid. p.91.
26 ibid. p.92, 93.
27 Lennard R. op.cit. p.12/13.
28 Turner W. 1568, op.cit.
29 Kellaway G A. 1991, *Hot Springs of Bath*, p16.
30 Cunliffe B. 1986, op.cit. p.12-14.
31 Stewart B. 1981, *The Waters of the Gap*, p.19, 25
32 Nielsen I. 1990, *Thermae et Balnea*, Vol.1, p.111.
33 Tomlin R S O. 1988, *Tabellae Sulis*, p.59, 60.
34 Cunliffe B. 1986, op.cit. p.40/1.
35 ibid. p.48.
36 ibid. 49, 51.
37 Hinde T. op.cit. p.16.
38 Cunliffe B. 1986, op.cit. p.62.
39 ibid. p.72.
40 ibid. p.74, 76.
41 ibid. p.81/2, 99.
42 Hinde T. op.cit. p.17.
43 ibid. p.17.
44 Kellaway G A. op.cit. p.18.
45 Hembry P. op.cit. p.27-29.
46 Hamilton M. op.cit. p.30.
47 Hembry P. op.cit. p.21.
48 Kellaway G A. op.cit. p.16, 17, 21.
49 Stanton W I, 1991, "Hydrogeology of the Hot Springs of Bath" in Kellaway G A. (ed.) 1991, *Hot Springs of Bath*; Edmunds W M. Miles D L. 1991 "The Geochemistry of Bath Thermal Waters" in Kellaway G A. (ed.) 1991, *Hot Springs of Bath*; Burgess W G. Black J H & Cook A J. 1991, "Regional Hydrodynamic Influences on the Bristol-Bath springs" in Kellaway G A. (ed.) 1991, *Hot Springs of Bath*.

50 Cunliffe B. 1993, *The Roman Baths*, p.2.
51 Cunliffe B. 1986, op.cit. p.4.
52 Kellaway G A. op.cit. Chapter 7.
53 Charleton R. 1754, *A Treatise on the Bath Waters*, p.63-73.
54 ibid. p.4/5.
55 Ord W M. Garrod A E. 1895, "Bath" in *The Climates and Baths of Great Britain*, p.518.
56 Kellaway G A. op.cit. p.22.
57 Hamilton M. op.cit. p.41.
58 Cunliffe B. 1986, op.cit. p.80.
59 Hamilton M. op.cit. p.42.
60 ibid. p.42.
61 Hembry P. op.cit. p.88, 89.
62 Illustrated in Freeman H W. 1888, *The Thermal Baths of Bath*, p.142-143.
63 Hembry P. op.cit. p.91.
64 Morris C. 1982, op.cit. p.191.
65 Heywood A. 1991, "Lead, Gout and Bath Spa Therapy", in Kellaway G A. 1991, p.79.
66 Hamilton M. op.cit. p.43.
67 Kellaway G A. op.cit. p.53.
68 ibid. Chapter 7.
69 Freeman H W. op.cit. p.142.
70 Winsor J. 1988, "A Case of Fraud and Skulduggery", *Independent*, 31 Dec.
71 Cunliffe B. 1986, op.cit. p.104.
72 ibid. p.142.
73 The Springs Foundation 1991, *The Cross Bath*, public relations leaflet.
74 Cunliffe B. 1986, op.cit. p.80, 104/5.
75 Kellaway G A. op.cit. p.25, 34, 54.
76 Cunliffe B. 1986, op.cit. p.136.
77 ibid. p.150.
78 Freeman H W. op.cit. p.143/4.
79 Hamilton M. op.cit. p.33.
80 Hinde T. op.cit. p.16.
81 Cunliffe B. 1993, op.cit. p.37.
82 Cunliffe B. 1986, op.cit. p.142.
83 Hembry P. op.cit. p.88-91.
84 Hamilton M. op.cit. p.38/9.
85 Kellaway G A. op.cit. Chapter 7.
86 Freeman H W. op.cit. p.136.
87 Hinde T. op.cit. p.15.
88 Boddely T. op.cit. p.9.
89 Hamilton M. op.cit. p.39.
90 Hinde T. op.cit. p.23.
91 Cunliffe B. 1993, op.cit. p.34.
92 Hinde T. op.cit. p.21.
93 Freeman H W. op.cit. p.139.
94 Hamilton M. op.cit. p.40/41.
95 Cunliffe B. 1986, op.cit. p.100.
96 Rolls R. 1988, *The Hospital of the Nation*, p.87.
97 Hamiltion M. op.cit. p.44.
98 Rolls R. op.cit. p.87.
99 Boddely T. op.cit. p.19/20.
100 Hamiltion M. op.cit. p.45.
101 Monro D. 1770, *A Treatise on Mineral Waters*, Vol.II, p.246-252.
102 Munro J M H. 1928, *The Radio-activity in the Bath Thermal Waters*.
103 British Spas Federation, c.1930, *The Spas of Britain, Official Handbook*, p.7.
104 Heywood A. 1990, "A Trial of the Bath Waters: A Treatment of Lead Poisoning", in Porter R. (ed.) 1990, *The Medical History of Waters and Spas*, p.82-101.
105 Rolls R. op.cit. p.84-86.

WELLS

On her Great Journey of 1698 Celia decided to pay a visit to Wookey Hole before visiting the city of Wells. Having seen Bristol she passed over the Downs to the Mendips.[1] Wookey Hole lies about 2 miles north-west of Wells.

"Oacky Hole", as she called Wookey Hole, was a large underground cavern similar, she thought, to Poole's Hole in Derbyshire. Wookey Hole however lay in a hollow which she likened to a quarry unlike Poole's Hole. She described various lofty chambers known as The Hall, Parlour and Kitchen. The entrance to each involved stooping below overhanging rocks, one leading to another. Beyond this was the cistern, which was permanently full of clear water.

In the light of the candles, she noticed how the water, as it fell in the caverns, appeared to congeal into stone, a process she likened to the making of candy. As the stone grew, so it met with other stone. Shapes were formed which were given names such as The Organ, Porter's Head, a dog and The Witch, who had a great belly. Some of the rock so formed glistened like diamonds and other was as white as alabaster. The floor was sandy and the roof so high that it gave a great echo. Dropping a stone caused a sound like firing a cannon and guides frequently demonstrated "shooting the cannons" for visitors. In the farthest reaches was the Well. It was of great depth and as cold as ice she noted, when she put her hands into the water in what she described as a cistern.

Celia then went on to the city of Wells which she described as only half a city, because it shared the Bishop's See with Bath. Besides two churches she described the cathedral, noted for its carved stonework. The west front was ornamented with many figures including the twelve apostles, the King and Queen and angels. When she visited Wells the Assizes were being held which made the town like a fair, with stalls in the streets for selling things. She saw the Town Hall and the large market place and the shambles. The Bishop's Palace was in a park and was moated. St Andrew's Spring was nearby. It was so quick (fast running) that it became the head for two small rivers which increased in volume a short way off.

Leaving Wells she then went to Glastonbury Tor where she passed the tower of St Michael on its summit. Now in ruins, it once had bells in it and was the subject of superstition.

COMMENT

Wookey Hole is a show cave of long standing. The locality is the issue of the River Axe as it emerges from the Mendip limestone which is largely drained below ground. This spectacular spring produces a daily average flow of about

23 million gallons.[2] The series of caves that Celia saw can be identified today. Caverns 1,2 and 3 are known as The Great Cave and sequentially designated The Kitchen, The Hall and The Parlour although the order appears to have varied from time to time. From Celia's journals it is apparent that the mythology of the caves has changed little over the centuries. Between the Kitchen and the Parlour the River Axe flows through a submerged tunnel. The third chamber still has a sandy floor and is renowned for its acoustics. At the end is the well that Celia described; we now know that it is the arched submerged passage to the fourth chamber.

William Schellinks, who also visited Epsom Wells, in 1662 recorded a visit to Wookey Hole.[3] His description of such features as the Great Hall, the Dining Room, the Table, The Witch, etc. all indicate that the location was already established as a tourist spot. He noted that often a bottle of wine was taken into the cave to enliven the visit. Subsequently, seventeenth century wine bottles were found by cave divers when charting the river bed between the 3rd chamber and the point of escape of the Axe.[4] Schellinks' journal is one of the earliest references to the stalagmite as The Witch. A woman, guiding by candle light, demonstrated the sound of cannon caused by throwing a heavy stone, just as was demonstrated to Celia Fiennes nearly 40 years later. Such acoustic displays were not limited to Wookey Hole however. A mysterious round boulder puzzled archaeologists during rubbish removal at the medieval Barons' Cave at Reigate, Surrey. Subsequently a hand written manuscript by an early visitor noted the demonstration of the echo using a round boulder. Twentieth century visitors continue to enjoy the experience at Reigate using the original boulder.

Other visitors contemporary with Celia Fiennes included a West Country physician who sent a party of six to see Wookey Hole in 1709. The was no guide but they were given candles and beer in exchange for 2s 6d.[5] Defoe also recorded early eighteenth century Wookey Hole in a somewhat dismissive tone. Having visited Poole's Hole near Buxton, he decided that the legend of the witch and the calcite formations were of little consequence.[6]

The Witch stalagmite is in the first main chamber, known as the Witch's Kitchen, overlooking the river Axe which flows through the cavern. The legend of the witch is more ancient than the likening of a stalagmite to her image and has been elaborated over time. The provenance appears to be linked with a figure of a woman - clad and holding in her girdle a distaff, described by William of Worcester in 1470. The old recluse is reputed to have lived in the cave from where she cursed the local populace, causing their cattle to die. A more likely interpretation, with the benefit of hindsight, is that lead mining contaminated the water causing the cattle that drank it to fall sick. Even earlier, King Arthur, in the legend of Kuhlwch and Olwen, is reputed to have slain the black witch who lived in the cave of the Stream of Sorrow on the confines of hell, in the year 577.[7] The location of this act is interpreted as Wookey Hole. The following poem was published in 1756 explaining how the Witch was petrified.[8]

> *Deep in the dreary dismal cell*
> *Which seemed and was ycleped hell*
> *This blear-eyed hag did hide:*
> *Nine wicked elves, as legends sayne,*
> *She chose to form her guardian trayne,*
> *And kennel near her side.*
>
> *From Glaston came a lernede wight,*
> *Full bent to marr her fell despight,*
> *And well he did, I ween:*
> *Sich mischief never had been known,*
> *And, since his mickle lerninge shown*
> *Sich mischief n'er has been*
>
> *He chauntede out his godlie booke,*
> *He crost the water, blest the brooke,*
> *Then - pater noster done,*
> *The ghastly hag he sprinkled o'er:*
> *When lo! where stood the hag before*
> *Now stood a ghastly stone.*
>
> *But tho; this lernede clerke did well:*
> *With grieved heart, alas! I tell*
> *She left this curse behind:*
> *That Wokey nymphs forsaken quite,*
> *Tho' sense and beauty both unite,*
> *Should find no lemon kind.*

The petrifying action of the waters, the old hag and the paranormal happenings all suggest that there are distinct similarities with Mother Shipton's legend at Knaresborough.

Celia's experience at Wookey was very limited compared with what has been learnt by subsequent research. Later knowledge does enable an appreciation to be gained of why Wookey appeared as a place of mystery and wonderment to early visitors. Celia knew nothing of modern geology, chemistry or evolution. The first serious underwater exploration of the underground River Axe and the Wookey Hole series of caves started in 1935 using, by modern standards, antiquated and clumsy diving gear.[9] Such exploration eventually revealed further chambers beyond the first three and in recent years the provision of man-made passages now enables the public to gain access to the 7th, 8th and 9th. In 1976 chamber 25 was discovered. A British cave diving depth record was broken in June 1977 when 45 metres was reached beyond chamber 25! This was broken in 1982 with a 60 metre record beyond chamber 25.[10]

Exploration, especially by Herbert Balch who spent much of his life associated with Wookey Hole, has yielded an immense amount of archaeological evidence in the twentieth century and it is now recognised that the cave has been in continual use, by animals, since time immemorial and by humans since 250 BC. Finds of coinage and Clement of Alexandria describing, in 189 AD, the sound of clashing cymbals peculiar to the cave, confirm Roman activity in the cave.[11]

Amongst the archaeological artifacts found by Balch between 1908 and 1913 were the skeletons of a goat and kid, the remnants of a stake and nearby various domestic remains including a milking pot, knives, combs etc. A skeleton was also found. Overlaying debris suggested that the finds were Roman or earlier. Balch interpreted this as the ancient witch who had died leaving her goats tethered and helpless, thereby giving credence to the legend. He also identified later supposed cannibalistic practices. Superstition and fear must have led to a reluctance to enter the cave. When it was eventually entered the bodies had decayed leading to the belief that the witch had disappeared by turning to stone. Overlaying material had resulted in the remains being undisturbed by humankind until the twentieth century.[12] The museums at Wookey and at Wells house many of the finds including the reputed skeleton of The Witch and her crystal ball.[13] Subsequent removal of much of the floor debris by archaeologists has rendered the entrance more convenient to visitors since the time of Celia Fiennes.

Other removal included the stalactites, the broken remains Balch noted as hanging from the roof in 1926.[14] These were shot down by Alexander Pope to adorn his Grotto at Twickenham about 1739/40.[15] Modern day conservationists have difficulty in comprehending the psychology behind the destruction of Wookey Hole in this manner. The truth is that the prevailing paradigm has shifted to a diametrically opposed stance. In Pope's day, such vandalism was justified by the intelligentsia as being in accord with the conventions of Rev. Borlase's *Natural History*. Such underground beauty was allied to the work of God but that nature was imperfect. This in turn could be legitimately re-perfected, and even improved upon, by Pope through art. This took the form of his Grotto, which became an expression of virtue, philosophy and true wisdom. As such it became a "musaeum" for the development of higher thought processes.[16] The Grotto was destroyed by a bomb in 1944. Such is the folly of humankind.

The Entrance to
Ochie Hole, 1719,
after a sketch by
Bernard Lens.[17]

As Wookey is the resurgence of the River Axe, the city of Wells, the next place visited by Celia Fiennes, is also the resurgence of underground waters. These waters originate from swallet holes up to six kilometres away. The waters emerge from a number of pot holes near the cathedral known collectively as St Andrew's Well. It is these pot holes that give Wells its name.

A characteristic of limestone country is the disappearance of surface water down through swallet holes. The water then traverses the bedrock, moving through natural cracks and fissures along the bedding planes that are slowly enlarged through solution. This in turn causes extensive cave systems, often totally or partially flooded. In the case of elevated limestone, the ground water eventually emerges at a resurgence. The calcium carbonate in solution is deposited as calcite when the water undergoes temperature change and evaporation, particularly in air-filled cave systems. Such phenomena give rise to many unique features associated with limestone country including spectacular watercourses, both above and below ground.

At Wells, subterranean water from the Mendips is forced to the surface from a single underground watercourse through a series of natural vents or pots. Such activity precipitates ground movement which is supplemented by man in attempts to contain and stabilise the outfalls. The activities of nature and man can result in the pots becoming partially or completely choked from time to time. As the water passage is barred or slowed, the water seeks alternative outlets and springs emerge nearby. Such activity is often exacerbated in times of flood. Efforts to reclaim part of the pond and prevent encroachment of the springs on adjacent buildings in the 1940s resulted in a new north pot erupting in the main pond. Intermittent infilling of the springs has also resulted in the pool level being considerably higher than the surrounding land area, as is demonstrated by the land contours on the east side. Efforts to control the outflow of the pots has resulted in water levels and resurgences being altered. Since Saxon times the water levels have risen about 1.5 metres at the springs as a result.

Five large springs and several smaller ones burst to the surface between the moated Bishop's Palace and the Cathedral of St Andrew. Today they generally emerge from the bed of the substantial artificial pond. The exceptions are in times of flood when they have a tendency to spring up elsewhere in the gardens. This pond has not always existed and was not there in the time of Celia Fiennes.

Dr Stanton's paper *The Ancient Springs, Streams and Underground Watercourses of the City of Wells* [18] provides an insight as to the configuration of the springs in the late seventeenth century. The main pot, known as Bottomless Pit, erupted into a short pond which also collected the outfall of the other springs. The water was divided and one channel ran into the fourteenth century Bishop's Palace moat nearby, the other ran between the moat and the cathedral, forming the Bishop's Mill stream. By 1735 this fed a large horse pond and the Bishop's Mill, on what is now the outer Palace green. It then went on to supply several mills in the city, after being supplemented by water from the moat. A satellite spring known as Scotland was then, and has remained since, separate and drained through its own watercourse. This runs west through the Camery to the "Dipping Place" in Palm Churchyard eventually joining the Mill stream beyond the market place. These watercourses would have been the two streams that Celia observed.

A well-house was built alongside the springs in 1451 by Bishop Beckington. This was fed by a tributary from the Bishop's Mill stream, which in turn found its way into the moat. The well-house still exists on the southern bank of the c.1824 substantial artificial pond seen today.

The city of Wells is unusual in that the streets are flushed clean by a stream of constantly flowing water from the St Andrew's Spring. Celia Fiennes would have seen this arrangement which dates from 1451 and Bishop Beckington. Today the gutter on the south side of the High Street is fed by a pipe from the moat installed in 1803 by public subscription. Intervention by man has resulted over the centuries in considerable inclosure of the waterways and the street flow has been reduced from earlier times.

Stanton makes no mention of the springs ever having been used for religious or curative purposes. The early springs are reputed to be where King Ina of Wessex founded a Saxon religious college in 766AD. There is evidence that they formed part of an early public water supply. As early as 1322 there were complaints of the Scotland stream being polluted. St Andrew's spring water supply was supplemented by local wells from the eighteenth century, for example Jacob's Pump is marked on a map of 1735.

Other tourist attractions in the City of Wells for Celia included the cathedral. Building was started in the thirteenth century and completed in the fifteenth. Celia does not appear to have entered the cathedral because she makes no mention of the contents which include a fourteenth century clock. A feature of the west front of the cathedral is over 400 statues, inspired by the sculptures of Continental cathedrals. These certainly inspired Celia's comment and today the modern traveller can equally enjoy the panorama of statuary.

Having seen Wells, Celia Fiennes next travelled past Glastonbury Tor noted for what she described as superstition. This mystical place lies just outside the town of Glastonbury and was supposedly created by Joseph of Arimathea. Reputed to be the burial place of King Arthur, the Tor is associated with Avalon and the Celtic Otherworld. The hill is 525 feet high and crowned by the fourteenth century tower which marks the site of a former chapel destroyed by a landslide in 1271. At the foot of the Tor on the western side is the celebrated Chalice or Blood Well. The name results from the reddish tinge to the water which has given rise to numerous myths concerning the blood of Christ from the Holy Grail. The water can be sampled from a fountain in the gardens in which the well is located.[19]

Footnotes:

1   Morris C. (ed.) 1947, *The Journeys of Celia Fiennes*, p.241-2.
2   Green G W. Welch F B A. 1965, *Geology of the Country around Wells and Cheddar*, Memoirs of the Geological Survey of GB, p.172.
3   Exwood M. Lehmann H L. (Trans.), 1993, *The Journal of William Schellinks' Travels in England, 1661-1663*, p.109.
4   Gatacre E V. Winsor D. 1977, *Wookey Hole*, p.10.
5   ibid. p.2.
6   Cole D. 1927, *A Tour through the whole island of Great Britain by Daniel Defoe*, p.Vol.1, p.278.
7   Gatacre E V. Winsor D. op.cit. p.30.
8   Mason E J. 1977, *Caves and Caving in Britain*, p.99-103. Balch, 1926, quotes a longer version of this poem but gives no provenance.
9   Mason E J. op.cit. p.55/6.
10   Farr M. 1984, *The Great Caving Adventure*, p.228/9.
11   Gatacre E V. Winsor D. op.cit. p.30.
12   Balch H E. 1926, *The Caves of Mendip*, p.24-27.
13   Mason E J. op.cit. p.165/6.
14   Balch H E. op.cit. p.39.
15   Mason E J. op.cit. p.165-7.
16   Miller N. 1982, *Heavenly Caves*, p.82-84.
17   One of a series of 10 pen and ink illustrations of a trip through Wookie Hole. see Williams A. 1952, *Early English Water Colours*, The Connoisseur, London, p.18.
18   Stanton W I. 1987/8, *The Ancient Springs, Streams and Underground Watercourses of the City of Wells*, 99th and 100th Annual Reports of the Wells Natural History and Archaeological Society.
19   Bord J & C. 1985, *Sacred Waters*, p.172.

ALFORD

Sometime in or before 1687 Celia Fiennes went on a tour of Wiltshire, Dorset, Devon, Cornwall and Somerset.[1] She remarked on the huge numbers of fruit trees in Somerset, particularly apples and pears, though was quick to point out that the inhabitants were far more interested in the quantity of their fruit at the expense of the quality. At cider making time rather than particular varieties being pressed separately, all sorts of apples were pressed together, producing mediocre ciders rather than the fine ciders found in Herefordshire. It was perhaps this careless attitude which caused her to remark that the country people in Somerset were *"clounish and rude"*.

Celia's route took her from Stonehenge via Yeovil and Castle Cary to the mineral well at Alford. She noted that the well had formerly been better attended by the Company, suggesting that it was declining in popularity. Her further comments indicate that this was probably due to the lack of accommodation for wealthier visitors and the behaviour of the local people, which was not at all welcoming. For these, and perhaps other reasons, no capital investment was made in promoting the waters and it never acquired the acclaim and popularity of some other spas. However, people within a several mile radius were sending for the water and making beer out of it. One is led to wonder, from the descriptions of the taste of the water mentioned below, just what the beer tasted like. It may have been that adding malt and hops slightly disguised the natural flavour whilst still having the desired purging effect.

Celia described the spring as quick and clear and coming off alum. There was no basin to catch the water, which flowed instead into a little well which had a bluish clay or marl at the bottom. From there it flowed quickly to waste. She confirmed that it was a quick purger, probably similar to Epsom and Barnet wells, and was good *"for all sharpe Humers or Obstruction"*.[2]

17ᵗʰ CENTURY ALFORD SPA?

Alford Well as it may have been at the time of Celia Fiennes' visit. She described the water flowing into a little well, which was probably set below ground level and so similar to that at Barnet.

260

COMMENT

Alford village is 24 miles south of Bath and 12 miles north of Sherborne. The well is situated at a farm called Alford Well, about three-quarters of a mile from the church. The saline spring was first discovered in 1670 by Thomas Earl, a local minister, when he noticed large numbers of pigeons congregating to drink.[3] The spring at Dulwich in London was also notable for the large number of pigeons which clustered round its saline spring.[4] Although the issue at Alford was not great, it was the only notable purging spring in the West Country, so was much in demand, and its efficacy compared with that of Barnet.[5] Writing in 1673, just three years after the spring's discovery, Henry Chapman wrote, *"... never was there a greater resort to any place (considering the small quantities of Waters it produced) then thither so much reputation it had gained that much people had the patience to stay their turns (for Gods mercies were much seen in that it was a (pitifully) barren Spring) till they could be supplyed from the Well."*[6]

Because of its strong purging effect Alford water was much sought after and by 1676 was being bottled and distributed in the south-west, certainly to Plymouth and Land's End, and also to Bath, where it was highly recommended by Dr Robert Peirce.[7] He sent some of his patients to Alford specially to take the waters, considering their purging qualities to be as effective as those of Epsom, Northaw and Barnet. Bath waters were renowned for alleviating gout, a side effect of which was costiveness. Dr Thomas Guidott of Bath recommended Alford waters in gouty cases, most probably because Bath's bitumen-sulphur waters were not effective in curing chronic costiveness.[8] *"The Bitumen and Niter which is in them, although it serves well for an alterative remedy, yet it is not sufficeient for an evacuate."*[9] Dr Musgrave frequently prescribed Alford waters in gout cases, and also where gout symptoms were produced by scurvy.[10] Dr Highmore of Sherborne also sent patients to Alford, after first visiting the spring himself to verify its efficacy.[11]

It is surprising that the water was being endorsed by Bath's finest physicians, and bottled and distributed, in the wake of Henry Chapman's remark in 1673 about its terminal effects. He wrote that the water must have been sent from hell rather than from heaven, because of the *"... Diseases and Mortality that seized an abundance of People, in a very short time after they had drunk them; insomuch, that ever since there is a Lord have Mercy written on the Door of him that made Merchandize of them."*[12] The explanantion for this comment may be found in Dr Peirce's preface to his *Bath Memoirs* of 1697, in which he says that the spring was very popular until some people started to take the water randomly, without a doctor's prescription. He recorded that some consumptives *"(who dying almost on the spot)"* had partly destroyed the spring's reputation.[13] This is a subtle reminder that, improperly used, water can kill as well as cure.

In view of this catastrophe, and since Alford's medicinal water resembled Epsom water, one might have anticipated a reduction in the popularity of Alford when Epsom salts became available in apothecaries' shops after 1700. This does not appear to have been the case and the waters continued to be sought as late as 26th and 27th March 1776. On those days, James Woodforde wrote in his diary that his niece was suffering from the King's Evil, which had prevented her from travelling with him to Norfolk. She had gone to Alford in the hope of being cured.[14]

As a nitrous water, like Epsom and Barnet, it was recommended *"to cool, cleanse, penetrate, and attenuate gross Humours; allay Acrimony; attemperate and suppress undue Fermentation; Good in the Spleen, Scurvy, Jaundice, and all Obstructions of the Mesentery and Bowels..."*[15] Dr Elliot in 1789 added that it was also effective in curing glandular obstructions, and that in promoting sweat and urine it was beneficial in shifting bladder and kidney gravel.[16] The water would hardly have been taken unnecessarily. Richard Gough described it as nauseous and bitter, which was attributed to the salinity being chiefly nitrous.[17] Benjamin Allen in 1699 described it as a cross between saltpetre and common salt, and Russel's book in 1769 described it as saturated with salt.[18]

ANALYSES

Analyses and experiments found nearly 6 drams of sediment to a gallon, and suggest an impregnation with calcareous nitre, sea salt and a little limestone.[19]

Thomas Guidott, c.1724, in his *De Thermis Britannica*, noted various experiments which he had conducted on this water. It curdled soap; yielded a white grumous sediment with a solution of potass; turned a dilute green when syrup of violets was added, indicating salinity; green with sumach, and a greenish cloud formed when powder of galls were applied, indicating iron. From one gallon he obtained nearly 6 drams of matter, consisting of calcareous nitre, marine salt and carbonic acid.[20]

Dr Rutty in 1757 was only able to obtain two drams of solid content from a gallon of Alford water. One scruple was a calcareous earth, the other five scruples were salt, two thirds of which were calcareous Glauber salt and one third sea salt.[21] These constituents clearly account for the excellent purging qualities of this water.

There are several reasons for the discrepancy in the solid content extracted during these two experiments. Dr Rutty may have taken his sample after heavy rainfall, when the water was diluted. Guidott may have taken his sample during a long dry spell, when the water was heavily mineralised. Alternatively, Rutty only managed to find two drams of solids because by 1757 the subsoil had already been leached of its minerals. In some Australian wells large variations in mineral content have occurred over time, particularly in the sodium and iron content.[22]

TODAY

By the 1920s the well was reported to be in a locked shed.[23] Today the spring is contained within a stone-lined well situated in the garden to the side of Well House Farm. The water, which is several feet deep and protected by a metal cover, is limpid and very faintly brackish to taste. There is no sign of saline encrustation on the stone lining. The well has now almost certainly been diluted with rain water which would account for the very slight salinity and the lack of encrustation.

Footnotes:

1   Morris C. (ed.) 1947, *The Journeys of Celia Fiennes*, p.16.
2   ibid. p.16.
3   R C. Hope mistakenly identifies this spring as chalybeate in his *Holy wells and their Legends and Traditions*, 1893, p.150.; P. Hembry, 1990, describes it as saline-chalybeate in *The English Spa 1560-1815*, p.76.
4   Russel R. 1769 (5th edition) *Dissertation on the use of Sea Water* with anonymous supplement *A Treatise on the Nature, Properties and Uses of the Mineral Waters*, p.267-269.
5   Rutty J. 1757, *A Methodical Synopsis of Mineral Waters*, p.128.
6   Chapman H. 1673, *Thermae Rediviviae, the City of Bath Described*, p.14.
7   Monro D. 1770, *A Treatise on Mineral Waters*, Vol.I, p.132.
8   Chapman H. op.cit. p14.
9   Jorden E.1631, *A Discourse of Naturall Bathes and Minerall Waters... especially of our Bathes at Bath in Sommersetshire*, p.130.
10 Rutty J. op.cit. p.130.
11 Hembry P. op.cit. p.76-77.
12 Chapman H. op.cit. p.14.
13 Rutty J. op.cit. p.130.
14 Beresford J. (ed.) 1978, *The Diary of a Country Parson, 1758-1802*. King's Evil was a scrofulous disease which was supposed to have been cured by the king's touch. Scurvy, caused by a lack of vitamin C, was widespread, and characterised by spongy and bleeding gums.
15 Guidott T. 1724, *A Century of Observations containing further Discoveries of the Nature of the Hot Waters of Bath*, 2nd edition, p.143.; John Andrews, Folio of maps 1796-8, Bodleian Library, G.A. Fol.B.2., p.113.
16 Elliot J. 1789, *Principal Mineral Waters of Great Britain and Ireland*, p.123.
17 Camden's *Britannia*, Gough R. (trans.) 1789; Guidott T. op.cit. p.142.
18 Allen B. 1699, *The Natural History of the Chalybeate and Purging Waters of England*, p.144; Russel R. op.cit..
19 Russel R. op.cit. p.256-258.
    According to Dr Monro in 1770, Dr Rutty was only able to obtain two drams of solid content from a gallon of Alford water.
20 Rutty J. op.cit. p.129.
21 Monro D. op.cit. p.132.
22 Wishart E. Wishart M. 1990, *The Spa Country*, p.27-31.
23 Horne E. 1923, *Somerset Holy Wells*, p.30.

BIBLIOGRAPHY

Primary Source

Manuscript

British Library
Sloane MS 2348 f34, Anon, 17th century, *A Ballad in Tunbridge Wells*.
Sl.640 ff.340-351, Anon. 1640, *Accounts of Hotwells by a physician*.

Hertford Record Office
D/P15 256 5/2, Barnet parish (churchwardens') records
54808-54820, Chandos Papers, 1734-1868.
Gerish Collection, Box 13, General Accounts, Medicinal Waters of Hertfordshire.

Printed

Allen B. 1699, *The Natural History of the Chalybeate and Purging Waters of England*.
Anon. 1668, *A Short Account of the Mineral Waters lately found in the City of Canterbury* (British Library ref. 1171.h.18 (2)).
Anon. 1668, *A Brief Account of the Virtues of the Famous Well of Astrop by a learned Physician*.
Anon. 1702, *Canterbury Wells: or, A discourse upon the mineral waters lately discovered in that city, and the many extraordinary cures which are daily performed by them* (The Beaney Institute, Canterbury, ref. CO20224011).
Anon. but believed to be T. Short 1765, *A General Treatise on Various Cold Mineral Waters in England*, W. Owen, printer.
Anon. n.d. *Journal of Excursions, 1819-23*, London.
Aubrey J. 1718, *The Natural History and Antiquities of the County of Surrey*, Curll, London.

Banister R. 1622, 2nd edition, *A Treatise of one hundred and thirteene diseases of the eyes, and eye-liddes*. Bodleian Library ref. Douce B582 (1)
De Beer E S. (ed.) 1955, *Diary of John Evelyn*, Clarendon Press.
Beresford J. (ed.) 1978, *The Diary of a Country Parson, 1758-1802*, OUP.
Blome R. 1673, *Britannia*, London.
Blundell M. (ed.) 1952, *Blundell's Diary and Letter Book 1702-1728*, Liverpool University Press.
Boddely T. 1755, *The Bath and Bristol Guide*, Bath.
Braun J. 1875, *Curative Effects of Baths and Waters*, Smith, Elder & Co, London.
Bray W. (ed.) 1891 and c.1946, *The Diary of John Evelyn*, Frederick Warne & Co. London.
Brome J. 1700, *Travels over England, Scotland and Wales*, London.

Camden's *Britannia*, P. Holland (trans.) 1610, London.
Camden's *Britannia*, R. Gough (trans.) 1789, London.
Capper B. 1808, *A Topographical Dictionary of the United Kingdom*, Richard Phillips, London.
Carey G S. 1799, *The Balnea: or, an impartial description of All the Popular Watering Places*, J Myers, London.

Chapman H. 1673, *Thermae Redivivae, The City of Bath Described*, London (British Library 1171.h.18).

Charleton R. 1754, *A Treatise on the Bath Waters*, T. Boddely, Bath.

Cobbett W. 1966 edition, *Rural Rides*, Dent, London.

A Tour Thro' the Whole Island of Great Britain by Daniel Defoe, 1927, P. Davies, London.

Deane E. 1626, *Spadacrene Anglica*, John Wright & Sons reprint, Bristol, 1922, with an introduction by Rutherford J. and bibliographical notes by Butler A.

Defoe D. *A Tour Through England and Wales*, J M. Dent, 1927.

Defoe D. *A Tour Through the Whole Island of Great Britain*, Penguin, 1971.

Dugdale J. 1819, *The New British Traveller or Modern Panorama of England and Wales*, J. Robins & Co.

Elliot J. 1789, 2nd edition, *An Account of the Nature and Medicinal Virtues of the Principal Mineral Waters of England and Ireland*, London.

Exwood M. Lehmann H L. (trans.) 1993, *The Journal of William Schellinks' Travels in England 1661-1663*, Royal Historical Society, London.

Floyer J. 1697, *Hot, Cold and Temperate Baths in England*, London.

Floyer J. 1722, *The History of Cold Bathing*, London.

Freeman H W. 1888, *The Thermal Baths of Bath*, Hamilton Adams & Co.

French J. 1652, *The Yorkshire Spaw*, printed for E. Dod & N. Ekins, London.

Fuller T. 1684, *Worthies of England*, London.

Gosling W. 1777, 2nd edition and 1825 edition, *A Walk in and about the City of Canterbury*, William Blackley, Canterbury.

Granville A B. 1841, *The Spas of England*, Adams and Dart reprint, 1971.

A Guide to All the the Watering and Sea-Bathing Places for 1813, by the editor of the Picture of London, London.

Guidott T. 1724, 2nd edition, *A Century of Observations containing further Discoveries of the Nature of the Hot Waters of Bath*.

Hoffman F. 1731, *New Experiments & Observations upon Mineral Waters*, Osborn and Longman, London.

Hooson W. 1747, *The Miners Dictionary*, reprint by the Institution of Mining and Metallurgy, London, 1979 .

Hunter J. (ed.) 1830, *The Diary of Ralph Thoresby 1677-1724*, London.

Jones J. 1572, *The benefit of the Auncient Baths at Buckstones*.

Jorden E. 1631, *A discourse of naturall Bathes and Minerall Waters...especially of our Bathes at Bath in Sommersetshire*, London (British Library 234.h.29).

Kelk J. 1841, *Scarborough Spa*, London.

Latham R C. Matthews W. (eds.) 1971, *The Diary of Samuel Pepys*, G. Bell & Sons, London.

Lehmann H L. (ed.) 1987, *The Residential Copyholds of Epsom*, Epsom and Ewell Borough Council, ref. 1B13.

Luke T D. 1919, *Spas and Health Resorts of the British Isles*, A & C Black Ltd, London.

Macky J. 1732, *A Journey Through England*, London.
Mackenzie P. 1820, *Practical Observations on the Medical Powers of Mineral Waters*, Burgess and Hill, London.
Macpherson J. 1869, *The Baths and Wells of Europe*, Macmillan, London.
Madden T M. 1974, *The Spas of Germany, France and Italy and their Uses*, Newby, London.
Marshall W. 1818, *Review and Abstracts of the County Reports to the Board of Agriculture*, T. Wilson.
Matthews W. (ed.) 1939, *The Diary of Dudley Ryder*, Methuen.
Mitchell L G. (ed.) 1973, *The Purfoy Letters 1735-1753*, Sidgwick and Jackson.
Moore-Smith G C. (ed.) 1928, *The Letters of Dorothy Osborne to Sir William Temple*,
Monro D. 1770, *A Treatise on Mineral Waters*, Wilson & Nicol, London. J M. Dent.
Morris C. (ed.) 1947, *The Journeys of Celia Fiennes*, The Cresset Press, London.
Morris C. (ed.) 1982, *The Illustrated Journeys of Celia Fiennes*, Macdonald & Co, London.

Ogilby J. 1698, *Britannia*, London.
Ord W M. Garrod A E. 1895, *The Climates and Baths of Great Britain*, Royal Medical and Chirurgical Society, Macmillan & Co. London.

Parry E A. (ed.) 1914, *Letters from Dorothy Osborne to Sir William Temple (1652-54)*,
Peter J. 1680, *A Treatise of Lewisham*, S. Tidmarsh, Cornhill. J M. Dent.
Pickering D. 1765, *Statutes at Large*, Grays Inn.
Pitt W. 1813, *General View of the Agriculture of the County of Worcester*, David and Charles reprint, 1969.
Pliny, A.D 77, *The Natural History*, J. Bostock (trans.) 1861, Henry Bohn, London.

Rogers P. (ed.) 1992, *Daniel Defoe, A Tour Through the Whole Island of Great Britain*,
Rowzee L. 1632, *The Queenes Wells, that is a Treatise of the Nature and* Penguin.
Vertues of Tunbridge Water.
Russel R. 1755, *Oeconomy of Nature*. Russel R. 1760 (4th edition) *Dissertation on the use of Sea Water* with anonymous supplement *A Treatise on the Nature, Properties and Uses of the Mineral Waters,*Russel R. 1769 (5th edition) *Dissertation on the use of Sea Water* with anonymous supplement *A Treatise on the Nature, Properties and Uses of the Mineral Waters,* W. Owen, London.
Rutty J. 1757, *A Methodical Synopsis of Mineral Waters*, (British Library 33.e.11).

Saunders W. 1805, 2nd edition, *A Treatise on the Chemical History of Mineral Waters*, Phillips and Fardon, London.
Scott Thomson G. (ed.) 1943, *Letters of a Grandmother, 1732-1735*, Jonathan Cape,
Shaw P. 1734, *An Enquiry into Scarborough Spaw Waters*, London. London.
Shiercliff E. 1793, *The Bristol and Hotwell Guide*, Bulgin and Rosser, Bristol.
Short T. 1734, *Natural Mineral Waters*, London.
Short T. 1734, 2nd edition, *The Natural, Experimental, and Medicinal History of the Mineral Waters of Buxton, and other warm waters in the Peak in Derbyshire.*
Short T. 1734, *The History of the Mineral Waters of Derbyshire, Lincolnshire and Yorkshire*, F Gyles, London.
Short T. 1740, *History of the Principal Mineral Waters*, Sheffield.
Smith J. (ed.) 1924, *Diary of Samuel Pepys*, J M. Dent.
Smith L T. (ed.) 1907, *Leyland's Itinerary in England, 1535-1543*, George Bell & Sons.
Sprange J. 1786, *The Tunbridge Wells Guide.*

Toland J. 1711, *The Description of Epsom*, A. Baldwin, London, D W. James reprint, 1978.
Trinder W M. 1812, 3rd edition, *The English Olive Tree; or a treatise on the use of oil and the air bath.... To which are subjoined chymical experiments on the Barnet Well Water, Harts.*
Turner W. 1568, *A Booke of the natures and properties as well as the bathes in Germanye and Italye.*

Wall M. 1806, *Malvern Waters*, OUP.
Wilson A P. 1805, *An Analysis of Malvern Waters*, J. Tymbs, Worcester.
Wilson E. 1675, *Spadacrene Dunelmensis, Treatise on the Vitrioline Spaw near Durham*, printed by W. Godbid, London.
Wilson J. Gully J M. 1843, *Prospectus of the Water Cure Establishment*, Cunningham and Mortimer, London.
Wittie R. 1660, *Scarbrough Spa*, Charles Tyus, London Bridge.

Secondary Sources

Addison W. 1951, *English Spas*, Batsford.
Allsop David G. 1992, *Visitor's Guide to Poole's Cavern*, Buxton & District Civic Association Ltd.
Anon. c.1850, *The Pipes, Pumps, and Conduits of Bristol*, Hamilton Adams & Co. London.
Anon. 1995, *The Discovery of Symonds Well*, Symonds Well Restaurant, Epsom.
Ashton Court Mansion and Estate, c.1994, Bristol City Council.

Balch H E. 1926, *The Caves of Mendip*, Folk Press, London.
Bantok A. 1980, *The Smyths of Ashton Court*, Malago Publishers.
Barbeau A. 1904, *Life and Letters at Bath in the 18th Century*, William Heinemann.
Barton M. 1937, *Tunbridge Wells*, Faber and Faber, London.
Bell W G. 1926, *Where London Sleeps: Historical Journeying into the Suburbs.*
Bevington M. 1990, *Stowe, A Guide to the House*, Capability Books, Buckingham.
Bevington M. c.1990, *Templa Quam Dilecta, Stowe, The South Front*, No.XI.
Bord J & C. 1985, *Sacred Waters*, Granada Publishing, London.
Bristow C R. Bazley R A. 1972, *Geology of the Country around Royal Tunbridge Wells*, HMSO.
British Spas Federation c.1930, *The Spas of Britain*, Pitman Press, Bath.

Calvert M. 1844, *A History of Knaresborough*, W. Parr, Knaresborough.
Canning J. (ed.) 1988, *Macaulay's History of England*, first published 1848-1861, Guild Publishing, London.
The Canterbury Guide, 1835, 5th edition, Henry Ward, Canterbury.
Church R. 1948, *Kent*, Robert Hale.
Clanny W R. 1807, *History and Analysis of the Mineral Waters at Butterby*, Pennington.
Clark F L. 1954, *New Light on Epsom Wells*, Pullingers, Epsom.
Clark F L. 1960, *The History of Epsom Spa*, Surrey Archaeological Society, Guildford.
Clarke F W. 1924, *The Data of Geochemistry*, Washington Government Printing Office, USA.
Cooper A H. Burgess I C. 1993, *Geology of the country around Harrogate*, HMSO.
Crismer L M. 1983, *The Extraordinary History of the Waters of Spa*, S.A Spa Monopole N.V.
The Cross Bath, 1991, The Springs Foundation, Bath.

Cunliffe B. 1986, *The City of Bath*, Alan Sutton, Gloucester.
Cunliffe B. 1993, *The Roman Baths*, Bath Arch. Trust.

David C. 1971, *St Winefride's Well, a history and guide*, n.p.
Davies D C. 1892, *Earthy and other Minerals and Mining*, Crosby Lockwood, London.
Denbigh K. 1981, *A Hundred British Spas*, Spa Publications.
Dropping Well Estate, c.1950, *The Life and Prophecies of Ursula Sontheil better known as Mother Shipton*.

Earp J R. Haines B A. 1971, *The Welsh Borderland*, British Regional Geology, HMSO.
Edwards T. 1951, *British Cities, Bristol*, Batsford.
Epsom Common Association 1981, *Epsom Common*, Living History Publications.
Lord Ernle, 1919, *Farming Past and Present*, Longmans.
Exwood M. 1989, *Epsom Wells, A New History of the Epsom Wells and Epsom Salts*, Epsom and Ewell Borough Council.

Farmer D H. 1978, *The Oxford Dictionary of Saints*, OUP.
Farr M. 1984, *The Great Caving Adventure*, Oxford Illustrated Press.
Farthing R. 1990, *Royal Tunbridge Wells*, Phillimore.
Foord A S. 1910, *Springs, Streams and Spas of London*, Fisher Unwin.
Ford T D. Gill D W. 1979, *Caves of Derbyshire*, Dalesman Books, Clapham, N. Yorks.
Fordyce W. 1857, *History of Durham*, Newcastle.
Fox A. 1971, *The Pictorial History of Westminster Abbey*, Pitkin Pictorials.
Fox C S. 1949, *The Geology of Water Supply*, The Technical Press, London.
Freeman H W. 1888, *The Thermal Waters of Bath*, Hamilton Adams, London.

Gatacre E V. Winsor D. 1977, *Wookey Hole*, Wookey Hole Caves Ltd.
Gill R. 1989, *Chemical Fundamentals in Geology*, Unwin Hyman, London.
Grainge W. 1871, *History and Topography of Harrogate and the Forest of Knaresborough*, M. Rigg Ltd reprint, 1988.
Green G W. Welch F B A. 1965, *Geology of the Country around Wells and Cheddar*, Memoirs of the Geological Survey of GB, HMSO.

Hall S C. and Llewellyn J. c.1890, *The Stately Homes of England* (paper from the Droitwich Heritage Centre).
Hamilton M. 1978, *Bath before Beau Nash*, Kingsmead Press, Bath.
Happerfield L. Hutton S. 1915, *Bath and Bristol*, A & C Black Ltd.
Harris J. 1907, *Great Horwood, Bucks*, unpublished.
Hart G. 1981, *A History of Cheltenham*, Alan Sutton, Gloucester.
Hembry P. 1990, *The English Spa 1560-1815*, Athlone Press.
Hibbert C. 1969, London, *The Biography of a City*, Penguin.
Hinde T. 1988, *Tales from the Pump Room*, Victor Gollancz.
Home G. 1901, *Epsom, Its History and Its Surroundings*, 1971 edition, S.R Printers, Yorkshire.
Home G. 1931, *Old London Bridge*, John Lane, London.
Hope R C. 1893, *Holy Wells of England*, Elliot Stock, London.
Hopkinson B. 1984, "The British Salt Industry and Droitwich", *Industrial Heritage*, Vol 2, No.4.
Hopkinson B. 1994, *Salt and Domesday Salinae at Droitwich A.D. 674-1690*,

Droitwich Brine Springs and Arch. Trust & Worcs. Arch. Soc.
Horne E. 1893, *Somerset Holy Wells*, Somerset Folk Press, London.
Hughes J. 1977, *Shropshire Folklore, Ghosts and Witchcraft*, Westmid Supplies, Shrewsbury.
Hurst J D. 1992, *Savouring the Past, The Droitwich Salt Industry*, Hereford and Worcester County Council.

James P R. 1938, *The Baths of Bath in the Sixteenth and Early Seventeenth Centuries*, Arrowsmith, Bristol.
Jennings B. (ed.) 1970, *A History of Harrogate & Knaresborough*, The Advertiser Press Ltd, Huddersfield.
Jennings B. 1974, *A History of the Wells and Springs of Harrogate*, Harrogate Borough Council.
Jewitt A. 1811, *History of Buxton*, London.
Johnson M. 1992, 6th edition, *Durham, Historic and University City*, Turnstone Ventures, Durham.

Kahn J E. (ed.) 1985, *The Right Word at the Right Time*, Readers Digest Association.
Kellaway G A. 1991, *Hot Springs of Bath*, Bath City Council.
Kellaway G A. Welch F B A. 1993, *The Geology of the Bristol District*, HMSO.
Kellett A. 1991, *Historic Knaresborough*, Smith Settle Limited.
Kershaw Mary J. 1987, *Knaresborough Castle*.
Kirkby W. 1902, *The Evolution of Artificial Mineral Waters*, Jewsbury and Brown, Manchester.
Kourimsky J. 1977, *Minerals and Rocks*, Artia, Prague.

Langham M. Wells C. 1986, *Buxton Waters, A History of Buxton the Spa*, The Derbyshire Heritage Series, J. Hall, Derby.
Latimer J. 1970, *The Annals of Bristol in the Sixteenth Century*, George's, Bristol.
Leach J. 1987, *The Book of Buxton*, Barracuda.
Lees E. 1856, *Pictures of Nature*, H W. Lamb, Malvern.
Lennard R. 1931, "The Watering Places", *Englishmen at Rest and Play*, Oxford.

Mackinlay J M. 1893, *Folklore of the Scottish Lochs and Springs*, W. Hodge, Glasgow.
Major H D A. 1922, *Memorials of Copgrove Registers*, Blackwell.
Mason B Moore C B. 1982, 4th edition, *Principles of Geochemistry*, John Wiley & Sons, New York.
Mason E J. 1977, *Caves and Caving in Britain*, Robert Hale, London.
Melville L. 1912, *Society at Royal Tunbridge Wells*, Eveleigh Nash, London.
Metropolitan Water Board, 1953, *London's Water Supply*, 1903-1953, Staples Press, London.
Middlemas B. Hunt J. 1985, *John Corbett, Pillar of Salt, 1817-1901*, Saltway Press, Droitwich.
Miller N. 1982, *Heavenly Caves*, Allen & Unwin, London.

Munro J M H. 1928, *The Radio-activity in the Bath Thermal Waters*, Fyson, Bath.
Musgrave C. 1981, *Life in Brighton*, J. Hallewell Publications.

Nash R. 1782, *Collections for the History of Worcester*.
Neesan M G. 1989, *Exclusively Harrogate*, Smith Settle.
Neville Havins P J. 1976, *The Spas of England*, Robert Hale, London.

Nickolls J F. Taylor J. 1881, *Bristol Past and Present*, J W. Arrowsmith.
Nielsen I. 1990, *Thermae et Balnae*, Aarhus University Press, Denmark.
Nott J. 1885, *Some of the Antiquities of Moche Malverne*, John Thompson, Malvern.

Paget-Tomlinson E W. 1978, *Canal and River Navigations*, Waine Research Publications, Wolverhampton.
Pevsner N. Williamson E. 1994, *The Buildings of England, Buckinghamshire*, Penguin.
Pitkin Pictorials 1988, *Durham Cathedral*, n.p.
Poole E G. Whiteman A J. 1966, *Geology of the Country around Nantwich and Whitchurch*, Geological Survey of Great Britain, HMSO.
Porter R. (ed.) 1990, *The Medical History of Waters and Spas*, Wellcome Institute.
Potter G W. 1904, *Hampstead Wells*, Carlisle reprint, 1978.
Pownall H. 1825, *History of Epsom*, W. Dorling, Epsom.
Priestley J B. 1969, *The Prince of Pleasure*, Sphere Books, London.
Proud K. 1992, *Durham City*, Phillimore.
Pryce G. 1861, *A Popular History of Bristol*, W. Mack.

Reid H. 1992, *A Chronicle of Clifton and Hotwells*, Redcliffe, Bristol.
Robertson W H. 1838, *Buxton and its Waters*, London.
Rochester M. c.1990, *Rock Salt Mining in Cheshire*, A Salt Museum Publication, Cheshire Libraries.
Rolls R. 1988, *The Hospital of the Nation*, Bird Publications, Bath.

Savidge A. 1975, *Royal Tunbridge Wells, A History of a Spa Town*, C. Bell reprint, 1995, Oast Books, Tunbridge.
Scott J. 1973, *Palaeontology an Introduction*, Kahn & Averill.
Searle M V. 1981, *Spas and Watering Places*, Midas Books.
Sheppard E J. 1962, *Bath in the Eighteenth Century*, Longmans, London.
Simmons D A. 1983, *Schweppes, The First 200 Years*, Acropolis Books, Washington DC.
Smith B. 1964, *A History of Malvern*, Leicester University Press.
Smith B. 1978, 2nd edition, *A History of Malvern*, Alan Sutton and The Malvern Bookshop.
Smith F W. 1899, *The Natural Mineral Waters of Harrogate*, Dawbarn & Ward, London.
Smith G C M. 1930, *Sir William Temple Bt.*, Clarendon Press.
Smith R A L. 1944, *Bath*, Batsford.
Spence K. 1973, *The Companion Guide to Kent & Sussex*, Collins.
Stamp L D. 1946, *Britain's Structure and Scenery*, Collins, London.
Stamp L D. Beaver S H. 1964, *The British Isles, A Geographic and Economic Survey*, Longmans.
Stevens J V. 1929, *Wells and Springs of Derbyshire*, HMSO.
Stewart B. 1981, *The Waters of the Gap*, Bath City Council.
Sunderland S. 1915, *Old London's Spas, Baths and Wells*, John Bale, Sons and Danielsson, London.
Surtees R. 1816-40, *The History and Antiquities of the County Palatine of Durham*, E.P Publishing Ltd and Durham County Library reprint, 1971.

Taylor D C. 1982, *The Book of Cobham*, Barracuda.
Thorold H. 1980, *County Durham*, A Shell Guide, Faber & Faber.
Tomlin R S O. 1988, *Tabellae Sulis*, Oxford University Committee for Archaeology.

Victoria County History for the County of Hertfordshire, 1908.
Victoria County History for the County of Surrey, 1911.

Waite V. 1960, *The Bristol Hotwell*, Hotwells and Clifton Wood Community Association republication, 1977.
Weaver C. Osborne B. 1994, *Aquae Malvernensis*, Cora Weaver, Malvern.
The Water Supply of Bristol, 1949, Bristol Waterworks.
Weber H. & F P. 1907, *Climatotherapy and Balneotherapy, the Climates and Mineral Water Health Resorts (Spas) of Europe and North Africa*, Smith Elder, London.
Widdicombe S H. 1912, *A Chat about Barnet and its History*, privately published.
Whittaker M. 1984, *Book of Scarborough Spaw*, Barracuda.
Willan T S. 1964, *River Navigation in England 1600-1750*, Frank Cass & Co., London.
Windsor D. 1990, *Mother Shipton's Prophecy Book*, Astroquail.
Wishart E. Wishart M. 1990, *The Spa Country*, Spa Publishing, Victoria, Australia.
Woodbridge K. 1995, *The Stourhead Landscape*, National Trust.
Wright T. 1826, *The History and Antiquities of Ludlow*, E J. Morten, Didsbury.

Articles

Barnard E A B. 1936, "The Pakingtons of Westwood", *Trans. Worcs. Arch. Soc.*

Bax A R. 1899, "Suspected Persons in Surrey During the Commonwealth", *Surrey Archaeological Collections*, 14, Surrey Archaeological Society.

Clarke F W. 1924, "The Data of Geochemistry", Bulletin 770, *U.S Geological Survey*, Washington.

"Diary of John Greene" 1929, *English Historical Review*, Vol. XLIV.

Edwards N. 1994, "Holy Wells in Wales and Early Christian Archaeology", *Source, The Holy Wells Journal*, New Series No.1, Autumn.

Hopkinson B. 1984, "The British Salt Industry and Droitwich", *Industrial Heritage*, Vol.2, No.4, Winter.

Hunt L. 1987, "Ancient, Healing and Holy Wells of Durham", *Source, The Holy Wells Journal*, No.7.

Lehmann H L. 1973, "The History of Epsom Spa", *Surrey Archaeological Collections*, Surrey Archaeological Society, LXIX.

Lehmann H L. 1980, *Surrey Archaeological Collections*, Surrey Archaeological Society, LXXVI.

Kershaw S W. 1897, "Surrey During the Commonwealth", *Surrey Archaeological Collections*, 13, Surrey Archaeological Society.

McIntyre S. 1973, "The Mineral Water Trade in the Eighteenth Century", *The Journal of Transport History*, New Series, Vol.II, No.I.

Pakington H. & R. 1975, "The Pakingtons of Westwood", *Trans. Worcs. Archaeological Soc.*

Rattue J. 1994, "Wells at the Bottom of the Garden", *Source, The Holy Wells Journal*, New Series No.2, winter.

Sakula A. 1983, "The Waters of Epsom Spa", *Surrey History*, Vol.2, No.5, Phillimore.

Shipton W. 1934, "A History of Buxton", *Buxton*, conference souvenir, National Association of Head Teachers, University of London Press.

Taylor I. 1987, "St Mungo's Well and the Devil's Stone, Copgrove", *Source, The Holy Wells Journal*, No.7.

Thornes R. Leach J. 1994, "Buxton Hall", *Derbyshire Archeaological Journal*.

Tongue C. 1970/1, "Thomas Thornton at Astrop Spa", *Northamptonshire Past and Present*, Vol.IV, No.5.

Newspapers

Barnet Press, 14 February 1975.

Independent, 31 December 1988, "A Case of Fraud and Skulduggery".

Telegraph, 12 October 1995, P. Elson, "Now Tunbridge Feels Distinctly Unwell".

Lloyds Evening Post, 14 - 16 August 1769, "British Chronicle, A concise historical Account of the old Epsom Wells, situated on Epsom Common, in the County of Surrey".

Nantwich Guardian, 1883, "The Nantwich Brine and Medical Baths".

Weekend Telegraph, 13 January 1996, R. Fairley, "Exploring the Crystal Maze".

Maps and Plans

Andrews J. 1797, *Map of the Mineral Waters and Bathing Places in England* (Bodleian Library ref. C 176.4 and G.A Fol.B.2).

Geological Survey of Great Britain, 1978, *Sheet 286, Reigate*, 1:50,000.

Jacobus Millerd's plan of Bristol, 1673.

Reports

Morris M. Penrose F. 1895, *The Climates and Baths of Great Britain*, a report by the committee of the Royal Medical and Chirurgical Society of London, Macmillan & Co., Vol.I.

Stanton W I. 1987/8, *The Ancient Springs, Streams and Underground Watercourses of the City of Wells*, 99th and 100th Annual Reports of the Wells Natural History and Archaeological Society, Wells Museum.

Williams C T. Horton-Smith P., *The Climates and Baths of Great Britain*, a report by the committee of the Medical and Chirurgical Society of London, Macmillan & Co, Vol.II.

Theses and Dissertations

Osborne B E. 1993, *Brighton's Past on Shifting Sands?*, unpublished dissertation, University of Birmingham.

INDEX

Acton 37 45 50 58 68
Acton Salts 49 50 58
Alford 65 86 260-263
Anaemia 14
Ashton Court, Bristol 217 227-228
Astrop Wells 11 89-101 108 113 160 212

Banstead, Surrey 40 42 47 71
Banstead Well 78
Barnet Wells 1 34 35 37 68 69 74 77-88 100 103 125 260 261 262
Bath 29 35 39 46 47 50 57 87 96 107 109 110 114 117 131 182 185 216 230-252 261
Bingham's Well, Buxton 112
Blackheath 34
Bone Well, Richard's Castle viii 202-203
Bottling 71 73 84 126-127 147 214
Box Hill 30 45 46
Brighton 33 39 49 220
Bristol 114 218-229 236 241
Bristol Diamonds 217 218-220
Bristol Hotwells 39 57 125 182 222-226
Burning Well, Wigan 150 173-177
Butterby, Durham 139 140 141 145
Buxton 34 102-119 150 155 178 183 185

Cannel coal 173 174 175 176-177
Canterbury Wells 1-10 11 13 34 103 136
Cheltenham 59 95
Cheltenham Salts 59
Cider-making 260
Cinchona Bark 7
Clifton Wells/Spa 224 225
Coal 124 144 145 173 216 241 (see also Mining)

Copgrove 110 148 150 152-159 (see also St Mungo's Well)

Dipper 7 16 82 84
Droitwich 189 192 194-201
Dropping Well, Knaresborough 151 161 169-171
Dropsy 94 140
Dulwich Wells 37 65-67 68 85
Durham 11 133-146 261

Ebbing Well, Tideswell 120 121
Elden Hole (Devil's Arse), Derbys. 120
Epsom 1 15 27-64 65 66 68 69 71 78 83 84 85 87 96 103 125 183 220 223 233 236 254 260 261 262
Epsom Salts 37 38 44 48 49 50 52 53 56 57 58 59 60 69 86 143 165 191 262
Eridge 24

Ffynnon Fair (St Mary's Spring) 181
Fishing 124 190

Glauber Salts 60 86 95
Gout 7 13 94 113 125 126 165 199 245 249 250 261
Great Horwood, Bucks. 11 89-93
Great Plague 16 31 96 108
Green sickness (chlorosis) 7 66 113 129 140

Hackney 68 74-75 82 84
Hampstead Wells 34 39 69-73 87 103 174 176
Harrogate 11 90 135 141 148 160-172
Holywell, Flints. viii 103 110 112 152 (see also St Winefride's Well)
Holy Well, Malvern 205 209 210 211

Infertility 13 113 126 140 249
Islington 34 87 96 174 176
Jaundice 94
Jessop's Well 49 55 56

Kepier Hospital, Durham 138
King's Evil 140 262
King's Sutton, Northants. 90 93 96 98 100
Knaresborough 87 125 147-151 154 160 161 165 166 169 255

Lead poisoning 249 250
Leprosy 28 66 126 248
Lewisham 65 67
Lewisham Wells 67
Liverpool 156 157 173 186

Malvern 153 184 199 202 204-215
Mam Tor, Derbys. 106 118 120
Mining:
coal 102 122 178
copper 102
crystal 104
iron 11 178
lead 102
marble 102 104
silver 102
tin 102

Nantwich 189-193
Nonconformist viii 123 134 135 136 182
Nonsuch 28 31 33 35
Northwich 39 189-193

Ordinary 99 102 109 122
Owen's Mineral Water Warehouse 48 128 208 226

Paper-making 2
Penshurst Place 23
Poole's Hole, Derbys. 103-106 118 120 253

Quakers 122 123

Reigate 254
Rheumatism 7 85 94 113 129 165 199 249
Richards Castle 202-203 204
Roman Catholics 29 94 112 134 148 149 152 153 154 179 181 182 183 184 187

St Andrew's Spring, Wells 253 257 258
St Ann's Well, Malvern 211-213
St Anne's Well, Buxton 1 28 29 34 39 42 43 46 50 90
St Bueno's Well (Ffynnon Bueno), Holywell 184 187
St Cuthbert's Well, Durham 139 145
St Mungo's (Magnus) Well, Copgrove 116 152-159 179
St Robert of Knaresborough 148
St Robert's Cave 147 150-151
St Robert's Chapel 149-150
St Rumbold's Well, Astrop 93 98 100
St Vincent's Rock/Well, Bristol 216 219 222 225
St Winefride's Well, Holywell 112 116 178-188 211

Salt 143 189-201
Scarborough 34 83 84 87 122-132
Scurvy 13 66 94 114 129 140 220 225
Seidlitz Water 37 58 86
Shooters Hill 37 45 49 58 60 67-69 71
Silk weaving 1
Somerhill 17 22 23
Spa (the town of) 14 15 16 19 28 155 160 162 233
Sydenham Wells 66 67
Symonds Well, Epsom 40 53 54 59

Tideswell, Derbys. 106 120-121
Tunbridge Wells 5 11-26 35 52 57
71 83 87 92 96 103 125 135 139 236

Wellingborough 96
Wells 253-259
Westwood House, Droitwich 194
200
Wigan, Burning Well 150 173 177
Wookey Hole 217 253 259

PEOPLE

Aubrey John 29
Banister, Richard 96 207-210 214
Blome, Richard 78 106 108 182 186
Blundell, Elizabeth 182 183
Blundell, Nicholas 131 182 183
Brome, Reverend James 114 115 149
156 186 202
Camden, William 78 93 106 110 113
120 139 153 154 174 186 196 202
208 209
Culpeper, Nicholas 65 67
Defoe, Daniel 46 47 70 71 74 87 106
114 116 117 124 130 174 176 182
183 254

Doctors:
Allen, Benjamin 53 54 67 84 127 262
Charleton, Rice 241
Clanny 140 141 142 144
Deane, Edmund 153 154 161 162
164
Elliot, John 141 169 174 176 262
Fallopio, Gabriele 94 113
Floyer, John 110 113 115 116 156
157 185
Fraizer, Alexander 237 246
French, John 154 155
Granville, A B. 59 115 140 141 143
144 149 210 225
Grew, Nehemiah 36 37 38 40 45 50
57 58 60 68
Guidott, Thomas 244 261 262

Highmore of Sherborne 126 261
Jones, John 106 107 112 116
Leigh 112 114 173
Lower, Richard 93
Monro, D. 61 113 127 130 175 248
des Moulins, Scipio 5 6 8
Peter, John 65 66 85
Peirce, Robert 96 238 261
Rowzee, Lodowick 14 15
Russel, Richard 49 50 52 57 60 67
113 175 208 220
Rutty, J. 86 95 262
Short, Thomas 95 105 110 114 115
120 126 141 143 144 164
Struve, Friedrich 39 48 60
Turner, William 235 248
Venner, Tobias 223 235
Wall, John 207-209 211 212
Wilson, Edward 140 141
Wilson, Philips 212
Wittie, Robert 83 125 126

Dugdale, James 141 143 144
Evelyn, Elizabeth 30 33 34 40
Evelyn, John 15 31 33 36 65 67 68
211 223
Evelyn, Richard 30 31 32 33
Fuller, Thomas 27 83 85 182 202
Gainsborough, Earl of 70 72 83
Leland, John 169 220 243
Livingstone, John 34 39 40 41-51 54
57 58 59 60 61 71
Macky, John 3 9 45
Moult brothers 37 38 45 49 58 60 61
68
Nash, Richard "Beau" 233 238
North, Lord Dudley 14 15 24 28
Ogilby, John 135 136 218
Osborne, Dorothy 28 29 35 83
Owen, William 48 49 67
Parkhurst, John 39 40-42 57 60
Pepys, Samuel 22 31 32 34 74 82 83
84 182 243
Purfoy, Henry 97

Royalty:
Anne, Queen and Princess 12 18 19
68 232 237
Anne of Denmark 247
Bladud 247
Catherine of Braganza 13 16 223 237
243
Charles II 15 31 32 33 69 223 237
Elizabeth I 5 14 22 27 183 193 240
243
Henrietta Maria 15 96 237
James II 235 237 243
Mary of Modena 181 182 230 243
Mary Queen of Scots 103 107
William & Mary 2 237 243

Ryder, Dudley 45 72
Sarah, Duchess of Marlborough 130
Schellinks, William 30 36 218 223
235 236 247 254
Schweppe, Jacob 48 60
Slingsby, Sir Thomas 150
Slingsby, Mr William 162
Temple, Sir Richard 89 97 99
Temple, Sir William 29 83
Thoresby, Ralph 105 165
Thornton, Thomas 98 99
Toland, John 42 43 44 46 51 58
Verney, Sir Ralph 90 92 96 97
Wicker, Henry 27
William of Worcester 110 222 254
Woodforde, James 182 262